INSTRUCTIONAL STRATEGIES FOR CHRISTIAN TEACHERS

How to Teach the Bible and Theology in the Church and School

James Riley Estep Jr. & Jay L. Sedwick
EDITORS

KREGEL
ACADEMIC

Instructional Strategies for Christian Teachers: How to Teach the Bible and Theology in the Church and School

Published by Kregel Academic, an imprint of Kregel Publications, 2450 Oak Industrial Dr. NE, Grand Rapids, MI 49505-6020

The subject index was created by Dr. Cynthia Stephens.

Cataloging-in-Publication Data is available from the Library of Congress.

ISBN 978-0-8254-4758-7

Printed in the United States of America

25 26 27 28 29 / 5 4 3 2 1

"My friends Jay Sedwick and James Estep Jr., along with several other of my Dallas Seminary colleagues, have teamed up to write *Instructional Strategies for Christian Teachers,* a foundational resource chock-full of not only biblical and theological principles for teaching the truth of the Bible in every ministry context, but also practical strategies for applying educational theory to the lives of God's people everywhere. This volume will be an essential textbook for Bible colleges and seminaries and missional settings tasked with training Christian teachers to deliver life-changing content with effectiveness and excellence."

—Mark M. Yarbrough, PhD
President, Dallas Theological Seminary

"*Instructional Strategies for Christian Teachers* stands as one of the most comprehensive and substantive contributions to the field of Christian pedagogy in recent years. It offers a thorough exploration of the teaching-learning process, thoughtfully integrating educational philosophy, psychological principles, and instructional theory with a sound biblical framework. Each chapter reflects a high level of scholarly engagement, incorporating current research and best practices that move well beyond introductory treatments. The volume thoughtfully addresses significant and often-overlooked topics related to teaching and learning, and also emphasizes the formative role of the teacher and the importance of the educator's character and calling. Each chapter reflects scholarly depth and practical insight, enriched by a collaborative team of faculty writing from their individual areas of expertise. This is an invaluable resource for Christian higher education committed to developing effective, theologically grounded educators and ministry leaders."

—Karen E. Jones, PhD
Professor and Chair, Institute for Christian Thought and Practice
Huntington University

"Jesus commanded his disciples to teach others everything he had taught them. But how? How do we faithfully and effectively teach the Scriptures for transformation? While many books focus on educational theory and others focus on educational methods, this compelling text uniquely offers a comprehensive approach to strategic biblical teaching that grounds practice in sound philosophy and theology. Fair warning! Engaging in this comprehensive approach to Christian education may lead to a complete demolition and renovation of your teaching ministry, requiring an altered perspective that necessitates a change in strategy. Significant change is never easy, but faithful Christian educators will embrace this challenge to carefully reexamine their approach to teaching and learning in ministry."

—Mark Cannister, EdD
Professor of Christian Ministries
Gordon College

"Estep and Sedwick have delivered a much-needed resource for the teaching ministry, whether at church or at school. The writers are skilled academics and practitioners in their fields, and the chapters cover the topics all teachers need to know as they submit to the Holy Spirit to guide them in his transformational work. Those of us who are passionate about Christian education are thankful for *Instructional Strategies for Christian Teachers*!"

—Chris Shirley, PhD
Dean, Terry School of Educational Ministries
Professor of Educational Ministries
Jack and Barbara Terry Chair of Religious Education
Southwestern Baptist Theological Seminary

"The church is called to multiply the ministry of the Word, teaching and encouraging one another to know the triune God better, understand his will more fully, love him more deeply, and walk with him more consistently in our lives. To do this, we need to equip more people to understand how people learn and grow in their walks with God, and how to design and lead learning opportunities that contribute to a vital, maturing faith. My thanks to Estep, Sedwick, and the whole team who put this book together. There is so much here that will help us all grow as teachers of the Word, whatever setting we serve in. Thanks for the reflection questions to help us all consider the impact of what we have read for how we teach. This is a blessing!"

—Kevin E. Lawson, EdD
Global Affiliate Professor of Educational Studies
Talbot School of Theology, Biola University

"Teaching represents a high vocation to help others learn. As followers of Christ, teaching receives an even higher divine calling for transformation in partnership with the Holy Spirit. This readable, practical, and insightful book, *Instructional Strategies for Christian Teachers*, is a helpful tool for those who take Christian teaching seriously and humbly and have a desire to continue growing in their journey to imitate Jesus, their Lord and master teacher."

—Octavio Javier Esqueda, PhD
Director, PhD and EdD programs in Educational Studies
Professor of Christian Higher Education
Talbot School of Theology, Biola University

"Absolutely foundational material for any disciple maker, especially those in teaching or educational settings. The whole text drives us toward practice through important tactics, examples, and robust resources. Every pastor and Christian educator should deeply explore the biblical and theoretical principles here. Doing so will dramatically increase effectiveness and fruitfulness in education and ministry."

—Mike Severe, PhD
Ministry Chair
Taylor University

"*Instructional Strategies for Christian Teachers* is a comprehensive instructional manual by teachers for teachers who want to teach others how to teach. In light of Ephesians 4:11–12 teachers who use this text will be engaged in 'the equipping of the saints for the work of service.' An approachable, practical theology text for teachers and learners that lays a theoretical and biblical foundation for teaching of the master teacher, Jesus Christ. Includes information gleaned from what the social sciences offer, like developmental human growth, the many ways people learn, and more. This book is pragmatic and thorough as it answers the why regarding teaching and learning for the church, the academy, and spiritual formation."

—Judy L. Glanz, PhD
Spiritual Director, Silent Retreat Facilitator
Adjunct Instructor
Western Seminary

"In his final words, Christ gave the church a clear mission: proclaim and teach his life and message. Yet Scripture also warns that in the last days, people will turn away from sound teaching (2 Tim. 4:3). That's why a book like *Instructional Strategies for Christian Teachers* is more vital than ever. Estep and Sedwick have assembled a team of trusted scholars and practitioners to equip pastors, small group leaders, and Sunday school teachers with both theological depth and practical strategies for faithful instruction. Whether you're formally trained or serving as a lay leader, this book will sharpen your ability to teach God's Word with clarity, conviction, and compassion—so the church may be found faithful when Christ returns."

—Steve Grusendorf, PhD
Director for the Alliance Center for Leadership Development

To our wives
Karen Lynn Estep
Laurie Eileen Sedwick
For your constant love and unwavering support
in what God has called us to do

CONTENTS

PREFACE

"And Jesus came and said to them, 'All authority in heaven and on earth has been given to me. Go therefore and make disciples of all nations, baptizing them in the name of the Father and of the Son and of the Holy Spirit, *teaching them to observe all that I have commanded you.* And behold, I am with you always, to the end of the age'" (Matt. 28:18–20 ESV, emphasis added). While disciple making may be the heart of the Great Commission and the church's mission, the teaching ministry of the church is indeed a major artery, a core essential to a healthy Christian congregation, organization, or campus.

Christian education as a ministry of the church is broader than teaching, but it cannot exist without it. The function and role of the pastor include more than preaching, but to excel pastors must be proficient in preaching. Likewise, Christian education includes more than teaching, but Christian educators must be capable of teaching if their ministries are to fulfill the mandate to "make disciples." No wonder that of all the qualifications for leadership in the earliest church, teaching was the only skill required. Overseers/elders/shepherds must be "able to teach" (1 Tim. 3:2; 2 Tim. 2:24 ESV) and "give instruction" (Titus 1:9; see also Eph. 4:11 ESV). Teaching is not *exclusively* a Christian activity, but it is indeed a Christian activity to propagate, pass on, and protect the faith.

Three years ago, we sat down at a Society of Professors in Christian Ministry annual meeting to discuss a writing project that would take teaching in the church to a different level. Familiar with books that highlighted methods of teaching and sensing a disconnect between books on the theory of Christian education and the task of teaching, we set out to create a book that would address teaching as ministry with a more serious look at weaving theology, theory, and practice into a unified resource for Christian educators.

Instructional Strategies for Christian Teachers is not just another book about creative teaching methods or endless lists of bells, balloons, and bubble gum designed to keep learners entertained. Creativity in teaching means more than entertaining methods. This book delves deeper into the teaching task of a Christian educator. It provides a macroview to the topic of teaching; and hence, rather than methods, it focuses on *strategies*, which in turn informs which methods would be most effective given the lesson objective.

After mapping out the initial contents of the book, the educational ministries and leadership faculty of Dallas Theological Seminary was brought into dialogue regarding the proposed contents, and modifications were made to the project. What followed was two years of writing, editing, dialogue, refinements, and finally the production of a manuscript in the fall of 2023, which you now hold in your hands as a book.

With the influence of these faculty members, the book was structured to be used in the primary teaching course in their curriculum: EML5105—Teaching Process and Media Presentations. While this book was tooled to fit the requirements of this particular course, it is not limited solely to it but is designed to benefit the reader with *instructional strategies* for contemporary ministry, as the title suggests. It is an academically informed, distinctively Christian, practical textbook on developing the art of teaching.

James Riley Estep Jr.
Director
Doctor of Educational Ministries Degree
Dallas Theological Seminary

Jay L. Sedwick
Department Chair
Educational Ministries and Leadership
Dallas Theological Seminary

CONTRIBUTORS

The book's authors are academically prepared practitioners who hold academic degrees, higher education positions, and a wealth of ministry experience in local congregations and various Christian ministries around the world.

Michael J. Anthony, *BA, MA, MRE, PhD, PhD.* Dr. Anthony taught nonprofit management and leadership studies for twenty-seven years at Biola University's Talbot School of Theology, where he is currently an emeritus professor. He has served on staff with five local churches in roles including interim senior pastor, associate pastor, family pastor, and youth pastor. He is president of Calibrate Global Consulting, a business that provides leadership development resources to ministry leaders and nonprofit organizations in North America. Most recently he was the COO and CFO at Dream Centers in Colorado Springs where his wife, Michelle, serves as the executive pastor to families at New Life Church.

Mark L. Bailey, *AA, BA, MDiv, ThM, PhD, DD.* Dr. Bailey assumed the role of DTS chancellor after serving for nineteen years as the seminary's fifth president and continues his role as senior professor in the Bible exposition department. He has pastored various churches in Arizona and Texas. He was a seminar instructor for Walk Thru the Bible Ministries for twenty years and is in demand for Bible conferences and other preaching engagements all over the country and world. His overseas ministries have included service in Venezuela, Argentina, Hungary, and China.

Jennifer Brooks, *BA, MSEd, MAMC/MACE, DEdMin.* For the past thirty-six years, Dr. Brooks has worked her way through the church, serving every age group as Christian educator director and as a member of the worship team. She has taught preservice teachers preparing for state certification. She and her husband have been on mission trips in Ukraine, the Philippines, and the Middle East. Dr. Brooks's passion is helping people discover what God designed them to do and encouraging them to find ways to achieve that.

Stacey Davis, *BA, MACE, PhD.* Dr. Davis's passion is helping others discover their gifts and talents for works of service that the Lord Jesus Christ planned for them. Prior to joining the DTS faculty, her vocational ministry experience included leadership roles at Saddleback Church, Willow Creek Community Church, and Mariners Church. During those years she pursued a doctorate in educational studies while serving as an adjunct faculty member at both the undergraduate and graduate levels at Biola University and other Christian colleges and universities.

John Dyer, *BS, ThM, PhD.* Dr. Dyer likes to say, "When I code, I can feel God's pleasure." This desire to glorify God by showing how our creativity is an important aspect of our role as image bearers drives Dr. Dyer's work and teaching. A former youth pastor, he enjoys working with students to see how the biblical story brings insight and clarity to the ideas found in science, sociology, and culture. Dr. Dyer is married to Amber, a literature and philosophy professor, and has two lovely children.

Sue Edwards, *BS, MA, DMin.* Dr. Edwards is professor emeritus of Christian education with a specialization in women's studies at Dallas Theological Seminary. She brings more than forty years of experience into the classroom as a Bible teacher, curriculum writer, and overseer of several megachurch women's ministries. As minister to women, she has worked with women from all walks of life, ages, and stages around the world. Her Bible studies have ushered thousands of women all over the country and overseas into deeper Scripture study and community experiences.

James Riley Estep Jr., *BA, MA, MA, MDiv, DMin, PhD.* Dr. Estep has a long history of service in Christian higher education, serving in Bible colleges, Christian universities, and seminaries, and has served in a variety of Christian education ministries. He is cofounder of e2: effective elders, a ministry exclusively focused on equipping church leaders to lead. His ministry has also taken him to teach internationally in Austria, Canada, and China. Dr. Estep has also taught and written on a wide variety of subjects and to a wide range of audiences. He is currently director of the DEdMin program and a professor of educational ministries and leadership at DTS.

Scott Harris, *BBA, ThM, PhD.* Dr. Harris finds great joy in helping men and women prepare for the task that God has called them to fulfill. He has a background of various ministry platforms. He served on staff with the local church. He has been the headmaster of a small private school, directed a graduate program at a Christian university, and has served on staff in the local church.

George Hillman, *BS, MDiv, PhD.* Dr. Hillman serves as the vice president for education and professor of educational ministries and leadership at DTS. He previously served as vice president of student life, and as chair of the educational ministries and leadership department, he oversaw the MA in Christian education degree program and the creation of the MA in Christian leadership degree program. Dr. Hillman came to DTS in 2002 with years of pastoral experience in churches and parachurch organizations in Texas and Georgia.

Phil Humphries, *BS, ThM, DMin.* Dr. Humphries served in pastoral ministry for thirty-five years in the roles of associate pastor, executive pastor, and senior pastor. He has experience in the areas of Christian education, small groups, administration, church planting, and pastoral leadership. He has an interest in emotional intelligence and personal and organizational leadership development. Dr. Humphries has a heart for both the congregant and the student.

Michael S. Lawson, *BA, ThM, PhD.* Dr. Lawson invested seventeen years in pastoral work and Christian education before returning to teach at DTS in 1986. His special concern for Christian education in the developing world has guided his international preaching and teaching schedule in scores of countries around the world, particularly China. In recent years numerous international Bible colleges and seminaries have requested his help in curriculum design and faculty development.

Michael A. Ortiz, *BA, JD, ThM, PhD.* Dr. Ortiz was born in New York City to Cuban immigrants. After receiving a law degree from Southern Methodist University in 1988 and developing his practice in Florida, he submitted his life to Christ. Most of his ministry prior to DTS involved theological education leadership and teaching in Spanish-speaking countries, especially Cuba. Since being at DTS, Dr. Ortiz served as the initial director of DTS en Español, a department developed to offer master's-level programs to the Spanish world. He currently serves as international director of the International Council for Evangelical Theological Education, which further positions him as a key leader in global theological education.

Jay L. Sedwick, *BS, ThM, MA, PhD.* Dr. Sedwick has more than forty years of youth ministry experience, combined with twenty-seven years of faculty service. He served on the board of the Association of Youth Ministry Educators and has served as president of the board for the Society of Professors in Christian Ministry. He also serves as vice chairman of the board for World Link Ministries, an evangelistic, church planting, and pastoral-training ministry around the world.

Jim Thames, *BA, ThM, PhD.* Dr. Thames has served in a variety of academic administrative roles since joining the DTS staff in 1984, including professor, registrar, and currently academic dean. His years of experience in academic administration at DTS have given him a unique perspective and backdrop for his classes. Dr. Thames has been involved in overseas ministry and is active in his local church, including several years of service as a teacher and as a member of the board of elders.

WHY WRITE SUCH A TEXT?

Why assemble such a team of contributors with their academic credentials and practical expertise in teaching and ministry? The real purpose of this book is threefold. First, the book is designed to equip ministry students to teach God's Word with both accuracy and with excellence. "Do your best to present yourself to God as one approved, a worker who has no need to be ashamed, rightly handling the word of truth" (2 Tim. 2:15 ESV). Second, it plumbs the depths of Christian teaching theory, not relegating it to mere creative methods of teaching but broadening it to include intentional strategies for instruction in the church. Just as they would commit themselves to sound exegesis of the Word (*orthodoxy*), ministry students can now equally commit themselves to embracing sound teaching practices (*orthopraxy*). Finally, as they enter the field of ministry to which God has called them, they will be supplied with a resource to train and equip others to become more effective teachers of the Word. As Paul encouraged Timothy, "What you have heard from me in the presence of many witnesses entrust to faithful men, who will be able to teach others also" (2 Tim. 2:2 ESV).

We pray that this book is both a blessing to your ministry and a resource to equip you and others for kingdom service.

CHAPTER 1

JESUS: THE MASTER TEACHER

James Riley Estep Jr. & Jay L. Sedwick

For three decades I (Jay) have led the sophomore boys' small group at my church on Sunday mornings. I ask them a lot of questions. The Sunday school answer to all those questions is "Jesus," or so the joke goes. When we talk about the ways many religious groups throughout the centuries have gone astray, it is most often related to a misunderstanding of who Jesus is and what he has done for us. Jesus is the center of everything (Col. 1:13–20). What God wants us to know and understand about Jesus's life and ministry was recorded for us by the four gospel writers. Who he was and is, what he did and does, how he worked and works are all described for us to study and emulate. It makes sense to examine the Savior and what made him the Master Teacher.

JESUS, THE MASTER TEACHER

Modern New Testament scholarship has tried to explain who Jesus was: a Cynic philosopher, a mystic, a magician/miracle-worker, the teacher of righteousness in the Dead Sea Scrolls, or a spirit-possessed sage.[1] In addition to being God's Son, our Savior and Lord, Jesus had many titles throughout Scripture. One of the most frequent is *Teacher*. He

1. Edward J. Young, "The Teacher of Righteousness and Jesus Christ," *Westminster Theological Journal* 18 (1956): 121–45; Craig A. Evans, *Fabricating Jesus: How Modern Scholars Distort the Gospels* (Downers Grove, IL: IVP Books, 2006).

is called *rabbi* fourteen times.[2] Nicodemus famously addressed Jesus saying, "Rabbi, we know that you are a teacher come from God" (John 3:2a ESV). John reports that Mary, upon realizing she was speaking to Jesus after his resurrection, "cried out in Aramaic, 'Rabboni!'" (John 20:16 NIV). John immediately explains the word means "teacher."

As Mark 10:1 describes, it was Jesus's "custom" to teach. The gospel writers utilize a variety of titles to describe Jesus's instructional activity: *Didaskalos* (Gk. "teacher"), *rabbi* (Heb. "teacher"), and *rabonni* (Heb. "honored teacher"), as well as the more generic *master* and *leader* are used in regard to Jesus's educational endeavors.[3] Obviously, teaching was an important part of his earthly ministry. As C. B. Eavy concludes, "Jesus regarded himself as a teacher. He spoke of Himself as such. He permitted others to address Him thus, and He was generally recognized by others as a teacher."[4]

WAS JESUS A "TRADITIONAL" RABBI?

While Jesus functioned as a teacher and was even referred to as *rabbi*, Jesus did not conform to the teachers of his day. This is readily attested to in the Gospels. On one occasion, "The officers then came to the chief priests and Pharisees, who said to them, 'Why did you not bring him [Jesus]?' The officers answered, 'No one ever spoke like this man!'" (John 7:45–46 ESV). Similarly, at the Sermon on the Mount, "The crowds were astonished at his teaching, for he was teaching them as one who had authority, and not as their scribes" (Matt. 7:28–29 ESV).

As a teacher, Jesus did bear some similarity to his contemporaries. For example, the metaphor of the "yoke" in Matthew 11:28–29 describes the relationship of a teacher to his pupil in rabbinic Judaism (cf. Sir. 51.26). New Testament scholar Donald Guthrie observes regarding Jesus's teaching methods,

> Jewish methods of teaching may give some help in understanding the methods of Jesus. . . . It must, of course, be recognized that Jesus was not a traditional rabbi. His unconventional purpose must have affected His methods, yet He could not have

2. Robert H. Stein, *The Method and Message of Jesus' Teachings* (Philadelphia: Westminster, 1978), 1.
3. Roy B. Zuck, *Teaching as Jesus Taught* (Grand Rapids: Baker, 1995), 25.
4. C. B. Eavey, *History of Christian Education* (Chicago: Moody, 1964), 78.

> been unmindful of the need for both memorization and interpretation. . . . His purpose was to adapt His teaching to make the most efficient use of the passing opportunity [to teach]. The mechanical character of most traditional Jewish methods was wholly unsuited to such a purpose. [5]

The methods Jesus used were unlike those of his contemporaries. Theirs was intended for the formal, scholastic settings of rabbinical Judaism and the synagogue; his was intended to transform lives. "In stark contrast to the general practice of the rabbis of his day, Jesus's overwhelmingly favored context was the open air. . . . Jesus's interaction with the religious leaders was done in places of worship . . . and even more the reverse is true—that in places of worship Jesus focused his attention on the religious leaders."[6]

Jesus's teachings were also different from the traditions and teachers of his day.[7] For example, we are all probably familiar with the Beatitudes that open the Sermon on the Mount (Matt. 5:1–12; Luke 6:20–23), but we may not be familiar with the wisdom literature of intertestamental Judaism, such as Ben Sirach (a.k.a. Ecclesiasticus). Its wisdom differs distinctly from what Jesus teaches. The following are several statements from Ben Sirach 25 (NAB Revised) entitled "Those Who Are Worthy of Praise":

- "Three kinds of people I hate, and I loathe their manner of life: a proud pauper, a rich liar, and a lecherous old fool" (25.2).
- "There are nine who come to mind as blessed, a tenth whom my tongue proclaims: The man who finds joy in his children, and the one who lives to see the downfall of his enemies" (25.7).
- "Happy the one who does not sin with the tongue, who does not serve an inferior" (25.8b).

This is quite different from Jesus's affirmation of the poor, the peacemaker, and the meek. Jesus's teachings centered on the good news! The synoptic gospel writers mention the good news fourteen times in

5. Donald Guthrie, "Jesus," in *A History of Religious Educators*, ed. Elmer L. Towns (Grand Rapids: Baker, 1975), 17–18.
6. Perry W. H. Shaw, "Jesus: Oriental Teacher Par Excellence," *Christian Education Journal* 1NS (1997): 89.
7. See Zuck, *Teaching as Jesus Taught*, 40–41.

various contexts, always as the thrust of his message.[8] The Gospels related this central theme to several other frequent subjects: (1) God, such as God's Fatherhood; (2) Jesus himself as the eschatological Son of Man; (3) the already–not yet kingdom of God (Matt. 12:28; Mark 13; and Luke 11:20, paralleled in Matt. 24 and Luke 21); (4) the Holy Spirit (John 14–16); and (5) humanity in relation to God and one another, such as in the Sermon on the Mount (see Figure 1.1).[9]

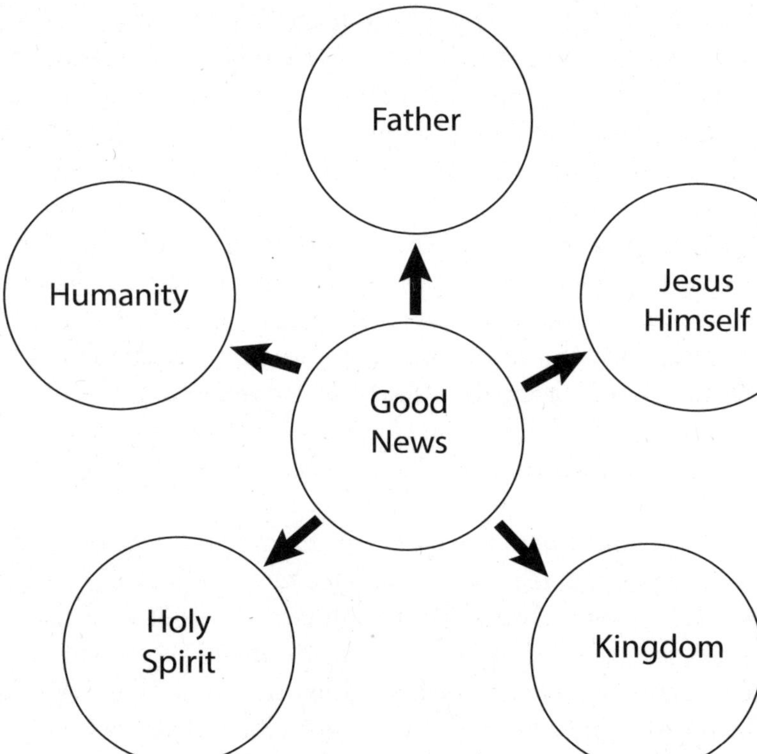

Figure 1.1: The Good News in relation to frequent subjects

Some of Jesus's teachings paralleled the subject matter of rabbinical Judaism,[10] but what Jesus said, who Jesus was, and how he taught

8. Matt. 4:23; 9:35; 11:5; Mark 1:14, 15; 16:15; Luke 1:19; 2:10; 3:18; 4:18, 43; 7:22; 8:1; 16:16.
9. Guthrie, "Jesus," 26–35.
10. Brad H. Young, *Meet the Rabbis: Rabbinic Thought and the Teachings of Jesus* (Peabody, MA: Hendrickson, 2007), 63–77.

captured the crowd's attention and admiration (Matt. 5–7). Lifelong Christian educator Warren Benson captures why Jesus is often referred to as the Master Teacher:

> The Savior was the quintessential teacher. Being God in human flesh He had no weakness as a pedagogue. He modeled the truth in an ultimate sense. Christ never lost touch with those He was teaching despite loftiness of His content or the holiness of his character. He knew how to adapt to their level of understanding and used the familiar to explain the profound.[11]

Ultimately, Jesus is the master teacher not because of what he did but because of who he was!

JESUS'S TEACHING PRINCIPLES

Understanding the life of Jesus and his activities is just as important as studying his methods for communicating and teaching God's truth. His life is an example for us to emulate. Several principles arise from studying the teaching ministry of Jesus.

Jesus Taught Persons

Jesus taught persons. Before saying "of course he did," note that Jesus saw the individual in the crowd, not just the masses. Jesus saw the individual among the religious leaders opposing him, not just an opposition party. Jesus became personal with his hearers. For example, in Luke 19, Jesus saw the small-statured Zacchaeus and called to him, "Zaccheaus, hurry and come down, for I must stay at your house today" (Luke 19:5 ESV). To what end? "Today salvation has come to this house, since he also is a son of Abraham. For the Son of Man came to seek and to save the lost" (Luke 19:9–10 ESV). While others may have seen the crowds of people, Jesus saw persons in a crowd.

Jesus Taught with Grace and Truth

John describes Jesus as "full of grace and truth" (John 1:14 ESV). Jesus's followers embraced this in their teaching, such as Paul's

11. Warren Benson, "Christ the Master Teacher," in *Christian Education: Foundations for the Future*, ed. Robert E. Clark, Lin Johnson, and Allyn K. Sloat (Chicago: Moody, 1991), 89–90.

instruction to the Ephesians, "Rather, speaking the truth in love, we are to grow up in every way into him who is the head, into Christ" (Eph. 4:15 ESV). He had to balance grace and truth because one without the other would be unremarkable. As Figure 1.2 illustrates, if Jesus had taught truth without grace, he would have sounded like the religious leaders of his day. Likewise, if Jesus had taught with grace without truth, he would have led his hearers to a licentious lifestyle. But Jesus avoided these extremes and shared a message that matched his life, full of both grace and truth.

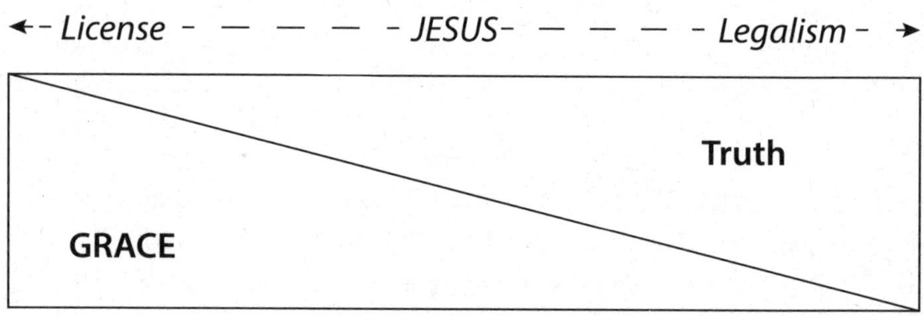

Figure 1.2: Jesus's life, full of grace and truth

In Matthew 23:23 (ESV), Jesus illustrates this principle when he pronounces, "Woe to you, scribes and Pharisees, hypocrites! For you tithe mint and dill and cumin, and have neglected the weightier matters of the law: justice and mercy and faithfulness. These you ought to have done, without neglecting the others." He condemns their "obedience" to the law without concern for the "weightier matters," a both-and approach, truth and grace; not either-or, truth versus grace. This is perhaps the rationale behind the slogan that pervades Dallas Theological Seminary's campus: "Teach Truth, Love Well."

Jesus Taught with Humility

The apostle John illustrates Christ's humility in John 13. The night before his death, Jesus was eating the Passover meal (what we as Christians call the Last Supper) with his twelve disciples, who were enjoying fellowship with him in the upper room. To their surprise, he got up from the table and prepared himself to do the nastiest job reserved for the lowliest servants of any household—foot washing. The climate was arid, the terrain dusty, and the feet sweaty, dirty, and smelly. Simon Peter objected. How could Jesus, the Messiah, humble himself to perform such a lowly, menial, servant's task? Jesus gently rebuked Peter and continued to wash their feet. Fortunately for us, Jesus helped us understand the purpose of his actions: "You call me Teacher and Lord, and you are right, for so I am. If I then, your Lord and Teacher, have washed your feet, you also ought to wash one another's feet. For I have given you an example, that you also should do just as I have done to you" (John 13:13–15 ESV). The creator Jesus, who spoke the universe into existence and holds it all together (Col. 1:16–17), demonstrated humility as he taught in a way that the disciples could not miss or forget. His example of humility is for teachers today to follow as well. If we strive to become teachers of God's Word, then we too must demonstrate humility in our teaching.

Jesus Leveraged Imagery

Jesus employed verbal imagery as a master teacher. Shaw lists thirteen items that capture the wide spectrum of speech devices Jesus utilized: inversion, parallelism, dualism, euphemism, hyperbole, irony, metaphor, parable, paradox, proverb, rhetorical questions, riddle, and simile.[12] Jesus selected his speech techniques based on the audience. Jesus's clever and creative use of verbal imagery is noteworthy, particularly in the frequent use of parables and illustrations, such as "You are the salt of the earth . . ." and "You are the light of the world . . . a city . . . a lamp" (Matt. 5:13–15 ESV).

Jesus Challenged the Status Quo

Jesus criticized religious leaders of his time, challenging the spiritual status quo. As previously discussed, while he used the terminology of traditional rabbinical instruction, such as *rabbi* and *yoke*, he did not copy their instructional content or strategies. Matthew 15 opens with one such example. "Then Pharisees and scribes came to Jesus from Jerusalem and said, 'Why do your disciples break the tradition of the elders? For they do not wash their hands when they eat.' He answered them, 'And why do you break the commandment of God for the sake of

12. Shaw, "Jesus," 87.

your tradition? . . . So for the sake of your tradition you have made void the word of God. You hypocrites!'" (Matt. 15:1–3, 6b–7a ESV).

Neither did the social status quo impede his ministry. For example, John 4:1–30 narrates the familiar story of the woman at the well. This was a Samaritan speaking to a Jew, a woman publicly conversing with a man, and about matters of theological concern at that! Still, Jesus did not hesitate to share with her and affirm her conclusion that he was indeed the Messiah, "I who speak to you am he" (John 4:26 ESV). Luke highlights marginalized people whom Jesus elevated and to whom he gave his personal attention and affirmation, such as children (Luke 18:16) and women (Luke 23:27–28). As Thomas R. Schreiner reminds us, in Luke's gospel there are "no little people."[13]

Jesus Taught Principles

Perhaps more directly, Jesus did not teach rules. He did not provide copious lists of dos and don'ts. Rather, he taught principles to guide his disciples' lives from their hearts instead of by external commands. Perhaps no passage demonstrates this better than the Sermon on the Mount. In Matthew 5–7 Jesus was not critiquing or replacing the Old Testament, which should be evident when he said, "Do not think that I have come to abolish the Law or the Prophets; I have not come to abolish them but to fulfill them" (Matt. 5:17 ESV). Throughout his lesson, he made reference to the teaching of the scribes and Pharisees, the oral traditions that expounded on the Old Testament, as should be evident from the repeated phrase "You have *heard* that" (Matt. 5:21, 27, 33, 38, 43 ESV, emphasis added), not the familiar phrase "It is written," which typically precedes a citation of Scripture (e.g., Matt. 2:5; 4:4, 6, 7, 10; 11:10; 21:13; 26:24, 31). Jesus moved his hearers from abiding by external rules and regulations to living in the proverbial "spirit of the law." He said, for example, "You have heard that it was said to those of old, 'You shall not murder; and whoever murders will be liable to judgment.' But I say to you that everyone who is angry with his brother will be liable to judgment; whoever insults his brother will be liable to the council; and whoever says, 'You fool!' will be liable to the hell of fire"

13. Thomas R. Schreiner, "Jesus's Love for the Marginalized of This World," Crossway.org, January 6, 2022, accessed October 13, 2023, https://www.crossway.org/articles/jesuss-love-for-the-marginalized-of-this-world/.

(Matt. 5:21–22 ESV). Notice, Jesus set a primary principle of managing one's anger (internal) that should then have an immediate influence on one's actions (external). "The positive quality in Christ's teaching indicates the type of good man the Master had it in mind to produce."[14]

Jesus's Teaching Was Transformational

Jesus's commission to his disciples was one of transformation. It called upon them to "make disciples," the only command in Matthew 28:18–20. How? By going, baptizing, and perhaps most significantly, "teaching them to observe all that I have commanded you" (Matt. 28:20 ESV). Putting it simply, Jesus changed lives. No one who encountered him was ever the same. "He taught that he might create, mature and direct a body of Christian impulse which would find expression in all the nobler forms of conduct and in the highest lines of service."[15]

JESUS'S TEACHING METHODS

Much has been written on Jesus's teaching methods—entire books in the field of Christian education focus exclusively on methods—and hence our treatment of Jesus as a teacher focuses on methods as well. Perhaps the most extensive statistical study of Jesus's teaching methods was produced in 1997 by Perry W. H. Shaw.[16] Focusing on Jesus's teaching ministry in all four Gospels, the biblical data is sorted by teaching contexts, initiative (Jesus or others), audience, methodologies (which are more like strategies, i.e., categories of teaching methods), and teaching techniques (which are in fact methods). Further, the data is analyzed in terms of Jesus as teacher, contexts of instruction, and his audiences. From this, Shaw makes several observations regarding Jesus's teaching ministry:[17]

- *Context*: Jesus favored teaching in the outdoors, especially in the Synoptic Gospels.
- *Methodology*: Jesus lectured when teaching outside and in homes, using more interactive methods in the synagogue/temple.

---

14. C. R. Brown, "Christ as a Teacher," in *The Encyclopedia of Sunday Schools and Religious Education*, ed. John T. McFarland, 3 vols. (New York: Thomas Nelson, 1915), 1:249.
15. Brown, "Christ as a Teacher," 249.
16. Shaw, "Jesus," 83–94.
17. Shaw, "Jesus," 89–90.

- *Initiative*: Jesus initiated the vast majority of his teaching sessions, especially with the disciples.
- *Audience*: All four Gospels portray Jesus focusing his teaching primarily with his disciples, as should be expected, and then with the multitudes and religious leaders; the Synoptics emphasize the multitudes and John's gospel the religious leaders.

In terms of methods, specific techniques in teaching, Jesus utilized a full spectrum of practices.

Teaching Through Discourse

Jesus was an articulate story teller. In the Synoptic Gospels, 86 percent of the times Jesus was teaching he was speaking through discourse, which includes parables, narratives, and other means of conveying content, as opposed to using dialogue or discussion.[18] Jesus rarely if ever used what could be described strictly as lecture, delivering a prepared monologue. Perhaps the two longest discourses in the Gospels are recorded in Matthew's gospel, namely the Sermon on the Mount (Matt. 5–7) and Jesus's eschatological discourse (Matt. 24–25). However, lengthy streams of content were not his typical method of instruction. Guthrie notes that Jesus's "general method was to impart His teaching more concisely,"[19] that is, in short talks. Even then, Jesus incorporated a variety of techniques such as parallelism, euphemism, hyperbole, metaphor, and rhetorical questions when conveying truth.[20]

Methods of Reasoning

Lectures are not always sufficient; methods that facilitate reasoning and critical thinking are required. In such instances, Jesus employed methods that caused his audience to pause and think, logical arguments and methods that were more dialogical. The Gospels depict Jesus using analogy (Matt. 7:10–11; John 10:11); *argumentum ad absurdum*—demonstrating the absurdity of an idea (Matt. 12:22–32; Mark 3:23; Luke 11:15–23); *argumentum ad hominem*—identifying the false

18. Shaw, "Jesus," 91–92.
19. Guthrie, "Jesus," 18.
20. Shaw, "Jesus," 87.

or erroneous motives and character of another (John 10:34–36; Matt. 21:23–27); *argumentum a fortiori*—providing a more certain reason for an idea than others can provide (Matt. 7:11; John 13:14–15); and question and answer (Matt. 16:26).[21]

Interactive Process Methods

Perhaps one of the most interactive teaching sessions recorded in the Gospels is Jesus's engagement with the disciples on the road to Emmaus in Luke 24:13–35. Jesus uses discussion (v. 14), inquiry (v. 17), correction (vv. 25–27), modeling (vv. 30–31), and response (vv. 33–35). Robert Pazmiño comments that Jesus's teaching in Luke 24 had three parts: question, listen, and exhort. Likewise, teachers must engage their students to think and reflect, not merely mimic.[22] A modern instructional method that parallels Jesus's is *scaffolding* (see chapters 11 and 16), wherein an instructor uses interaction with the learner designed to guide and support the learner to a desired objective, so that ultimately the student can reach a conclusion without the aid of the instructor.[23]

Teaching by Action

Jesus oftentimes performed miracles not merely to exhibit his authority and power, but to accentuate a lesson. George Barker Stevens said, "The miracles of Jesus may also be reckoned among the methods of his teaching, since they were never mere exhibitions of power, but were regarded by him as a part of his revealing, saving work—a method of disclosing the grace of God which wrought in his beneficent ministry."[24] However, the action does not have to be miraculous to be instructional. It can be a symbolic act designed to reinforce instruction, such as when Jesus washed the feet of the disciples (John 13:12–38). Jesus reminded us that words accompanied by action make a more significant impact.

21. Guthrie, "Jesus," 19–21.
22. Robert W. Pazmiño, *Foundational Issues in Christian Education: An Introduction in Evangelical Perspective* (Grand Rapids: Baker Academic, 1997), 38.
23. Lori McDonald, "What Is Scaffolding and How to Use It," TeachHub.com, July 9, 2020, accessed October 14, 2023, https://www.teachhub.com/teaching-strategies/2020/07/5-scaffolding-teaching-strategies-to-try-today/.
24. George Barker Stevens, *The Teaching of Jesus* (Whitefish, MT: Kessinger Publishing, 2010), 38–39.

Teaching with Parables

Scholars differentiate between parables and proverbs, as well as between metaphor and simile. For example, Stevens outlines the difference between parables and various forms of literary types as follows:

- *Fable*: "moves on a lower plane," simplistic stories, like the moralism in Aesop's fables
- *Myth*: "wears the guise of truth," such as Homeric myths
- *Proverbs*: brief statements of "practical wisdom, and seldom deals with truths which are distinctly religious"
- *Allegory*: closely resembles parables, but "the allegory identifies the symbol and the thing signified," such as John 10 where the shepherd imagery is identified with Christ[25]

However, this distinction is more modern than ancient. Lutheran New Testament scholar Joachim Jeremias cautions that the category of literature called *mashal* in Hebrew included all manner of figurative forms of speech, including parables, proverbs, fables, riddles, and even humor.[26]

Jesus was not the first person to teach with parables. We find them in Judges (9:8–15) and during the reign of King David (2 Sam. 12:1–4). Stevens divides Jesus's parables into "two general classes": "(1) those in which some fact in the actual world is adduced as illustrating a moral or religious principle; and, (2) those in which some imagined event . . . is narrated to illustrate a spiritual truth or process."[27] The most readily recognized teaching method employed by Jesus was the parable.

> Parables were Jesus's characteristic teaching technique for his provocative, symbol-redefining, dangerous mission. First, their oblique way of presenting truth was (and is) difficult to resist. Second, their storytelling form invites hearers to identify themselves in the narrative and to implicate themselves in their response. Third, they fulfill scriptural predictions of Israel's lack

25. Stevens, *The Teaching of Jesus*, 40–42.
26. Joachim Jeremias, *The Parables of Jesus*, 2nd ed. (Norwich, England: SCM Press, 1972), 20–21.
27. Stevens, *The Teaching of Jesus*, 39.

> of response. And finally, Jesus prevented early termination of his mission through these opaque stories.[28]

Perhaps this is why Jesus only interpreted two of his parables (Matt. 13:18–23 and 13:36–43), leaving all the others to be understood by his hearers.

In the past, according to Philip Chia, some questioned the value of parables as a teaching method, suggesting that they do not really aid in memorization, even to the extent of questioning the recollection of the gospel authors to recall what Jesus taught them, particularly the parable of the Mustard Seed and the parable of the Sower. However, more recent studies have actually challenged this notion, noting that the use of parables led to enhanced memory and lessons learned.[29]

JESUS TEACHING THE DISCIPLES

The term *disciple* literally means "student" and is used 142 times in the Synoptic Gospels (cf. Matt. 28:20; Mark 6:30; Luke 12:12). Although the disciples received regular instruction from Jesus, they were often still at a loss for understanding the depth of his instruction (Mark 8:15–16; John 6:5–9; Acts 1:6). Disciples adhered their lives to the instruction of their teacher, requiring from Jesus a distinctive approach to instruction and relationship with his followers. Disciple making was his instructional context and method, with his followers learning through socialization and non-formal teaching.[30]

"Jesus . . . did not establish a school with a philosophical doctrine or special method of interpreting the law. His followers learned by observing what he said and did in different situations."[31] Jesus's relationship with his disciples matured them from being his students to being his apostles. How? His relationship was developmental. The gospel of Mark makes this progression evident. Early in their relationship, Jesus does

28. Ted Newell, "What Kind of Teacher Is Jesus?" Crossway.org, February 8, 2009, accessed October 14, 2023, https://www.crossway.org/articles/what-kind-of-teacher-is-jesus/.
29. Philip Suciadi Chia, "Analysis of the Effectiveness of Jesus' Parable: A Cognitive Psychology Approach," *Journal of Research on Christian Education* 29, no. 3 (2020): 272–84.
30. Cf. Raymond Calkins, *How Jesus Dealt with Men* (New York: Abingdon-Cokesbury, 1962); Herman Harrell Horne, *Jesus: The Master Teacher* (New York: Association Press, 1920); Herman Harrell Horne, *Teaching Techniques of Jesus* (Grand Rapids: Kregel, 1982).
31. Pheme Perkins, *Jesus as Teacher*, Understanding Jesus Today (Cambridge: Cambridge University Press, 1990), 1.

and the disciples watch (Mark 1:14–3:12). Then the disciples become more involved: Jesus does and the disciples help (Mark 3:13–6:6). Then the disciples do while Jesus supervises (Mark 6:7–13, 30). This process crafted the twelve into his apostles, wherein the disciples do and Jesus is in the background (Mark 16:15–16, 20).

The twelve took their marching orders seriously. After Jesus gave them the Great Commission in Matthew 28:18–20, the Lord brought a harvest of three thousand new disciples through Peter's bold proclamation on the day of Pentecost. Luke tells us the new believers "devoted themselves to the apostles' teaching" (Acts 2:42 ESV). Teaching the new believers all that Jesus had commanded the twelve was a critical aspect of the Jerusalem church's development. Jesus's former pupils, the apostles, assumed the task of teaching through instruction, preaching, and writing. The apostles perpetuated Jesus's mission by making disciples for Christ (Acts 14:21). Doctrine assumes a crucial role in the church through their instruction (Acts 2:42; 5:28; 13:2; 17:19). The apostle Paul was perhaps the most prolific educator among the apostles, particularly through his correspondences and established missionary endeavors.[32]

The apostles had learned how to teach from the Master Teacher for three and a half years, both by watching and personally experiencing his message and methods. Jesus was the model and example for them to follow in every way.

JESUS AND US AS TEACHERS

When Luke opened his second volume, Acts, he wrote, "In the first book [the gospel], O Theophilus, I have dealt with all that Jesus began to do *and teach*" (Acts 1:1 ESV, emphasis added). Luke goes on to pen a first-century account of the ministry of the church, the body of Christ. Our ministry of Christian education is the continuation of Jesus's teaching ministry. Yes, Jesus finished his work of salvation, but we are continuing to fulfill his teaching ministry today!

Jesus's final marching orders, as recorded in Matthew's presentation of our Savior's life, is called the Great Commission (Matt. 28:18–20). We are to make disciples of all nations. But how? The commandment has two inseparable components that must function together for either of them to work at all: *baptizing* and *teaching*. Like an airplane that cannot

32. Roy B. Zuck, *Teaching as Paul Taught* (Grand Rapids: Baker Books, 1998).

fly if either wing is damaged, so making disciples will not work if either component does not function properly. *Baptizing* represents identification with and acceptance of the gospel. Jesus essentially told the disciples to take the message of the gospel to the world by winning others to the faith through evangelism in the name of the triune God. *Teaching* those who believed is the required next step for new disciples in order for them to mature in the faith and reproduce additional disciples. The assumption is the current disciples will teach new believing disciples everything Jesus had taught them. The chain of disciples stretches from today all the way back to the day Jesus spoke these words.

CONCLUSION

As Christian educators we need to follow not only the mission of Jesus but his model of instruction, as Shaw observed: "Although Jesus followed the general patterns of his day, he was in no way bound by them. Rather he spoke in forms that were understandable to those around him, but broke through the tradition to communicate more effectively and to a wider audience."[33] We should do the same!

REFLECTION QUESTIONS

1. How can you better reflect and embrace Jesus's example as a teacher?
2. What about Jesus's approach to teaching do you find most challenging? Why?
3. How could your church's teaching ministry reflect and embrace Jesus's model of teaching?
4. How might you introduce your teaching team to Jesus as Master Teacher?
5. Describe how Jesus's strategy for teaching is still relevant for the twenty-first–century church and society.

RECOMMENDED READING

Andrews, Edward D. *Jesus Christ: The Great Teacher*. Cambridge, OH: Christian Publishing House, 2019.

Carlson, Gregory. *Rock-Solid Teacher*. Grand Rapids: Baker, 2006.

Perkins, Pheme. *Jesus as Teacher*. Understanding Jesus Today. Cambridge: Cambridge University Press, 1990.

33. Shaw, "Jesus," 92.

Rixon, L. D. *How Jesus Taught: Methods and Roles of Jesus Christ the Teacher*. Croydon, Australia: S.M.B.C., 1997.
Stein, Robert H. *The Method and Message of Jesus' Teachings*. Philadelphia: Westminster, 1978.
Wilson, Clifford A. *Jesus: The Master Teacher*. Grand Rapids: Baker, 2001.
Zuck, Roy B. *Teaching as Jesus Taught*. Grand Rapids: Baker, 1995.

CHAPTER 2

A THEOLOGY OF TEACHING

Michael J. Anthony

Assumptions are powerful influencers. Everyone has them and they shape our perspective on the world around us, influence our values, and ultimately mold our behavior. The danger comes when we become blind to our own assumptions, or they are based on false information. Assumptions can be either explicit or implicit. When we bring these assumptions, true or false, into the learning environment, we run the risk of significantly impacting the learning that takes place. That's why identifying our own personal assumptions about teaching and learning is so important prior to walking into the classroom. One of the more prominent false assumptions about teaching and learning is that all students learn the same way. It simply isn't true. We know from research that there are at least four different preferences, or styles, of learning. Each is based on a preference for thinking, feeling, watching, or acting. When combined, this matrix significantly impacts how an individual learns.[1]

Another false assumption about teaching and learning is that children and adults learn the same way. Again, we know this to be false because children have a completely different worldview from adults based upon their limited life experience. Adults bring their wealth of experience and

1. For greater development of this concept, see "About 4MAT," accessed September 25, 2024, https://4mat4learning.com.au/what-is-4mat/. I also recommend Marlene D. LeFever, *Learning Styles: Reaching Everyone God Gave You to Teach* (Colorado Springs: David C. Cook, 2004).

prior knowledge to the learning context and therefore possess different objectives, motives, strategies, and priorities for learning.[2]

A final false assumption about teaching and learning is that people rarely change once they become adults. Fortunately, as Christian educators we partner with the Holy Spirit, who can change the condition of the heart and mind and reshape us into the image of Christ (Rom. 8:28–29). Destructive patterns of thoughts and behaviors, which may have plagued us in childhood or early adolescence, do not have to have long-term influence on our lives in adulthood.

Assumptions we know to be true and that influence the teaching and learning process are evident throughout Scripture. Chief among them is that God created us (Gen. 1:1) and desires to engage us in a personal relationship with him. We reject the deistic tenet that God set the universe in motion and subsequently retreated from further influence, thus leaving humans to fend for themselves.

Second, God has given us a written account of his engagement with humans in his Word, and this record provides us with all that we need to enjoy a robust and meaningful relationship with him. One of the primary purposes of God's written Word is instruction. Paul instructed his young disciple Timothy that "all scripture is God-breathed and is useful for teaching, rebuking, correcting and training in righteousness" (2 Tim. 3:16 NIV).

Perhaps one of the most striking true assumptions we have as Christian educators is that we work in partnership with God to fulfill his objectives, not our own. Our goal is not simply to instill knowledge about God into people's minds, like pouring biblical knowledge into a mental silo, but rather to see the learner formed into the very image of Christ himself. Paul refers to this in his letter to the believers in Rome: "For those God foreknew he also predestined to be conformed to the image of his Son, that he might be the firstborn among many brothers and sisters" (Rom. 8:29 NIV).

Each of these biblical assumptions serves as a foundation for the Christian teacher. They help shape the very nature of the learning environment, instructional methodology, curriculum choices, and learning outcomes.

2. For an excellent explanation of this concept, see Sue Edwards, "Overwhelmed Adults," in *Invitation to Educational Ministry*, ed. George M. Hillman Jr. and Sue G. Edwards (Grand Rapids: Kregel, 2018), 174–92.

BIBLICAL PERSPECTIVES ON TEACHING AND LEARNING

Teaching and Learning in the Old Testament Era

We must consider all of Scripture as we form a biblical theology of teaching and learning. While it is possible to hand select a few choice verses, it is far more responsible to look across the entire testament of Scripture, both Old and New, to see the broad range of what God says regarding how he created us to learn and provide instruction.

One of the primary purposes of the Old Testament was to give believers a better understanding and awareness of their Creator. This involved instruction in the Torah, or law of God. While the term *Torah* may refer to all Jewish teachings and beliefs, it has a more specific and reverenced reference to the Pentateuch, the first five books of the Old Testament. In addition, the twenty-four books of the Jewish Bible, known as the *Tanakh*, also include the eight books of the Prophets (Joshua, Judges, Samuel, Kings, Isaiah, Jeremiah, Ezekiel, the twelve minor prophets) and the eleven books of the Writings (Psalms, Proverbs, Job, Song of Songs, Ruth, Lamentations, Ecclesiastes, Esther, Daniel, Ezra/Nehemiah, and Chronicles).[3] When viewed in a combined manner, these books form a wealth of material that guides, forms, and shapes our understanding of the very nature of God and his involvement with mankind.

A secondary purpose of the Old Testament was to provide instruction and guidance in the more practical issues of life such as dietary rules and regulations, matters of personal hygiene, guidance on parenting, regulations regarding washing clothes, crime, divorce, inheritance, court proceedings, sexuality, marriage, interpersonal relationships, and a host of other important and practical matters.

The home was considered the primary institution for instruction. Parents were responsible to ensure that their children had a basic understanding of God's laws, rules, and regulations. A child learned first at home and then in relationship within his or her community.[4] These early forms of homeschooling formed the basis of passing down Hebrew culture, norms, values, and religious practices from

3. "The 24 Books of the Hebrew Bible," Torah.org, https://torah.org/learning/basics-primer-torah-bible/.
4. Michelle D. Anthony, *Dreaming of More for the Next Generation: Lifetime Faith Ignited by Family Ministry* (Colorado Springs: David C Cook, 2012), 38.

one generation to the next.[5] "The role of teaching in Israel's family life must be seen in the context of teaching in the Old Testament community. Moses commands parents to teach their children (Exod. 13:9; Deut. 6), teaches Israel's elders how to adjudicate civic matters (Exod. 18:20), and assigns responsibility for teaching the law to Aaron and his descendants, the priests and Levites (Lev. 10:11; Deut. 33:10; cf. 2 Chron. 15:3)."[6]

Perhaps one of the most stalwart passages reflecting this Old Testament theme is found in Psalm 78:5–7 (NIV):

> He decreed statutes for Jacob and established the law in Israel, which he commanded our ancestors to teach their children, so the next generation would know them, even the children yet to be born, and they in turn would tell their children. Then they would put their trust in God and would not forget his deeds but would keep his commands.

This isn't to say that home life was the only means of instruction. Hebrew culture and community were replete with formal and informal instructional curricula. Stone monuments were scattered across the land as memorials to God's faithfulness and interactions with his people, annual festivals were constant reminders of important historical events in Israel's past, and from time to time Levitical priests would gather the people together for public readings of Scripture. Children were expected to attend and participate in these events as they provided significant reinforcement of God's teachings, which in turn made lasting impressions on their minds and the subsequent character development of Israel's children.

Teaching and Learning in the New Testament Era

Jesus rarely referred to himself as a teacher. However, history will always know him as the Master Teacher for his unique ability to penetrate the human heart with wisdom, understanding, and insight like no other. Though he never attended any of the "universities" of his day,

5. Michael J. Anthony and Warren S. Benson, *Exploring the History and Philosophy of Christian Education: Principles for the 21st Century* (Grand Rapids: Kregel, 2003), 25.
6. David L. Turner, "Teach, Teacher," in *Evangelical Dictionary of Biblical Theology*, ed. Walter A. Elwell, Baker Reference Library (Grand Rapids: Baker, 1996), 758.

he possessed a God-given ability to instruct his followers in ways that no formal instruction could have provided. For example, he occasionally taught using lectures but preferred object lessons, parables, poetry, metaphors, storytelling, and the occasional miracle. He was just as comfortable teaching in a small hamlet or village as he was on the steps of the ornate temple in Jerusalem. All learners were treated equally, whether rich or poor, healthy or infirm, members of the elite or the destitute and poor. He was not influenced by partiality but spoke truth regardless of consequences.

Jesus passed on an imperative to his disciples to go and instruct others using the same methods and values by which they had been instructed. Their ultimate mission was to go and make disciples throughout the world, and this would be accomplished primarily through teaching and instruction. "Therefore go and make disciples of all nations, baptizing them in the name of the Father and of the Son and of the Holy Spirit, and teaching them to obey everything I have commanded you. And surely I am with you always, to the very end of the age" (Matt. 28:19–20 NIV).

Evidently this approach took effect immediately, for soon after Christ's death and resurrection, Peter and John were arrested and subsequently put on trial before the Sanhedrin. Annas, the high priest, along with other members of his priestly family were in attendance. In their defense the disciples "schooled" these members of the Jewish elite regarding the prophetic words from Psalm 118:22 about their rejection of Jesus the Messiah. So humiliated were these religious leaders that they sat back and were amazed at how such unlearned, common men could have such an astute understanding of Old Testament teachings. Those in attendance "took note that these men had been with Jesus" (Acts 4:13 NIV).

It wasn't long before persecution broke out and Christian believers fled Jerusalem for safety. Wherever these bands of believers settled, they established churches where the teachings of Christ would be communicated. These church schools became the basis for training new Christian converts. Curriculum was pretty basic at first, but eventually a sixteen-chapter book, called the *Didache*, was published to instruct new believers in matters pertaining to living the Christian life (chapters 1–6); baptism, communion, and fasting (chapters 7–10); distinguishing between false teachers and true prophets, as well as qualifications for church leaders (chapters 11–15); and finally how to live a godly life in the midst of a fallen world while keeping hope alive in the imminent return of Christ (chapter 16).[7]

As those who had been personally trained by Christ (i.e., the apostles) died, there arose a need to codify Christ's teaching to guarantee orthodox theology. Councils of trusted spiritual leaders were formed to establish documents for churches to follow, such as the Apostles' Creed (second to fourth century AD) and the Nicene Creed (fourth century AD). Other councils that documented church dogma include the pre-ecumenical Councils of Rome in 155 and 193, the pre-ecumenical Council of Ephesus in 193, the pre-ecumenical Council of Carthage in 251, and perhaps most importantly, the ecumenical Council of Nicaea in 325. These written records helped refute false teachings and doctrines circulating among the churches. Some of these false doctrines included Gnosticism, Docetism, antinomianism, and asceticism.

During this period, early church fathers wrote and circulated letters that would form the basis for teaching curriculum. These letters provided a detailed defense to refute false teachings that were beginning to manifest in some churches. Among the more prominent letters of these early church fathers include those of Justin Martyr (AD 100–165), who wrote the *First Apology* to Emperor Antonius Pius; Tertullian (AD 150–230), who wrote *Apologeticus* to aid Christian believers who were being persecuted by Roman authorities; Origen (AD 185–254), who wrote *First Principles*, which introduced basic Christian doctrines according to systematic order; and Augustine (AD 354–430) who wrote *Confessions* and *The City of God*, the latter drawing distinctions between our earthly kingdom and the heavenly kingdom to come.

The Old and New Testaments form a broad and firm foundation upon which believers could come to a thorough understanding of the nature of God, his desired relationship with humans, and instruction pertaining to how we relate and conduct ourselves in association with one another. Reading and studying these biblical texts provided early church believers with the essential teachings of the faith.

---

7. *Didache: The Teaching of the Twelve Apostles* (Zeeland, MI: Saint Ignatius Orthodox Press, 2024), https://legacyicons.com/content/didache.pdf.

THE NATURE OF GOD'S REVELATION

The Bible, throughout the Old and New Testament eras, was the primary resource for believers to learn what it meant to become dedicated followers of Yahweh and Jesus. In the Old Testament we read, "These are the commands, decrees and laws the LORD your God directed me to teach you to observe in the land that you are crossing the Jordan to possess, so that you, your children and their children after them may fear the LORD your God as long as you live by keeping all his decrees and commands that I give you, and so that you may enjoy long life" (Deut. 6:1–2 NIV).

One of the primary texts, known as the Shema, was to be taught to all Hebrew Jewish children at an early age. It formed the basis of God's personal relationship with his people and for their relationship with him. "These commandments that I give you today are to be on your hearts. Impress them on your children. Talk about them when you sit at home and when you walk along the road, when you lie down and when you get up. Tie them as symbols on your hands and bind them on your foreheads. Write them on the doorframes of your houses and on your gates" (Deut. 6:6–9 NIV). This emphasis on teaching God's Word was ingrained in Hebrew Jewish culture and formed a foundation for their faith.

Likewise, the church has affirmed God's ability to communicate with humans through two means. General revelation speaks of God's unique communication to all humanity through nature, his providential care, and the basic moral instinct of right and wrong embedded in human conscience.[8] Verses that support this viewpoint include "the heavens declare the glory of God; the skies proclaim the work of his hands" (Ps. 19:1 NIV), and also "since what may be known about God is plain to them, because God has made it plain to them. For since the creation of the world God's invisible qualities—his eternal power and divine nature—have been clearly seen, being understood from what has been made, so that people are without excuse" (Rom. 1:19–20 NIV).

Special revelation refers to God's communication to a particular group of people at specific times and in supernatural ways. Special revelation includes miraculous events, the person of Jesus Christ, and his divinely inspired Scriptures.[9] Some examples of this in the Old Testament include

8. Gregg R. Allison with Michael J. Anthony, "Revelation, Scripture, and Christian Education," in *A Theology for Christian Education*, ed. James R. Estep, Michael J. Anthony, and Gregg R. Allison (Nashville: B&H Academic, 2008), 73.
9. Allison and Anthony, "Revelation, Scripture, and Christian Education," 74.

God's provision of the Ten Commandments to Moses on top of Mount Sinai (Exod. 20) and Jacob wrestling with the "angel of the Lord" (Gen. 32). Likewise, the prophetic books were God's instructions to a specific group of people within a specific historical setting.

New Testament examples include Jesus's ability to reveal the invisible nature of his Father (Col. 1:15; Heb. 1:3) and prophetic words being communicated to the apostles, which were subsequently recorded for our use (i.e., the New Testament). Scripture, in and of itself, is God's special revelation of himself to his people so that they might know and understand how to enjoy a relationship with him.

The apostle Paul states that "all scripture is God-breathed and is useful for teaching, rebuking, correcting and training in righteousness" (2 Tim. 3:16 NIV). The apostle Peter went on to state, "Above all, you must understand that no prophecy of Scripture came about by the prophet's own interpretation of things. For prophecy never had its origin in the human will, but prophets, though human, spoke from God as they were carried along by the Holy Spirit" (2 Peter 1:20–21 NIV). In summary, the apostles understood that the written record of God's revelation of himself to humans resulted from God reaching out to humanity rather than the other way around. Therefore, it stands to reason that God, who initiated this revelation of himself, desires for us to learn about him, commune with him, dialogue with him in prayer, and worship him as Creator.

The Christian teacher must believe beyond any doubt that his or her foundational textbook for discipleship and heart transformation is the Bible. The Chicago Statement on Biblical Inerrancy affirms that "the authority of Scripture is inescapably impaired if this total divine inerrancy is in any way limited or disregarded or made relative to a view of truth contrary to the Bible's own; and such lapses bring serious loss to both the individual and the Church."[10]

Speaking of the priority of believers to teach God's Word, William (Rick) Yount writes, "Unless our teaching produces a clearer understanding of the Bible, with its call to personal commitment to Christ and His church, all our teaching efforts produce little more than 'hay, wood, or straw' (1 Cor. 3:12). For education to be rightly called 'Chris-

10. The Chicago Statement on Biblical Inerrancy (1978), as quoted in Wayne Grudem, *Systematic Theology: An Introduction to Biblical Doctrine* (Grand Rapids: Zondervan Academic, 1994), 1204.

tian,' it must be built upon the sure foundation of God's Word."[11] Klaus Issler puts it this way: "Bible study is at the heart of Christian education. Our job is to take the living word of God and write it on the hearts of believers. The result should be a slow process of life transformation that draws them closer in their relationship with God. Bible teaching requires a firm conviction of the origins and purposes of scripture."[12]

Theology intersects with teaching when it transforms people's lives, shapes their characters, and changes their hearts. "Christian education must avoid teaching the Bible and theology as ends in themselves, reducing them to purely cognitive constructs. Rather, studies must be designed so that students learn to think in biblical ways, using theology as a guide to categories of thinking."[13] This distinctive difference is seen as the process of spiritual formation. It leans heavily on the work of the Holy Spirit for effectual work and in many respects is set apart from more formal constructs found in the field of Christian education.

Instructional Outcomes of Biblical Teaching

Bible study has always been a fundamental discipline among faithful followers of Christ. However, it eventually became evident that curriculum was also needed to take the biblical text and form it into meaningful and systematized units of instruction to form a cohesive awareness of all that Scripture had to say about the faith. If we jump forward in history and review the North American context, it becomes evident that during the early days of colonial America there was little difference between the aims of church education (for example, Sunday school) and public schools. Both used the Bible as their primary textbook because "integrating biblical values into the structure of America was what the Founding Fathers intended from the beginning."[14] Four additional books were also used as the basis for school curriculum. These

---

11. William R. Yount, *Created to Learn: A Christian Teacher's Introduction to Educational Psychology*, 2nd ed. (Nashville: B&H Academic, 2010), 7.
12. Klaus Issler, "Theological Foundations of Christian Education," in *Introducing Christian Education: Foundations for the Twenty-first Century*, ed. Michael J. Anthony (Grand Rapids: Baker Academic, 2001), 35–36.
13. Warren S. Benson, "Philosophical Foundations in Christian Education," in Anthony, *Introducing Christian Education*, 33.
14. Anthony and Benson, *Christian Education*, 288.

were the hornbook,[15] the New England Primer, the Psalter, and a book titled *Spiritual Milk*, which also included the Westminster Primer.[16]

In time, as more and more immigrants from across Europe arrived on the shores of America, it became imperative to allow a more inclusive curriculum that was less religious in nature. Christian education gave way to religious education, which eventually morphed into a more secular format. This trend continued throughout the eighteenth and nineteenth centuries as many of our churches in their religious education began to take on many of the elements of public schools in terms of formal curriculum with a scope and sequence, lesson plans, and learning outcomes.

During the twentieth century, public education experienced new ways of thinking, new technologies, and experimented with a variety of new instructional methods. It was inevitable that many of these new approaches found their way into the local churches as well. This resulted in proven ways to increase learning and retention in biblical knowledge. Programs began to flourish in local churches that emphasized Scripture memory. However, in time, growing tensions arose regarding this integration with social science as seen in the public school system. The emphasis on rote memory without critical-thinking skills challenged the notion of what it meant to be a "disciple."

Clearly, the aim of Christian instruction is far more than the transmission of biblical knowledge. Jesus frequently condemned and ridiculed those religious leaders who had a deep knowledge of God's Word but had failed to put it into practice. Many of these strict religious leaders held to the more legalistic details of the law but neglected the spirit under which it was presented. As a result, a false sense of spirituality built upon moralism crept into the church down through the ages. Our heavenly Father gave us the Holy Spirit to guide us into the proper interpretation and application of his Word. What is needed today is Spirit-led discernment to apply his Word in the complex cultural settings we find ourselves in today.

The ultimate aim of biblical instruction is *not* some strict adherence to religious legalism. His Word was not given to beat people

15. The hornbook was a commonly used educational teaching device that resembled a paddle listing the alphabet and other rudimentary content for the student to memorize.
16. Anthony and Benson, *Christian Education*, 294–95.

down like an abusive parent but rather to conform us into the image of Christ (Rom. 8:29), an image characterized by grace, mercy, redemption, and forgiveness. When the Holy Spirit is evident in the life of the teacher, he or she is marked by character qualities such as love, joy, peace, patience, kindness, goodness, faith, gentleness, and self-control (Gal. 5:22–23).

CHRISTIAN EDUCATION VS. SPIRITUAL FORMATION

Christian education and spiritual formation are not at odds with each other. They both desire the same learning outcomes: to be conformed into the image of Christ (Eph. 4:24). However, they are accomplished by different means. This section highlights distinctives of *each* so that readers might be more able to determine which approach is best given the audience, learning outcomes, and educational resources available.[17] Figure 2.1 illustrates some of the differences between these two educational approaches.

Christian Education	Spiritual Formation
▪ Intellectual	▪ Experiential
▪ Dogmatic and didactic	▪ Subjective and intuitive
▪ Memorization	▪ Meditation
▪ Exegetical study	▪ Devotional study
▪ Corporate	▪ Personal
▪ Recitation	▪ Reflection
▪ Rubric assessment	▪ Personal assessment
▪ Application	▪ Response
▪ Extrinsic motivation	▪ Intrinsic motivation

Figure 2.1: Difference between two educational approaches

17. Much of this material is extrapolated from a presentation that my wife and I did at the headquarters of David C Cook Publishing on November 20, 2017. It has been published in Michelle Anthony and Megan Marshman, *7 Family Ministry Essentials: A Strategy for Culture Change in Children's and Student Ministries* (Colorado Springs: David C Cook, 2015), chapter 3.

Intellectual vs. Experiential

One of the more common mistakes made in our churches today is the assumption that if we present enough Bible content, some of it will stick and eventually show up in the behavior of our students. As a result, we teach Bible content much like we would teach any other academic subject. But Bible facts alone do not facilitate lasting behavioral change or heart transformation. What is needed is learning that impacts more than the brain but reaches deep into the student's soul. This is best accomplished through experiential learning. Anyone who has ever participated in an overseas short-term mission trip knows the difference between memorizing a Bible verse on serving others and actually serving people through personal participation. The latter is far more influential and memorable.

Dogmatic and Didactic vs. Subjective and Intuitive

Christian education teaches students based on the authoritative Word of God. It is powerful and commanding and because it can be relied on as truth, it can be taught with confidence and systematic delivery. Dogmatic teachers leave little room for disagreement or ambiguity. Lessons are delivered with authority and confidence. The approach used by those who advocate spiritual formation is to leave room for questions and not knowing all the answers to life's complex issues. They embrace uncertainty and don't need to have the answers to all the questions asked in class. In essence, they invite the Holy Spirit into the classroom, and they're more subjective about defining truth and open-minded about the outcomes. They approach life's answers with more grace and less dogmatic intensity. What is communicated through the lesson to one student may be different to another—each as the Holy Spirit takes the lesson and speaks into the unique needs of each learner.

Memorization vs. Meditation

One end of Christian education is that students memorize Scripture in keeping with Psalm 119:11 (NIV): "I have hidden your word in my heart that I might not sin against you." By memorizing the Scriptures, the Holy Spirit will one day be able to draw up to remembrance the Bible passage(s) just when the learner needs it most. In essence, the student cannot apply what they do not know, and Bible memorization plays a critical role in that process of learning. To those with more of an emphasis on spiritual formation, Bible memory is more a means than an end. To this teacher, Bible memory games, quizzes, and competitions have far less value than simply meditating on a passage of Scripture and asking God to reveal the deeper meaning and response that should be prescribed to each student.

Exegetical Study vs. Devotional Study

While related to one another, exegetical study and devotional study are still distinct from one another in several ways. Like a Venn diagram, they do overlap and share some common elements, but they are also different in others. To the teacher who values Christian education, studying the Scriptures is a hallowed responsibility, and the focus is on detailed examination of the specifics of the passage, the historical setting, the grammatical context, and the author's intent. Studying God's Word involves taking a deep dive into the text and comparing it to other related passages. This person's Bible is characterized by handwritten notes and highlighted with colored marker pens. The teacher who emphasizes spiritual formation also highly values the Word of God but approaches its examination differently. This individual sees the examination of God's Word as a profound encounter with the living God. The teacher is standing/sitting on holy ground and invites God into the moment and reads slowly with an attitude of anticipation and expectancy.

Corporate vs. Personal

This describes best how spiritual growth takes place in the life of the believer. One approach values the gathering of believers in Bible study, worship, and small groups while the other camp prefers personal prayer, reflection, and individual soul searching. The former views spiritual growth taking place best in the context of the local body of Christ while the latter sees a smaller community as the place for growth. This will include the local church but may also incorporate other, more intimate settings such as small groups, retreats, and seasons of personal reflection.

Recitation vs. Reflection

This describes what we do with the Word of God once it has been studied and put to memory. We can either recite it back to someone to show we have learned it (for example, this has historically been the emphasis of the popular Awana children's program), or we can sit quietly and reflect on what the Scripture is saying in relation to how we are living it out in daily practice. The former places an emphasis on corporate gatherings to facilitate spiritual maturity while the latter emphasizes individual work of the Spirit in the heart of the believer.

Rubric Assessment vs. Personal Assessment

The rubric is an approach for measuring student learning outcomes. It is a common method used in public schools across North America to determine the degree to which a student has achieved a measured degree of learning. This approach compares the student's progress to a standardized set of criteria that is the norm for an individual of the same age. The difficulty of this approach lies in trying to measure one's heart and soul. Spiritual growth is not the same as cognitive development. Knowing is not the same as doing, and Jesus was free in his condemnation of those who knew the Word of God but rarely lived it—or worse yet, used it to judge others while escaping its conviction upon themselves. The former approach uses a standard for comparison while the latter is more adaptive to the individual; it sheds light on the motives of the heart and desires of the soul.

Application vs. Response

Early on in my Christian education training I memorized the hook-book-look-took approach (as will be presented in chapter 8) for lesson plan development. Everything in the lesson, from its introduction to the Bible teaching, drove toward practical application. The "look" portion of the lesson was more general in nature, while the "took" portion was more specific and explicit. There was no escaping how the lesson was to be lived out in the life of each student. The latter approach prefers to let the Holy Spirit dictate how the passage is to be manifested in the life of the learner since each person is different and has a unique spiritual journey. The emphasis of spiritual formation is seen in the lesson response as meditation, confession, praise, worship, and/or instruction about some personal response. It is different for each learner, and time needs to be provided at the end of each lesson for necessary soul searching and reaction.

Extrinsic Motivation vs. Intrinsic Motivation

This describes how we are motivated to learn, adapt, change, or adopt newly learned materials related to faith formation. In the extrinsic camp we are rewarded or disciplined on the basis of what we receive so that others can see our progress (for example, patches on a vest, plaques or a wall, public recognition, etc.). Intrinsic motivation is more concerned with learning that is motivated by deeper issues such as a love for Christ and personal inner convictions, and less about what others can see.

Anthony and Marshman, in their book *Seven Family Ministry Essentials*, summarize these differences as follows:

Christian Education

- *External listening*—gaining knowledge through books, teachers, and resources
- *Obedience*—changing behavior
- *Trying harder*—striving to work harder after disobedience occurs

Spiritual Formation

- *Internal listening*—learning to discern God's voice
- *Desiring to obey*—wanting to follow God's voice
- *Obeying in the power of the Holy Spirit*—recognizing that it's more about learning to abide in Christ[18]

We can learn valuable lessons from either approach. Neither is right or wrong, but rather they should both be relied upon for building up the body of Christ. Discipleship requires a balanced approach of each philosophy. The emphasis should not be on one approach versus the other but rather on both being integrated and blended. Each has a role to play in the healthy creation of fully devoted followers of Christ. Too often we get caught up in arguments about the "means" versus the "ends" without taking the time to realize that both are essential and necessary. You can't apply what you don't know, and both instruction and reflection are necessary to facilitate spiritual maturity. It is the blending of information and formation that creates transformation.

18. Anthony and Marshman, *7 Family Ministry Essentials*, 68.

THE ROLE OF THE HOLY SPIRIT IN THE TEACHING AND LEARNING PROCESS

The Holy Spirit as Teacher

There are fifty-two designations ascribed to the Holy Spirit in the Scriptures. Of these, at least seven are assigned to the work of teaching: Spirit of understanding, Spirit of wisdom, Spirit of wisdom and understanding, Spirit of knowledge and the fear of the Lord, Spirit of counsel and might, Spirit of Truth, Paraclete (Greek for *helper, comforter, advocate*), and the Spirit of wisdom and revelation.[19] Speaking of these designations given to the Holy Spirit, Roy Zuck comments, "These seven titles add support to the scriptural evidence of the personality and deity of the Spirit. The quality of personality, the possession of understanding, the position of divine Teacher, Revealer, Guide, and Instructor can all be based on these interesting titles ascribed to the third Person of the Trinity. Just the title Paraclete alone suffices to point to the personality of the Spirit."[20]

The New Testament highlights teaching as a major role of the Holy Spirit. He accomplishes this through a variety of actions. First, he instructs us into a knowledge of the truth (John 14:26; 16:12–15). Second, he reminds us of his Word that we have faithfully studied (John 14:25–26). Third, the Spirit guides us into a deepening knowledge of the truth (John 16:13). He declares God's truth to us (John 16:13–15). Finally, he also clarifies God's Word for us (1 Cor. 2:9–10). The Holy Spirit delights in helping us come to know, understand, and communicate our heavenly Father's Word to his people.[21]

The Teacher's Reliance on the Holy Spirit

Humans are born separated from God due to their sinful nature (Rom. 3:10–23; 1 Cor. 2:14; 2 Cor. 4:4; Eph. 2:1). When individuals confess their sins and accept God's provision of salvation, God offers his Spirit to indwell them and guide their life going forward (Luke 11:13; John

19. W. E. Biederwolf, *A Help to the Study of the Holy Spirit*, 2nd ed. (New York: Fleming H. Revell, 1903), 17.
20. Roy B. Zuck, *The Holy Spirit in Your Teaching* (Wheaton, IL: Scripture Press, 1963), 23–24.
21. For a more robust presentation of these elements, see Roy B. Zuck, "The Teaching Ministries of the Holy Spirit" in *Spirit-Filled Teaching: The Power of the Holy Spirit in Your Ministry*, ed. Charles R. Swindoll (Nashville: Word, 1998).

3:5; Acts 2:38). Paul describes this individual as a "new creation" (2 Cor. 5:17 NIV). He also states that unbelievers cannot understand the things of God and therefore cannot be relied upon to teach the things of God (Rom. 8:7–9). Only those who have the Holy Spirit inside them can understand the things of the Spirit because such things are spiritually discerned (1 Cor. 2:14). Therefore, since knowing and teaching the Scriptures is a spiritual phenomenon, only those indwelled by the Spirit are qualified to teach his Word.

However, being indwelled by the Holy Spirit does not guarantee successful teaching. There is a difference between being indwelled by the Holy Spirit and being yielded to the Spirit. The latter takes place when the teacher relinquishes control to the Spirit prior to service. Service through the power of the flesh will yield no lasting fruit. In the ideal teaching scenario, the teacher allows the Spirit to guide, enable, and enlighten during the preparation and teaching of the lesson that God can move freely between the teacher and the student.

As the Spirit of God and the Word of God work in tandem, the teacher and learner are able to receive all that God has for them. The movement of the Holy Spirit is essential for a fruitful learning encounter (1 Cor. 2:12–16; Eph. 1:17–18). This spiritual encounter leads the heart of the learner into regeneration (John 3:5–7; Titus 3:5), sanctification (2 Thess. 2:13; Heb. 10:14–15; 1 Peter 1:2), and enlightenment (John 14:26; 16:13; 1 Cor. 2:10–15). As the Holy Spirit is allowed a free course of movement in and through the teacher, that teacher is able to make a lasting and significant impact in the lives of the students. In essence, the teacher is merely the conduit for the work of the Holy Spirit in the life of the learner.

The Spiritual Gift of Teaching

The Bible identifies approximately twenty-eight spiritual gifts.[22] By far, most of them are listed in the New Testament (see Eph. 4:7–13; Rom. 12:3–8; 1 Cor. 12–14; and 1 Peter 4:10–11).[23] "The four lists of spiritual gifts demonstrate significant overlap as well as important variations.

22. In no particular order: apostle, wisdom, knowledge, faith, healings, miracles, prophecy, discerning spirits, tongues, interpretation of tongues, teaching, service, administration, exhortation, evangelism, giving, pastor, mercy, leadership, artisanship, celibacy, intercession, hospitality, voluntary poverty, deliverance, missions, martyrdom, and worship.
23. The gift of artisanship is identified in Exod. 31:1–5.

This suggests that none of the lists, taken either individually or together, is intended to be comprehensive."[24] Each believer is given at least one gift for the purpose of building up the body of Christ (1 Cor. 12:7). These are given with diversity in mind so that we recognize our interdependence (1 Cor. 12:6). Only God determines who receives what gift(s), although we are not precluded from asking for additional or different gifts (1 Cor. 12:6, 31a). Ephesians 4:11–16 seems to imply a ranking of gifts (for instance, apostles, prophets, evangelists, pastors, and teachers), but this ranking may indicate the order of gifts needed to start and develop a new church rather than a hierarchy of value.

"The gift of teaching can be described as a supernatural, spiritually endowed ability to expound (explain and apply) the truth of God."[25] The gift of teaching differs from that of prophecy. Prophecy declares or preaches God's Word, while the teacher provides additional understanding, clarity, and focused application of the prophet's declarations. The teacher provides organization, structure, and order, which in turn bring about greater clarity and understanding. Ephesians 4:11 links teaching with pastoring in the original language, indicating that a pastor should also be able to teach. However, Romans 12:7 informs that not all teachers are pastors.

Ephesians 4 helps us understand that the outcome of the spiritual gifts is to build up the body of Christ until we all reach unity in the faith and the knowledge of the Son of God, "until we all reach unity in the faith and in the knowledge of the Son of God and become mature, attaining to the whole measure of the fullness of Christ" (v. 13 NIV). The end result is a mature and stable church that is not susceptible to false doctrines but characterized by love, mutual devotion to one another, and spiritual maturity.

The following passages illustrate the role of the Holy Spirit as he interfaces with the gift of teaching:

> But the Advocate, the Holy Spirit, whom the Father will send in my name, he will teach you all things and will remind you of everything I have said to you. (John 14:26 NIV)

24. Craig L. Blomberg, "Gifts of the Holy Spirit," in Ewell, *Evangelical Dictionary of Biblical Theology*, 348.
25. Byron D. Klaus, "The Gift of Teaching," in *Evangelical Dictionary of Christian Education*, ed. Michael J. Anthony (Grand Rapids: Baker Academic, 2001), 680.

> You gave your good Spirit to instruct them. You did not withhold your manna from their mouths, and you gave them water for their thirst. (Neh. 9:20 NIV)

> But when they arrest you, do not worry about what to say or how to say it. At that time you will be given what to say, for it will not be you speaking, but the Spirit of your Father speaking through you. (Matt. 10:19–20 NIV)

> Whenever you are arrested and brought to trial, do not worry beforehand about what to say. Just say whatever is given you at the time, for it is not you speaking, but the Holy Spirit. (Mark 13:11 NIV)

> The Holy Spirit will teach you at that time what you should say. (Luke 12:12 NIV)

> As for you, the anointing you received from him remains in you, and you do not need anyone to teach you. But as his anointing teaches you about all things and as that anointing is real, not counterfeit—just as it has taught you, remain in him. (1 John 2:27 NIV)

CONCLUSION

A theology of teaching takes into consideration not only the content of what is taught but also the assumptions, both true and false, of the learning environment. It also informs the scope and sequence of the lesson(s) to help organize the material into a cohesive and natural flow. It shapes the philosophy of the instructor and provides helpful parameters to ensure orthodox instruction.

One's theology of teaching is formed in partnership with the Holy Spirit of God, for it is this same Spirit that brings us into fellowship with our heavenly Father. This indwelling sets the stage for further outpouring and filling. Once filled, the teacher's heart is open to hearing the things prompted by the Spirit. As such, the teacher is able to understand, discern, instruct, guide, and articulate the Word of God. The teacher, in partnership with the Spirit of God, is able to construct lessons that speak to the learner's heart. The relevance of what is spoken to one learner may be completely different from its relevance to another as the Spirit of God takes what is spoken and applies it differently to each learner. In unison with the Holy Spirit, the teacher is in alignment with the eternal God of this universe for the purpose of helping to form each student more fully into the image of Christ our Savior.

REFLECTION QUESTIONS

1. What personal false assumption(s) do you have about teaching that influences the way you approach class?
2. How do you see the home as being part of the child's educational journey today?
3. Can you identify any other teaching methods used by Jesus that weren't covered in this chapter?
4. From your understanding of Christian education and spiritual formation, can you identify any other differences between the two constructs?
5. Have you been able to identify your own personal spiritual gift? How are you able to use it in the context of serving in the local church?

RECOMMENDED READING

Anthony, Michael J., ed. *Introducing Christian Education: Foundations for the Twenty-first Century*. Grand Rapids: Baker Academic, 2018.

Estep, James R., Michael J. Anthony, and Gregg R. Allison. *A Theology for Christian Education*. Nashville: B&H Academic, 2008.

Hendricks, Howard. *Teaching to Change Lives: Seven Proven Ways to Make Your Teaching Come Alive*. Sisters, OR: Multnomah, 1987.

LeFever, Marlene D. *Creative Teaching Methods: Be an Effective Christian Teacher*. Colorado Springs: David C. Cook, 2004.

Wilkinson, Bruce. *The Seven Laws of the Learner: How to Teach Almost Anything to Practically Anyone*. Portland, OR: Multnomah, 2005.

CHAPTER 3

PREPARING TO TEACH: THE TEACHER AS STUDENT OF THE BIBLE

Mark L. Bailey

To be an effective Bible teacher requires one first and foremost to be a diligent Bible student. A commitment to Bible study in anticipation of sharing its riches with others is best grounded on a firm set of convictions: divine inspiration, heart preparation, spiritual illumination, diligent effort, and the anticipation of life change. First, the real value of the divinely inspired Word of God is its ability to teach, reprove, correct, and instruct in righteousness, with the end benefit of adequately equipping one for effectively serving God (2 Tim. 3:16–17). Second, the need for preparation before proclamation is well modeled by Ezra's heart purpose to study, to live, and to teach the statutes and ordinances in Israel (Ezra 7:10). Third and central to these foundational commitments is a humble dependency upon God to guide the interpretive process. This is expressed in a prayer for illumination in Psalm 119:18 (NASB): "Open my eyes, that I may behold wonderful things from Your Law." Fourth, there is no getting around the fact that it takes diligent and careful effort for the appropriation of truth God has communicated in his Word in order to stand approved in his sight (2 Tim. 2:15). The fifth commitment is to remember that the goal of all Bible study is personal transformation. Second Corinthians 3:18 capsulizes the multifaceted dynamic of the Christian life. The goal is God's step-by-step transformation of the believer into the glorious image of Christ, by the Word of God, through the power of the Spirit of God, in fellowship with the people of God. These foundations suggest a four-step process of diligent study in preparation for teaching the Bible: observation, interpretation, preparation, and application.

OBSERVATION: SEEING THE COMPONENT PARTS OF THE TEXT

As H. T Kuist defined, "Observation is the art of seeing things as they really are."[1] Such ability is developed by asking the right questions of the text and seeing the details in the text. Asking the standard journalism questions gives valuable insights on what the biblical author has included in a passage and why.

- Who: Is speaking? Is being spoken to? Is being spoken about?
- What: Is the subject? Is said about the subject? Are the supporting truths?
- When: Was it written? Did or will the actions of the passage happen?
- Where: Was the writer? Are the readers? Did the events of the passage occur?
- Why: Was the passage written? Should it be accepted or obeyed?
- How: Will the action take place? Is the exhortation supported?

In addition to asking the right questions, observation involves paying attention to four key components of the text: terms, structure, literary form, and atmosphere. A *term* is a word used in a particular context. Each term is a grammatical part of a sentence that serves a specific function in that sentence. That function may be the subject, verb, or object. It may be an adjective, adverb, conjunction, or preposition. Key terms worthy of special attention include unusual or difficult words and those used repeatedly throughout a section or book. Terms can be stated in plain language or with figurative language. Both may be employed by the author to communicate a literally intended meaning. Ironically and maybe surprisingly, figurative language makes meaning even more concrete by specifying or qualifying a description.

1. H. T. Kuist, *These Words upon Thy Heart: Scripture and the Christian Response* (Richmond, VA: John Knox, 1900), 79.

A second component of the passage to observe is its *structure.* The student of Scripture should use both the close-up lens of the grammatical structure and the wide-angle lens of the literary structure to see the complete picture. Working outward from individual terms, for grammatical structure one should study the clauses and phrases that make up the sentence, and then how the sentences are arranged to create a paragraph. A paragraph is the basic unit of study for observation in prose, while a stanza is the basic unit to observe in poetry. Key words that connect the parts of the sentence are those conjunctions used to link sentences as a whole or to introduce clauses and phrases. It is often in these connectors that form (the what) leads to function (the how or why) and makes the passage come alive.

Literary structure is the result of how paragraphs are connected to form multiple sections or divisions that make up the whole book. How these structures are arranged is how the author develops the argument or emphasis of the book as a whole. Argumentation is achieved through the artistic employment of certain methods of literary composition. Identifiable examples include cause and effect, contrast and comparison, summary and explanation, movement between general and specific, alternation or inversion, repetition or proportion, climax or pivot, and question and answer.[2]

The third component of a passage to be observed is its *literary form.* God, in the revelation of his mind through human authors, creatively utilized a variety of literary genres to reveal his will and purposes to humanity. At the initial step of observation, note simply whether the passage is written as narrative, in poetry, through parable, as a letter (epistle), or as prophetic literature. Specific principles of hermeneutics appropriate to each will need to be employed in the interpretive step.

The final consideration in the step of observation is to discern the background or *atmosphere* of the passage. This entails identifying, as much as possible, the author, the date of composition, the place of origination, the intended reader(s) and their location, and what specific purposes can be observed within the text for the writing. Also pay attention to whether the atmosphere within the passage is one of instruction, correction, exhortation, expectation, or a combination.

2. Robert A. Traina, *Methodical Bible Study* (Grand Rapids: Zondervan, 1985), 50–52.

An observation is a positive statement of what can be seen in a particular pericope (i.e., a paragraph). One cannot overstate the benefit of listing everything that can be observed in the passage under consideration. The goal at this point is not to interpret but simply to record what can be seen from the text itself; interpretation comes next.

INTERPRETATION: DISCOVERING THE INTENDED MEANING OF THE TEXT

Properly called *hermeneutics*, interpretation is the science and art of interpreting the Word of God. It is asking and answering the question, "What did God mean by what God said?" What God said through the writers of Holy Scripture and the purpose he intended by how it was said is the proper concern of interpretation. The most significant challenges in interpretation are the gaps in time, culture, literature, and language between the world of the writer and the world of the reader.

While observation is designed to develop the inductive skill to give the interpreter a firsthand exposure to the Scripture, interpretation involves the deductions resulting from an informed understanding of the historical, cultural, literary, and grammatical contexts. This is often referred to as the historical-grammatical method of interpretation. Tools to help this process include Bible dictionaries, encyclopedias, atlases, special introductions, and reliable commentaries.[3]

Historical Backgrounds

The books of the Bible are primarily occasional literature. In other words, they were written to communicate God's revelation at a particular *occasion* to address the real needs existing in the community during that time and in that place. Therefore, understanding the author and the audience as much as possible is a primary step in interpretation. Questions to ask about the author include the following: What can we know about the author's ethnicity, family, education, occupation,

3. Important hermeneutics textbooks include Gordon D. Fee and Douglas Stuart, *How to Read the Bible for All Its Worth*, 4th ed. (Grand Rapids: Zondervan Academic, 2014); Roy B. Zuck, *Basic Bible Interpretation: A Practical Guide to Discovering Biblical Truth* (Colorado Springs: David C. Cook, 1991); Walter C. Kaiser and Moisés Silva, *An Introduction to Biblical Hermeneutics: The Search for Meaning* (Grand Rapids: Zondervan Academic, 1994); and Andreas J. Köstenberger and Richard D. Patterson, *Invitation to Biblical Interpretation: Exploring the Hermeneutical Triad of History, Literature, and Theology* (Grand Rapids: Kregel Academic, 2011).

and spiritual journey? Questions to ask and answer about the intended audience are the following: Who are they? Where are they located? When did the writing take place? What were their circumstances at the time of writing? Why was the book written? Answering the last question requires paying attention to explicit statements, implicit clues, repetition of themes, and the imperatives in the text.

Cultural Backgrounds

The cultures of the Old and New Testaments are very different from our own. "Culture is all learned behavior which is socially acquired, that is, the material and nonmaterial traits that are passed on from one generation to another."[4] What makes a culture unique is how people think as reflected in what they say, do, and make. The Bible was written within the cultural milieu of its day and therefore reflects both social and material aspects of that culture. Social aspects include marriage customs, political structures, agricultural practices, military strategies, athletic competitions, and religious rituals. Material samples include denominations of coinage, styles of pottery, legal treaties, business documents, architectural designs, geographical or topographical locations, and water systems for collection, storage, and irrigation. All of the above can help illuminate the meaning of various passages of Scripture. Illustrations of both the social and material culture of the first century can readily be found in the parables Jesus told and the illustrations used in the discourses he preached.

Literary Forms

Understanding the nature of the particular genre of a passage is critical to its correct interpretation. Some genres are familiar to the average reader of the Bible, but others demand additional study. Probably the most familiar is narrative, while poetry and prophecy are probably the most unfamiliar and difficult.

Narrative is a literary genre that is made up of scenes containing descriptions, dialogues, speeches, and editorial commentary. Biblical narrative is the record of what God did for and through his people. The primary function of individual narratives in the Bible is to support the

4. Eugene Nida, *Customs and Culture: Anthropology for Christian Missions*, 9th ed. (Pasadena, CA: William Carey Library, 1986), 28.

larger biblical narrative of God's historical dealings with humanity for achieving his divine purposes. His presence, or references to him, are keys to the interpretation of the events portrayed. Narrative is the result of an author's selection of materials arranged for theological presentation for an intended rhetorical effect on the reader. To understand a narrative, one should pay close attention to settings, character depictions, and plot development. Setting includes the physical, temporal, and social details of the narrative. Characterization is achieved by direct description or as an author reveals the words, thoughts, and actions of a character. Plot traces the movement of episodes and activities as they revolve around some kind of conflict. Conflict can be physical or moral and can take multiple formats.[5] The arrangement of plot sequences with repetition, chiasm, and inclusions helps the reader grasp the authorial emphasis. Editorial comments by the author also help frame the point of view presented. According to Ryken, the purpose of narrative is to define reality, clarify morality, and disclose what really matters and what matters most.[6]

The Gospels are a unique species of narrative. Mark Strauss concludes, "The Gospels are historical narratives motivated by theological concerns."[7] They are historical in that they contain selected events and sayings of Jesus. As narratives they reflect plot sequencing, characterization, and setting. They are theological in that they present Jesus as the Messiah, the Son of Man and Son of God who, through his death and resurrection, provided redemption for fallen humanity and will victoriously bring the kingdom of God to full reality. Each gospel should be read vertically to appreciate its unique presentation to a particular audience before being read horizontally in comparison with the other gospels.

Narrative scenes are framed and connected by different progressions. Biographical progressions follow the lives of people and their conversations. Historical progressions follow the ordered sequences of events. Times, seasons, and reigns indicate chronological progression. Movement and travel trace geographical progression. Logical

5. Leland Ryken, *How to Read the Bible as Literature . . . and Get More Out of It* (Grand Rapids: Zondervan Academic, 1984), 165–75.
6. Ryken, *How to Read the Bible as Literature*, 58.
7. Mark L. Strauss, *Four Portraits, One Jesus: A Survey of Jesus and the Gospels*, 2nd ed. (Grand Rapids: Zondervan Academic, 2007), 36.

progression is the result of ideas and themes that get developed. While these may be used in combination, a change in progression marks the beginning or end of a narrative episode. Charting the paragraphs and sections of a book is a good way to see the literary structures and how these structures are stitched together.

It is important to see the narrative movement across the ages in the pages of biblical history in the light of Scripture's movement from the old covenant to the new covenant. Not all explicit teaching, for example, in the history of Israel is directly applicable to the church. However, the principles underlying the specifics are the same principles of righteousness and holiness evidenced across all the pages of Scripture.

Poetry is the most compact genre and utilizes many figures of speech. More can be said with less in poetry than in any other genre. Poetry appeals to the heart as a vehicle to the mind since the use of imagery not only communicates information but also evokes an emotional response in its listeners. A familiarity with the most common figures of speech is necessary to appreciate and interpret poetry.[8] The most prominent books of poetry are the Psalms and the wisdom literature of Job, Proverbs, and Ecclesiastes. The Hebrew Psalter contains both psalms of lament and psalms of praise. The psalms have been further classified according to styles, themes, and function.[9] Proverbs is comprised of axiomatic statements, which are both descriptive and prescriptive, that reveal the practical wisdom that comes by both divine revelation and the norms of human experience. Those norms get challenged in Job and Ecclesiastes. The mystery of wisdom is debated through the odyssey of Job's suffering and addresses the questions as to why God sends or allows suffering into the lives of even righteous people, and how they should respond. The futility of human wisdom and its limitation for discovering the real meaning of life is depicted through the speculation and philosophical musings of Ecclesiastes. To rightly interpret both Job and Ecclesiastes, one must see the whole of each book to see how the search for wisdom is to be successfully navigated.

The patterns of Hebrew poetry include imagery, sound, word meaning, and especially meter called *parallelism*, or *stereometrics*.

8. For basic lists and samples of figures of speech see Kaiser and Silva, *An Introduction to Biblical Hermeneutics*, 92–98, and Zuck, *Basic Bible Interpretation*, 143–68.
9. For a brief classification of the Psalms, see Fee and Stuart, *How to Read the Bible for All Its Worth*, 175–77.

Parallelism is "the practice of using similar language of approximately the same number of words and length, and containing a corresponding thought, phrase, or idea over succeeding lines."[10] The providential genius of Hebrew poetry is "thought rhyme" more than "sound rhyme," which makes translation into other languages possible without a loss of meaning. That interaction may be through a synonymous repetition where the second line repeats the thoughts of the first line but in different words. When the second line affirms the truth of the first line with an opposite or contrasting statement, it is called *antithetical* parallelism. Sometimes there is an additional element in a second line that is not found in the first, and that is termed *synthetic* or *climactic* parallelism. At times, while still reflecting the bouncing-like meter, a single statement is made without a second line of amplification; this is known as a formal statement. Any one of the above styles of parallelism is said to be emblematic whenever a figure of speech is used in either of the lines. Parallel lines or sets of lines can be structured alphabetically, acrostically, or with chiasm to make up larger units called stanzas. Laying out the lines of thought that go together, connecting what is parallel between them, and identifying what kind of parallelism one sees is a great start for the appreciation and analysis of poetry.

Parables are a specific kind of wisdom literature and were a frequent vehicle of the Lord's communication. A parable is a figurative narrative that is true to life and designed for the historical and pedagogical purposes of conveying through analogy some specific spiritual truth, usually relative to the kingdom program of God.

According to Jesus, parables were designed to reveal new truths about God's kingdom program to receptive hearts and to conceal those same truths from rejecting hearts (Matt. 13:10–17). As parables are a particular rhetorical form of narrative, they can best be interpreted working through the following five steps. First, recover the setting of the parable in its historical and literary setting as discovered in the context. Second, discover the solution to the problem or the answer to a question the parable addresses. Third, trace the flow of the narrative and its details. Fourth, uncover the central truth or truths of analogy between the story and their relationship to the kingdom of God.

10. Köstenberger and Patterson, *Invitation to Biblical Interpretation*, 266.

Finally, state the intended appeal of the parable for the historical audience and then its application for a present-day readership.

Epistles in the Bible are letters written to the early churches and pastors in the foundational days of Christianity. The New Testament authors adapted the basic form of letter writing current in their culture. The general epistolary outline consisted of an opening, a body, and a conclusion with their component parts. The opening consisted of a salutation, health wish, and a prayer. The salutation began with the mention of the author, the identification of the audience, and then a greeting. The health wish was a report on the welfare of the writer and a wish of goodwill for the readers. Many times, the opening comments introduced a preview of themes the rest of the letter would address in detail. The body of the letter normally contained an introduction of the major subject or purpose for writing, and then an extended section of requests or admonitions. New Testament letters were designed to address specific issues for the churches to whom they were addressed or ministry instructions for the pastors. The Epistles reveal a wide freedom of adaptation of the epistolary form depending on the subject matter presented. Typical to the conclusion of a first-century letter was a closing greeting, a final health or welfare wish, and a farewell salutation. Sometimes these could be combined into a benediction, as seen at the end of Hebrews and Jude. With a knowledge of the historical and cultural background, the Epistles are probably the easiest to interpret, utilizing the paragraph as the basic unit of thought for serious study. Attention should be paid to the main imperatives and exhortations along with their supporting argumentation.

Prophetic literature can be classified in three broad configurations. Some ethical prophecy is more sermonic in nature. By far the greater majority of prophetic literature is forthtelling more than foretelling. The first is more instructive and sermonic for the present while the second is predictive of future events. Second, futuristic prophecy is concerned with God's promises and warnings for the future. And finally, there is visionary prophecy which is often termed *apocalyptic*.[11]

11. Visionary or apocalyptic literature contains a narrative revealed through a vision or dream often accompanied by an explanation by God himself or an interpreting angel. Biblical examples would include portions of Isaiah, Ezekiel, Daniel, Zechariah, and Revelation. For a concise approach to interpreting visionary literature, see Ryken, *How to Read the Bible as Literature,* 165–75.

The exhortations of the prophets are rooted in the covenant law of Moses. Key principles for interpreting prophecy include the need to see the cyclical literary design of the messages of judgment and salvation. No single prophetic book gives an ordered chronology of all that is predicted for the future. A look at the first chapter of Isaiah will reveal this roll-over effect of the messages of salvation and judgment. The blessings of salvation are promised for repentant faith and obedience to God's commands. Judgment or discipline is warranted for unbelief or unfaithfulness, respectively. Judgment prophecies can take the form of woe oracles, lamentations, or a covenant lawsuit whereby summons, charges, and sentences are announced. The most common sins that God surfaces through his prophets include spiritual adultery, injustice, idolatry, and false worship. Spiritual adultery is the repudiation of God's love by being unfaithful to the covenant relationship, pictured with marital imagery throughout the prophets. Injustice is sin against others in the community. Idolatry is the rejection of the one true God in favor of another. False worship is the attempt to worship God in ways other than those prescribed by God.

The "mountain peak perspective" is another key principle for correctly interpreting prophecy. The imagery of seeing one mountain peak behind another without seeing the valley between has been used to illustrate that phenomena where the near view and the far view are placed side by side in the same passage.[12] Some aspects of prophecy have an immediate fulfillment for the audience contemporary to the times of the prophet, while other aspects await their ultimate fulfillment. Sometimes both are future and yet still separated by an extended period of time. An obvious example is Isaiah 9:6, which speaks of both the future birth of the Messiah and his ultimate rule. A third consideration is that much of prophecy is poetic and therefore utilizes a vast range of figurative language. While figurative language still has intended meanings, one must take care to interpret those figures correctly.[13]

12. A classic example is Isaiah 9:6 where the incarnation is inferred from the first part of the verse and the consummation of the messianic kingdom is referenced in the second half.
13. For an insightful discussion on the hermeneutics of prophecy, see Kaiser and Silva, *An Introduction to Biblical Hermeneutics*, 139–58, and Köstenberger and Patterson, *Invitation to Biblical Interpretation*, 346–58.

Grammatical Interpretation

As was discussed under "Observation," when two or more terms are linked together, there is structure. In order to interpret the meaning of a word in a context, we must understand the relative value of a word's root meaning and its meaning in a particular context. The etymological origins of a word may not be how an author is using the word. For example, the English word *precise* at its root means "to cut before," but that is never how the word is used now. Word meanings can change over time, and while that diachronic path may bring some illustrative insight, the immediate context must be determinative. Working outward through the concentric circles of context helps validate the intended meaning. At the center is how a term is used in the immediate context of the passage. The next ring out is how that term is used in the particular book being studied. A third ring is how the same author uses the word in other books. A fourth ring is how other authors in the Bible, and especially of the same genre, employ the term. Finally, it can be helpful to see how the term was used in an extrabiblical context within the surrounding culture of the same time period.

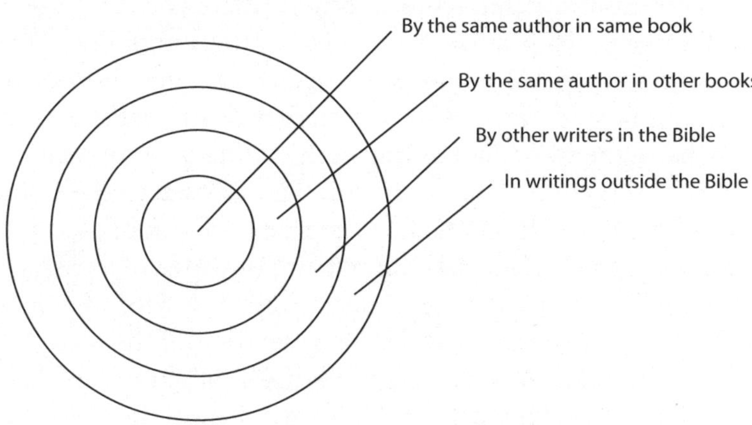

Figure 3.1 The Concentric Circles of Contextual Word Studies

Once the meaning of the word has initially been determined, how that word functions within the sentence needs to be discovered. A noun, for example, may function as a subject or the object of a verb or preposition. An infinitive can function as a subject. The study of synonyms and antonyms of a term can yield further clarity as well.

The goal in grammatical analysis is to see the importance of the interplay of main statements and the supporting clauses or phrases that modify them. While different genres have different structures, most non-poetic literature can best be studied at the paragraph level as a basic unit of thought. Main statements can take the form of an affirmation, question, command, or request. Dependent clauses modifying the main statements may show cause, comparison, concession, condition, purpose, result, time, relation, or location. Prepositional, infinitival, and participial phrases all add direction and relationship to that which they modify. Most serious Bible students find it helpful to do a grammatical layout of the passage to identify each of the main statements and what clauses, phrases, and other modifiers are subordinate to them. The benefit of such an exercise is to understand the form and function of each sentence and its constituent components. Modifying clauses and phrases reflect how an author is structuring the material for maximum rhetorical impact. They reveal the how and why of what is being presented.

PREPARATION: SURFACING THE CENTRAL THRUST OF THE TEXT

Before one can effectively appropriate the truth of a pericope to oneself or effectively communicate that truth to others, there is a need to discover the central thrust of the passage as intended by the author and communicate it in a way that can be both remembered and applied. While a passage may have a number of truths, all of which may be important, it is helpful to decide what is the most demanding in the immediate context. The diligent work in observation and interpretation is designed to give a complete familiarity of the text in its contexts. With that background, the following process can help one surface the central truth or thrust of a passage.[14]

First, re-ask the basic journalistic questions with the informed perspective of having completed the interpretation of the passage. Next, record all truths great and small to see all that is taught in the text within its context. Third, classify what are the most demanding truths and what are the more supporting truths. Fourth, collate and combine statements that revolve around the major themes. Fifth, compose between three and five principles that capture the truth of the passage. For our purposes

14. For the value of seeing the big idea or central thrust, see Haddon W. Robinson, *Biblical Preaching: The Development and Delivery of Expository Messages* (Grand Rapids: Baker, 1980), 73–75.

here, a principle is defined as an outstanding and abiding truth that is not limited to a moment in time. Sixth, with one eye on the text and one eye on those principles, determine the outstanding subject, action, and the how or why of the passage that most clearly represents the circumstance of the passage. With that information in mind, state the central theme or big idea of the passage in a simple, succinct sentence that accurately and adequately represents the true interpretation of the passage. Nothing should be lost by the formation and communication of this main idea as it finds its validation in the supporting principles and other details that explain and support the main idea. The other principles serve as the support structure and can be wedded into the message along with other insights from the textual details.

When teaching or preaching the message of a given text, one will need to decide how to structure that message for maximum rhetorical impact. Here the skills of pedagogy and homiletics find their place. For purposes of this summary, the message can be structured around the components of the main theme or reflect the main statements as seen in the grammatical or literary layout of the passage.

AN EXAMPLE

Adequate work in the steps of observation and interpretation will provide complete familiarity of the text in its context necessary for this step of preparation. Assuming all of that has been done, here is an example of what that process could yield for Romans 12:1–2.

All Truths Great and Small

1. Believers can be motivated to spiritual dedication.
2. God is a merciful God.
3. The mercies of God were the motivation Paul used to challenge the Roman Christians.
4. Paul urged the Roman Christians to sacrificially commit themselves to God.
5. God wants the whole person for an agency of worship and service.
6. God desires his people to live holy lives as a reflection of their commitment.
7. Living for God is the logical result of the believer's experience of God's mercy.

8. Serving God is one way the Christian worships God.
9. An acceptable sacrifice is a living and holy sacrifice to God.
10. Being conformed to the ways of the world is a constant danger.
11. Believers bear the responsibility of avoiding worldliness.
12. The correction to worldly conformation is personal transformation.
13. Transformation is a continual need in the life of a Christian.
14. The renewal of the mind is essential to a transformed life.
15. God has a perfect will for every believer to discover and accept.
16. God's will is always be right and should be accepted as such.
17. A proper relationship with God is a prerequisite for effective ministry.

Collated Truths

1. Personal dedication is motivated by God's mercies.
2. Consecration involves the whole person.
3. Self-sacrifice is an act of worship.
4. Worldliness is an enemy of a transformed life.
5. Transformation is the result of a renewed mindset.
6. A believer can know the perfect will of God.
7. Knowing God's will is always the best preparation for effective service.

Concluding Principles

1. Exhortation to Christian service is grounded in God's mercy.
2. The personal dedication of the believer is an act of worship.
3. An approved sacrifice is a personal and pure sacrifice.
4. Renewed thinking is an effective means of a transformed life.
5. Discerning God's perfect will is the benefit of a transformed life.

Central Truth

Personal dedication is a prerequisite to acceptable Christian service.

Possible Basic Outline

I. Dedication and the Worship of God
II. Transformation and the Will of God

APPLICATION: RESPONDING TO THE SPIRIT'S APPEAL IN THE TEXT

By now the preparation necessary for proper application should be no secret: observe well, interpret accurately, and develop an aptitude for communication. Critical to good application is awareness, both of the teacher and of the learner. Ezra 7:10 provides the ideal model for anyone teaching God's Word to others. "For Ezra had set his heart to study the Law of the LORD, and to do it and to teach his statutes and rules in Israel" (7:10 ESV). The order of the four verbs in the verse is instructive. The intention of the heart is for the diligent study of the Scripture. The commitment to personal application by the teacher before instructing others reflects the admirable order modeled by Ezra. For both the teacher and student, the mirror illustration in James 1:19–25 warns against the danger of rationalizing away the need for personal change in conformity to the Word of God. Honesty and humility are underlying attitudes foundational to good application for both. An honest understanding of one's strengths and weaknesses opens to receive and apply God's Word. Strengths are the ground for gratitude for God's grace and gifting in our lives. Weaknesses remind us of God's extended mercy and drive us to depend on him.

Two different models are here suggested as examples of a matrix that can help facilitate and focus application. First, Second Timothy 3:16–17 could be called God's "inspired" method of application. The profitability of the Scriptures mentioned in verses 16 and 17 can be tuned into a series of questions to ask of any passage of Scripture:

- What does the passage *teach* about God? About salvation? About the Christian life?
- How does this passage *reprove* sinful actions? Wrong thoughts? Fleshly motives?
- What *correction* does this passage provide? What should stop? What should start?
- What are the key *training* points that direct one toward a more righteous life?
- How does this passage *equip* for ministry?
- What *good work* would God want done as stated in this passage?

Although not written specifically for application in Bible study, J. Grant Howard's *Balancing Life's Demands* helps raise awareness for more consciously applying God's truth.[15] In an exposition of Matthew 22:34–40, Howard probes the priorities of Jesus's two great commandments (love God and love neighbor; see Deut. 6:5 and Lev. 19:18). Challenging the traditional ladder of sequential priorities, Howard builds a construct of nested circles with God in the center, the believer in the ring, and at the circumference five significant relationships every person has based on the groups of "neighbors" identified in the context of Leviticus 19: family, work, government, church, and world. He concludes that: (1) God should be at the center of all of life and all relationships; (2) the Bible contains multiple commands for each relationship sector identified; (3) loving God and others is best evidenced by obeying God's commands concerning those relationships (John 14:23); (4) to fail with one of the commands is to break the whole law (James 2:10); and (5) since no command of the Lord is optional, we are simultaneously responsible for all the commands in every relationship. Using the model as a grid through which to "pour the passage," specific directions for applications not otherwise immediately apparent may come to mind. Some passages will appeal to one's individual relationship to the Lord, but some truths will link more closely to responsibilities in the relationships with others. Howard and William Hendricks discuss a somewhat similar approach and offer a spiritual inventory to assist in applying the truth in the interplay of such interpersonal relationships.[16]

Applications should be specific courses of action that are accurate to the text, relevant to contemporary needs, and measurable. Any given text has one interpretation intended by the author but multiple applications possible for the readers, depending upon their spiritual maturity and present circumstances. Well-stated applications must align with the truth taught in the text. Applications also need to have immediate connection to the culture. Howard Hendricks wrote "As John Stott once said to me, 'I've discovered that it's not hard to be biblical if you don't care about being contemporary. And it's certainly

15. J. Grant Howard, *Balancing Life's Demands: A New Perspective on Priorities* (Portland, OR: Multnomah, 1983).
16. Howard G. Hendricks and William D. Hendricks, *Living by the Book: The Art and Science of Reading the Bible* (Chicago: Moody, 1991), 295.

not hard to be contemporary if you don't care about being biblical. Being biblical and contemporary—that's the art of Christian communication.'"[17] This was the strength of the men of Issachar who understood their times and knew what Israel should do (1 Chron. 12:32). To be effective, applications must result in action. Intentionality with regard to when, where, and how one will obey ensures Bible study and Bible teaching will result in dynamic transformation and not simply the collection of dormant information.

CONCLUSION

Like first learning to drive a car, each step of the process is separate and conscious: for driving, it's starting the car, positioning the hands on the steering wheel, shifting, and braking. Time and experience make these steps more automatic and integrated. With an understanding of the value of each step in the Bible study process, the student of the Bible can become a better student *and* a better teacher of the Bible. The communication of God's Word is an awesome privilege to enjoy and a sober responsibility to fulfill.

REFLECTION QUESTIONS

1. Why are the five personal commitments mentioned in the introduction to the chapter so important?
2. How do the six journalistic questions guide the observational step of Bible study?
3. In what ways do the four key components of terms, structure, literary form, and atmosphere provide the necessary foundation on which to build the interpretive process?
4. How does paying attention to the historical and cultural backgrounds protect against misinterpretation and misapplication in Bible study?
5. Read Matthew 7:24–27 and James 1:22–25. What is lost when one stops their Bible study with interpretation and doesn't move on through to application?

17. Howard Hendricks, "Teaching That Motivates" in *Mastering Teaching*, ed. Earl Palmer, Roberta Hestenes, and Howard Hendricks (Portland, OR: Multnomah Books, 1993), 80.

RECOMMENDED READING

Fee, Gordon D. and Douglas Stuart. *How to Read the Bible for All Its Worth*. 4th ed. Grand Rapids: Zondervan Academic, 2014.

Hendricks, Howard G. and William D. Hendricks. *Living by the Book: The Art and Science of Reading the Bible*. Chicago: Moody, 1991.

Vanhoozer, Kevin J. *Is There a Meaning in This Text? The Bible, the Reader, and the Morality of Literary Knowledge*. 10th anniversary ed. Landmarks in Christian Scholarship. Grand Rapids: Zondervan Academic, 2009.

Yarbrough, Mark. *How to Read the Bible Like a Seminary Professor: A Practical and Entertaining Exploration of the World's Most Famous Book*. New York: FaithWords, 2015.

Zuck, Roy B. *Basic Bible Interpretation: A Practical Guide to Discovering Biblical Truth*. Colorado Springs: David C. Cook, 1991.

CHAPTER 4

TEACHER AS LEARNING STRATEGIST

Michael S. Lawson

We are teachers because Jesus commanded us to make students, but not just any students: disciples who follow Jesus. That is the Great Commission. The Bible defines a standard for learning that exceeds knowledge. According to the Bible, no one has truly learned truth until they act on the truth. Jesus's command to "observe" everything he taught radically shifts the goal of our task from information dispensing to life changing (Matt. 28:20 NASB). God models the ideal learning *strategist* throughout his Bible. The God of the Bible (and author of our central content) set a massive, multi-generational plan in motion to:

- redeem humans from their own sin (John 1:29),
- place Christ as ruler over his chosen people, Israel (Matt. 2:2),
- reveal Jesus as head of his body, the church (Eph. 5:23), and
- establish his beloved Son as King of kings over all nations (Rev. 19:11–16).

This carefully crafted plan emerges from within the organized character of God. Just like the God we represent, our teaching ought likewise to reflect a carefully crafted strategy. After all, we are guiding people through a process of embracing truth, considering personal implications of that truth, and making intentional decisions for ongoing change. The apostle James warns teachers and students alike about the delusion of hearing good teaching without making necessary changes in behavior (James 2:17–26). Granted, these changes occur incrementally over time, but change represents the essential ingredient. Ongoing change in teacher and student offers evidence that God's plan works in us. Obeying truth ultimately bursts forth in visible fruit produced by the Spirit. Does anyone object to producing more love, joy, peace, patience, kindness, goodness, faithfulness, gentleness, or self-control (Gal. 5:22–23)?

If our task were not challenging enough, in the church we work with volunteer learners. Unlike a formal schooling context, we cannot screen students for their suitability or background. Nor do we normally use tests and grades to evaluate their learning. And finally, we do not withhold graduation as a motivator. We must draw upon students' internal motives to move their learning process forward. We teach by order of the King, our goal is learning evidenced by change, and to accomplish our assignment we carefully plan a strategy modeled by the God we worship.

On our best day, teaching requires more than our best effort. In chapter 3, Mark Bailey carefully explains the process of each teacher studying the Bible to make sure that teacher is clear on what God's Word says and means. And, while we definitely want to prepare excellent lessons, we must prepare ourselves first. This step requires serious personal reflection. Are our hearts right with God? Have we talked with God before we talk with students? Are we teaching them God's truth or has our own opinion crept in? Are we doing in our walk with God what we tell our students to do? Never take your personal preparation lightly; after all, you are representing God himself.

In this chapter we will first observe various ways the Bible reflects strategic planning on behalf of learners. Then, we will explore three phases of our strategic plan: preparation, implementation, and evaluation. Along the way, we will compare how several classroom models guide the learning process toward different objectives. We will also note how much of what we plan for the physical classroom can be translated into an online environment.

THE BIBLE WE TEACH

The Bible reflects not only the organized character of God but strategic planning on behalf of readers and learners. Even those who do not believe the Bible's message honor it as a great, perhaps the greatest, piece of literature ever written. The Bible's structure on the behalf of the learner offers impressive examples of strategic planning. After all, good literature does not happen by accident, it happens on purpose! The following are six obvious examples of how God organizes his Bible on behalf of the reader/learner. These are not the only examples, but as you will see, each author organizes his material with the reader/learner clearly in mind.

Psalm 119

Anyone who has bumped around in the Bible very long notices the length of this psalm, about five pages depending on your translation and font size. Since very few ordinary Israelites had personal copies of the Scriptures, this (along with all the psalms) was designed to be sung from memory because music offers one of the strongest aids to memory. If you do not believe it, just ask anyone associated with the advertising industry. They spend millions to create unforgettable tunes associated with their products. Although the psalms have come down to us without their musical score, Israel sung them from memory in both formal and informal settings. But there is more! Psalm 119 offers a rich educational design.

> This psalm is written in an acrostic (alphabetical) arrangement. In each paragraph (strophe) of eight verses each line begins with the same letter of the Hebrew alphabet. (The 22 strophes correspond to the 22 letters of the alphabet.) So verses 1–8 each begin with the first Hebrew letter, verses 9–16 each begin with the second letter, and so on.[1]

Perhaps you can sing the English alphabet even to this day. How could we ever forget it? Unfortunately, my song about each letter does not also represent eight lines of pristine theology that begin with that same letter. Children generally enjoy the experience of memorizing their respective alphabets. Hebrew children would quickly learn how each letter in their alphabet reminded them of essential devotional and

1. Allen P. Ross, "Psalms," in *The Bible Knowledge Commentary: An Exposition of the Scriptures*, ed. J. F. Walvoord and R. B. Zuck, vol. 1 (Wheaton, IL: Victor Books, 1985), 879.

theological truth. If you are supposed to love God, you need to know as much as you can about him. When you teach, will you provide meaningful memory devices?

Jude 1:3

In his opening verses, Jude's tiny letter surprises us with a change of direction. Jude alerts us to his "every effort" at writing to his readers about their "common salvation" (soteriology). Instead, something deep inside him urges a letter about the need to "contend earnestly for the faith" (Jude 1:3 NASB). We do not know for sure why he changed his mind. Perhaps he remembered a previous conversation with someone from that group, or perhaps he got a report from someone who had just returned from where these folks lived, but certainly the Holy Spirit activated his thinking to turn his attention to a different "lesson plan," if you will.

Anyone who has taught for very long has experienced something similar. One curious class insisted we explore a particular thought more deeply and destroyed my original lesson plan. Unfortunately, the next section did not share their enthusiasm for the change of direction, which caused me to shift back to the old plan. Our best planned strategy for a lesson may need to be changed for a variety of reasons—such as class enthusiasm or, in Jude's case, his sense that his readers needed a different letter. Should our strategies be held lightly and be sensitive to the real or perceived needs of our students?

John 20:31

Unlike Jude, John follows through on a soteriological purpose for his gospel. Notice that John chooses particular events in Jesus's life that he expects will prompt readers to conclude that Jesus (son of Mary) is the Christ, Son of God. Having come to that conclusion, each one should place their trust in him to receive eternal life. This thematic arrangement of material reveals John's strategy, which differs from the other gospel writers. John did not randomly collect stories of Jesus because they were his favorites. Instead, he followed a premeditated collection and arrangement strategy. As he himself states, he could have included much more.

As one wise professor once said to me, "You cannot teach everything, but you must teach something!" So, what will guide your selection of material to teach? Hopefully, those selections accommodate such things as the size of the group, their intellectual sophistication, their spiritual maturity, their age, the time allotted, their perceived and unperceived needs, and their previous biblical and theological knowledge or the lack thereof. How will you determine a guiding purpose for your students even as John did for his readers?

Hebrews 8:5

The author of Hebrews recounts God's warning to Moses about precisely following the pattern for the tabernacle as revealed to him. The earthly tabernacle needed to be built carefully because it copied heavenly things. Although Solomon's temple became the gold-plated version, both had the same essential pieces representing that heavenly pattern. The unapproachable holiness of God, mandatory blood atonement, necessary mediator to offer sacrifices, and repeated washings and cleansings for everyone and everything represent just a few of the spiritual issues addressed by the tabernacle's architecture and ministry.

The tabernacle and Solomon's temple exemplify the grandest visual aid of all time. This living, breathing, "walkthrough" visual aid, exquisite in every detail, revealed more than an art museum. Instead, the buildings and furnishings and activities called God's worshipers to a highly participatory experience of everything necessary to begin and maintain a healthy relationship with God. These monuments to God's expectations stood at the center of Hebrew national life for hundreds of years—from the time of Moses through the final days of the Davidic dynasty. Experiential learning as a strategy did not originate with modern educators. This powerful model needs to be adapted to our modern contexts. What kind of meaningful activities will you plan for your students?

Luke 1:4

Luke makes his chronological strategy clear from the opening verses of his gospel. Theophilus (Greek for *friend of God* or *lover of God*) has already been taught a great deal about Jesus. Now he needs to have the events and teaching of Christ put in a systematic order. We all owe Dr. Luke for his hard work. During Jesus's life, stories about his illegitimate birth circulated, his enemies frequently promoted misquotes, and after his death, false rumors were circulated about his stolen body. Sorting through and arranging the various events, both true and false, must have taken considerable time. Western holiday tradition helps us with Jesus's birth and his resurrection, but that leaves a lot of material in between to be put in order.

Luke's strategy of writing a chronological account offers a wonderful record of Jesus's activities and teachings. But what will be our strategy for teaching Luke's record to those who love God today? Will we be in a Sunday school setting limited to thirty-five to forty-minute weekly increments? Will we be in a home Bible study full of irregular attenders? Will we be in some kind of retreat where we can stack multiple sessions throughout an evening or day? We may be called upon to repackage Dr. Luke's record in multiple creative ways to accomplish objectives limited by various factors. In what ways will your plan reflect strategic thinking on behalf of your students?

Luke 24:27

Jesus's strategy covers the entire Old Testament christologically in about two hours. Did Jesus ever deliver a more amazing lesson? My first introduction to the Old Testament took an entire semester, and the lessons focused more on the authorship of the Pentateuch than tracing the predictions about its central character, the seed of the woman (Gen. 3:15). In dramatic contrast to that professor's approach, a recent publication by Moody Press goes right to the heart of the matter by tracing the messianic prophecies through the entire Old Testament.[2]

In contrast, Jesus's strategy in disclosing his presence throughout the Old Testament in a two-hour time frame offers an impressive model. Where, when, and how do we plan strategic overviews of large bodies of material? Jesus's strategy varied from time to time and place to place. On one occasion he centered his entire lesson around the tense of a verb (Matt. 22:32). On another he lifts out a personal pronoun from Psalm 110 to establish the divinity of David's son/Messiah (Matt. 22:41–46). His most famous sermon (Matt. 5–7) takes only about fifteen minutes to read . . . but a lifetime to digest. Clearly, the Savior had multiple strategies associated with his teaching to provoke learning and so must we. How will you keep the notion of multiple strategies before you as you plan your lessons?

---

2. Michael Rydelnik and Edwin Blum, eds., *The Moody Handbook of Messianic Prophecy: Studies and Expositions of the Messiah in the Old Testament* (Chicago: Moody, 2019).

Fortunately, we possess the unlimited resources of our Creator. The gifting and empowering of the Holy Spirit enliven us as teachers while at the same time enlightening our students with his inerrant Word. And our message could not be more timely or needed by everyone in every culture. Because we represent our triune God on his teaching mission, we approach a three-phased strategy carefully, responsibly, and prayerfully.

THREE PHASES OF A STRATEGIC PLAN

The three phases of our strategy involve careful *preparation*, responsible *implementation*, and prayerful *evaluation*.[3] Each step deserves our full attention and appropriate time allocation. Historically, many if not most teachers assumed they only needed a relatively firm grasp on the material to be taught. The "firm grasp" largely depended on the amount of training experienced by the teacher, and teaching involved little more than telling. Students bore the complete responsibility for learning. In any case, *preparation* meant conquering the material; *implementation* meant saying what you intended to say; and if *evaluation* was done, only students in academic settings experienced it—and that through testing.

Our understanding of how to craft teaching to maximize learning has come a long way since Robert Raikes started the Sunday school movement in 1780. We honor the incredible efforts of those brave mothers who launched the Sunday school movement by opening their kitchens, collecting neighborhood children (who worked a six-day week in English pin factories), and teaching them how to read the Bible.[4] We would dishonor their memory if we did not make every effort to utilize the amazing resources and sophisticated understanding of our present age. With their sacrificial example clearly in mind, let us examine more carefully a three-phased strategy.

3. Great minds think alike! I began using the P.I.E. acronym, representing *preparation*, *implementation*, and *evaluation* in 1997 in my seminary classroom at Dallas Theological Seminary. Almost simultaneously, Robert Pazmiño put a parallel planning process for Christian education in print as P.I.E, representing *preparation*, *instruction*, and *evaluation* in 1998. See Robert Pazmiño, *Basics of Teaching for Christians: Preparation, Instruction, and Evaluation* (Eugene, OR: Wipf and Stock, 1998).
4. For a fun read about the details of the amazing start of the Sunday school movement, see Wesley R. Willis, *200 Years and Still Counting! Past, Present, and Future of the Sunday School* (Wheaton, IL: Victor, 1979).

Preparation

Unlike teaching in the public sector where the subject matter is first and foremost and rarely tied to the teacher's spiritual condition, Christian teachers must first pay attention to their own spiritual health. As previously stated, there is more to effectively teaching God's Word than just knowing what it says and means. If we declare our message represents God, then we must be talking with him frequently and depending on him constantly. One of my favorite seminary teachers took time to pray in his office before each and every lesson. He did that even though he may have taught that same lesson dozens of times. On one occasion, I made the mistake of thinking I knew my own material well enough to teach it without that prayerful preparation. Needless to say, the lesson, which had been well received on many other occasions, did not go well.

Every teacher realizes the need to know the subject. But if we have had a measure of success, we find it easy to believe we can teach a lesson on our own. Jesus exposed this misconception when he returned from the Mount of Transfiguration only to find his disciples defeated by a problematic demon. When they asked him why they could not cast the demon out, he responded, "This kind can come out only by prayer" (Mark 9:29 NIV). They needed prayer, you need prayer, all God's children need prayer to fulfill their responsibilities.

In reality, we need to string successful lessons like pearls in our long-term disciple-making endeavor. We all want those who study with us to become mature followers of Jesus Christ. Jesus himself said, "The student is not above the teacher, but everyone who is fully trained will be like their teacher" (Luke 6:40 NIV). The obvious implication? Your students will become more like you than will make you comfortable. Each of us must be what we want our students to become. Preparation begins with our own spiritual life.

The teachers in the New Testament, whether Jesus or one of the apostles, normally address something their listeners need. Those needs can be divided into two categories, namely: (1) a need the listener is aware of (felt need) and (2) a deep need the listener is not aware of (real need).

The gospel of John illustrates these two need categories back-to-back. In John 3 Nicodemus comes to Jesus because he senses something needful within himself. He feels it but cannot put his finger on it. But, of course, Jesus goes right to the heart of the matter by giving him and us the most quoted verse in the Bible, John 3:16. Nicodemus needed to be born again, and so do we, and so do those we teach.

Following that story, we read about a lady filling her bucket with water. She too had a need, but layers of painful experiences had hidden it deep within her. Jesus teases her deep need to the surface through his gentle conversation about water, living water, and who can provide such amazing water. In the first story, Jesus works with the top of Jewish intellectual society. In the second story, he works with the social silt at the bottom of a despised Samaritan village. In these cases, the need was the same. Nicodemus had a sense of his need; the nameless woman did not. Our task often involves exposing a real need at a felt-need level, just as Jesus did.

Next, we turn our attention to deciding *what* to teach. *Who* and *what* are so tightly interconnected that *who* often determines *what.* Our lessons can legitimately revolve around a word, a phrase, a verse, a paragraph, a chapter, a collection of chapters, an entire book, a theological issue, or a common misconception in our culture. Figure 4.1 offers a series of questions in the left-hand column to stimulate your thinking. The right-hand column shows examples of where that kind of question could anchor a Bible lesson.

Possible Directions for a Study	An Example of That Direction in the Text
1. What question will you answer?	1. Is it lawful to heal on the Sabbath?
2. What problem will you raise?	2. Was John the Baptist from God?
3. What concept will you explain?	3. "You must be born again!"
4. What new truth will you discover?	4. "A new commandment I give you . . ."
5. What passage will you explore?	5. How is David's Son his Lord? (Ps. 110)
6. What old truth will you ponder?	6. The first and great commandment
7. What notion will you challenge?	7. Does wealth equal God's blessing?
8. What warnings will you consider?	8. "Woe to you . . ."
9. What characters will you evaluate?	9. Philip and Nathaniel
10. What chapter will you summarize?	10. Luke 24
11. What passages will you compare?	11. Genesis 1:1 and John 1:1
Note how the biblical text suggests different approaches for students to consider.	

Figure 4.1: Possible directions for study with examples

Church ministry offers the distinct advantage of long-term exposure to our students. We have time to get to know the people in our classes. Their needs help determine our selection of material as well as procedures. As has been and will be discussed in this volume, we must become students of our students as well as students of the Bible. Adults more than children in either academic or church settings always ask the question, "Why do I need this?" Unless we answer that question for our adults, our lessons often fall on deaf ears.

Assuming an understanding of our students' needs and a reasonable grasp of the material we hope to teach, the next task in our strategy requires a clear objective or lesson aim. Each and every lesson should have one major objective around which the lesson revolves. Lesson aims have received a great deal of attention in modern educational research. However, modern educators were not the first to explore this more precise way of teaching. Dr. Luke alerts us to Jesus's aim in several of Jesus's lessons. For instance, in Luke 10:25–37 Jesus answers a specific question about how to inherit eternal life. Unfortunately for this man, he simply wanted to justify himself. Fortunately for us, Jesus answers this man's deeper need with the wonderful story of the good Samaritan.

In Luke 12:15 a man appeals to Jesus to settle an inheritance problem. Jesus in return looks past what the man thinks is his problem to his deeper problem of greed. To cement his perspective in the minds of his listeners, he gives the parable of the rich fool. Who can forget it?

As Jesus was teaching along the way, he was asked a question about how many will actually be in the kingdom. Many in Israel assumed Jewish descent guaranteed inclusion in the kingdom. Jesus's shocking lesson expanded their notion of the kingdom and concluded with his unforgettable words about the reversal of their thinking by saying, "Some are last who will be first, and some are first who will be last" (Luke 13:30 ESV). Over and over again Luke records the precise nature of Jesus's lessons. Look for yourself at how Jesus focuses his lesson on a single issue. The following passages are a good place to start, since Luke points out the issue somewhere in the text. If you plan to imitate Jesus as your Master Teacher, you might find this exercise helpful: Luke 14:1–6; 15:1–10; 16:14–16; 17:5–6; 18:1–30.

Although modern educational researchers did not invent the focused lesson, they have helped us think more precisely about how we can construct our lessons around one. For example, researchers have identified three kinds of learning: information processing, operating values and attitudes, and skills acquisition. The first two speak to the heart of our teaching. We want people to know the truth (information) because the truth will make them free (attitudes).[5]

We want to help students easily embrace the biblical text at each and every level. We want our students to know the material so well that they can put it to a variety of appropriate uses, but we really want more. As we mentioned earlier, we are guiding people through a process of embracing truth, considering personal implications of that truth, and making intentional decisions for ongoing change. We expect students of Scripture (including ourselves) to embrace the truth so that they experience a realignment of their core values and attitudes. We are not talking about the values or attitudes that we verbalize. Rather, we are talking about our internalized values and attitudes. Those values and attitudes begin with merely acknowledging that a single value or attitude exists. As humans grow, they classify attitudes as important or not, choose or eliminate values as desirable or not. Mature adults integrate a whole range of values and attitudes that characterize the individual. Those consistently integrated sets of biblical values and attitudes govern all choices and decisions.

The affective domain (discussed in detail in chapter 6) reveals where a particular value or attitude lies in our process of decision-making. For instance, many Christians in the modern era "believe" in the value of personal Bible reading. The affective domain provides descriptive words to be more precise. In this case, does "believe" mean Bible reading is a good idea; does it mean I actually practice Bible reading; does it mean Bible reading is so high among my values that I read my Bible every day before I do anything else? In each case, a person could affirm Bible reading as important but that person's actions will rank it higher or lower in his or her personal value system. As people grow in this value, they will act on that value, beginning with periodic and advancing to regular Bible reading. Ultimately, they will treasure Bible reading above all other reading.

5. Indeed Editorial Team, "3 Domains of Learning: Cognitive, Affective and Psychomotor," Indeed.com, accessed September 1, 2023, https://www.indeed.com/career-advice/career-development/domains-of-learning.

Until I became a Christian in April 1963, I would have affirmed the value of the Bible but never read it for myself. My inexperience with King James English made the intermittent efforts bewildering. By September 1965, I was enrolled at Dallas Theological Seminary, where reading the Bible became a way of life. But the Bible was still not the companion it is today. Now, the Bible dominates my interests and choice of reading material. I read it for teaching, preaching, and sheer enjoyment. I do not need academic requirements to motivate me anymore. My Bible-reading journey illustrates how values and attitudes change over time. The journey of changed values begins with information but does not end there.

Public education about language or mathematics can teach information without any regard for whether the student has proper values or attitudes. We cannot. For us, truth must be connected to God's value system. Return once again to the lessons in Luke. Can you find which lessons address such values and attitudes as self-righteousness, repentance, humility, or greed? The strategy of Jesus and every New Testament author moves students past satisfying their curiosity toward spiritual maturity. Another description of spiritual maturity involves conformity to the image of Christ (Rom. 8:29). In other words, when Christ's values and attitudes characterize all our choices, then we have arrived at our spiritual destination.

So far we have reviewed how the written material of the Bible provides a variety of strategies that help students learn. As we have followed those strategies, we discussed the need for our personal preparation before we embark on lesson preparation driven by the needs of our students. Our chosen scriptural text or texts should lead us to a central purpose, often called a lesson aim. Our aims combine both cognitive and affective elements as we seek to lead our students through an incremental process of spiritual growth. When truth influences our values and attitudes, we and our students move toward maturity.

Once we are spiritually prepared, have chosen appropriate text(s), and defined a clear objective that combines both truth and values/attitudes, we are ready to put a lesson plan together. Three models represent different time allocations between information presentation and student participation: *presentation*, *discovery*, and *discussion*. These models represent various levels of time commitments between teacher and student involvement. These work in an inverse relationship. In other words, the more time the teacher takes to *present* material, the less time there is for *student participation* (with the teacher or each other). These models move in order from low student participation/high teacher involvement to high student involvement/low teacher participation. As a general rule, in the presentation model the teacher uses about 90 percent of the class hour speaking, while students get about 10 percent of class time for questions about the presentation. In the discovery model, the teacher uses about 25 percent of the time for instruction at the beginning and 25 percent of the time debriefing students' discoveries at the end, while students use about 50 percent of the time to interact with material presented in oral or printed form. In the discussion model, the teacher sets up the parameters and issues of the discussion, using 10–15 percent of the time while the rest of class time is entrusted to student interactions among themselves. The results of the discussion may be used at a different time. What is our rationale for time allocation? This requires us to understand the three models and select the most appropriate one for the lesson at hand.

Presentation Model

The presentation model provides the best opportunity to give information not normally available through books, articles, or recordings. For verbal information transfer, this clearly represents the most efficient model since most of the time is consumed by teacher presentation and only a small amount of time for student participation.

Ordinarily, teachers allocate some time for student questions about clarification, meaning, or use of the information. Too often, teachers become preoccupied with what they want to say and neglect the student participation time. Innumerable lessons in my experience ended with, "That's all for today, we will pick up here the next time." Students listened passively with no specific time devoted to active student processing. When that happens, only the most courageous students interrupt the presentation to even ask a question. The teacher assumes that what they have to say is more important than what students are trying to understand.

One possible way to improve this model breaks a lecture into three to four smaller pieces of ten to twelve minutes with three five-minute question breaks.[6] It looks like this:

Introduction	2–3 minutes

6. Israel Galindo, "How to Keep Learners Engaged," Columbia Theological Seminary, https://www.ctsnet.edu/how-to-keep-learners-engaged/.

Point 1	10–12 minutes
Question break	3–5 minutes
Point 2	10–12 minutes
Question break	3–5 minutes
Point 3	10–12 minutes
Final questions	3–5 minutes
Total	41–54 minutes

Figure 4.2: Three-point lecture example

Breaking a presentation into pieces honors the adult attention span of ten to twelve minutes and maximizes student participation even in a presentation model.[7]

Discovery Model[8]

As Figure 4.3 shows, the discovery model allocates an almost equal amount of time to both teacher presentation and student participation.

The student participation section usually has students divided into work groups of three to four. Groups larger than that allow at least one person to be silent. The goal in the discovery model focuses on participation by all members. Time allocation can deviate either way, devoting more time to either the teacher or the students. The teacher's role in the discovery model changes substantially from the presentation model. Notice how a lesson might break down and then what role the teacher plays in each section.

7. I republished Dr. Haddon Robinson's "Proper Outline Form" in *The Professor's Puzzle: Teaching in Christian Academics* (Nashville: B&H Academic, 2015), 289. His whole sentence outline protocol has helped my presentations hold together better than anything else I have found. Using whole sentences disciplines your thinking and exposes where you need better connections between major thoughts.
8. I was first introduced to this model through Gospel Light's ICL (International Center for Learning) workshops. Their *Bible Activity* books are priceless, and Lowell Brown's *Sunday School Standards* (1997) is clearly the most helpful resource I have ever found to evaluate the effectiveness of the Sunday school or whatever you call the hour before or after the worship service.

Teacher: Welcome and introduction	2–3 minutes
Teacher: Giving lesson background information	5–10 minutes
Teacher: Explaining guidelines for and expected result of student participation	5–7 minutes
Students: Participating in discovery groups	15–20 minutes
Teacher: Moderating student-group results report	10–12 minutes
Teacher: Summarizing and synthesizing group reports along with providing additional information as needed	5–7 minutes
Total Teacher Student Teacher/Student	42–59 minutes 17–27 minutes 15–20 minutes 10–12 minutes

Figure 4.3: The Discovery Model

As a general rule, the higher the participation of students, the deeper their satisfaction and the longer they retain the material. The most difficult part of this model is designing the student participation section. Students must have clear explanations about what their group must produce and how they will present it. This approach allows your imagination to run free to create the student activities.[9]

In recent years, the cognitive domain's taxonomy has been revised and upgraded to include these kinds of activities.[10] Now labeled the *Padagogy Wheel*, Allan Carrington utilizes ubiquitous iPhone apps as a mechanism for student activity. But the wheel's suggested activities can be used without any apps at all. A thorough understanding of this wheel and the taxonomy makes lesson design less overwhelming. The process in linear fashion might be:

1. Study the text;
2. Determine the preferred taxonomy level;
3. Select an appropriate verb for a lesson aim;

9. Jesus used "learning activities" many times in his teaching. My favorite occurs in the story of the shekel in the fish's mouth (Matt. 17).
10. Used by permission. The wheel is available online at https://designingoutcomes.com/english-speaking-world-v5-0/.

4. Choose an appropriate group activity or individual app; and
5. Flesh out a lesson plan.

Most importantly, don't forget or neglect the personal spiritual preparation necessary to teach.

Discussion Model[11]

This model utilizes discussion and works best when leaders have some sense of group dynamics and members understand basic guidelines for group behavior.[12] The best groups have developed strong interpersonal relationships. The stronger the relationships, the more likely people are to share. Discussion groups with short lives, say four to eight weeks, seem to have the best attendance patterns. Every group needs someone who will faithfully do the following four things:

1. Monitor the time with questions like: Have we spent enough time on this question? Are we ready for the next question? Any final thoughts before we move on?
2. Keep the discussion on the subject with questions like: Can you help us understand how that relates to the original question? Have we wandered off the question, or does this really deal with some portion of it? Can we put that over to one side, perhaps discuss it over coffee, and return to the main question?

11. Stephen D. Brookfield and Stephen Preskill, *Discussion as a Way of Teaching: Tools and Techniques for Democratic Classrooms* (San Francisco: Jossey-Bass, 1999). This volume provides a comprehensive look at real discussion, the kind that goes on among students, not between leader and student. The principles will need to be downsized for Sunday school purposes. This resource is highly recommended for anyone designing discussions for adults.
12. University of Waterloo Centre for Teaching Excellence, "Facilitating Effective Discussions," accessed February 24, 2021, https://uwaterloo.ca/centre-for-teaching-excellence/teaching-resources/teaching-tips/alternatives-lecturing/discussions/facilitating-effective-discussions. The key to good discussion lies in the quality of the questions. You will do yourself a favor by acquiring the following older works. Although no longer in print, they were the gold standard for great questions; they also include helpful and extensive bibliographies. Marilyn Kunz and Catherine Schell wrote Bible-study booklets for several decades. These can still be found in the used-book market and some are on Amazon. Marilyn Kunz and Catherine Schell, *Neighborhood Bible Studies, Four Sample Discussions* (Dobbs Ferry, NY: n.d.). *The Serendipity Bible* is a classic with built-in discussion studies through the whole Bible. *The Serendipity New Testament* does not duplicate material from the Bible. These are great tools for those who are learning to write questions. Lyman Coleman, ed., *Serendipity Bible for Groups, NIV* (Littleton, CO: Serendipity House, 1988) and Lyman Coleman, ed., *Serendipity New Testament for Groups, NIV*, 3rd ed. (New York: Paulist Press, 1990).

3. Limit those who tend to dominate the discussion with questions/statements such as: [Name], can we put your comments on hold at this point and see if others have some contribution? [Name], let me interrupt right here and invite some of the others to share their thoughts. [Name], in the interest of everyone having an opportunity to share, let me interrupt and ask others to contribute some of their thinking.
4. Invite the silent members to participate with questions like: [Name], you have been quietly listening to everyone else, but we have not heard from you. What are your thoughts? [Name], since you have listened to everyone, what do you think are the most important points so far? [Name], we haven't heard from you. Can you help us with some of your thinking?

The leader tries to stay out of the discussion except to keep the discussion flowing and maximizing participation. Sometimes an errant comment may be left hanging until a group member raises a question or concern. If not, the leader might probe the group with something like, "Has anyone heard a different point of view?" Or, "I've heard people say XYZ, which seems very different. What do you think?" Again, note that the leader has not corrected anyone or taken control and begun instructing the group.

Regardless of how long the study lasts, the first session ought to include getting acquainted, along with a brief overview. The final session should include celebrating the end and saying goodbye. Like any skill set, quality group facilitation requires an understanding of group process as well as practice. The effort to acquire both skill and understanding pays off in the actual learning of students. If the student can discuss questions without having to consult the text, we have failed. We are not just looking for pooled opinions. On the other hand, the power of discussing the text to activate long-term memory ought to lift it high in our model selection.

> Discussion produces greater change in beliefs, preferences, and attitudes than do lectures, documentary presentations, or any other passive exposure to information. Questioning to stimulate discussion develops active participation, the key to attitude change. The Socratic approach to teaching may be

> less comfortable for students than other approaches, because it forces involvement, but it is more effective in development of student commitment to believe and the ability to put belief into practice.[13]

Mixing, matching, and modifying these models can create a classroom where students come to expect the unexpected. For example, brief activities can be used to introduce, expand, or conclude any lesson in any model.

In an effort to rescue the Sunday school, some well-meaning pastors and churches changed its name. Some new monikers include "adult learning centers," "adult Bible studies," and "adult Bible fellowships." The list could go on. Unfortunately, whatever label was hung on the hour, the internal teaching/learning mechanisms remained largely the same. Namely, the teacher did all the talking while students listened passively. The alternate models presented in this chapter can help adults begin to take responsibility for their own learning. After all, we are guiding people through a process of embracing truth, considering personal implications of that truth, and making intentional decisions for ongoing transformation.

Implementation

At this point, we assume you have a workable lesson plan that looks something like this three-part model: (1) *Begin* answers these questions: How will I introduce this lesson to my students? What is the first thing I plan to say? How can I help students make the transition from their immediate experiences to an orientation about the issue our text and their life needs will address? (2) *Develop* answers the questions: How will students handle the biblical material? In what ways can they handle the text for themselves? Will I have guided them to think more deeply about the text and how will I know? Finally, (3) *conclude* answers questions like: How will the summary reinforce the lesson aim? Will this time prepare students to make necessary changes suggested by the study? Will the students sense the study was a productive use of their time?

13. Donald K. Smith, *Creating Understanding: A Handbook for Christian Communication Across Cultural Landscapes* (Grand Rapids: Zondervan, 1992), 139.

This model parallels the more familiar pattern proposed by Larry Richards,[14] and later in partnership with Gary Bredfeldt,[15] of hook-book-look-took fame discussed at length in Cchapter 8. The *hook* parallels the "begin" stage above, arresting the students' attention and facilitating a disposition of questioning on the lesson's subject. It prepares the students to learn by stirring their interest and bringing to their awareness a life need. *Book* parallels the "develop" stage. Students are led to engage relevant biblical material to address the subject matter and questions raised in the hook. It is the Bible study on the subject of the lesson, applying God's Word to the students' inquiries. The *look* and *took*, while separate in Richards and Bredfeldt, are combined into the singular step of "conclude." In this phase the student is asked to make application of the biblical material in relation to the life need addressed by the lesson. The look is a more general application, "How might we (plural) apply this?" "What should the church (plural) do about this?" Such discussions are general, not personal, providing space for a noncommittal dialogue on the implications of the Bible. However, after the look is the took, which calls for a more specific, personal commitment to a tangible change implemented in the student's life. It is usually measurable and should reflect the lesson objective. It is an actual exercise of application, not a challenge to apply the Scriptures. For example, you could provide a 3x5 card and ask each student to identify one (measurable) way they could live out this biblical passage this week. Implementation begins where the lesson plan leaves off. The lesson plan is on a piece of paper. Now you are going to live by implementing the lesson in front of real students.

You will do yourself a favor if you plan to arrive early, maybe even an hour early. As a friend of mine used to say, "Class begins when the *first* student arrives!" But before students arrive, double-check:

- Is the room's seating appropriate for the activities you planned?
- Are the supplies handy that the students will need to complete their activities? (Markers, tape, note paper, pencils, poster board, etc.?)

14. Lawrence O. Richards, *Creative Bible Teaching* (Chicago: Moody, 1973).
15. Lawrence O. Richards and Gary J. Bredfeldt, *Creative Bible Teaching* (Chicago: Moody, 1998).

- Is the equipment ready?
- If there is a screen, what is on it to alert students to begin thinking about the lesson?
- Was the whiteboard/blackboard cleaned? Should something be written on it to indicate you are eager to begin this lesson with them?
- Will coffee, tea, hot chocolate, and/or donuts greet them upon their arrival?
- Is there a name-tag table near the door (first name only, printed in large capitals, like MIKE, large enough for you and others to see from a distance)?
- Are you ready to greet each student personally? Don't let the shy student slip by you.[16]

As the lesson unfolds:

- Spend as little time behind a lectern as possible.
- Move out among the students whenever you can.
- Walk toward anyone asking a question.
- Address students by name.
- You may not want to or be able to answer every question at that moment, but you can say things like:
  - I plan to address that later today (next week?), so can you hold that until we get there? Then let me know if you need more than my answer provided.
  - Can I answer that for you after class? Anyone also interested is welcome to listen in.
  - That is a good question. I do not know a really good answer right at the moment. Can I think about it and consult some resources before I get back to you? It's a good question; will you be sure and raise it again?
  - Before I answer, let me ask the class how they would answer your question.
- Make eye contact with individual students while you are speaking.

16. See additional discussion in chapter 14, "Pedagogical Uses of Technology."

- Watch the body language of each class member. More than once I have observed a student not really engaged with the lesson. After class I made it a point to approach the student and ask, "Are you OK?" Sometimes that elicited a brief conversation; sometimes that prompted an invitation to a more personal visit over coffee. Often the student shared genuine fatigue from some life events for which I prayed right then.

As soon as the class is concluded with prayer, ask yourself:

- What could I say or do to build anticipation or curiosity about the next lesson?
- What could I suggest for the "eager beaver" who would like to read or view something in addition to the lesson just concluded or in preparation for the next lesson? We should always challenge our best students as we are always looking for those who will become teachers themselves.

Evaluation

In reality, you construct evaluation devices in the planning phase. You execute evaluation after the lesson has concluded. Evaluation, like teaching, is more of an art form than a rigid science. You want to answer three questions as best you can:

1. How well did the plan work?
   a. My opinion
   b. Students' opinions
2. How well did I execute the plan?
   a. My opinion
   b. Students' opinions
3. How well did students embrace the lesson?
   a. My opinion
   b. Students' opinions

Let's look at each of these in turn. What is your opinion of the lesson? No matter how many times you teach a lesson, something seems to always happen with real students that causes you to think of something that would have made the lesson better. The best teachers never stop evaluating their work. Sometimes the idea comes during the lesson; making a quick note on the lesson plan helps remind you later. If you become a student of the teaching/learning process, you will likely notice many variable possibilities that go unnoticed by your students. The best time to make "notes to self" comes quickly after the lesson is over. Inevitably, long delays will steal fresh insights from you.

What is your students' opinion of the lesson? Although course evaluations have become the new norm in academics, they have rarely found their way into the church. Their value depends entirely on how well the questions are constructed and whether students can remain anonymous. To get something helpful for church evaluations, a downsized evaluation works in both formal and non-formal settings. Give the students each a 3x5 card, and have them answer one question on the front and an alternate question on the back. You can vary the question from time to time but always pair them. Here are some samples:

> Front: What did you like the best?
> Back: What did you like the least?
> Front: What do you wish we had done more of?
> Back: What do you wish we had done less of?
> Front: What would you have added to this lesson?
> Back: What would you have deleted from this lesson?

Students tend to appreciate the brevity and focused nature of the expected answer. In a church setting, select four to six different people to answer the questions and vary the people each time you use this technique.

How well did I execute the plan? Did I fail to do something that with a little tweak would improve that section? Did I make adequate transitions from one section to another or fail to give careful enough instructions about what I was expecting the students to do? Did I leave something important out completely? This is not the time to be kind to yourself. Ruthless honesty will help you get better. Careful evaluation truly helps you improve over time. If you choose to avoid evaluation, then just like when you shanked the golf ball into the woods, you have no one to blame but yourself.

How well did my students think I executed the plan? One of the best evaluation tools is found in the well regarded online resource *The*

Teaching Professor, established 1987. The questionnaire was reproduced with permission and can be found in my book, *The Professor's Puzzle.*[17] The tool offers eight major categories with questions or statements to be rated on a Likert scale of 1–5. The categories to evaluate: clarity, enthusiasm, interaction, organization, pacing, disclosure, speech, and rapport. I have used the questions and statements to guide areas to work on from lesson to lesson in a personal attempt to improve my skills.

How well did students embrace the lesson? This one is difficult to evaluate in any objective manner. Some students make immediate adjustments while others mull over information for an indefinite period before making any changes at all. The most helpful device I have found is a personal journal where students write down their own reactions to each lesson. That works poorly in a church setting where, in my experience, many adults and most men do not write down personal responses to lessons. My best results have come by putting adults in groups of three or four where they are asked to verbalize insights, responses, or personal applications prompted by the study. I still use the 3x5 card, but simply ask students to write down one application they wish to remember. After a time of group sharing, open the sharing to the whole class. Sharing in groups first makes sharing with the whole class much easier. By the way, when you ask a question or open up for sharing insights, you may have to wait for an uncomfortable length of time.[18] Your silence and patience will clue the class that you actually expect a response.

CONCLUSION

Teaching is not just telling, and learning is not just listening. Like the Master Teacher, we seek to engage people with truth that causes them to make choices aligned with God's value system. Our strategy is not casual nor is it modeled after the public school. We want our students to integrate truth in such a way that their new and improved value system reflects what God had in mind in the first place. Like the Bible itself, our strategy reflects a variety of approaches that show learners how to

17. Michael S. Lawson, *The Professor's Puzzle: Teaching in Christian Academics* (Nashville: B&H Academic, 2015), 283.
18. Mary Budd Rowe, "Wait Time: Slowing Down May Be a Way of Speeding Up!" *Journal of Teacher Education* 37, no. 1 (1986): 43–50.

be more like Christ. We evaluate our effectiveness by their consistently forward movement more than distance traveled. In other words, are we teaching them in such a way that day by day marks incremental transformation?

We have looked at three phases in our learning strategy which involve careful *preparation*, responsible *implementation*, and prayerful *evaluation*. The Bible itself illustrates lessons planned with its readers clearly in mind. We exert a great amount of effort in planning, implementing, and evaluating our teaching because we offer our lessons up as our worship to the great King. I asked one of my mentors how long it takes to develop a top-quality lesson. He replied, "A lifetime." In other words, we bring everything we have to each and every lesson. Over time, our lessons ought to get better as we grow closer to Christ in our personal devotion. In our early experiences, we may have the mechanics of a good lesson but not the spiritual depth we will bring as we mature. What a blessing to know that God can use even our feeble efforts when offered in worship to him.

By mixing and matching various elements from the three models, our lessons can offer an endless variety of interesting combinations. The Bible is not a boring book. It deals with essential life challenges on each and every page. When we bring our students to the text, we ought to help them linger on the truth long enough for it to sink deep within.

The treasury in Moscow collects Russia's most valuable art and treasures. One Fabergé egg contains a tiny gold replica of the Trans-Siberian train. If you look closely, you can see tiny gold people inside the gold cars. You find yourself wanting to stand and stare at the incredible craftsmanship. Can we as teachers showcase the Bible in such a way? On a table near the Trans-Siberian train rests a small bucket of stones tilted in such a way that they appear to have spilled slightly onto the table. Why in this amazing collection of Russian treasures does a bucket of rocks (not pebbles) lie on the table? Then you realize these rocks, some really good size, are uncut diamonds larger than any diamond you have ever seen. You ask yourself, "What is that bucket of diamonds worth?" The priceless treasure takes your breath away. When we take our students into the text, will it appear to them like a priceless treasure that takes their breath away?

May God help us all to bring everything we can find to bear on each and every lesson we teach as we fulfill the great King's Great Commission.

REFLECTION QUESTIONS

1. What three or four suggestions from this chapter would you make as personal priorities for change the next time you teach?
2. Which teaching strategy most appeals to you? What could you do to include a broader variety of strategies?
3. Did something in this chapter touch your personal "affective domain"? If so, how and what will you plan to do differently because of that change in your personal values or attitudes?
4. Thinking into the future, what will you plan to constantly improve (even if incrementally) in your teaching?

RECOMMENDED READING

Brookfield, Stephen D., and Stephen Preskill. *Discussion as a Way of Teaching: Tools and Techniques for Democratic Classrooms.* San Francisco: Jossey-Bass, 1999.

Hendricks, Howard G. *Teaching to Change Lives: Seven Proven Ways to Make Your Teaching Come Alive.* Sisters, OR: Multnomah, 1987.

Horne, Herman Harrell. *Teaching Techniques of Jesus.* Grand Rapids: Kregel Publications, 1982.

McKeachie, Wilbert J., and Marilla D. Svinicki. *McKeachie's Teaching Tips: Strategies, Research, and Theory for College and University Teachers.* 14th ed. Belmont, CA: Wadsworth Cengage Learning, 2014.

Smith, Donald K. *Creating Understanding: A Handbook for Christian Communication Across Cultural Landscapes.* Grand Rapids: Zondervan, 1992.

CHAPTER 5

RENEWING OF THE MIND: THE COGNITIVE DOMAIN

Scott Harris

"What is truth?" (John 18:38 NASB). Pilate's words echo through the corridors of time. You could argue that this is the most important question we can ask. The answer determines our eternal destiny. Men and women have sought the answer to this question from the beginning of time. One might even wonder if this question briefly ran through Eve's mind in the garden when she was tempted to question God's instructions. Did she think, "What is true?"

From Greek philosophers to Eastern mystics to modern-day courtrooms, we continue to ask, "What is the truth?" Implicit in this question—when asked sincerely—is the embedded desire *to know* what is true—to learn. After all, if truth exists, don't we want to know it? This desire to know truth leads us to another question, "*How* can I know truth?" For the purposes of this chapter, let me rephrase the question to "*How do I learn* truth?" An understanding of the *cognitive domain* helps us answer this question.

But before we get to the cognitive domain, let's contemplate the scene with Pilate a few moments longer. Picture yourself standing there as an attendant to Pilate. You hear the commotion of the Jewish leaders outside the praetorium calling for Jesus's execution. You listen to the conversation as it carries on. Jesus mentions people who are of the truth hearing his voice. Then Pilate asks that most profound question, "What is truth?" How he asks his question suggests his rhetorical aloofness—he is not interested in the answer. In fact, he smugly walks away from the very answer to his question: Jesus. The crucifixion narrative continues, and Pilate's question is left hanging in the minds of all in the room.

The irony of the setting astounds those who truly understand the situation. Jesus was not standing before Pilate. Pilate stood before Jesus, the Truth. The scene had been set in motion before time began. In fact, Jesus later corrected Pilate on who truly possessed the authority, "You would have no authority over Me at all, if it had not been given to you from above" (John 19:11 NASB). This was truth, yet Pilate's understanding of truth was wanting because his perspective was off.

PERSPECTIVE MAKES ALL THE DIFFERENCE

John Milton Gregory once wrote, "A truth can be fully seen only in the light of other truths."[1] In other words, true knowledge emanates from other truths. He argues that new knowledge is reached from that which is already known. Therefore, since we acquire knowledge from prior knowledge, it only makes sense to maintain a correct perspective on learning and by staying oriented to what is true. Ancient sailing gives us a clear example of this. Sailors could navigate at night by orienting themselves to the North Star. It is true. It is constant. This orientation gave them direction. When coupled with prior knowledge of shorelines, they could move freely at sea by night.

In the book of Proverbs, Solomon gives us a starting point and process for acquiring true knowledge. He writes, "The fear of the LORD is the beginning of knowledge" (Prov. 1:7 NASB). He later adds, "The fear of the LORD is the beginning of wisdom, and the knowledge of the Holy One is understanding" (Prov. 9:10 NASB). The book of Proverbs is about true knowledge and the proper use of that knowledge—wisdom. From the very outset of his writings, Solomon, in essence, tells his readers, "You must build your learning and practice from the perspective that God is God. He is sovereign over you, and your actions will either please or displease him. Having a healthy fear of God keeps you in alignment with him and what he possesses—true knowledge

1. John Milton Gregory, *The Seven Laws of Teaching* (Lancaster, PA: Veritas, 2004), 36.

and wisdom." Therefore, if we want to know truth and its proper application, God must be the plumb line of our orientation. The Bible tells us that "God must prove to be *true*," that Jesus is "the way, and the *truth*, and the life," and that the Holy Spirit is "the Spirit of *truth*" (Rom. 3:4; John 14:6; 16:13 NASB, emphases added). Our North Star for truth resides solely in God.

In ancient times when a stone building or temple was being constructed, the builders would first lay or set a large cornerstone. This stone then provided perspective for all other components of the building or temple. This stone gave proper orientation for true alignment of the entire structure. As long as the builders added to the structure with correct alignment to the cornerstone, the structure would be square and accurate. A building slogan might be, "Build it right from the cornerstone."

The same is true for us. It's not a question of *if* we will learn, but *what* we learn. Is our learning true? Our orientation must stay on God if we want to learn the truth. One wonders if Adam and Eve had maintained their orientation to who God is, whether they would have listened to the Serpent's temptation. They did not, though, and the consequences are beyond devastating. Knowledge of God helps us make sense of everything, which is why the book of Genesis orients us to him with, "In the beginning God" (Gen. 1:1 NASB). After accepting these words, we are now ready to learn truth and come to know, "All truth is God's truth."[2]

LEARNING IS A PROCESS

The term *cognitive* has been defined as "of, relating to, being, or involving conscious intellectual activity (such as thinking, reasoning, or remembering)."[3] The cognitive domain is a concept made popular by Benjamin Bloom and others in the 1956 classic *Taxonomy of Educational Objectives.* Bloom stated, "The cognitive domain . . . includes those [learning] objectives which deal with the recall or recognition of knowledge and the development of intellectual abilities and skills."[4] The cognitive domain explains how we learn, evaluate, and use knowledge.

2. Frank E. Gaebelein, *The Pattern of God's Truth: The Integration of Faith and Learning* (Kettering, UK: Oxford University Press, 1968), 20.
3. *Merriam-Webster Online Dictionary*, s.v. "cognitive," accessed August 18, 2023, https://www.merriam-webster.com/dictionary/cognitive.
4. Benjamin Bloom et al., eds., *Taxonomy of Educational Objectives: Handbook I: Cognitive Domain* (Harlow, UK: Longman, 1956).

This domain works in conjunction with two other domains: the affective (feelings, values) and the psychomotor (skills, certain behaviors). These are discussed in chapters 6 and 7 of this volume. All three domains contribute to the learning process.

Bloom argued we learn knowledge through increasingly complex mental processes. He organized his taxonomy (classification) of learning into six levels using the nouns: knowledge, comprehension, application, analysis, synthesis, and evaluation (see Figure 5.1). These are levels of learning that progress in complexity as one moves from knowledge to evaluation.

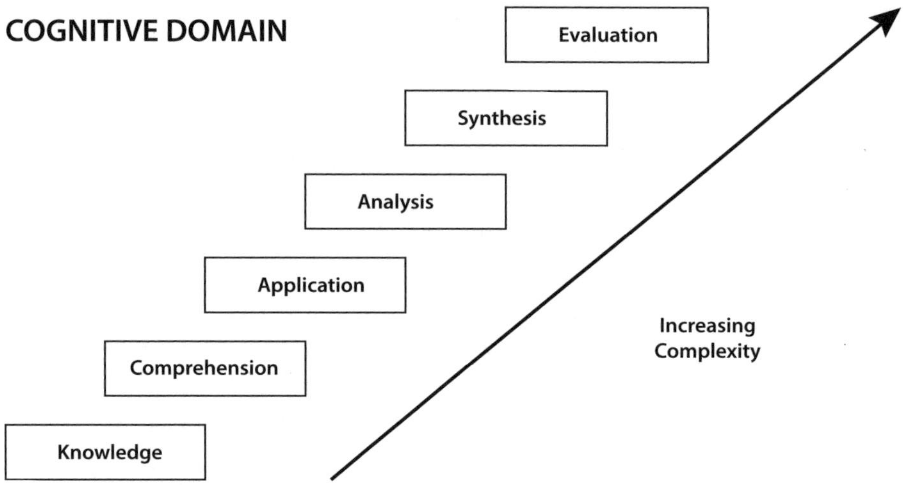

Figure 5.1: Levels of Learning

In 2001 Lorin Anderson, David Krathwohl, and others revised Bloom's Taxonomy in *A Taxonomy for Learning, Teaching, and Assessing*. They still identified six levels of increasing complexity in learning, but their revision renamed the six levels to reflect the active nature of the learning process. The six levels are: remember, understand, apply, analyze, evaluate, and create.[5] They also revised the order of the last two levels based on their understanding of where learning leads. The deductive skills of "evaluate" are not as complex as the inductive skills

5. Lorin W. Anderson and David Krathwohl, eds., *A Taxonomy for Learning, Teaching, and Assessing: A Revision of Bloom's Taxonomy of Educational Objectives* (Harlow, UK: Longman, 2001).

of "create." This revised version is what will guide our discussion in this chapter. A summary of the six processes can be seen in Figure 5.2.

Categories of Cognitive Processes	Expressions of Each Category
Remember	Recognizing Recalling
Understand	Interpreting Exemplifying Classifying Summarizing Inferring Comparing Explaining
Apply	Executing Implementing
Analyze	Differentiating Organizing Attributing
Evaluate	Checking Critiquing
Create	Generating Planning Producing
Note: The categories of cognitive processes increase in complexity from top to bottom. The expressions of each category identify various means each category may be demonstrated.	

Figure 5.2: Bloom's Revised Taxonomy of Learning

It is good to desire that our students pursue the highest (more complex) levels of learning, but successful teachers must understand their students' knowledge base and mental capacities. Students cannot think deeply about a subject before they possess the necessary information to be evaluated. We should not expect first graders to think critically about world events. That would be a fool's errand. In a similar manner, we should not teach adults as if they were still in first grade. Vygotsky's "zone of proximal development" echoes this idea. We cannot teach too far above or below the student's knowledge and cognitive abilities.[6] While children love to show off memorization skills, the same activities would probably drain the life out of adults. So, be mindful of where your students are developmentally, then craft your instruction accordingly.

Bloom's taxonomy is simple, but it is not simplistic. There is a difference. We may comprehend the essential elements of his taxonomy, yet we all have room for deeper understanding and application

6. Lev Vygotsky, *Mind in Society: The Development of Higher Psychological Processes* (Cambridge, MA: Harvard University Press, 1978).

of that taxonomy as we continue to grow in our learning. To illustrate how this taxonomy guides instruction, the remainder of this chapter will operate at the *analyze* level of the revised taxonomy. A cognitive learning objective for this chapter could read as follows: *The reader will analyze Bloom's revised taxonomy by distinguishing between its six levels of cognitive processes.*

As we proceed, I give you a question for consideration: Did Bloom develop something novel, or is his work a refined reflection of prior understanding?

THE PROCESS IS TIME-TESTED

The concept of a progressive cognitive learning process is not new. Learning and working with new knowledge at distinct levels has been seen throughout history. Three thousand years ago Solomon described the purpose of his writings in Proverbs, "The proverbs of Solomon . . . for gaining wisdom and instruction; for understanding words of insight; for receiving instruction in prudent behavior, doing what is right and just and fair" (Prov. 1:1–3 NIV).

Observe the progression of learning. First, the attentive student is gaining (learning) wisdom and instruction (knowledge that is outside the student). Understanding of knowledge comes next. (Understanding can often be demonstrated by rewording instruction in one's own words.) After understanding, the student advances to prudent behavior—application of understanding that is evaluated against standards. The learner arrives eventually at the intended purpose—doing what is right and just and fair in new settings in relation to truth and others. This is nothing less than a version of Bloom's taxonomy in ancient Hebrew. As in Bloom, knowledge and understanding are the foundation for higher levels of learning. But wait, there's more.

The process can be seen also in classical education. This educational model has grown in notoriety over the past few decades, yet its essential components have been present in educational practices throughout the centuries. Classical education reaches back through medieval times to Greek and Roman culture and even in some capacity back to Egypt and Mesopotamia.[7]

7. Circe Institute, "What Is Classical Education?," accessed December 27, 2024, https://circeinstitute.org/what-is-classical-education/.

Classical education seeks to help people interact with ideas that have shaped Western civilization, think about those ideas, and then wisely apply them (note the progression of knowledge, understanding, and expression). Classical education helps students learn how to learn. For the purposes of this discussion, we merely need to examine the first level of classical education, the Trivium.

In her 1947 essay *The Lost Tools of Learning*, Dorothy Sayers extolled the virtues of the Trivium, an organization of learning processes. She explained how the Trivium was the medieval syllabus that recognized children progress through three stages of learning: grammar, logic, and rhetoric (see Figure 5.3). These stages correspond to children's natural age and mental development. She also noted that every subject has a "grammar," "logic," and "rhetoric" stage.[8] Again, these stages align with knowledge, understanding, and expression.

Stage	Grammar	Logic	Rhetoric
Learning focus	Knowledge acquisition	Critical-thinking skills	Expression of ideas
Approximate developmental level	Elementary school years	Middle school years	Upper high school years
Note: The Trivium illustrates the overall learning progression of students from grammar to rhetoric. There is also a similar progression of learning for each subject one may study.			

Figure 5.3: Trivium

Fifty years later, Susan Wise Bauer described these three levels in *The Well-Educated Mind*. The grammar stage of learning corresponds to the early elementary years of a child. This is when children soak up new information like sponges. They acquire the building blocks, or "foundational knowledge of each academic subject."[9] Their capacity to remember new information is unparalleled. They learn to read,

8. Dorothy Sayers, *The Lost Tools of Learning* (Louisville, KY: GLH, 2017).
9. Susan Wise Bauer, *The Well-Educated Mind: A Guide to the Classical Education You Never Had* (New York: Norton, 2016), 18.

to write, and to work with mathematical facts. They learn history and cultural norms. They are not expected to evaluate knowledge at this stage. That comes in the next stage.

Evaluation comes during the middle-school years, or logic stage. She writes, "Once a foundation of information is laid, students begin to exercise their analytical skills; they decide whether information is correct or incorrect, and make connections between cause and effect, historical events, scientific phenomena, words and their meanings."[10] This stage fits their natural inclinations; they are starting to argue. This stage is intended to help them argue their thoughts well.

The final stage of rhetoric corresponds to the final secondary years. "Students learn to express their own opinions about the facts they have accumulated and evaluated."[11] Study focuses on eloquence in speaking and writing. This is where they learn to take their knowledge and reason from the prior two stages to express or create new applications of their learning. Again, the learning process fits the student's natural progress.

To illustrate the relevance of working with adults in a similar manner, let us consider the idea that every subject has a grammar, logic, and rhetoric stage. Consider law. First-year law students begin law school and are introduced to the foundational knowledge of legal theory and rulings (grammar). They are next guided in the finer art of thinking and argumentation about law (logic). Last, they are called upon to practice law and try mock cases (rhetoric). This progressive instruction aims at the wise use of law by the students.

Consider theology. Students show up at seminary and take an introduction to theology class where they begin the study of God (grammar). The next semester they take a class where they analyze how their understanding of God addresses current hot-button cultural topics (logic). Later, in other classes they are instructed to develop sermons, lessons, or podcasts that creatively communicate their knowledge of God to a world that needs him (rhetoric). The wise use of theology is the aim.

Pick any area of knowledge. People progress through these three learning stages (grammar, logic, rhetoric) whether they be a teenager flipping burgers at the local Burger Doodle or a pilot flying an Airbus.

10. Bauer, *The Well-Educated Mind*, 18–19.
11. Bauer, *The Well-Educated Mind*, 19.

Knowledge (in a specified area) is the assumed prerequisite for all subsequent learning activities.[12] You cannot expect someone to reason through a problem or present an appropriate solution if they don't understand the essential facts that give context to that problem. They must work through the process.

As Solomon wrote, "There is nothing new under the sun" (Eccl. 1:9 NIV). We learn in progressive steps. Solomon and classical education summarize these steps with different terminology. Bloom's revised taxonomy captures this proven understanding in current terminology that helps us apply the process. You can see the three models for cognitive learning set side by side in Figure 5.4. The three expressions of the learning process complement each other well.

Proverbs 1:1–3	Trivium	Bloom
Know wisdom and instruction Discern sayings of understanding	Grammar (Knowing)	Remembering Understanding
Receive instruction in wise behavior Righteousness Justice	Logic (Thinking)	Applying Analyzing Evaluating
Equity	Rhetoric (Expression)	Creating
Note: Each model increases in complexity from top to bottom.		

Figure 5.4: Comparing Three Models of Progression in Learning

Readers familiar with Bloom may have already noticed this chapter has taken them through the first two levels of his taxonomy (remembering and understanding) with the illustrations from Solomon and classical education. Did you see it? The chapter provided information you need to know, namely Bloom's taxonomy (remembering). Next, the cognitive progression of restating what is known in different terms was illustrated by using Solomon and classical education (understanding).

Now that we have established the idea of learning truth in progressive stages, let's analyze these stages as explained by Bloom's revised taxonomy.

12. Bloom, *Taxonomy of Educational Objectives*, 33.

COGNITIVE PROCESSES

In each of the six sections below you will find the given cognitive process identified and defined. You will then be given illustrations of how you might utilize these cognitive learning levels when teaching students in a variety of settings. Consider this chapter as an introduction to or review of the main ideas found in Bloom.

Remember

To retrieve relevant knowledge from long-term memory.[13]

In *How We Learn*, Klaus Issler and Ronald Habermas write, "The most popular understanding of learning views it as the acquisition of new information."[14] For instance, children learn their colors or the alphabet. They learn what "dog" or "cat" means. These are pieces of information they did not know when first born. Anderson and Krathwohl label this cognitive activity of learning as "remember." They assign this activity to the most basic learning level.

The cognitive process of remembering can be broken up into two main categories: *recognizing* and *recalling*. The learning activity of recognizing is demonstrated if you ask kindergarten students to identify red from a group of colors or pick out triangles from a group of shapes. They are retrieving information from long-term memory that matches material placed before them. It is basic, but it is necessary for later learning. You cannot study geometry if you cannot recognize a triangle.

If you want children to recall information, you are now asking for more than simple recognition. Perhaps you want your students to complete a sheet of math problems. When they see the problem 2 + 2 = _____, they will demonstrate their knowledge of mathematics by correctly answering (recalling) "4." This cognitive process is more than simple recognition. They are now recalling information from long-term memory and providing the correct response.

Two examples of learning objectives at the remember stage are:

---

13. Bloom, *Taxonomy of Educational Objectives*, 33.
14. Klaus Issler and Ronald Habermas, *How We Learn: A Teacher's Guide to Educational Psychology* (Grand Rapids: Baker, 1994), 31.

- The student will identify the twelve disciples from a list. (recognize)
- The student will recite John 3:16 before class starts. (recall)

These examples are basic, but knowledge at one level is required to move to the next. Gregory reminds the teacher that "truth to be taught must be learned from truth already known."[15] Connect the dots for and with your students. Let them see how bits of information relate to one another. Now let us build upon this knowledge of *remember* and move to the cognitive process of *understand.*

Understand

> To construct meaning from instructional messages, including oral, written, and graphic communication.[16]

For our purposes here, a person is said to understand an idea if they can restate or communicate the idea in a different form without compromising the meaning of the original idea. This is the next level of learning. You do this all the time. For instance, if you are not able to work your shift, you may call a friend from work and say, "I can't work my shift. Can you work my shift for me?" Your coworker responds, "I'll cover for you." She demonstrates understanding by replacing, "I'll work your shift for you" with "I'll cover for you." It's the same meaning with different words.

Earlier in the chapter, we demonstrated the cognitive process of *understanding* Bloom's revised taxonomy by using summaries of increasingly complex levels of learning from Solomon and classical education. If you wish to determine whether your students have progressed to the second stage of understanding a subject, have them restate what you have taught in their own words. If they can do that correctly, they understand.

Anderson and Krathwohl tease out multiple facets of understanding by explaining this can be done through activities of interpreting,

15. Gregory, *The Seven Laws of Teaching*, 84.
16. Anderson and Krathwohl, *A Taxonomy for Learning, Teaching, and Assessing*, 70.

exemplifying, classifying, summarizing, inferring, comparing, or explaining. Here are two specific examples:

- The student will explain the hook-book-look-took lesson plan model.
- The student will summarize the role of the Holy Spirit as explained by Jesus in the Upper Room Discourse.

Once students remember and understand a subject, using that subject is the next step.

Apply

> To carry out or use a procedure in a given situation.[17]

Bloom's revised taxonomy contains two levels of applying. The first is the concept of *executing*, where you demonstrate a procedure in a familiar setting. This can be likened to you making your bed while your mom watches. The second is that of *implementing*, where you demonstrate the procedure in an unfamiliar setting. This can be likened to you making your bed regularly in your dorm room while away at college. Consider this example of the procedure of a hard stop in a car.

> When I was sixteen, I earned my driver's license—that coveted plastic passport to freedom. As part of my driving test, the instructor told me to prepare to execute a hard stop at his command during the test. Later in the drive, he barked, "STOP!" and I complied—test passed. I *executed* the knowledge of "stop" for him in a planned and familiar setting.
>
> Periodically I have the opportunity to apply my driving instructor's teaching by implementing a hard stop during rush hour when some yahoo decides he wants to be in my driving space at the same time I occupy it. My instinctive application of "STOP!" is *implemented* in an unfamiliar setting, and I avoid having to call a tow truck.

17. Anderson and Krathwohl, *A Taxonomy for Learning, Teaching, and Assessing*, 77.

Application learning objectives are fun. They may be in familiar settings or unfamiliar settings. Consider these examples:

- The student will develop a hook-book-look-took[18] lesson plan for her teaching process class assignment. (execute)
- The student will share the Four Spiritual Laws on spring break when appropriate. (implement)

Ideally you will have the opportunity to observe executed application under supervision in the classroom and then can hear reports of implemented application after the lesson as a manner of life change. Application is a wonderful way to help students demonstrate knowledge they have acquired and come to understand.

As students progress, the analyze stage will demand remembering, understanding, and applying at an entirely new level.

Analyze

> To break material into its constituent parts and determine how the parts relate to one another and to an overall structure or purpose.[19]

In analyzing, we seek to *differentiate* the various parts of a topic: for example, we might identify the different sections of the Sermon on the Mount. In analysis, we should also consider how those different sections are *organized* by asking, "What is the relationship between the different sections of the Sermon on the Mount?" Lastly, we should seek to *attribute* or assign this observed organization to an overall intended purpose. We weigh what the intended meaning or conclusion of the Sermon on the Mount is based on how the various sections are organized.

Bloom explains the significance of analysis when he writes, "Although analysis may be conducted merely as an exercise in detecting the organization and structure of a communication and may therefore become its own end, it is probably more defensible educationally to consider analysis as an aid to fuller comprehension or as a prelude

18. The hook-book-look-took lesson plan format will be developed in chapter 8.
19. Anderson and Krathwohl, *A Taxonomy for Learning, Teaching, and Assessing*, 79.

to an evaluation of the material."[20] For instance, what is the lasting benefit of listing the various sections of Abraham Lincoln's Gettysburg Address and their relationship to one another without considering his intended purpose for developing and delivering such a speech? Bloom would argue, "Not much." That shortsighted analysis falls short of its intended impact. You don't just break a topic down. You seek to understand the whole by looking at its parts.

Analyzing knowledge properly is like a jigsaw puzzle. Jigsaw-puzzle pieces were never meant to be poured out of the box and just *differentiated* from one another. They also were never meant to just be *organized* on the table based on the related color schemes they possess. The intended purpose of jigsaw-puzzle pieces is to be connected by tabs and blanks in relationship to one another in order that they might *attribute* (or point out) the wonderful picture they create together.

Analysis, therefore, allows us to think deeply about the parts and how they are related, which leads to a deeper understanding of the meaning formed by these relationships. Analysis can lead us back to prior knowledge for more study, or it can propel us forward to a more robust evaluation of knowledge. In similar fashion, our analysis of these six levels of learning is designed to help you understand their relationship to one another and their contribution to how we learn.

As you plan analysis learning objectives for your students, they may look something like these:

- The student will *distinguish between* the necessary and unnecessary elements of the *ABC* after-school ministry program for kids. (differentiating)
- The student will *structure* elements from the book of Jonah that support "God is a merciful God." (organizing)
- The student will *identify the underlying problems* present in the church of Galatia based on the book Galatians. (attributing)

Throughout life people progress in the learning stages of remembering, understanding, applying, and analyzing, but from time to time they need to stop and measure their learning against plumb lines of truth. This is where the next stage of *evaluating* fits in the learning process.

20. Bloom, *Taxonomy of Educational Objectives*, 144.

Evaluate

> To make judgments based on criteria and standards.[21]

Evaluation continues the analytical thinking process. At this level students are looking at knowledge to see how it measures up. You might wonder, "Measures up to what?" Well, that standard is established back in the remember stage and strengthened in subsequent stages. Before we discuss *how* to evaluate in this learning process, it seems appropriate to briefly discuss what the standards for evaluation are.

All cultures have standards—that which they say is "right" or, in other words, true, beautiful, and good. For Christians, as explained above, that standard is defined by God. Yet, even for non-Christians, standards remain. If they did not, there would be no culture, no continued evaluation of "right." C. S. Lewis borrows the term *Tao* from Chinese culture in his book *The Abolition of Man* to give name to the universal concept of standards. He writes, "What is common to [all cultures] is something we cannot neglect. It is the doctrine of objective value, the belief that certain attitudes are really true, and others really false."[22] When it's time to evaluate, this doctrine of objective value is the standard.

The Christian looks to God and his Word to define what is true, beautiful, and good. Paul writes, "Finally, brothers and sisters, whatever is *true*, whatever is noble, whatever is right, whatever is pure, whatever is *lovely*, whatever is admirable—if anything is excellent or *praiseworthy*—think about such things" (Phil. 4:8 NIV, emphasis added). We practice evaluation even in the focus of our thinking. You cannot escape this. Hopefully you learn how to do it well.

With that established, let us return to Bloom. We can practice evaluation at two levels of engagement. First, students can carry out *checking* by looking for internal inconsistencies or fallacies of a procedure. Second, students can participate in *critiquing*. Critiquing occurs when students look for inconsistencies between a product and external criteria or determine if a procedure is appropriate for a given problem.[23]

---

21. Anderson and Krathwohl, *A Taxonomy for Learning, Teaching, and Assessing*, 83.
22. C. S. Lewis, *The Abolition of Man* (New York: MacMillan, 1950), 12.
23. Anderson and Krathwohl, *A Taxonomy for Learning, Teaching, and Assessing*, 84.

Every time you listen to a sermon, you should engage in evaluation. As you contemplate that same sermon later in the week, you can search the Scriptures to see if what has been preached is true, like the Bereans did in Acts 17. Churches practice critiquing each year as they evaluate ministries. They might ask, "Does ABC program care for widows as Scripture instructs us?" If they never evaluate, they may never know if they are doing it right—are aligned with the standard.

Evaluation is hard work in education. Remember, this is best suited for students who have critical thinking skills built upon a strong foundation of learning. It is not as effective with young children. If introduced well, your students will engage in the process because they are being asked to think and freely express their ideas on the question at hand. Remember, though, that perspective makes the difference in evaluative learning. We evaluate ideas in the context of established truth, and truth (learning) is established in the prior steps of remember, understand, apply, and analyze.

Here are two ideas that illustrate this practice:

- The student will evaluate how closely his thought patterns align with Philippians 4:8. (checking)
- The student will evaluate which proposed mission project best matches the student leadership team's student engagement goals. (critiquing)

When we have remembered, have understood, know how to apply procedures, can analyze, and can evaluate, we have the opportunity to create. This is the final and highest expression of cognitive learning according to Bloom's revised taxonomy.

Create

> To put elements together to form a coherent or functional whole; to reorganize elements into a new pattern or structure.[24]

Creating as a learning process truly makes the acquisition of knowledge enjoyable. As touched on above, Anderson and Krathwohl

24. Anderson and Krathwohl, *A Taxonomy for Learning, Teaching, and Assessing*, 84–85.

moved the create (synthesis in the original Bloom taxonomy) category to the highest cognitive-process level. They deemed creating as a more complex activity than evaluating. Evaluating involves looking at what is there and considering if it is right. Creating involves looking around at various elements that are not currently together, judging if they possibly could go together, and then making something completely new to address a problem or opportunity.[25] The prior levels of learning are all a part of the creating process. In fact, *each* level has elements of the simpler, prior levels in them. When I apply, I must remember. When I evaluate, I must understand.

There are three distinct avenues for creating. The first is *generating* or hypothesizing. The second is *planning* or devising procedures. The third is *producing* or inventing a product.[26] Imagine how these concepts might play out in the life of Sherry, the soon-to-graduate seminary student.

Sherry ponders her imminent graduation. She wonders why God continues to close doors that looked open just six months earlier. She prays, analyzes, and evaluates information to generate (create) hypotheses for her situation. One day, a new ministry opportunity that matches her desires emerges out of nowhere. Her hypotheses are confirmed. She pursues this opportunity by creating new plans based on remembering, understanding, and evaluating ideas God brings before her. God answers her prayers, and she soon lands in this new ministry. It's now time for her to get to work—to produce. She remembers her training. She shows *understanding* of ministry needs through proper *application* and *analysis*, and after *evaluating* her best option, she begins *creating* new ministry activities to meet the needs of those around her. This story is fictional, but it can be evaluated as containing truth.

Here are some final examples of learning objectives for the create level:

- The student will *generate* three hypotheses from available data to explain why the men's ministry sometimes struggles to cause life change.
- The student will *design a plan* to research the men's ministry needs.

25. Anderson and Krathwohl, *A Taxonomy for Learning, Teaching, and Assessing*, 85.
26. Anderson and Krathwohl, *A Taxonomy for Learning, Teaching, and Assessing*, 86–88.

- The student will create (*produce*) a men's ministry program that helps meet the top three reported needs of men in the church.

This chapter illustrates the progressive learning process. Writing this chapter required *remembering* knowledge gained through research on cognitive learning. This recall was transferred through *understanding* into my words. The activities of research, reading, and writing broadened the *application* process of learning. Revisions abounded during the *analyzing* stage of breaking down and organizing ideas to communicate the chapter's intended meaning. The red-penned editor passed out endless stars and dots on the work during *evaluation*—let's trust they don't stick.[27] Finally . . . the finished *created* product emerged. Lord willing, it has communicated the cognitive learning process as intended.

CONCLUSION

Life involves learning and learning truth is crucial for true life. Return with me to Pilate one last time. "What is truth?" How might his actions have changed if he recognized Jesus? We believe Jesus's death on the cross was ordained before the foundations of the earth, but if Pilate had understood that Truth was standing right before him, would he have waited for an answer to his question?

C. S. Lewis once wrote, "The head rules the belly through the chest."[28] This quote from *The Abolition of Man* is given in the context of the necessity of fueling the passions of men and women in education—the affective domain discussed in the next chapter. I would like to use it though to show the importance of knowing the truth.

It may seem simplistic to distill our daily lives down to three elements—head, belly, chest—but if you will engage in a moment of analysis with me, Lewis captured the essence of how we live. Our head is the keeper of knowledge. We learn of the physical and spiritual world around us and store that knowledge in our minds. The belly represents our actions—what we do both by choice and by instinct. It's the "living out" of our daily lives. Lastly, our chest, as Lewis argues, is the keeper of our affections, passions, and values. The strength of these determines

27. Max Lucado, *You Are Special* (Wheaton, IL: Crossway, 1997).
28. Lewis, *Abolition of Man*, 15–16.

whether we will or will not do what we know we ought to do. The three work together to create the lives we experience. Our knowledge (head) guides the application of our actions (belly) based on the strength of our affections (chest).

As Lewis said, it all starts with the head. So let us teach truth in such a way that when our students ask, "What is truth?" they run to Jesus and cling to him.

REFLECTION QUESTIONS

1. What are the six levels of Bloom's revised taxonomy? After you have listed them, come up with three synonymous terms for each level.
2. In your own words, explain the progression of learning from *remember* to *create*. In other words, how do these six levels relate to one another?
3. How can analysis inform greater understanding, and how can it inform better evaluation?
4. Refer to Figure 5.2 in the chapter and the expressions of each category in Bloom. What are the key components in each expression? For example, what is involved in recalling when you remember? What is involved in classifying to understand? What is involved in critiquing when you evaluate?
5. Evaluate one of your recent classes at school or in church. At what level of Bloom's taxonomy was most of the instruction? How did it vary? Was it appropriately placed for the class members' current level of understanding?
6. Imagine you have been assigned to teach Psalm 23 to a group of high school students. After studying chapter 8, "Lesson Objectives and Lesson Plans," develop a separate cognitive lesson aim for each level of Bloom's taxonomy that could guide your lesson preparations.

RECOMMENDED READING

Bauer, Susan Wise. *The Well-Educated Mind: A Guide to the Classical Education You Never Had*. New York: Norton, 2016.

Gaebelein, Frank E. *The Pattern of God's Truth: The Integration of Faith and Learning*. Kettering, UK: Oxford University Press, 1968.

Gregory, John Milton. *The Seven Laws of Teaching*. Lancaster, PA: Veritas, 2004.

Issler, Klaus, and Ronald Habermas. *How We Learn: A Teacher's Guide to Educational Psychology*. Grand Rapids: Baker, 1994.
Sayers, Dorothy. *The Lost Tools of Learning*. Louisville, KY: GLH, 2017.
Vygotsky, Lev. *Mind in Society: The Development of Higher Psychological Processes*. Cambridge, MA: Harvard University Press, 1978.

CHAPTER 6

TEACHING TO THE HEART: THE AFFECTIVE DOMAIN

Stacey Davis

"I will give them an undivided heart and put a new spirit in them; I will remove from them their heart of stone and give them a heart of flesh" (Ezek. 11:19 NIV). A colleague invited me to co-lead a discussion on ministry to the next generation with students in his seminary course. This was going to be a time of discussion and fellowship including lighthearted Q&A, a game about next-generation pop culture, and a dialogue on best practices with children and youth in the local church. During this session a student asked a question every person who disciples another ponders: "How do we ensure young people love Jesus after high school?" Spoken with what appeared to be a broken heart and genuine frustration, the student finished his question and eagerly awaited a solution from either his peers or the professors.

As a former minister to children and a professor of Christian education, I have learned that teaching for life change is no easy task. In both a seminary classroom and the local church, I have taught the Shema (Deut. 6:4–9) and the power of loving the Lord with all your heart, soul, and mind. The student's question reveals a genuine desire to assist another in the transfer of knowledge not just to the cognitive domain but to the affective domain as well—to the heart. This chapter will discuss the biblical and educational definitions of teaching to the heart and how one can teach for transformation and Christlikeness, and finally will conclude with practical ideas for a Christian education setting.

TEACHING TO THE HEART IS BIBLICAL

My ministry to the Lord began during junior high by serving children at my local church. Throughout the years children astounded me with their knowledge of the plagues in Egypt, their ability to recite all the Ten Commandments word for word, and their attention to every detail in the story of David and Goliath. However, one day I was teaching a child baptism class and asked one of the eight-year-olds present, "Why do you want to be baptized?" The child gave a simple response: "Because I love Jesus." This statement moved me to tears, as these four words revealed the beauty of the heart. Why do we teach others the knowledge of God? So they may one day declare, "Because I love Jesus."

To begin a discussion on teaching to the heart, it is important to define that word through a biblical perspective. Usage of the word *heart* varies throughout Scripture, including referring to the actual bodily organ itself; to human beings, meaning the range of emotions and passions such as fear, love, courage, anger, joy, or sorrow; to intellectual and moral faculties; and even to the human soul.[1] After analyzing the Old and New Testament, Gary Newton discovered a connection between the word *heart* and "innermost person."[2] Howard Hendricks complements Newton by demonstrating the Hebrew connection of the word *hear*t to a human personality, including the intellect, emotions, and will.[3]

What does Scripture desire of the human will or innermost person? Why does one teach to the heart? God is the Creator and changer of his creation. God created humanity (Gen. 1:26–31), designed a means of relationship with him (John 3:16), and can assist in the alteration of the will, or innermost person, by creating a new heart and spirit within his creation (Ezek. 36:26). Christian tradition calls this "conversion," referring to the ability of a person to turn toward a new "loyalty" and

1. Johannes. I. Marais. "Heart," in *The International Standard Bible Dictionary*, ed. by James Orr (Grand Rapids: Eerdmans, 1939), 1350–51.
2. Gary Newton, *Heart-Deep Teaching: Engaging Students for Transformed Lives* (Nashville: B&H Academic, 2012), 17.
3. Howard Hendricks, *Teaching to Change Lives: Seven Proven Ways to Make Your Teaching Come Alive* (Sisters, OR: Multnomah, 1987), 105.

begin to express "new patterns of behavior."[4] Therefore, after considering these various definitions of the word *heart* and what exactly God desires of the heart, it can be concluded that teaching to the heart refers to the "innermost person" or the human will for the result of developing a new conviction expressed through change of conduct.

TEACHING TO THE HEART IS EDUCATIONAL

Basics of the Affective Domain

Humans, being made in the image of God, have moral and spiritual capacities, giving them the ability to judge right from wrong regardless of their belief in Jesus Christ (Rom. 2:12–16).[5] Therefore, scholars in educational psychology possess a God-given capacity to do good work and to teach believers how human beings learn and how teachers can assist the changing of convictions.

Educational psychology refers to teaching to the heart as one of the three objectives created by a teacher for the purpose of instructing another in an educational setting. Prior to this chapter, it was established that objectives teach to the "human experience and development"[6] through three learning domains. The cognitive domain, discussed in chapter 5, refers to "remembering or reproducing" knowledge, while the psychomotor domain, to be discussed in chapter 7, indicates "muscular or motor skill."[7] David Krathwohl created the affective taxonomy in 1964. Scholars of educational psychology consider affective educational experiences as those that utilize sentiments as a means of influence for human behavior.[8] Scripture and educational psychology declare value in education that is transformational, and these interactions may even be able to alter the will and emotions of a human being.

---

4. A. Kreider, "Conversion," in *The Cambridge Dictionary of Christian Theology*, ed. Ian A. McFarland (Cambridge: Cambridge University Press, 2011), 115–16.
5. Millard Erickson, *Christian Theology*, 2nd ed. (Grand Rapids: Baker Academic, 1998), 180.
6. Ron Best, "The Development of Affective Education in England," in *Affective Education: A Comparative View*, ed. Peter Lang, Yaacov Katz, and Isabel Menezes (London: Cassell, 1998), 72.
7. David. R. Krathwohl, Benjamin. S. Bloom, and Betram B. Masia, *Taxonomy of Educational Objectives: The Classification of Educational Goals, Handbook II: Affective Domain* (New York: David McKay, 1964), 6–7.
8. Best, "Development of Affective Education," 73.

Value of the Affective Domain

Educational psychology reveals the value of teaching to the affective domain, or the heart. Krathwohl enhanced this taxonomy after the 1957 publication of *Changing Values in College* by Jacob found that a college experience did not produce any alteration of "values, belief or personality."[9] The study found teaching was not holistic in nature, instead simply transferring facts and skills to individuals. Other scholars believe the affective is equal to or may even be more essential than the cognitive domain.[10] One reason for this is the power of the emotional state. Researchers in childhood education discovered that emotional states can either encourage or hinder absorption of knowledge in the cognitive (mental) or psychomotor (skill) domains.[11] Anyone who has engaged in teaching has seen this occur. Global events or personal experiences such as a presidential election, a local school shooting, a new friendship, or personal or family illness can cloud the mind and block knowledge transfer. Of course it can also have the opposite effect. The learner is consumed by stress or concern in tragedy and joy or elation during times of victory, making it difficult for the teacher to reach the cognitive or psychomotor domains.

A teacher must also consider how teaching to the heart, or the affective domain, relates to the other domains of learning. A primary goal of teaching to the affective domain is to develop and understand character and conscience. As such, those who study transformational learning have found that a learning experience that teaches to the heart can enhance the cognitive domain as these moments usually answer "life's big questions."[12] The combination of remembering or recalling facts from Bloom's taxonomy (see chapter 5) and developing and characterizing ideas in Krathwohl's affective taxonomy enhances a learning experience as one begins to appreciate and value the content being shared.

---

9. Krathwohl, Bloom, and Masia, *Taxonomy of Educational Objectives*, 21.
10. A. D. Hauenstein, *A Conceptual Framework for Educational Objectives: A Holistic Approach to Traditional Taxonomies* (Lanham, MD: University Press of America, 1998).
11. Best, "Development of Affective Education," 73.
12. Elizabeth J. Tisdell, "Themes and Variations of Transformational Learning," in *The Handbook of Transformative Learning: Theory, Research, and Practice*, ed. Edward. W. Taylor and Patricia Cranton (San Francisco: Jossey-Bass, 2012), 22.

Krathwohl's Five Levels of the Affective Domain

Krathwohl's affective taxonomy contains five levels. The taxonomy is created in a hierarchical manner "along a continuum of internalization" in which the subsequent category takes the learner to a deeper level of learning than the prior.[13] The five levels of affective learning according to Krathwohl are: receiving, responding, valuing, organizing, and characterizing. Figure 6.1 contains a summation of these affective learning levels from Krathwohl's taxonomy, as well as learning measures based on Yount's treatment of the affective domain.[14]

Krathwohl's Taxonomy	Yount's Measures of Affect: A Learner . . .
Receiving Invitation to the educational process	listens, concentrates, observes, follows, watches, views, is attentive to, and/or focuses on
Responding Actual involvement in the educational process	shares, answers, asks, volunteers, complies, assist and/or testifies
Valuing Acceptance of the idea, forming a conviction or perspective	justifies, commits, defends, initiates, appreciates, selects, values, and works
Organizing Restructuring of value system to incorporate new conviction	prioritizes values, integrates, reorders, compares, and/or combines
Characterizing Lifestyle or behaviors reflect the newly affirmed value(s)	reflects, displays, practices, acts, and/or demonstrates

Figure 6.1: Affective Taxonomy Chart

The taxonomy signifies the student's progression from an inactive learner, to affirming and valuing new information, to actively participating in applying the newly acquired value to his or her life.

13. Krathwohl, Bloom, and Masia, *Taxonomy of Educational Objectives*, 95.
14. William R. Yount, *Created to Learn: A Christian Teacher's Introduction to Educational Psychology* (Nashville: Broadman and Holman, 1996), 277–81.

TEACHING TO THE HEART IS TRANSFORMATIONAL

An educational setting that seeks to be Christian requires transformation. Moral piety, declaring the correct answer, or distinguishing the righteous from the unrighteous kings in the Old Testament is not the primary goal of the teachings of Jesus. Transformation of the learner involves the educator assisting the learner in the sanctification process of becoming Christlike.[15]

Transformation in Scripture

The pages of Scripture contain hundreds of stories of life change, revealing how the heroes of the faith displayed a heart transformation that sought the kingdom of God. Joseph's brothers once sold their brother into slavery and told their father he had died. Yet, after time had passed, when they were seeking food due to a famine, they encountered their brother again in Egypt and it was evident to Joseph they had changed through their expression of love for Benjamin (Gen. 44).

Matthew was a tax collector and labeled a sinner by the Pharisees, yet when Jesus told him to "follow me," he responded by getting up and following Jesus (Matt. 9:9–13). Zacchaeus, too, was a tax collector and labeled a sinner, yet he desired to see Jesus and due to being small in stature climbed a tree. After seeing Jesus face-to-face, he declared he would give money to the poor and rectify his past financial wrongs. Hearing this, Jesus declared that salvation had come to his home (Luke 19:1–10).

A criminal next to Jesus on the cross knew of Jesus's innocence, declared his fear of God, and sought to be remembered in the kingdom of God. Jesus granted this request and delivered more by declaring the criminal would be in heaven (Luke 23:32–43).

Saul had a personal encounter with Jesus Christ that changed his life. He went from a man who murdered Christians to one who proclaimed the gospel and wrote nearly 25 percent of the New Testament (Acts 9). Christian educators should follow the example of these lives in Scripture by desiring that their students be transformed.

Transformation Is Beneficial

Transformation of the heart has many interpersonal benefits that can influence society. The affective domain can transform human interac-

15. Lois. E. Lebar, *Education That Is Christian* (Colorado Springs: Chariot Victor, 1995), 47.

tion and is needed in the childhood schoolyard and the adult office. Learning to socialize is key to thriving in childhood, making engaging the affective domain essential to these ages. A work environment provides the opportunity for an adult to control his or her emotions during times of stress, to value enduring during times of hard labor, and to appreciate colleagues through times of friendship at the water cooler or when collaborating on projects.[16] Society itself benefits from affective change, as a new conviction can challenge the wicked heart and address issues such as deceit, theft, bigotry, bias, and dishonesty.[17]

Transformation and heart change not only influences society, but it enhances the life of the individual. Although this point seems rather straightforward, considering how transformation influences the individual is vital. Howard Hendricks believed in emphasizing this aspect of education as he knew "teaching that impacts is not head-to-head, but heart-to-heart."[18] Transforming the heart can encourage lifelong learning. After a learner experiences heart change, he or she can apply this learning to a variety of avenues such as art, music, reading, sports, or hobbies.[19] Teaching to the heart assists learners in being aware of their emotions. Understanding the heart enhances life satisfaction, as one will understand how to handle various situations such as addressing common fears or anxiety. Affective learning can also build confidence as one begins to understand he or she can achieve various activities in this life.[20]

Teaching to the affective domain can be enhanced when considering the process of educational transformation. As mentioned earlier, Scripture reveals God's power to transform the human heart. Romans 12:2 and Psalm 51 likewise emphasize human involvement in transformation. A key seventeenth-century Christian educator, John Amos Comenius (1592–1670), contributed to our understanding of teaching to the heart by declaring that a person must have a "desire to learn" if they are to be educated, and emphasized teaching with the senses.[21] He recommended teachers appeal to the five senses, allowing children to learn the world around them through real objects rather than simply

16. Best, "Development of Affective Education," 73.
17. Hauenstein, *Conceptual Framework for Educational Objectives*, 59.
18. Hendricks, *Teaching to Change Lives*, 105.
19. Hauenstein, *Conceptual Framework for Educational Objectives*, 60.
20. Best, "Development of Affective Education," 73, 78.
21. Lebar, *Education That Is Christian*, 52.

hearing words.[22] Utilizing these types of techniques allows a teacher to assist spiritual growth as these will engage both outward measurable activities such as writing or computing math as well as the inner person through their feelings and attitudes resulting in teaching to the heart.[23]

Jack Mezirow contributed to our understanding through creating the transformational learning theory. Transformational learning theory seeks to understand how one is transformed by making meaning from a life experience.[24] This theory concludes that a person who engages in ten phases of deep reflection can create a new habit or new way of thinking.[25] The ten phases are:

1. a disorienting dilemma;
2. self-examination;
3. a critical evaluation of previous assumptions;
4. recognition that one's discontent and the process of transformation are shared;
5. exploring new things in life, such as identities, people, and actions;
6. changing a prior method to a new plan of action;
7. acquiring the correct knowledge and skills to implement a plan;
8. temporarily trying new identities or roles;
9. building competence and self-confidence in new things such as roles or relationships; and
10. a restoration of life based on the findings of a new perspective.[26]

The creation of a new mental habit or conviction will impact the learner's behavior and attitudes, revealing life change. Higher education institutions and human resource departments have incorporated transformational learning phases into their practices to develop the

22. Lebar, *Education That Is Christian*, 52.
23. Lebar, *Education That Is Christian*, 56–61.
24. Sharon B. Merriam and M. Carolyn Clark, "Learning and Development: The Connection in Adulthood," in *Handbook of Adult Development and Learning*, ed. Carol Hoare (Oxford: Oxford University Press, 2006), 35.
25. Jack Mezirow, "Learning to Think Like an Adult: Core Concepts of Transformation Theory," in *Learning as Transformation: Critical Perspectives on a Theory in Progress*, ed. Jack Mezirow (San Francisco: Jossey-Bass, 2000), 17.
26. Mezirow, "Learning to Think Like an Adult," 22.

heart and assist lifelong learning in their organizations.[27] Christian educators can follow this example by including questioning, challenging and reflecting on experiences to assist learner heart change.

TEACHING TO THE HEART IS PRACTICAL

"Yes, Jesus loves me. For the Bible tells me so." Very young children who grow up in a Christian environment learn this classic Sunday school song at their local church or at home with their families. Some children will grow up singing daily the powerful words that "Jesus loves me." Ministries to children and families who sing this song demonstrate that teaching to the heart is truly practical.

Lesson Distinctives

Teaching to the heart requires educators to examine their explicit curriculum and include essential components that address the affective domain. To begin, teaching to the heart demands learner engagement. After all, engaging the brain or the heart allows the teacher to help transfer knowledge transfer to the learners, ensuring they have received the "study of the day."[28]

Those seeking to teach to the heart should not neglect classic teaching methods found in many educational environments. These include times of discussion, small groups, and the use of questions, reflection, literature, and stories. Those who desire to create collective moments where learners can develop affectively in groups should consider including times of discussion in their educational environments. Group discussion assists the development of values and convictions in a manner different from merely listening to material. Including times of discussion provides participants opportunities to learn by sharing personal perspectives and gives time to wrestle with thoughts. Discussion can be with the entire class or with smaller groups. The use

27. Jack Mezirow, *Fostering Critical Reflection in Adulthood: A Guide to Transformative and Emancipatory Learning* (San Francisco: Jossey-Bass, 1990); Michelle K. Shuler and Elizabeth A. Keller-Dupree, "The Impact of Transformational Learning Experiences on Personal and Professional Counselor-in-Training Identity Development," *Professional Counselor: Research and Practice* 5, no. 1 (2015): 152–62; Carolin Kreber, "Critical Reflection and Transformative Learning," in *The Handbook of Transformative Learning: Theory, Research, and Practice*, ed. Elizabeth W. Taylor and Patricia Cranton (San Francisco: Jossey-Bass, 2012), 323–41.
28. Yount, *Created to Learn*, 278.

of small groups can enhance interpersonal relationships by forming bonds between participants, allowing more learners to express their emotions and convictions.[29]

Educators can engage the heart through individual moments of questioning or reflection. Times of question provide learners the opportunity to engage all learning domains and can ensure the application is included in the lesson itself. Questions can be designed by the educator to give learners time to express their opinions on a topic at hand, or learners can create their own questions. As mentioned earlier during the discussion of Mezirow's transformational learning theory, the use of reflection in an educational environment can lead to transformation, as these moments allow a learner to study his or her personal feelings of spirituality and religious belief.[30] Reflection guides that include biblical passages, questions to answer, pictures to draw, or prayers to journal are particularly helpful.[31]

Literature and stories are classic methods that engage individuals or groups by taking the learner on an emotional journey through another's experiences. Jesus taught in parables. The Psalms remind Christians to share the stories of God with the next generation as a means of developing confidence in God's power, resulting in obedience to his commands (Ps. 78:1–8). Literature also encourages empathy.[32] Stories can be a catalyst to life change, as this method enhanced by the Holy Spirit creates new convictions in the learner, resulting in new actions and behavioral change.[33]

Educators can also consider trying creative methods of engaging the heart. These methods work with a variety of age groups and include times of simulation, case studies, creative arts, cultural experiences, and sharing experiences. Simulation games provide moments of experiencing real-life situations, giving learners a safe environment to wrestle with difficult problems and life experiences. Case studies provide similar benefits. To truly engage human emotions, educators should include times of analysis and decision-making in these experiences.[34]

29. Newton, *Heart-Deep Teaching*, 125, 135.
30. Best, "Development of Affective Education," 78.
31. Newton, *Heart-Deep Teaching*, 133, 197.
32. Best, "Development of Affective Education," 78.
33. Newton, *Heart-Deep Teaching*, 124.
34. Newton, *Heart-Deep Teaching*, 123–24, 127.

The creative arts have been utilized as a means of activating the affective domain. Creativity itself in a learning environment not only provides an outlet for expression but also a time to imagine and hypothesize. Arts and music can refresh the cognitive elements of a lesson and motivate the learner to further engage in the material. Drama and role-playing provide an experimental environment for learners to engage in a range of emotions.[35] After completing the hypothetical activity, the learner may experience a "spark that ignites a change of heart" since role-play challenges prior convictions as the learner simulates confession of sins, moments of sadness during suffering, and times of joy during a victorious event.[36]

Sharing personal stories or cultural experiences can develop the affective domain and reveal true Christian character. Sharing a cultural experience can inspire learners as well as provide insight into how others experience life with God.[37] Educators or other learners can also share personal testimonies and stories to teach to the heart and reach the highest level of the affective domain. Christian doctrine informs us that life experiences can develop godly character.[38] When learners share their personal experiences that enhance their godly character, they are informing observers how to grow in the fruit of the spirit (Gal. 5:22–23). Not only do they remind the observers of how to display godly character while on earth, but they also show how Christians are being prepared for their Christian calling with Jesus Christ in heaven.

Teacher Distinctives

After addressing lesson distinctives, educators who desire to teach to the heart can address the implicit, or hidden, curriculum. Implicit curriculum "covertly" teaches the learner as it is what the student experiences in the lesson itself rather than what is "overtly" learned through explicit curriculum.[39] To begin, a teacher who desires to teach to the heart must create a welcoming environment, one that facilitates relationship between

35. Best, "Development of Affective Education," 78.
36. Newton, *Heart-Deep Teaching*, 122–23, 130.
37. Best, "Development of Affective Education," 78.
38. Henry W. Holloman, "Tribulation," in *Kregel Dictionary of the Bible and Theology* (Grand Rapids: Kregel, 2005), 546–47.
39. James R. Estep, Roger White, and Karen L. Estep, eds., *Mapping Out Curriculum in Your Church: Cartography for Christian Pilgrims* (Nashville: B&H Academic, 2012), 272, Kindle.

students and the teacher, and ensure students feel known. Being personal with students is one means of ensuring this occurs. Educational humanism began to personalize a learning environment. In order to make an impact, Christian educators must know their students. Through personal connection teachers can better address learner needs while assisting in transformation and life change. Once educators know their learners' needs, they can truly care for them. Caring for learners in an educational setting creates an environment that has "a positive emotional tone" and involves being "friendly and caring."[40] This is a matter of emotional intelligence on the part of the teacher, which is discussed in chapter 15. By actively caring for a learner, an educator develops the learner's trust, which is essential to teaching to the heart. As Hendricks states, "You can impress people from a distance, but you can impact them only up close," and "No one cares what you know until they know that you care."[41] Throughout my years as a teacher, Hendricks has proven to be right. Students have informed me countless times that they believe they learn best from a teacher who cares for them.

After teachers address their teaching environment, they can include intentional actions that assist the heart change of their learners. During the actual educational experience, educators must express the value of these moments to the learners. By expressing the importance of small groups, discussion, or reflection, the learners will engage in the material as they understand its value.

Every person made in the image of God has needs and thus can relate the teachings of Scripture to his or her own life, hopefully finding the answer to his or her greatest questions. Humanistic learning theory supports this perspective through the emphasis of teaching to the whole person. A way to address needs in an educational setting is by providing learner autonomy—giving students room for choices and freedom of expression—and connecting the subject matter to real life.

CONCLUSION

Howard Hendricks once said, "Until the mind has been changed, and the emotions have been changed, and the will has been changed, bibli-

40. Yount, *Created to Learn*, 334.
41. Hendricks, *Teaching to Change Lives*, 111, 117.

cal teaching and learning has not taken place."[42] What a great reminder that for education to be Christian it must assist another person in becoming more like Jesus Christ. The Great Commission admonishes Christian educators to go make disciples of all ages, realizing they have the capacity for life change and acknowledging that a changed life impacts society (Matt. 28:16–20). Right now, take a moment to remind yourself that teaching to the heart is biblical, educational, transformational, practical, and doable.

REFLECTION QUESTIONS

1. Consider your perceptions of teaching to the heart prior to reading this chapter. How have they stayed the same or changed? Are there any questions you still have regarding teaching to the heart?
2. Why is the affective domain important in an educational setting?
3. Have you seen transformation in your educational settings? If yes, describe an example.
4. What heart change would you like to see in your educational settings?
5. What are ways that you as a teacher can work with the Holy Spirit to transform the heart of a student?

RECOMMENDED READING

Hendricks, Howard. *Teaching to Change Lives: Seven Proven Ways to Make Your Teaching Come Alive*. Sisters, OR: Multnomah, 1987.

Lebar, Lois E. *Education That Is Christian*. Colorado Springs: Chariot Victor, 1995.

Newton, Gary. *Heart-Deep Teaching: Engaging Students for Transformed Lives*. Nashville: B&H Academic, 2012.

Yount, William R. *Created to Learn: A Christian Teacher's Introduction to Educational Psychology*. 2nd ed. Nashville: B&H Academic, 2010.

42. Hendricks, *Teaching to Change Lives*, 115.

CHAPTER 7

SKILLS FOR LIFE: THE PSYCHOMOTOR DOMAIN

George Hillman

When I was growing up, my family had a "weekend farm" just north of the town where we lived. It was a great place to explore nature and learn many life skills. On the farm I learned how to build a campfire, pitch a tent, cast a fishing reel, safely use a chainsaw, and even do basic electrical work. Some of my best childhood memories were created there.

It was also on the farm that I learned how to drive a manual transmission pickup truck even before I could legally drive on a street. It started off by first watching my dad drive the truck with me on the passenger side of the front bench. Then it progressed to me sitting in front of my dad while he drove around the farm. The next step was my dad letting me get behind the wheel with him offering guidance from the side as I ground the gears and ran into mesquite bushes. But each time I drove I was learning the skills to drive a truck, and I got better. My dad could not tell you what he was doing, but he was tapping into what educational theorists call the "psychomotor domain" in giving me hands-on instructions on how to drive a pickup truck and then letting me actually learn by doing.

DEFINITION OF PSYCHOMOTOR DOMAIN

This chapter is about the psychomotor domain (sometimes called the behavioral or volitional domain). The focus in this domain is on the bodily or physical skills—the movements, dexterity, reflex actions, motor control, coordination, and even interpretive movements—needed to perform a specific task.

The psychomotor domain includes both gross motor skills and fine motor skills. Gross motor skills include whole body actions like standing, walking, and running. Fine motor skills include actions like manual dexterity (handling without gripping as well as gripping with one's palm), finger dexterity (fingering without gripping, gripping with fingers, or movement), foot and toe dexterity, and facial muscular activity.[1] Progress is measured in the psychomotor domain with terms such as *speed*, *precision*, *distance*, *procedures*, or *techniques*.

While much has been written and analyzed regarding both the cognitive and affective domains of learning, it was not until the late 1960s and early 1970s that educational theorists even started describing the psychomotor domain in tangible terms.[2] But the idea of the psychomotor domain has existed as long as the knowledge of how to perform a specific trade or practical skill has been passed down from one generation to the next. How did people learn to hunt for food, make a fire, domesticate livestock, plant fields, build houses, or even create masterpieces of great art centuries ago? Someone more skilled took the time to train them. They allowed the learner to try to perform the skill and slowly improve in the trade or craft. This would later be codified in the trade or craft guilds with the progression from apprentice to journeyman to master in a particular area, and these terms are still in use today in fields like plumbing and electrical work.[3]

While some limit the psychomotor domain to athletics, vocational trades, and the arts, many of our everyday, real-life skills have a physical component. In preschool and elementary school we learned how to hold a pencil to write the alphabet and how to give a presentation in

1. Elizabeth Jane Simpson, *The Classification of Educational Objectives: Psychomotor Domain* (Urbana: University of Illinois Press, 1966), 6.
2. Walter Pierce and Charles Gray, *Teaching in the Three Learning Domains of Learning* (Lanham, MD: University Press of America, 1981), 165–66.
3. Simon Paul Atkinson, "Psychomotor Domain," Sijen.com, accessed February 15, 2021, https://sijen.com/research-interests/taxonomies/psychomotor-domain.

"show and tell" by actually performing those physical skills under the guidance of a caring teacher.[4] Later in high school we learned chemistry and biology by experimenting in lab exercises with Bunsen burners, test tubes, and balance scales, and maybe we even dissected a frog. But our hands-on learning is not limited to academic pursuits. Learning how to teach a Bible study or even share the gospel with someone requires a focus on correctly and accurately performing a skill in a real-life context.[5]

Learning happens best when a student is active and engaged in what is being taught.[6] Someone can read about how to ride a bicycle and can even watch another person ride a bicycle, but a student has not really learned how to ride a bicycle until she or he actually climbs on the bicycle and starts pedaling. In the psychomotor domain, learning happens with the student "trying, initiating, practicing, stretching, exceeding limitations, overcoming barriers, preserving, struggling, and repeating."[7] And there is no greater motivator for any student than the opportunity to perform a skill and to get it right.[8]

Broadly speaking, learning in the psychomotor domain advances through four stages (see Figure 7.1). In the first stage (observing), a student watches a more experienced person perform the skill. In the second stage (imitating), a student copies the skill of the more experienced person. In the third stage (practicing), a student repeats the skill until it becomes more automatic and smoother. Then in the final stage (adapting), a student fine-tunes the skill and makes minor adjustments to perfect the skill and to make it the student's own. All the while in each stage, the role of the more experienced person (the teacher) shifts from a model at the observing and imitating stages to a coach or mentor at the practicing and adapting stages.

---

4. Robert Gagné, Leslie Briggs, and Walter Wager, *Principles of Instructional Design*, 4th ed. (Fort Worth, TX: Harcourt Brace Jovanovich, 1992), 92.
5. William R. Yount, *Created to Learn: A Christian Teacher's Introduction to Educational Psychology* (Nashville: Broadman and Holman, 1996), 148–49.
6. Gary Newton, *Heart-Deep Teaching: Engaging Students for Transformed Lives* (Nashville: B&H Academic, 2012), 106–7; Bernice McCarthy, *About Teaching: 4MAT in the Classroom* (Wauconda, IL: About Learning, 2000), 13, 15, 112.
7. Newton, *Heart-Deep Teaching*, 106.
8. Wilbert J. McKeachie and Marilla Svinicki, *McKeachie's Teaching Tips: Strategies, Research, and Theory for College and University Teachers*, 14th ed. (Belmont, CA: Wadsworth Cengage Learning, 2014), 192.

1.Observing → 2. Imitating → 3. Practicing → 4. Adapting

Figure 7.1: Four Stages of the Psychomotor Domain

PSYCHOMOTOR TAXONOMIES

Unlike the cognitive domain (with Bloom's taxonomy in chapter 5) and the affective domain (with Krathwohl's taxonomy in chapter 6), educational theorists have never centered on a primary taxonomy to describe development in the psychomotor domain. What follows are three of the primary psychomotor taxonomies prevalent today, each with its unique expression of the same foundational domain.

Elizabeth Simpson's Taxonomy

One of the most well-known psychomotor taxonomies is by Elizabeth Simpson. Originally developed at the University of Illinois in 1966 and expanded in 1972, Simpson's psychomotor taxonomy lays out a progression from watching someone else perform the skill (perception and set), to being told specifically what to do (guided response), to not having to think about what you are doing (mechanism and complex overt response), to inventing new ways to perform the skill (adaptation and origination). Simpson saw the relevance of this in vocational and technical education such as industrial arts, agriculture, home economics, music, art, and physical education. These areas require a high degree of ability and skill in the physical domain as well as in the cognitive and affective domains.[9]

Perception (Awareness)

The first level of Simpson's taxonomy is *perception*. This is the essential opening step in performing any motor skill by becoming aware of objects or situations based on sensory cues that will guide future steps. Sensory cues can be auditory (volume, pitch, timbre, pattern of sounds, and distance), visual (color, spatial relations, shape, motion, light, and shade), tactile (texture, temperature, shape, size, pressure, position, state of motion, and weight), gustatory (saltiness, sourness, bitterness, and sweetness), olfactory (ethereal like fruit, fragrant like flow-

9. Simpson, *Classification of Educational Objectives*. All the following descriptions come from Simpson.

ers, burned like tar, putrid like bad fish, resinous like pine, and spicy like cloves), or kinesthetic (sensitivity from activation of receptors in muscles, tendons, and joints). Based on the sensory cue, a student decides what he or she must respond to, and then translates the cue into some action in a motor skill.

Phase 1: Preparation
▪ Perception: becoming aware of objects and their qualities through one or more of the human senses ▪ Set: possessing the readiness to perform a particular action
Phase 2: Supervised Practice
▪ Guided Response: performing under the guidance of a skilled trainer
Phase 3: Increasing Excellence in Performance
Mechanism: performing a task consistently with some degree of confidence and proficiency
Complex Overt Response: performing a task with a high degree of confidence and proficiency
Adaptation: performing new but related tasks based on previously learned motor skills
Origination: using understanding, abilities, and skills developed in the psychomtor area, the student creates new performances[10]

Figure 7.2: Overview of Simpson's Taxonomy for the Psychomotor Domain

Examples of this level are a student observing the grip on a golf club, estimating where a ball will land after it is thrown, adjusting the heat of a stove to correct temperature by smell and taste of food, relating the taste of food to a need for seasoning, recognizing a malfunction by the sound a machine is making, identifying music with a particular dance step, listening to the sounds made by guitar strings before tuning them, or adjusting the height of the forks on a forklift by comparing

10. Modification of Simpson's model by Klaus Issler and Ronald Habermas, *How We Learn: A Christian Teacher's Guide to Educational Psychology* (Grand Rapids: Baker, 1994), 38.

where the forks are in relation to the pallet. Examples of action verbs in writing learning objectives targeting the perception level are chooses, describes, detects, differentiates, distinguishes, identifies, isolates, relates, selects, and separates.[11]

Set (Mindset)

The second level of Simpson's taxonomy is *set*. This is possessing the mental (knowing the proper motor steps and appropriate tools), physical (being properly positioned such as in posture, balance, or aiming), and emotional (being willing to perform the action) mindsets and readiness to act or perform a particular motor skill. These three sets (mental, physical, and emotional) are dispositions predetermining a response to different situations.

Examples of this level are a student knowing the steps in varnishing wood, demonstrating proper bodily stance for batting a ball, knowing how to use a computer mouse, having a musical instrument ready to play and watching the conductor, or knowing a sequence of steps in a manufacturing process. Examples of action verbs in writing learning objectives targeting the set level are begins, displays, explains, moves, proceeds, reacts, responds, shows, starts, volunteers.

Guided Response

The third level of Simpson's taxonomy is *guided response*. This is the first attempt at performing a complex skill, including imitation (repeating the skill demonstrated by the instructor) as well as trial and error (trying various responses with some rationale until an appropriate response is achieved). Adequacy in performing the complex skill is achieved by repeated practice.

Examples of this level are a student completing a math equation on the board as demonstrated by the teacher, following instructions to build a model, performing a golf swing as shown by the coach, applying first-aid bandages as demonstrated by the instructor, or responding to

11. Norman E. Gronlund and Susan M. Brookhart, *Gronlund's Writing Instructional Objectives*, 8th ed. (Upper Saddle River, NJ: Pearson, 2009), 132–33; Yount, *Created to Learn*, 149; University of Connecticut Office of Institutional Research and Effectiveness, "Learning Taxonomy: Simpson's Psychomotor Domain," accessed February 15, 2022, https://assessment.uconn.edu/wp-content/uploads/sites/1804/2016/06/LearningTaxonomy_Psychomotor.pdf. All the following examples and action verbs of Simpson's taxonomy come from these sources.

hand signals of the foreman while learning to operate a forklift. Examples of action verbs in writing learning objectives targeting the guided response level are assembles, builds, calibrates, constructs, dismantles, displays, dissects, fastens, fixes, heats, manipulates, measures, mends, mixes, organizes, sketches.

Mechanism (Basic Proficiency)

The fourth level of Simpson's taxonomy is *mechanism* (also known as basic proficiency). At this level the student is consistently performing the skill on his or her own. If the previous level (guided response) was the introductory stage in performing a complex skill, this level (mechanism) is the intermediate stage in performing a complex skill. The skill is becoming habitual, with the movements being performed with some level of confidence and proficiency on a consistent level.

Examples of this level are a student using a personal computer, repairing a leaking faucet, driving a car, writing smoothly and legibly, setting up laboratory equipment, operating a projector, demonstrating a simple dance step, or making basic maneuvers in an airplane. Examples of action verbs in writing learning objectives targeting the mechanism level are the same action verbs as used in guided response (the student assembles, builds, calibrates, constructs, dismantles, displays, dissects, fastens, fixes, heats, manipulates, measures, mends, mixes, organizes, or sketches), but the student is doing this with more consistency (for example, the student consistently assembles).

Complex Overt Response (Expert)

The fifth level of Simpson's taxonomy is *complex overt response*. This level is the move from basic movement skills (first modeled in the guided response level then demonstrated in the mechanism level) to even more complex movement skills, possibly combining two or more basic skills together. This is when someone would be referred to as an expert at performing the skill. Proficiency is demonstrated by a quick, smooth, and accurate coordinated performance with a high rate of success, requiring a minimum of expended time or energy. At this level a student instinctively knows what the physical movement should feel like and knows immediately if the skill was performed successfully or not. For example, an athlete often utters sounds of satisfaction or frustration as soon as he or she hits a tennis ball or shoots a basketball because the athlete can tell by the feel of the act what the result will produce.[12]

There are two subcategories in describing the complex overt response level. One is a student performs the skill with a "resolution of uncertainty,"[13] where she or he acts thoughtfully using a mental picture of the task sequence. Second is a student gives an automatic performance resembling instinct, where she or he can perform a finely coordinated motor skill with ease and muscle control.

Examples of this level are a student maneuvering a car into a tight parallel parking spot, typing on a computer quickly and accurately, playing the piano or violin effortlessly, operating a power saw confidently, correcting her or his form in swimming, or dismantling and reassembling various components of an automobile quickly with no errors. Examples of action verbs in writing learning objectives targeting the complex overt response level are the same action verbs used in both the guided response level and the mechanism level (assembles, builds, calibrates, constructs, dismantles, displays, dissects, fastens, fixes, heats, manipulates, measures, mends, mixes, organizes, or sketches), but there will be an adverb or adjective indicating the performance is quicker, better, more accurate, and so on (such as "the student assembles with greater skill").

Adaptation

In her original research in 1966, Simpson had not yet fully developed these final two levels of adaptation and origination. But even at the early stages of the development of her taxonomy, Simpson recognized the need to go beyond the complex overt response. In the sixth level, called *adaptation*, a student can modify his or her well-developed skills to fit a new situation or to solve a new or different problem.

Examples of this level are a student adapting from swimming in a swimming pool to swimming in the open ocean, taking the skills to operate a typewriter to operate a computer word processor, or performing a task with a machine that it was not originally intended to do. Examples of action verbs in writing learning objectives targeting

12. Arkansas State University, "Bloom's Revised Taxonomy: Cognitive, Affective, and Psychomotor," accessed September 25, 2021, https://www.astate.edu/a/assessment/assessment-resource-links/files/Revised-Bloom%20s-Taxonomy-All-Domains.pdf.
13. Gronlund and Brookhart, *Instructional Objectives,* 132–33.

the adaptation level are adapts, adjusts, alters, changes, converts, elaborates, enhances, extends, improves, integrates, modifies, rearranges, reorganizes, revises, varies.

Origination

In the final level of *origination*, the student is so comfortable in performing the skill that he or she is now creatively expressing the skill in new ways. This is performing the skill at the highest developed level, doing so effortlessly, and now exploring creativity and originality to fit a particular situation or specific problem.

Examples of this level are a student constructing a new theory, developing a new training program, creating a new gymnastic or dance routine, writing an original musical composition, or designing a new dress style. Examples of action verbs in writing learning objectives targeting the origination level are arranges, builds, combines, composes, constructs, creates, designs, initiates, invents, makes, or originates.

Ravindrakumar Dave's Taxonomy

Besides Elizabeth Simpson's taxonomy, educational literature will usually mention two other psychomotor taxonomies. One is by Ravindrakumar Dave. Unlike Simpson's work (and Harrow's work that will be mentioned shortly), Dave's work is harder to trace in its initial development. It appeared in a conference paper from 1967 and then again is cited in a collection printed with publication dates of both 1970 and 1975. The descriptions are only two pages long. The five levels of Dave's taxonomy represent different degrees of competence in performing a skill, moving from initial exposure to final mastery.[14]

Imitation

At this level a student is merely observing and copying someone else perform the skill. This could be copying a work of art or mimicking a dance move while watching another dancer. The performance at this level is imperfect and lacking coordination, but at least the student is willing to try something never done before. Example verbs to describe

14. Ravindrakumar H. Dave, "Psychomotor Levels," in *Developing and Writing Behavioral Objectives*, ed. Robert Armstrong (Tucson, AZ: Educational Innovators, 1970), 33–34. All the following descriptions come from Dave.

the action at this level are copies, follows, mimics, repeats, replicates, or reproduces.

Manipulation

At this level a student is guided by written or verbal instruction in how to perform a skill. This is a move from mere observation to guided instruction, learning the "executive routine" or series of steps needed to perform the skill.[15] The performance skill is still unpolished and lacking coordination (as with imitation), but the skill is performed with the aid of written and verbal instruction, not just visual demonstration. Example verbs to describe this action at this level are acts, builds, executes, implements, performs, or recreates.

Precision

At this level accuracy, proportion, and exactness exist in the skill performance without help or referencing the original source material. The student performs the skill or produces the product with a high degree of precision (minimum errors). Example verbs to describe the action at this level are calibrates, completes, controls, demonstrates, executes, masters, or perfects.

Articulation

At this level two or more skills are combined, sequenced (in control of speed and time), or performed consistently and in harmony. Also at this level, the student's skills are so well developed he or she can modify the movement to fit special requirements or to meet a problem situation. Example verbs to describe the action at this level are adapts, combines, coordinates, creates, develops, integrates, or modifies.

Naturalization

At this level the performance is routine and automatic with little physical or mental exertion. Example verbs to describe the action at this level are automated designs, develops, or spontaneous events, such as what is commonly called "muscle memory."

15. Robert A. Reiser and Walter Dick, *Instructional Planning: A Guide for Teachers*, 2nd ed. (Boston: Allyn and Bacon, 1996), 52.

Anita Harrow's Taxonomy

The other psychomotor taxonomy usually mentioned is by Anita Harrow. Harrow originally developed her taxonomy in 1972 for children with special physical needs. The emphases in the six levels of Harrow's taxonomy are physical fitness, dexterity, agility, and body control organized from involuntary responses (reflex movements) to learned capabilities.[16]

Reflex Movements

At this level are the involuntary automatic movements that are not learned but are essential as a psychomotor base. Examples would be involuntary muscle contractions or blinking one's eyes to sunlight or dust.

Basic Fundamental Movements

At this level are simple movements (motor patterns) based upon reflexes that emerge without training. These are the simple movements (broken down as locomotor movements, non-locomotor movements, and manipulative movements) that can be built upon for more complex sets of movements. These are basic movements like walking, running, jumping, pushing, pulling, grasping, and manipulating.

Perceptual Abilities

At this level the various environmental cues (visual, auditory, tactile, or kinesthetic) are interpreted so a student can adjust with the environment. Examples are tracking a moving object, recognizing a pattern, jumping rope, catching a ball, or following instructions. This level is especially interesting for preschool and elementary school teachers. It contains a good example of a battery for testing the perceptive abilities of pupils, diagnosing difficulties, and proposing appropriate remedial exercises.

Physical Abilities (Fitness)

At this level proficiency in movement is developed. These are physical skills requiring endurance, flexibility, agility, dexterity, and strength. This may include activities of strenuous effort for long periods of time, muscular

16. Anita Harrow, *A Taxonomy of the Psychomotor Domain: A Guide for Developing Behavioral Objectives* (New York: David McKay, 1972). All the following descriptions come from Harrow.

exertion, range of motion, or precise movements. Examples include lifting weights, running a race, or performing basic ballet exercises.

Skilled Movements

At this level a student builds simple, compound, and complex movement skills. A student can also be categorized as beginner, intermediate, advanced, or highly skilled in the particular movement skill. These advanced movement skills would be found in sports, dance, acting, or the arts.

Non-Discursive Communication

At this level all a student's movements are used in expressive and interpretive ways to communicate meaning in nonverbal ways (i.e., body language). This includes posture, gestures, facial expressions, and/or creative movements like those in mime or in skilled dance movements.

Simpson (1966)	Dave (1970)	Harrow (1972)
Perception Sensory cues guide motor activity.	None	**Reflex Movement** (involuntary) Automatic reactions
Set Mental, physical, and emotional dispositions that makes one respond in a certain way to a situation	**Imitation** (Copy) Observing and copying someone else	**Basic Fundamental Movements** Simple movements that can build more complex sets of movements
Guided Response First attempts at a physical skill; trial and error coupled with practice lead to better performance	**Manipulation** Guided via instruction to perform a skill	**Perceptual Abilities** Environmental cues that allow one to adjust movements
Mechanism The intermediate stage in learning a physical skill; responses are habitual with a medium level of assurance and proficiency	**Precision** Accuracy, proportion and exactness exist in the skill performance without the presence of the original source	**Physical Abilities** Things requiring endurance, strength, vigor, and agility

Simpson (1966)	Dave (1970)	Harrow (1972)
Complex Overt Response Complex movements are possible with a minimum of wasted effort and a high level of assurance they will be successful	**Articulation** Two or more skills combined, sequenced, and performed consistently	**Skilled Movements** Activities where a level of efficiency is achieved
Adaptation Movements can be modified for special situations	**Naturalization** Two or more skills combined, sequenced, and performed consistently and with ease. The performance is automatic with little physical or mental exertion	**Non-discursive Communication** Body language
Origination New movements can be created for special situations	None	None

Figure 7.3 Comparison of Simpson's, Dave's, and Harrow's Psychomotor Taxonomies[17]

Writing Psychomotor Objectives

Whether you choose to use the psychomotor taxonomy outlined by Simpson, Dave, Harrow, or someone else, the next step is to write learning objectives based on your chosen taxonomy. Learning objectives in the psychomotor domain are specific, observable, measurable descriptions of what a student will be able to do or perform after receiving instruction on a particular skill. The action needs to be observable because you should be able to actually see your student's skill in action (like throwing a frisbee) or the artifact your student produces (like sculpting a statue).

17. Adapted from Simon Paul Atkinson, "Psychomotor Domain," accessed February 23, 2022, https://sijen.com/research-interests/taxonomies/psychomotor-domain/.

Each learning objective will include three parts. First is the action: What skill should your student be able to do? Second are the conditions: Under what conditions will your student perform the skill? And third is the criterion: What standard must be met for the skill of your student's performance to be acceptable?

1. Action What skill should the student be able to do?	→	**2. Conditions** Under what conditions will the student be required to perform the skill?	→	**3. Criterion** What standard must be met for the performance of the skill to be acceptable?

Figure 7.4: Parts of a Psychomotor Learning Objective

Some examples of a learning objective in the psychomotor domain are the following:

- The student will be able to swim the breaststroke for fifty yards using correct body movements.
- The student will be able to correctly assemble the biology lab equipment to demonstrate osmosis without the use of a diagram.
- The student will be able to perform an overhand baseball throw with ease during gameplay.
- The student will be able to sing before a jury with acceptable quality, a reasonable variety of color tone, dynamic range, and musical sensitivity.
- The student will be able to demonstrate drawing blood samples correctly and safely on multiple patients under supervision.[18]

A clearly written learning objective helps both your student and you. The learning objective will provide your student with a well-defined standard as to the precision, speed, and quality with which you expect your student to perform the skill. This allows your student to

18. Myron Dembo, *Applying Educational Psychology*, 5th ed. (New York: Longman, 1994), 255; Atkinson, "Psychomotor Domain"; Leroy Ford, *A Curriculum Design Manual for Theological Education: A Learning Outcomes Focus* (Nashville: Broadman, 1991), 257.

focus energy and time on actual performance improvement. The learning objective will assist you to impartially assess if your student has attained the prescribed outcome.[19]

GROWTH THROUGH CHALLENGING OPPORTUNITIES

Learning any new skill does not come automatically. Students learn new skills by stepping out of their comfort zones in trying new things. When placed in these new experiences, students have the chance to be curious, test themselves, make mistakes, and keep moving forward in the learning journey beyond familiar boundaries into new territory. The new territory requires new "maps" and new skills. Experimenting with new concepts and new ways of doing things is at the heart of the cycle of continual learning and meaning making. When students merely keep doing what they know they can do, no real change occurs.[20]

Leadership development experts James Kouzes and Barry Posner state it this way:

> Challenging opportunities often bring forth skills and abilities that people don't know they have. . . . Maintaining the status quo is the breeding ground for mediocrity. . . . If you are going to learn to lead, then you need to be restless when it comes to the status quo, adopt the leadership attitude of looking for opportunities to challenge your skills and abilities, and be willing to experiment with changing the business-as-usual environment. . . . Challenges, difficulties, setbacks, and hardships are all familiar sights on the leadership landscape. And one of the things they cause you to do is to come face-to-face with yourself. . . . It's clear that if

19. Reiser and Dick, *Instructional Planning*, 23, 34; Robert Mager, *Preparing Instructional Objectives: A Critical Tool in the Development of Effective Instruction*, 3rd ed. (Atlanta: Center for Effective Performance, 1997), 16; Gagné, Briggs, and Wager, *Principles of Instructional Design*, 26.
20. James Kouzes and Barry Posner, *Learning Leadership: The Five Fundamentals of Becoming an Exemplary Leader* (San Francisco: Wiley, 2016), 97–100; Ellen Van Velsor and Cynthia McCauley, "Our View of Leadership Development," in *The Center for Creative Leadership Handbook of Leadership Development*, ed. Cynthia McCauley and Ellen Van Velsor, 2nd ed. (San Francisco: Jossey-Bass, 2004), 7–9; Richard Hughes, Robert Ginnett, and Gordon Curphy, *Leadership: Enhancing the Lessons of Experience*, 3rd ed. (Boston: Irwin/McGraw-Hill, 1999), 91; Mihaly Csikszentmihalyi, *Flow: The Psychology of Optimal Experience* (New York: Harper and Row, 1990), 3; McCarthy, *About Teaching*, 39; George Posner and Alan Rudnitsky, *Course Design: A Guide to Curriculum Development for Teachers*, 7th ed. (Boston: Pearson, 2006), 168.

> you want to develop your leadership capabilities, you need to take the initiative and volunteer for assignments that stretch you beyond your current comfort zone. . . . The only way that you can learn is when you are doing things that you've never done before. . . . The fact is that when learning something brand-new, no one ever gets it right the first, or second, or even possibly the third time. You're going to make mistakes while learning. . . . Each failure produces valuable lessons that can be applied to the next iteration.[21]

Figure 7.5 Growth Through Challenging Opportunities[22]

These challenging opportunities are seen specifically in four areas in life. The first is *novelty*, where a student encounters experiences requiring new skills and new ways of understanding. The second is *difficult goals*, where a student encounters experiences requiring a different way of work instead of just working harder. The third is *conflict*, where a student must work through a conflict with another person, understanding the other person's perspective. And fourth is *hardship*, where

21. Kouzes and Posner, *Learning Leadership*, 102–3, 105–6.
22. Developed from Ellen Van Velsor and Cynthia McCauley, "Our View of Leadership Development," in *The Center for Creative Leadership Handbook of Leadership Development*, ed. Cynthia McCauley and Ellen Van Velsor, 2nd ed. (San Francisco: Jossey-Bass, 2004), 7–9.

a student deals with loss, failure, and disappointment, stimulating a search for new meaning and understanding. All of these challenging experiences create "disequilibrium" in our students, causing them to question the adequacy of their previous skills and approaches.[23]

As a teacher, you need to be able to safely lead your students out of their comfort zones to grow in their skills. It is riding the bicycle without training wheels for the first time. It is jumping into the deep end of the swimming pool without floaties for the first time. It is giving a speech in front of the class for the first time. It is speaking a foreign language in front of someone else for the first time. It is sharing the gospel with a neighbor for the first time. It is only in these challenging experiences that your students are required to develop new capacities or advance their ways of understanding that ultimately results in growth.[24]

Your students need opportunities to practice in a safe environment where mistakes can be tolerated and skills developed.[25] You may even want to consider rewarding certain kinds of mistakes that show your students are "trying new skills or approaches, formulating new ideas, putting old ideas together in novel ways, or otherwise taking intellectual risks."[26] This will help to create a safe and supportive environment for learning to take place.

FEEDBACK ON PRACTICE

Feedback on this practice is the only way your students know if they are making progress toward the new or improved skill.[27] Your role is to set up situations where your students can receive intentional and constructive feedback before the final product or performance. Sometimes it is clear if your students did or did not perform the skill correctly. An example of this is in archery. Either the archer hits the bull's-eye or not. But other times it is not as clear. Maybe in swimming the backstroke, a swimmer is not drowning in the pool; however, he or she is expending too much energy getting across the pool. Slight tweaks and suggestions

23. Van Velsor and McCauley, "Our View of Leadership Development," 7–9.
24. Van Velsor and McCauley, "Our View of Leadership Development," 7–9.
25. Gagné, Briggs, and Wager, *Principles of Instructional Design*, 94.
26. Posner and Rudnitsky, *Course Design*, 168.
27. Mager, *Preparing Instructional Objectives*, 17.

by a more experienced swimmer could make all the difference for a smoother (and less tiring) swim.[28]

Feedback is important because wrong behaviors without correction become habits that are counterproductive in the long run.[29] The lack of constructive feedback can also result in disillusioned students who are frustrated by their lack of progress.[30] You do not want your students practicing bad habits on a particular skill (which get much harder to break over time), and you do not want your students to be discouraged.

Some teachers have a natural instinct of what the proper steps are a student should follow and what proper technique looks like. But for both you and your students, it is more helpful to have a formalized checklist outlining step-by-step what successful completion of the skill looks like. For example, a baseball coach could work with a baseball player through the following progressions in learning how to throw a baseball (using Dave's taxonomy):

1. The baseball player will be able to copy the teacher's demonstration of an overhand throwing technique.
2. The baseball player will be able to perform in the presence of the teacher the overhand throwing technique from memory.
3. The baseball player will be able to consistently (80 percent success rate) demonstrate the overhand throwing technique.
4. The baseball player will be able to combine a mature overhand throwing pattern with running.
5. The baseball player will be able to perform an overhand throw with ease during gameplay.[31]

Or an English teacher may use the following checklist to guide and assess an oral report given in class:

- The student states the topic at the beginning of the report.
- The student speaks clearly and loudly enough to be heard.

---

28. Reiser and Dick, *Instructional Planning*, 52–53.
29. Reiser and Dick, *Instructional Planning*, 50.
30. Ken Blanchard, Patricia Zigarmi, and Drea Zigarmi, *Leadership and the One Minute Manager: A Situational Approach to Leading Others* (New York: William Morrow and Company, 1985), 40.
31. Atkinson, "Psychomotor Domain."

- The student uses language appropriate for the report.
- The student uses correct grammar.
- The student speaks at a satisfactory rate.
- The student looks at the class members when speaking.
- The student uses natural movements and appears relaxed.
- The student presents the material in an organized manner.
- The student holds the interest of the class.[32]

This can be a simple yes or no checklist (either your student performed the skill or did not), or it can take the form of a rubric with some type of rating from satisfactory to unsatisfactory performance at each level. A checklist of steps and criteria of success shows students what is expected, and it provides the teacher an objective set of criteria for assessment and ongoing instruction even when you are not there (instead of you always having to be present to instruct).[33]

Eventually, you want to develop students who self-assess their own learning.[34] As a student develops in a skill, she or he may start experiencing internal feedback independent of external feedback. Internal feedback is where a student's own muscles and joints can feel if the motor skill was performed correctly.[35] Internal feedback is where a student has a sense if the skill was performed properly or the learning goal was met. Instead of the teacher having to give all the feedback (both praise and correction), the student starts decision-making and problem-solving the task on her or his own. This is the self-reliant achiever who demonstrates high competence, confidence, and motivation. These students need less supervision or praise as long as they know how well they are doing.[36]

REFLECTING ON LEARNING EXPERIENCES

Education pioneer John Dewey believed that "all genuine education comes about through experience. . . . [However, this] does not mean that

32. Gronlund and Brookhart, *Gronlund's Writing Instructional Objectives*, 86–87.
33. Reiser and Dick, *Instructional Planning*, 88–89, 94; Gronlund and Brookhart, *Gronlund's Writing Instructional Objectives*, 88; Posner and Rudnitsky, *Course Design*, 210.
34. Posner and Rudnitsky, *Course Design*, 167.
35. Gagné, Briggs, and Wager, *Principles of Instructional Design*, 93.
36. Blanchard, Zigarmi, and Zigarmi, *Leadership and the One Minute Manager*, 35, 42, 49–50, 57.

all experiences are genuinely or equally educative."[37] Learning is not just facing (and overcoming) a challenging experience or practicing a skill over and over. Impactful learning comes when a student practices the new skill, receives specific feedback on how to better perform the skill, and then reflects on what he or she has just done.[38] This is called an action-observation-reflection model (see Figure 7.6). Action asks, "What did you do?" This is thinking about the actual experience itself. Observation asks, "What happened? What were the results? What was the impact on others?" This is thinking about ways to deal with the experience (problem-solving). Reflection asks, "How do you look at it now? How do you feel about it now?" This is examining assumptions, beliefs, and values about the experience or problem. It is difficult to learn from challenging experiences and fundamentally change without engaging in some kind of reflection.[39]

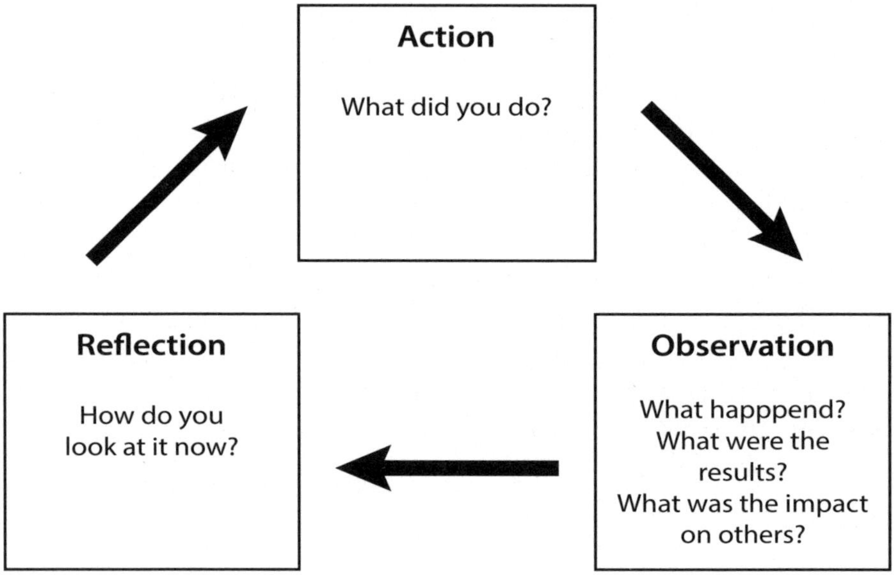

Figure 7.6 Action-Observation-Reflection Model[40]

---

37. John Dewey, *Experience and Education* (New York: Collier Books, 1938), 13.
38. Susan A. Ambrose et al., *How Learning Works: Eight Research-Based Principles for Smart Teaching* (San Francisco: Jossey-Bass, 2010), 3–4; Jane Vella, *Learning to Listen, Learning to Teach: The Power of Dialogue in Educating Adults* (San Francisco: Jossey-Bass, 2002), 14, 51.
39. Hughes, Ginnett, and Curphy, *Leadership*, 87.
40. Adapted from Richard Hughes, Robert Ginnett, and Gordon Curphy, *Leadership: Enhancing the Lessons of Experience*, 3rd ed. (Boston: Irwin/McGraw-Hill, 1999), 79–81.

Adult educational theorists Sharan Merriam, Rosemary Caffarella, and Lisa Baumgartner note, "Reflection is a cognitive process. We can think about our experience—muse, review, and so on—but to reflect critically, we must also examine the underlying beliefs and assumptions that affect how we make sense of the experience."[41] The teacher is to create space for reflection both during and after the learning cycle.[42]

CONCLUSION

At the end of his Sermon on the Mount, Jesus issues this challenge to his hearers:

> Therefore everyone who hears these words of mine and puts them into practice is like a wise man who built his house on the rock. The rain came down, the streams rose, and the winds blew and beat against that house; yet it did not fall, because it had its foundation on the rock. But everyone who hears these words of mine and does not put them into practice is like a foolish man who built his house on sand. The rain came down, the streams rose, and the winds blew and beat against that house, and it fell with a great crash. (Matt. 7:24–27 NIV)

As important as knowledge (cognitive domain) and emotions (affective domain) are, neither is the end goal, or *telos*, of Christian education. It is one thing for your students to know what is right (which can descend into mere Bible trivia) or even to affirm what is right (which can descend into mere emotionalism or even emotional manipulation). It is another thing for your students to actually *do* what is right.[43] The goal of education is transformation in the lives of your students such that "obedience to truth is practiced."[44] Your role as a

41. Sharan Merriam, Rosemary Caffarella, and Lisa Baumgartner, *Learning in Adulthood: A Comprehensive Guide*, 3rd ed. (San Francisco: John Wiley and Sons, 2007), 145.
42. McCarthy, *About Teaching*, 23.
43. Gary Parrett and Steve Kang, *Teaching the Faith, Forming the Faithful: A Biblical Vision for Education in the Church* (Downers Grove, IL: IVP Academic, 2009), 270, 272, 295; Allen Jackson, "The Contribution of Teaching to Discipleship," in *Teaching the Next Generations: A Comprehensive Guide for Teaching Christian Formation*, ed. Terry Linhart (Grand Rapids: Baker Academic, 2016), 7; Lawrence Richards and Gary Bredfeldt, *Creative Bible Teaching*, rev. ed. (Chicago: Moody, 1998), 138.
44. Parker Palmer, *To Know as We Are Known: Education as a Spiritual Journey* (San Francisco: Harper and Row, 1983), 69.

Christian educator is to create an environment for the Holy Spirit to bring this obedience to life, where the image of Christ is formed in your students as they grow as disciples. We want students to grow in "love, joy, peace, forbearance, kindness, goodness, faithfulness, gentleness and self-control" (Gal. 5:22–23 NIV) as they pray, evangelize, worship, teach, and serve (all of which have psychomotor aspects). And as they move up in the psychomotor level in these endeavors, more fruitfulness should be seen in students as a way of life (habit) and an expression of their heart.[45]

REFLECTION QUESTIONS

1. Which practical physical skills (psychomotor domain) do you personally feel most equipped to teach to others?
2. What are the skills of ministry that best fit in the psychomotor domain?
3. Out of the three psychomotor domain taxonomies presented in this chapter (Simpson, Dave, Harrow), which one resonates the best with you and how you think of your own teaching?

RECOMMENDED READING

Ambrose, Susan, et al. *How Learning Works: Eight Research-Based Principles for Smart Teaching*. San Francisco: Jossey-Bass, 2010.

Kouzes, James, and Barry Posner. *Learning Leadership: The Five Fundamentals of Becoming an Exemplary Leader*. San Francisco: Wiley, 2016.

McCall, Morgan. *High Flyers: Developing the Next Generation of Leaders*. Boston: Harvard Business, 1998.

McCauley, Cynthia, and Ellen Van Velsor, eds. *The Center for Creative Leadership Handbook of Leadership Development*. 2nd ed. San Francisco: Jossey-Bass, 2004.

McCauley, Cynthia, et al. *Experience-Driven Leader Development: Models, Tools, Best Practices, and Advice for On-the-Job Development*. 3rd ed. San Francisco: Wiley, 2014.

45. Parrett and Kang, *Teaching the Faith*, 295; Newton, *Heart-Deep Teaching*, 52–53; Barrett McRay, "How People Develop Their Thinking," in Linhart, *Teaching the Next Generations*, 78–79; Klaus Issler and Ronald Habermas, *How We Learn: A Christian Teacher's Guide to Educational Psychology* (Grand Rapids: Baker, 1994), 39.

CHAPTER 8

LESSON OBJECTIVES AND LESSON PLANS

Jennifer Brooks

I love to cook. I love to teach. And I see some commonalities between the two activities. First, it is difficult to come up with a good product without making a mess. The best meals cost me the most time in the kitchen after my family enjoyed the meal. And my classroom has often looked like structured chaos just before I began to see lights come on in the students' eyes. My favorite teachers—whether in home economics, Bible exposition, or education classes—created an atmosphere of experimentation that said, "It is OK not to get it right the first time. This is a safe place for you to try things, make messes, and learn from your mistakes." But creating that atmosphere can cause teachers a certain amount of angst. What if our students don't discover what we want them to discover? What if our activities lead us in a completely different direction than we had planned? What if we run out of time? What if this activity does not take as much time as we thought it would? That leads to a second similarity between the kitchen and the classroom.

All good products need to begin with a plan (a good recipe, if you will) even if you deviate from that plan in the process. Knowing where we plan to go from the beginning will help us guide students before they wander too far on unrelated paths. The following pages will lay out a biblical foundation for structure in the classroom, a guide for creating structure, and a few constructs you may want to try.

FOUNDATIONS: DO NOT START UNTIL YOU KNOW WHAT YOU ARE BAKING

We are creating something here. Lessons do not just happen. They are designed, built, and crafted. Contrary to the belief of some, creativity needs structure and discipline. How do we know?

God's Order in Creation

Consider the creation account in Genesis. Life could not have survived on a planet that was "formless, and empty [with] darkness over the face of the deep" (Gen. 1:2 NIV). God took something dark, formless, and empty and created a beautiful universe with a habitable planet in it.

God's creation had an orderliness and structure to it. Good stories have a first-next-last, or beginning-middle-end, sequence. Good cooking has a preparation-cooking-presentation process. Good teaching has a planning-preparation-presentation progression. While the creation of the universe is more than just a story, it does have a distinct order.

Animals and humanity need food to live. Plants will not live long without light for photosynthesis. What if the sequence of creation had been different?

God's Order in the Church

Creation was a long time ago. God does things differently in the New Testament, right? Sometimes he does. But his principles and character always remain the same. We still see God's desire for order in the church age. The church in Corinth was a mess. The people reflected the chaotic culture surrounding them. Dio Chrysostom (8.6) describes the chaos of the culture this way.

> That was the time, too, when one could hear crowds of wretched sophists around Poseidon's temple shouting and reviling one another, and their disciples, as they were called, fighting with one another, many writers reading aloud their stupid works, many poets reciting their poems while others applauded them, many jugglers showing their tricks, many fortune-tellers interpreting fortunes, lawyers innumerable

> perverting judgment, and peddlers not a few peddling whatever they happened to have.[1]

The people of Corinth lived with a circus atmosphere surrounding their public places. What was a familiar scene in front of Poseidon's temple must have been an assumed tradition for any Corinthian temple, including God's house. God did not agree.

In 1 Corinthians Paul describes a church setting similar to the confusing picture Chrysostom (writing later than Paul) paints above. Divisions, pride, immorality, tolerance of evil in the church, idolatry, and greed were all prominent. Confusion created by the mixture of multiple prophecies and languages caused Paul to say in 14:23 that people coming into the church from outside will "say that you are out of your minds" (NIV). However, in verses 1–12 Paul gives the purpose for what happens in the church. Four times he refers to prophecy, teaching, and instruments all being for the purpose of edification or building up of the church.

> What then is the conclusion, brothers? Whenever you come together, each one has a psalm, a teaching, a revelation, another language, or an interpretation. All things must be done for edification. If any person speaks in another language, there should be only two, or at the most three, each in turn, and someone must interpret. But if there is no interpreter, that person should keep silent in the church and speak to himself and to God. (1 Cor. 14:26–28 HCSB)

There is an orderliness to the church service Paul describes. Many may participate, but they should do it one at a time. There is a purpose for everything that happens in the church. People must be edified, and the body must be built up by any activity we allow to be part of our worship. And whether we are teaching in a parachurch setting or a church setting, the principle remains the same. We need order. Paul concludes, "But everything should be done in a fitting and orderly

1. Dio Chrysostom, Oration 8 in *Diogenes of Sinope, Life and Legend: Handbook of Source Material*, ed. Frank Redmond, 2nd ed. (Chicago: Menin, 2016), 57.

way" (v. 40 NIV). What a great principle to follow, whether in a church service, classroom, or small group.

TEACHERS' RESPONSIBILITIES

It may seem simplistic, but the teachers' responsibility is to teach. This becomes much less simplistic when we think about everything that comes before we walk into the teaching scenario. The following pages will lead through a recipe for creating good lessons. Creating an effective lesson involves:

- following a scope and sequence (see chapter 9),
- formulating goals (see chapter 9),
- crafting objectives to fulfill goals,
- developing a big idea (see chapter 3 for additional help),
- designing a lesson plan (see chapters 4, 9 for additional help), and
- evaluating the lesson (see chapters 4, 9).

GOALS: A GOOD RECIPE MAKES A GOOD COOKIE

"Begin with the end in mind." This is a common directive that has been so used it is almost a cliché, but clichés are often underestimated. Beginning with the end in mind is another way to say it's important to establish a target or goal for your teaching. Goals are overarching statements declaring what you want to produce in the students through a lesson or unit. To develop an appropriate goal, look at your scope and sequence and ask yourself what students should know, value, and do with that content.

Perhaps the most important concept is teaching for transformation. There is no other reason to teach. News stories abound with reports of theft on a variety of levels. One day we read about a petty theft in a neighborhood store. The next day we hear about a CEO who embezzled millions of dollars. Morally, there is not a lot of difference between the two thefts; the distinction is that the CEO knows how to get more money than he would by shoplifting in a mom-and-pop store in the neighborhood. We expect the CEO to be educated enough to earn a living, provide for a family, live quite comfortably without stealing, and know not to treat people with the disrespect and disregard that allows such behavior. So why does the educated CEO behave worse than the hoodlum? We might say education should have prepared the CEO to use skills and talents to help people. But education has not transformed the CEO who embezzled from a company and cheated people out of their hard-earned savings and retirement. The CEO knows a lot. But that knowledge has not developed a good person. We need to *teach*, not to just transfer information from our heads to the students' heads. That is not a worthy goal for teaching anything, but teaching to encourage godly servant leadership is a worthy goal. Teaching to provoke love and good works is a worthy goal. We must teach for transformation.

You Have Not Taught Until They Have Learned

We have made a very simple statement: the teacher's responsibility is to teach. However, if the students have not learned, has the teacher really taught? And how do we know the students have really learned? The short answer is this: What the students have learned must somehow be seen in *their lives*. It is about the student, not the teacher.

- How should a lesson on Hebrews 12 show up as the peaceable fruit of righteousness in students' lives following the lesson?
- How does a student demonstrate gracious treatment of others (even those they do not know or do not like) in the weeks following a lesson on the Good Samaritan from Luke 10:25–37?
- Does a unit on Joseph from Genesis 37–50 show up as faithfulness despite hurt, rejection, fear, and accusations?

We teach whole people. Therefore, we must be careful not to rely solely on information dumps that unload content from our brains to theirs. While lecture is sometimes an appropriate teaching method, it should be paired with some type of activity which allows students to exhibit understanding, valuing, and doing what they learned. Students are not just brains to be filled. They are made of head, heart, and hands. They are image bearers of God and created to be thinkers, feelers (or valuers), and doers.[2] That means our preparation to teach must involve a design to reach all parts of our students to encourage the transformation we strive for in our lessons. So, when establishing goals for a unit or lesson, ask three questions.

2. William R. Yount, *Created to Learn: A Christian Teacher's Introduction to Educational Psychology*, 2nd ed. (Nashville: B&H Academic, 2010), 336–37.

Head: What do I want them to know?

Knowing involves the cognitive part of us, the brain, what we think. Certainly there is something to know as we open Scripture. Proverbs tells us, "The mind of the discerning acquires knowledge, and the ear of the wise seeks it" (18:15 CSB). As we read Scripture and prepare to teach it, we ask the Holy Spirit to show us what we should learn from the text and what to share with our students. Who are your students? What do they already know? What do they need to know? What is their age level mentally, physically, and spiritually? Do they have previous knowledge that enables them to grasp the depth you want to provide? Or are they from a more limited church or educational background that will necessitate time to work through foundational material before being confronted with more comprehensive Bible and theology concepts? The answers to all these questions give us a picture of our students that helps us to know what is appropriate for our teaching and what should be eliminated or at least saved for later. The student-needs list shows what they need to know and how we need to teach the content. From that information, we create goals for a unit or lesson. More on that in a bit.

Heart: What do I want them to value?

Valuing is the affective part of us, the heart. It is where we feel. We can memorize a verse of Scripture so that it easily falls out of our mouths on demand. We have placed it in our brain. But do we value it? It is possible to earn awards for memorizing Scripture and never really apply the Scripture we have memorized. When the psalmist said, "I seek you with all my heart; do not let me stray from your commands. I have hidden your word in my heart that I might not sin against you. Praise be to you, LORD; teach me your decrees" (Ps. 119:10–12 NIV), he demonstrated that he valued what he found in God's Word. This was no mere head knowledge. God's Word took hold of the writer's heart and therefore changed his life. The result was remaining close to God and far from sin because that was what the writer valued.

Hands: What do I want them to do?

We can ask students for information we have taught, and they can spit it out automatically as rote memory. That may or may not change their lives. They can value what we have taught, whether we can see it overtly or not. But we do want to be able to see what we have taught worked out practically in their lives.

THE BIG IDEA

Doing is behavioral. This is where we discover whether students have actually made the content a part of their lives. Our students should never leave a lesson without knowing what they are expected to do. But in order for the students to carry the lesson with them throughout the week in a way that does transform their lives, they must be able to remember what happened in the classroom. That is where the *big idea*[3] can help both students and teachers.

There are two very good reasons for developing a big idea. First, the human mind strives for unity. If you do not provide it throughout the lesson, the students' brains will be spinning to find that unity, even if only subconsciously. By the time they discover it, *if* they discover it, they may have missed the most important thing you wanted them to catch. Second, a well-developed big idea can help students remember the lesson at least until they get to the car, but sometimes for a lifetime.

Before thinking about a big idea, immerse yourself in the passage you will teach until you internalize it. See chapter 3 for help in studying the passage. This requires that you read it for several days, sometimes several times in one day. Once you have become familiar with the text, you will begin to see themes stand out. Something jumps off the pages that reminds you of a discussion you have had with your students. This may make it easier to formulate a big idea, but please do not try to pull a big idea out of thin air or try to build a lesson on some fun saying you have heard going around social media. Your big idea must not control your text. The text determines your big idea.

A big idea is a short (three to five words), pithy sentence that encompasses the heart of your chosen passage. It must be strong and repeatable. Repeating it several times throughout your lesson will help students remember. If you cannot repeat it before each point or as part of each point, you likely have a point that does not fit your lesson. Weed

3. Haddon Robinson, *Biblical Preaching: The Development and Delivery of Expository Messages*, 3rd ed. (Grand Rapids: Baker Academic, 2014). Robinson's classic work on preaching is invaluable not only for preachers but also for teachers. His chapter on the *big idea* gives a detailed explanation of the purpose of a big idea and examples of how to develop it.

it out. A few years ago while a student was teaching a lesson on Haggai, she had the class participate in a very effective activity. The big idea for the lesson was "Let first things be first." The student was trying to make the point that we do what we prioritize. The student asked everyone in the room to take out their phones and set an alarm to pray for the person to their left, thereby setting a priority. Everyone was assigned something to do that transformed them. That class is still praying for each other.

The teacher's responsibility certainly is to teach. That involves knowing our students, planning the content and order of lessons, and crafting goals for what we hope the students will carry away from our teaching. Goals are general in nature, and they are the foundation on which our instructional objectives will be built. So it is important to spend enough time and thought on them. Look at the following goals for a unit on the life of Joseph.

- Students will apply biblical responses to life struggles of jealousy, fear, and temptation.
- Students will discover God's faithfulness as a characteristic to depend on.

Notice several things about these goals. First, they are student-centered, meaning they are telling what the student will do, not what the teacher will do. Next, an action verb identifies the student's action. In the first goal the student will *apply*. In the second goal the student will *discover.* Finally, an object tells who or what the completion of the action is. In the first goal, students apply *biblical responses.* In the second goal, students discover *God's faithfulness.*

Goals do not indicate how the concepts will be taught. They do not indicate how the student will apply or discover the concepts, or how the instructor will know whether the students have applied or discovered them. These goals lack anything measurable, but they give direction. They demonstrate a general plan for what students are expected to do, which influences the shape of objectives.

OBJECTIVES: INSTRUCTIONS FOR THE RECIPE

Instructional objectives are also called learning objectives, learning outcomes, lesson aims, or terminal indicators. Christian educators in church and parachurch settings more often prefer the term *lesson aims*. If you come from an educational background, you are more familiar with the terms *learning objectives* or *instructional objectives*. An instructional objective is a statement giving student-centered performance, specific conditions, and measurable criterion outcomes to a lesson.[4] Norman Gronlund says, "Learning outcomes provide the criteria for judging the quality of the performance."[5] This is one place where we really should be judging. Teachers measure our own teaching as much as we judge the students' ability to do what we want to teach them to do. This is not the hypocritical judgment Jesus prohibits in Matthew 7.

Student-centered performance means these statements are crafted to identify what the students should know, value, or do as a result of a lesson. An action verb tells specifically what the students will *do* to fulfill the objective. A teacher-centered objective may read: *The teacher will design a scope and sequence for lessons presenting the life of Joseph that will encourage application of biblical principles for handling life's circumstances.*

There are several problems with this objective. The most important may be that it does not tell us *anything* about the student and what the student is supposed to do. It might be the student's responsibility to apply biblical principles. But the way the objective is written, a reader could infer that it is the teacher's responsibility. If an objective is to be student-centered, it must begin by identifying the student as the doer of the action. The easiest way to make sure objectives are student-centered is to begin them with, "The students will . . ." This signals you to think of the students as you are writing the objective.

Specific conditions involve eliminating questions about your intent. Imagine the following objective for a Thursday evening Bible study for which the teacher gets sick on Thursday afternoon. Paula is called in to substitute for her friend. Here is what she is asked to have the students do: *The students will explain Joseph's characteristic of faithfulness.*

Paula wants to call the teacher after reading the lesson and objective, but the teacher's phone is turned off because she is just so sick. Paula wonders, "How are these students supposed to explain? Is this a

4. Robert Mager, *Preparing Instructional Objectives: A Critical Tool in the Development of Effective Instruction*, 3rd ed. (Atlanta: Center for Effective Performance, 1997), 166.
5. Norman Gronlund, *Writing Instructional Objectives for Teaching and Assessment*, 7th ed. (Upper Saddle River, NJ: Prentice Hall, 2004), 110.

question-and-answer session to do during class? Are students supposed to go home and write about this after study and reflection?" The teacher would have served both Paula and the students better if she had written her objective this way: *The students will orally describe, during class, three ways Joseph showed faithfulness during his prison term.*

Measurable criteria have to do with the extent to which a student is able to do something. How will you know the students have achieved what you wanted them to achieve? Put it in the objective. The following objective shows all three parts of an acceptable learning objective. It includes three elements, as follows:

> Cognitive objective: *Students will be able to recall the major events of Joseph's life in Genesis 37–50 by writing a list of the events with 90 percent accuracy.*
>
> a) Student-centered performance: *Students will be able to recall*;
> b) Specific conditions: *the major events of Joseph's life in Genesis 37–50*;
> c) Measurable criterion: *by writing a list of the events with 90 percent accuracy.*

That may look an awful lot like school. It reeks of a paper-and-pencil test to follow. But it does not have to. We ought to be able to justify assessment of our students in spiritual formation. Maybe we will give them a paper-and-pencil test. Maybe we will assess with the use of oral questions and answers. But whichever we chose, we may decide it is not wise to move on to the next lesson or stop reviewing the last one until most of the students are answering with 90-percent accuracy. More on that later.

Objectives are written with just one task evident. You can tell if you have more than one task if you see the word *and* in your objective. When it is time to determine whether the students achieved what you expected, how will you evaluate that when one part of your objective may have been achieved but the other part of it was not? Observe the following: *The student will orally explain Joseph's faithfulness and compare it to a moment of faithfulness from one person found in Hebrews 11.* Maybe the student can orally explain Joseph working in Potiphar's house, facing Potiphar's wife every day, and running when she tries to trap him. But providing information about any characters in Hebrews

11 stumps the student. Or maybe the student can name some of the people in Hebrews 11, but comparing their experience with Joseph's is beyond their ability right now. It is important to craft objectives so that measurements of their achievement are clear.

If we are teaching for transformation (and we are), we ought to build it into our planning, even at the objective stage. It is wise to write objectives for what you want the student to know (cognitive) and what you want the student to value (affective). We saw this in the Psalm 119 passage. If we turn those verses into objectives, they might look like this.

> Cognitive objective: *The students will identify the advantages of memorizing Scripture based on Psalm 119:10–12 by listing at least two of the benefits.*
>
> Affective objective: *The students will appreciate the value of Scripture memory by paraphrasing a personally meaningful verse from Psalm 119.*

The cognitive objective in the first statement above is student-centered, telling who the doer of the action is. It has a cognitive action verb: *identify*. This one falls at the lowest level of the cognitive domain, but there is value to hiding God's Word in our hearts.[6] Some learning at Bloom's lower levels is necessary.[7] The specific conditions are given: *advantages of memorizing Scripture*. It shows how the action will be measured: *listing at least two of the benefits* (assuming the teacher will be checking for accuracy). The affective objective is also student-centered and tells what the student will do. The affective action verb is: *appreciate*. This is at the *valuing* level of the affective taxonomy.[8] The specific conditions are given: *value of Scripture memory*. The measurable

6. Please see chapter 5, "Renewing of the Mind: The Cognitive Domain," for further explanation of the cognitive taxonomy.
7. Bloom's taxonomy is an organizational system of learning developed by Benjamin Bloom, David Krathwohl, Max Englehart, Edward Furst, and Walter Hill in 1956. It was revised by Loren Anderson and David Krathwohl in 2001. Six levels of learning progress from lower to higher order thinking. The six levels for the latest edition of the taxonomy are as follows: remember, understand, apply, analyze, evaluate, and create. See Iowa State University's Center for Excellence in Learning and Teaching at https://iastate.app.box.com/s/z0otio95lflaii1l2ro3h42kp8q6fdmm.
8. Please see chapter 6, "Teaching to the Heart: The Affective Domain," for further explanation of the affective taxonomy.

criterion is: *paraphrasing a personally meaningful verse*. Paraphrasing a personally meaningful verse forces the mind and the heart to work together to formulate ideas about the value of hiding God's Word in the students' hearts.

Formulas can feel uncomfortable and wooden, but they are helpful if you are just beginning to write instructional objectives, especially if you know this task will get easier the more you do it. There will come a time when you no longer need a formula. In the meantime, try this one out to see if it makes your life easier.

- (Decide the student-centered performance desired) *The students will* followed by an action verb
- (State the specific condition) object of the action verb
- (Identify measurable outcome) *by* or *based on*.

One day you may wake up to discover you are teaching others to do what you struggle to do today.[9]

LESSON PLANS: IT'S ALL ABOUT THE PRESENTATION

You have already put in a lot of work. You have studied both your passage and your students and prayed for wisdom about what your students need and how to teach them. You have organized a scope and sequence, formulated goals, crafted objectives, and developed a big idea. Now it is time to put it all in separate lessons. But you still have some more decisions to make. What kind of format is a specific lesson going to take? How are you going to present it?

Basics: Introduction, Body, Conclusion

Just as you will choose an order for the unit in your scope and sequence (see chapter 9), you will want to select a structure for each lesson. This will vary from lesson to lesson and group to group. But a very basic starting place is to identify your lesson's introduction, body, and conclusion. The body is the heart of the lesson. Typically, teachers spend most of their preparation time there. You are unpacking the passage, observing the text,

9. Writing learning objectives is a skill that takes time and practice. Robert Mager and Norman Gronlund have written classic works on building instructional objectives. These are invaluable resources for every teacher, clearly written, easy to follow, and give plenty of opportunity for practice.

and analyzing, interpreting, and applying it. This can be the fun part. But do not stop there. Once you know what you are doing in the body, give significant thought to how to get started. The intro should capture attention and prepare the students for what they will be hearing (and doing) in the body of the lesson, but do not let it take over the lesson.

The conclusion may be the most important part. If you do not have a plan to finish, you may drone on until you run out of wind, or someone pulls you offstage with a shepherd's crook. Here you should review the main point(s) and leave students with a powerful reminder of what they need to do because of what they have experienced during this lesson. Try writing your intro and conclusion word for word. Practice them. They need to make a powerful impact.

The law of primacy and recency tells us that we tend to remember best what we hear first (primacy) and what we hear last (recency).[10] Unfortunately, for some students, that means they are remembering the roll call, announcements, or a joke the teacher heard and wanted to use. Have somebody else keep attendance records. Hand out the announcements on a sheet or send them electronically during the week. See that everything clearly fits your lesson topic, including jokes. Make sure the intro and conclusion to your lesson are reserved for catching your students' attention at the beginning and reminding them of what is most important at the end.

Classics: Hook-Book-Look-Took[11]

Introduction, body, and conclusion is the most basic structure in any communication. The hook-book-look-took structure builds on that basic idea and adds depth and flexibility to the lesson structure. It is a classic plan developed by Lawrence Richards decades ago and later championed by Gary Bredfeldt. It has seen great success, and we will probably be using it until Jesus calls us to heaven.

Hook

Introduction correlates to the hook, and it does exactly what it implies. Imagine you have a room full of business executives who have an

10. David A. Sousa, *How the Brain Learns,* 4th ed. (Thousand Oaks, CA: Corwin, 2011), 95.
11. Lawrence O. Richards and Gary J. Bredfeldt, *Creative Bible Teaching*, 3rd ed. (Chicago: Moody, 2020).

end-of-year board meeting tomorrow, or a group of noisy sixth graders, or a group of busy women responsible for a house, a family, meal planning and writing a real estate portfolio. How are you going to catch the attention of any of these groups (are you tired yet)? You need a pretty good attention-getter. But a hook is more than just an attention-getter. A good hook (1) captures attention, (2) raises a need, (3) sets a goal, and (4) leads them into the Word.

Capture the students' attention: You have studied the text. You have studied the students. So you should know something about what from the text might capture the interest of the students. For example, what might appeal to a business executive from the life of Joseph? Eventually, Joseph is given the responsibility of providing for all of Egypt during a famine. Might a business executive want to know how a person can go from being the family outcast, to prisoner, to major decision-maker for a country?

Raise a need: How many of the people in that room might be suffering from imposter syndrome? They are asking themselves, "How did I get where I am and how long will it take my boss to figure out I do not belong in this position?" They just might need to hear how God is in control and can give wisdom and direction in the middle of their major decisions.

Set a goal: You could let students know that by the end of the lesson, they will discover God was faithful in Joseph's life and they can depend on him too. Then be sure not to disappoint them.

Lead them into the Word: You caught their attention. You put a finger on their need(s). You set a goal. Now they are ready for you to open the Word of God and give them truth. Remember: directly connect your hook to the text you are about to study. How is your hook like the text you are about to present? You may have heard teachers or preachers lay the groundwork. While reading the text does not belong in the hook (unless you are only teaching from one verse, your passage is probably too long to fit in the intro), an effective transition statement tying the hook to the book is critical.

Book

The body of the lesson is where we find the book. If you have had a good hermeneutics course, you know the importance of observing the text. It was important for you as you studied the passage in your preparation. It is just as important to lead students in observing it. Teach them how and expect them to do it. Each student should have a copy of the Bible text in hand, either physically or electronically. Ask them about their observations.

Discovering what the biblical text means is the main task to complete during the book section. Howard Hendricks says, "Tell the learner nothing and do nothing for him that he can learn for himself."[12] All the time you are leading students in observation, you are listening for any misunderstanding or confusion. You are helping to clarify the text.

Look

This is where good discovery learning can happen. Allow students some time to wrestle with questions. Disequilibrium is a great teaching strategy. Just as the human brain strives for unity, it struggles to find answers and equilibrium. When all the answers are not provided immediately, discovery becomes like finding gold. And the learning is then long-term. Provide unity with your big idea but let students discover answers that provide equilibrium as long as they are not heading the wrong direction.

You have a multitude of methods at your disposal during the look portion of the lesson.[13] How are you going to use those methods to help students dig into the text? You might start with a lecture in the book section. Then ask a question and break students up into pairs or small groups to dig for the answer in the look portion. After some group discussion time, bring them back together again to share their discoveries.

Change methods each time you teach. Your weakest method is the one you use all the time. Boredom sets in, and people tune out. The more variety you use, the more students you will reach. They are all different, and it will take a variety of methods to connect with each of them. Some get stressed about having to share in a small group.

12. Howard Hendricks, *Teaching to Change Lives: Seven Proven Ways to Make Your Teaching Come Alive* (Sisters, OR: Multnomah, 1987), 39.
13. Wilbert McKeachie and Marilla D. Svinicki, *McKeachie's Teaching Tips: Strategies, Research, and Theory for College and University Teachers*, 14th ed. (Belmont, CA: Wadsworth Cengage Learning, 2014). *McKeachie's Teaching Tips* can be a great help to the teacher who wants to expand methods. It can also be a great resource for a variety of issues that new teachers often struggle with, such as what happens when you decide to use discussion, buzz groups, and peer learning, but one student does not want to participate, and another student takes over every discussion.

Some are visual learners; others are auditory. Many need to move frequently. So the use of lots of visuals, allowing for students to share their thoughts, and having them switch seats and positions will help the variety of students in the room maintain focus on what is important from the passage.

The students are hooked. They have discovered some good things in the text. But what difference will it make in their lives in the coming weeks?

Took

Took is what you want students to carry out of the room with them. This is another great place to use the creativity God gave you. Give students something specific and personal to do in the coming week as a direct result of the lesson. You could give them something tangible to remind them of the lesson. They can set it in a prominent place so every time they see it throughout the week, they are reminded they are not forgotten. God is faithful. You can tell them you will ask for a report of God's faithfulness next week. Then email or text them to remind them to look for God showing his faithfulness. That is a good place to start next week. There should be reports of how God was faithful throughout the week. Be consistent in expecting feedback from them about the previous lesson.

Long-Term Effects: John Dewey's Spiral

John Dewey may have written much that we are uncomfortable with as Christians, but where there is good material to use, we ought not reinvent material. Dewey believed strongly in experiential education. He saw the importance of connecting concepts to experience while looking at his students' futures outside the classroom to show how the students would use what they had learned. He called his teaching process a learning "spiral" that grew and expanded throughout the education of a child into adulthood.[14] He reviewed previously taught material, introduced new material, and connected it all to what he was currently teaching as well as to the student's experience. David Kolb took Dewey's learning spiral a step further and developed the four stages of learning: concrete experience, reflective observation, abstract conceptualization,

14. John Dewey, *Experience and Education* (New York: Macmillan, 1938), 30–34.

and active experimentation.[15] Kolb does what all teachers hope their students will do. He expands on Dewey's spiral model. In the process, he shows how different students receive and act on particular learning events. The spiral learning strategy is a great practice for teaching Scripture because the Word of God is not a series of disconnected stories. It is his story that stretches from creation through eternity and that remains applicable to our lives today. We must show good stewardship in the way we teach it.

Once you have decided on the format you want to teach, you need to put it all on paper. While hook-book-look-took is regarded as the standard lesson format, other formats exist. For example, Dr. Michael Lawson's alternative format—begin-develop-conclude—parallels but does not duplicate Richards's hook-book-look-took.[16] Figure 8.1, located at the close of this chapter, is a blank template for writing lesson plans. Figure 8.2 explains the various parts of the template. They include a final step of evaluation. It will be efficient to take a few minutes alone after everyone has left the room to think about what worked well and what did not work so well. Make notes of both in the "evaluation" space, and then adjust accordingly before you teach the lesson again.

ASSESSMENT: "THE PROOF IS IN THE PUDDING"

"Test? At church [YWAM, Bible study, Good News Club, Women's Life Group, Men's Life Group]? I am not in school, and I am NOT taking a test." Is this what you are afraid of hearing? Yes, another name for *assessment* can be *test*. But there is value in assessing what we are doing before we teach (diagnostic), while we teach (formative), and after we teach (summative). Assessment gives us proof that the "pudding" is set.

Diagnostic Assessment

Maybe you will not want to call this a test or assessment. But you do want to find out what your students know before you begin teaching them things they already know or are not ready for yet. So, try a game. Ask

---

15. University of Florida Center for Instructional Technology and Training, "Kolb's Four Stages of Learning," accessed August 15, 2023, https://citt.ufl.edu/resources/the-learning-process/types-of-learners/kolbs-four-stages-of-learning/.
16. Michael S. Lawson, *The Professor's Puzzle: Teaching in Christian Academics* (Nashville: B&H Academic, 2015), 150–51.

questions that lead students toward the subject matter you are about to launch. The questions should tell you something about what they already know and what they need to know. This information will help you develop a strategy for a unit. It can also help you finalize details in specific lessons as you discover things that should be reviewed as reminders and things that need introduction before you jump in over students' heads.

Formative Assessment: Testing Along the Way Prevents Disasters

Class discussions give you an opportunity to hear the thought processes of students. Some students learn by hearing themselves work through content. You may want to let it play out, depending on what you hear. Discovery learning is great, and disequilibrium promotes discovery learning as people dig for information to settle their questions. Embrace the questions but beware of statements that signal someone has made a wrong turn and is now headed toward something unorthodox or unbiblical. Stop that student with a question or two to explore their thinking.

- Did I understand you to say . . . ?
- When you say . . . do you mean . . . ? (Do not lead the question. You want to hear exactly what they are thinking, so fill in the blank with what you believe they are thinking. Then deal with it graciously.)
- Help me understand what you meant by . . .

Sometimes you may want to stop and ask questions just to check, even if nobody has spoken.

- How does this response from Joseph fit what happened in the last scene?
- Why do you think he responded that way?
- What do you think the writer meant when he said, "Be angry and sin not?"
- When Jesus turned over the tables on the Temple Mount, how was it different from sinful anger?

Asking questions in the middle of teaching has several advantages. First, the teacher discovers when students begin to stray from either the topic or correct theology. In addition, it allows students to hear more voices than the teacher's voice. Hendricks says, "Everyone . . . can be motivated to learn. But not at the same time . . . and not by the same person . . . and not in the same way."[17] A student in the room may say something you are trying to communicate in a slightly different way that attaches in another student's brain better than the way you said it. And maybe it will stick better in your brain for future use as well. Finally, questions break up the time and call wandering minds back into the room to participate.

Summative Assessment: They Ought to Be Different by the End

We have mentioned transformational learning throughout this chapter. Summative assessment is another place you get to see if and how the students have been transformed. In an academic setting, unless visual art or a performance is being evaluated, this is almost always done with a paper-and-pencil test. That can be a challenge in the church or para-church setting. What are you going to do with that paper-and-pencil test once the students have completed it? Will they put their hearts into it if they know they are not going to receive a grade? Will they mutiny if you suggest you are going to grade it?

Gronlund says, "Affective outcomes based on inner feeling, such as attitudes, typically are assessed with self-report methods."[18] Testimonials make for good self-report assessment in the Christian education setting. You get to hear what the students value. Remember, affective learning promotes transformation. It is unlikely that you will have a person formulate words, sentences, and paragraphs and then speak out loud to a group of peers about something they do not value. There is a risk to that attempt. You know what they value when they are willing to take the risk of speaking out loud in a group of their peers.

What about those who just cannot take that risk? There are a lot of people who cannot or will not speak in public. Since fear does not create the best learning scenario, try the written word. Hand out 3x5 cards and ask students to write one thought they want to take away from this lesson, unit, or year. Have them draw a picture of their lives before and life after this unit.

17. Hendricks, *Teaching to Change Lives*, 110.
18. Gronlund, *Writing Instructional Objectives*, 119.

Whatever you do at the end, make sure you are checking to see if their lives are different following the learning/teaching experience than they were before.

LEAVING IT TO GOD

There are no guarantees that our efforts will create godly, well-developed, mature believers. We are working with real people who are both created in God's image and have a fallen sin nature. There is comfort in knowing that we teach with the Holy Spirit. He is at work in our students' lives even when we are no longer with them. But that does not mean we can sit back and expect him to work alone. We are given the gift of teaching, and we are expected to be good stewards of our gifts. So we work hard to create the best lessons possible for the Holy Spirit to use. As we prepare, we are praying for the students who will receive those lessons. We pray that they will come to us softened by the Holy Spirit and ready to receive God's Word. We pray for their internal motivation to apply and follow the instruction. And we trust that God's promise to accomplish his purpose with his Word will be fulfilled in our students (Isa. 55:11). Then we entrust them to God who created them and loves them more than we do.

CONCLUSION

There is an adage in education circles that goes like this:

> I do, you watch.
> I do, you help.
> You do, I help.
> You do, I watch.

Teaching with this proverb in mind is a helpful strategy. Our students are always watching us. We should be giving them something to emulate. In addition, we ought to be teaching in such a way that we are prepared to set them free to teach. There are a couple of very good reasons to prepare to let go and let them do it. First, all teachers know that we learn more while preparing to teach than we ever did as students. And we learn more in our study than we could ever hope to present to our students. We ought to want to see our students begin to study to get more than we can give them.

But the most important reason to teach them to be independent from us is that Jesus did it with his disciples. We will not always be with our students. They will move on. We will move on. We ought to be teaching them to go out and multiply. We pray that as they are discipled, they will also go and make disciples.

Figure 8.1 Lesson Plan Template (Bible Study)

Date & Place:
Title & Scripture:
Name:

LESSON PLAN

Time	Content	Activities	Equipment
	Hook (Intro):		
Transtition (TR)			
	Book (Message):		
TR			
	Look (Life Application):		
TR			
	Took (Commitment):		
TR			

	Summary:		
Evaluation:			

Figure 8.2 Lesson Plan Explanation (Bible Study)

Date:
Title/Topic:
Group:

The students will (TSW) . . . What is the one thing I want the student to accomplish? Am I teacher-centered or student-centered? What cognitive and affective objectives am I aiming for?			
Time	**Lesson Focus**	**Activities**	**Equipment/Facilities**
Note time in 2 ways: by hour and minute reference—8:10–8:20, and by quantity—10 Min.	Hook (Intro): What will you do to signal the beginning? capture interest? create a need? prepare students for learning?	List and/or describe the activities you will use, e.g., sentence completion brainstorm contrast list SGI (small group interaction) LGI (large group interaction) IR (individual reflection)	List equipment you will need, e.g.,– Document camera HOs (handouts) TV/DVD Data projector Make note of special facility needs or room set up, e.g., turn lights down turn lights up arrange seating by groups arrange seating theater style need tables

<table>
<tr><td colspan="4">Transition: How will you transition from one section of your lesson to the next?
A transition provides:
a bridge from one part of your lesson to the next,
a connection from what you have just completed to what you are about to begin, and
a signal to your audience that you are shifting gears, moving on to something new.
A transition should not simply be:
a summary of what you have just said,
an introduction of what you are about to say, or
an introduction of the next member of your teaching team.</td></tr>
<tr><td></td><td>Book (Message):
How will you communicate God's word?
What are you going to say?
How will you convey the content of your lesson?
How will you get the student directly involved, directly interacting in God's word?
90% of lessons end here!</td><td>Lecture
Q&A
Personal discovery exercise
SGI
Poster board exercise</td><td>• Data projector
• Laptop
• Flip chart
• HOs
• Bibles</td></tr>
<tr><td colspan="4">Transition: How will you move from one section of your lesson to the next?</td></tr>
</table>

Look (Application): ▪ How will you move from the content of God's word to the application of God's Word? ▪ How will the students examine their lives in light of God's word? ▪ How will you help the students connect the Bible with their environment?	▪ IR (individual response) ▪ SGI ▪ LGI	▪ Markers ▪ Data projector ▪ Handouts ▪ Construction paper
Transition: How will you move from one section of your lesson to the next?		
Took (Commitment): How will the student demonstrate a planned response toward application?	Index card for a commitment statement	3x5 cards pencils/pens
Transition: How will you move from one section of your lesson to the next?		
Summary: Concluding remarks Land the plane		
Evaluation: Strengths Weaknesses Changes to make for next time		

REFLECTION QUESTIONS

Select one of the following passages: Hebrews 12, Luke 10, or one scene from Genesis 37–50.

1. What might be a big idea for the passage you chose?
2. What should students know, value, and do following a lesson from your selected passage or scene?
3. What is one goal for each of the domains: *know* (cognitive), *value* (affective), and *do* (psychomotor)?
4. How might you construct an instructional cognitive objective for a lesson on your selected passage?
5. How might you write an instructional affective objective for a lesson on your selected passage?

RECOMMENDED READING

Hendricks, Howard. *Teaching to Change Lives: Seven Proven Ways to Make Your Teaching Come Alive.* Sisters, OR: Multnomah, 1987.

Lawson, Michael S. *The Professor's Puzzle: Teaching in Christian Academics.* Nashville: B&H Academic, 2015.

Mager, Robert. *Preparing Instructional Objectives: A Critical Tool in the Development of Effective Instruction.* 3rd ed. Atlanta: Center for Effective Instruction, 1997.

McKeachie, Wilbert J., and Marilla D. Svinicki. *McKeachie's Teaching Tips: Strategies, Research, and Theory for College and University Teachers.* 14th ed. Belmont, CA: Wadsworth Cengage Learning, 2014.

Richards, Lawrence O., and Gary Bredfeldt. *Creative Bible Teaching.* 3rd ed. Chicago: Moody, 1998.

Robinson, Haddon. *Biblical Preaching: The Development and Delivery of Expository Messages.* 3rd ed. Grand Rapids: Baker Academic, 2014.

Yount, William R. *Created to Learn: A Christian Teacher's Introduction to Educational Psychology.* 2nd ed. Nashville: B&H Academic, 2010.

CHAPTER 9

CURRICULUM DESIGN

Jay L. Sedwick

Our youth minister decided to reorganize the entire curriculum for our ministry. The tenth-grade year was my teaching team's responsibility. The task was to survey the entire Old Testament in forty-eight weeks. The team was excited to tackle the challenge and began to discuss writing the curriculum ourselves. I stepped in to tamp down their enthusiasm. Oh, I had every confidence in the abilities of my team to pull it off. They had many years of Sunday school and small group teaching experience and were well versed in the Bible and theology. A few were certified school teachers. But when I challenged them with the time commitment required to accomplish this feat, there was immediate hesitation from the whole group. At minimum, weekly mandatory meetings outside of normal church commitments would be necessary for the entire year until we had everything in place. If we were going to do this, I insisted we do it right.

Writing sloppy curriculum is fairly easy. In fact, people do it all the time. However, writing quality curriculum is really hard. Most people are not willing to spend the time it takes to do it well. Most people are not aware of the systematic process to follow that will ensure consistent success in the endeavor.

My team quickly decided to look for a curriculum already on the market to help us meet the need. We found a forty-eight–week survey of the Old Testament written for adult learners and adapted it for our tenth-grade students. It worked very well and saved us hundreds of hours of effort.

I instruct my seminary students to do an exhaustive search for a curriculum to meet whatever need they have in their ministry context. Only commit to writing your own curriculum if you cannot find something that will work or is adaptable. And if possible, do not attempt this on your own. You will find curriculum writing more rewarding and encouraging if you engage others to join you on the journey.

The term *curriculum* comes from the Latin word *currere*, which means "to run." *Curriculum* means the course of a race.[1] The word is elastic and can be used to mean various things, all valid meanings, depending on the context. Within the context of the local church or ministry, curriculum can refer to the aggregate of all that is taught from the pulpit, in Sunday school, through small group Bible studies, at vacation Bible school, and in all other programs. Curriculum can also describe the collection of Bible study courses designed for a specific age range or special interest group. Curriculum can be used to identify a single Bible study lesson. *Curriculum* as used in this chapter describes a singular Bible study course within the church or ministry comprising a series of individual related lessons. If you are willing to take the time to do it with excellence, follow the process outlined in this chapter to give yourself confidence in writing curriculum for your ministry context.

THE CURRICULUM DESIGN PROCESS

The task may seem daunting at first, but when the curriculum design process is divided into individual and interdependent steps, the experience becomes more manageable and enjoyable. There are several curriculum design models in use today that share many common steps and procedures; a fuller discussion of these models is beyond the purpose of this chapter. One of the traditional models was proposed by Ralph Tyler, who laid a foundation many others have followed and built upon over the years.[2] Hilda Taba, one of Tyler's colleagues, gave his process more specific steps and championed the participation of

1. Leroy Ford, *A Curriculum Design Manual for Theological Education: A Learning Outcomes Focus* (Nashville: Broadman, 1991), 33–34.
2. Ralph Tyler, *Basic Principles of Curriculum and Instruction* (Chicago: University of Chicago Press, 1949).

the teachers in the development of the curriculum.[3] Taba suggested the following seven steps for any curriculum design regardless of topic:

1. Diagnosis of needs
2. Formulation of objectives
3. Selection of content
4. Organization of content
5. Selection of learning experiences
6. Organization of learning experiences
7. Determination of what to evaluate and of the ways and means of doing it[4]

Taba's system has been used for decades to help designers methodically work through the process to effectively produce a final curriculum product primarily for the public-school context. Here is an adaptation and reordering of Taba's process for our purposes in designing Bible study curriculum for the local church or ministry:

1. Discover the cognitive, affective and behavioral needs of the learners to establish a rationale for the curriculum (see chapters 5, 6, 7).
2. Select the biblical content to address identified needs (see chapter 3).
3. Prioritize topics and organize the biblical content into units and lessons (see chapters 3, 4).
4. Formulate goals and objectives based on the biblical content (see chapters 4, 8).
5. Select and organize learning experiences into lesson plans (see chapter 8).
6. Teach the Bible study curriculum.
7. Evaluate the curriculum design, the process of teaching the curriculum, and the effectiveness of the curriculum (see chapters 4, 8).

---

3. Allan C. Ornstein and Francis P. Hunkins, *Curriculum: Foundations, Principles, and Issues*, 4th ed. (New York: Pearson, 2004), 198.
4. Hilda Taba, *Curriculum Development: Theory and Practice* (New York: Harcourt, Brace and World, 1962), 12.

In our modified system, step 6 represents the actual implementation of the curriculum. It is difficult to evaluate the design in step 7 without the experience of using the curriculum. And of course, Taba's belief that the teachers of the curriculum should be directly involved in its creation should be wholeheartedly embraced. The rest of what follows expands on the steps listed above.

Step 1: Discover Needs

The first step in the production of a quality Bible study curriculum is to identify the needs of the intended audience. Peter Oliva identifies five main sources of needs-assessment data that curriculum developers should give attention to. They are:

1. The needs of the students in general;
2. The needs of the society;
3. The needs of the particular students;
4. The needs of the particular community; and
5. The needs derived from the subject matter.[5]

Let us apply Oliva's five sources of data to a specific example, though reordering them for our purposes. You have been asked to develop a curriculum for high school students in your church. First, and the most obvious step, is to surface the needs identified by the Bible, our subject matter. What are the commands, imperatives, attitudes, values and behaviors the Scriptures tell us we need to embrace? The second step involves discovering the general needs of the broader society in which high school students live. The next step takes the second step to the more specific level of understanding the needs of the community in which the church ministers. Fourth, discover the needs of high school students in general. What is typical of high school students in your neighborhood, city, state, and the country? The fifth and final step requires an in-depth look at the needs of the high school students attending your church.

5. William R. Gordon II, Rosemarye T. Taylor, and Peter F. Oliva, *Developing the Curriculum: Improved Outcomes Through Systems Approaches*, 9th ed., Pearson Educational Leadership (New York: Pearson, 2019), 139.

Obviously, the needs of a fifteen-year-old teenager greatly differ from the needs of her forty-year-old parents. Different stages of life have different challenges, and therefore different needs. *Needs assessment* is a planning process for identifying gaps between the current situation and the desired one and addressing those gaps in priority order.[6] A proper needs assessment will provide the necessary information for designing the more effective curriculum, one that produces the desired results. *Evaluation* is a retrospective concern to determine the gaps between what has been achieved through the teaching of a curriculum and the targets previously set beforehand. However, a needs assessment is forward looking and determines the gaps between the current situation and what will hopefully be attained, as illustrated in Figure 9.1. To put it simply, a needs assessment measures the difference between "what is" and "what should be."[7]

Figure 9.1: Needs Assessment

Consider the following three conditions to help determine the extent to which teaching a Bible curriculum will produce a desired change. First, conduct a thorough assessment of the current state of the learner's general knowledge, attitudes, and skills related to the Christian life. Second, everyone involved should have a clear understanding and agree on the desired state of the learner's knowledge, attitudes, or skills. Third, all should understand and agree that any differences (the needs) observed between the current state and the desired state can be diminished or eliminated by the learner's experience with the curriculum. To put it simply, the learner's starting position is A. The learner's desired ending position is B. The curriculum should move the learner from position A to position B. And more

6. Fenwick W. English and Roger A. Kaufman, *Needs Assessment: A Focus on Curriculum Development* (Alexandria, VA: Association for Supervision and Curriculum Development, 1975), 3–4.
7. Tyler, *Basic Principles of Curriculum and Instruction*, 8.

directly, can the Bible study curriculum you develop help to transform the students who complete it?

Needs can be delineated into two broad categories: *real* needs and *felt* needs. A real need is something that must be addressed in the life of the learner for optimal satisfaction and flourishing. The learner may not be conscious of the need and therefore not be motivated to satisfy the need. If the need is not met, the consequences will more than likely be detrimental. A felt need is something the learner is conscious of and motivated to meet for optimal satisfaction and flourishing. The felt need may or may not be a real need, so meeting the need may or may not be essential for optimal satisfaction or flourishing.

A simplistic way to illustrate both real and felt needs is hunger. Every living person *really* needs to eat. There are no other options. If no food is available for a long enough time, death is certain. Eating is a real need. However, we do not need to eat all the time. At certain times the body internally demonstrates the felt need for food with hunger pains to motivate the person to eat. Those hunger pains manifest the felt need to address the real need for food. In many cases, real needs are not addressed until they become felt needs. For example, all people have a real need to trust in Jesus Christ's death on the cross to pay the penalty for their sins. The Bible is clear in Romans 6:23 that "the wages of sin is death" (ESV). Without Christ, spiritual death is certain. Our task is to partner with the Holy Spirit in helping people experience the felt need for a Savior, which will motivate them to seek a relationship with Jesus to meet the real need for salvation (Eph. 2:1–10).

Various strategies for collecting needs-assessment data exist. One way is through your own personal experiences. What personal needs have been met throughout your life experiences? Living the Christian life day to day provides a breadth of data to help determine the needs others have, because chances are high that many others share life experiences similar to yours.

Another helpful way is by consulting others who are knowledgeable about the learners. There are sources of information like the Census Bureau, the Barna Research Group, the Pew Research Center, the Springtide Research Institute, to name just a few, which can provide a general overview of the needs of people. More specifically, there are experts who can help identify the needs of particular learners from their research, experience, and wealth of knowledge. Anecdotal information from those who have direct, hands-on experience with a group of learners can also provide valuable needs-assessment data.

Direct data-gathering techniques can also help discover the needs of your intended audience. Conducting interviews with the intended audience of the curriculum should yield very specific information about a variety of topics and issues, depending on the questions asked. The interviewer should follow a consistent and designed protocol and be trained on how to conduct interviews.[8] Using focus groups is another great technique that incorporates a guided response to questions discussed in a group and usually provides more personal information on feelings, attitudes, and values. The facilitator of the focus groups should also be trained on how to guide the discussion without directing the conversation toward predetermined answers due to bias.[9] Direct observation by the curriculum developer is another valuable source of needs-assessment data. Paying close attention to the intended audience over time can supply a wealth of information helpful to designing the curriculum for maximum impact. Care must be taken not to let personal bias influence the interpretation of the information gathered.

One of the more common ways to gather needs-assessment data is to survey the intended audience by using a locally constructed questionnaire.[10] Very specific questions can be asked to gain an understanding of people's current state or condition. Take care in the construction and design of the questionnaire to ensure the maximum number of people will respond so that you will have enough useful information to draw insightful conclusions.[11] For instance, make sure it is not too long and can be completed in a short amount of time. The longer the questionnaire, the more likely people will not complete it. Use a balance of close-ended (can be answered quickly) and open-ended (take more thought and time to answer) questions. A Likert-type rating scale can be used to ask respondents to choose a range value, for example between (1) never, (2) rarely, (3) sometimes, and (4) always. Decide if

8. Gary J. Dean, *Designing Instruction for Adult Learners*, Professional Practices in Adult Education and Human Resource Development (Malabar, FL: Krieger, 1994), 44.
9. Richard A. Krueger and Mary Anne Casey, *Focus Groups: A Practical Guide for Applied Research*, 5th ed. (Los Angeles: SAGE, 2015), 2–9.
10. Gordon, Taylor, and Oliva, *Developing the Curriculum*, 154.
11. Dean, *Designing Instruction for Adult Learners*, 48, 50.

the questionnaire will be anonymous (more honest answers, typically) or identified with the respondent.

Once sufficient data has been collected, a general report should be written to compile the findings for current and future use. The generalized findings can be used for several years without conducting another needs assessment, which is fortunate, because the needs-assessment process is time-consuming. In addition, the components of the needs assessment that are broader in scope and not specific to the intended audience can be used for other needs-assessment considerations and do not need to be repeated. If you regularly write curriculum for different age groups within your church, then the first three steps of the process outlined above would apply in all cases: (1) needs from Scripture; (2) broader society and cultural needs; and (3) church and community needs. Only the two steps specific to the intended audience would need to be completed for each age group.

Step 2: Select Biblical Content

The next step in the design process is to select the biblical content to be taught to address what the needs assessment has surfaced. The Bible provides us with all we need to live our lives according to the purpose God has set before us: to be "ambassadors for Christ" (2 Cor. 5:20 ESV). There are commandments to obey, instructions to follow, and warnings to heed that lead to salvation, righteousness, and wisdom so that believers will be "equipped for every good work" (2 Tim. 3:15–17 ESV). This step assumes the curriculum designers have at least a basic knowledge of the entire Bible, essential doctrines, and theological concepts. It will be difficult to choose biblical content to address surfaced needs if you do not know what the Bible says about those needs.

The process of discovering what God's Word says and explaining its meaning is called *exegesis*. *Eisegesis*, on the other hand, is the process of making God's Word say something it does not say to fit an agenda or prescribed issue by inserting one's own opinion. Essentially eisegesis is reading into the text something that is not there. We need to strongly resist making the latter mistake and to trust that Scripture will address all that needs to be addressed as we understand it and teach it faithfully. For example, if the needs assessment identifies a deficiency in the practice of prayer, the writer should select passages in Scripture that teach about prayer, and then study them carefully as instructed in chapter 3.

By the way, selecting the right biblical content must also be bathed in prayer. Ask the Lord for guidance as you consider the counsel of God in his Word.

There are a variety of useful categories for Bible study curriculum, all of which you will use, depending on the needs to be addressed. Examining the life and significance of David would be an example of a character study. While walking through the sections of the Old Testament that tell the stories of his life, many helpful topics and issues will be encountered, such as obedience, patience, confession, friendship, loyalty, worship, and the consequences of sin. The book of Nehemiah could serve as both a character study and a Bible book study. Principles of leadership, perseverance, the importance of prayer, dependence on God, and faithfulness are all touched on in the book. If you need to teach a deeper appreciation for and greater understanding of the person and work of Christ (Christology), then select specific passages like Philippians 2:1–11 and Colossians 1:13–20 that address who he is and what he has done for us.

Step 3: Organize Biblical Content

Once the biblical content is selected, you must decide how much to teach and in what order. This is referred to as scope and sequence. The scope of the curriculum encompasses the entirety of subject matter to be taught. It includes everything you plan to teach from the first lesson to the last. The sequence refers to how the curriculum subject is organized to maximize effectiveness in communicating the material. In my opening example to this chapter, the entire Old Testament was the scope—a *huge* scope. However, calendar parameters will usually limit the scope to fit the context for which the curriculum is being written. The calendar parameter for the Old Testament curriculum was forty-eight weeks. The typical Sunday school curriculum produced by the mainline denominational publishing houses is based on the quarterly calendar. Each quarter is thirteen weeks long, so the curriculum is broken up into thirteen-week segments for the year. These publishers also offer special study curriculum products that do not fit the quarterly system but instead are designed for small group studies, which are typically six or eight weeks long. Someone in your ministry, maybe you, will determine the calendar limitations to work with so everyone understands the scope of the task to fit your context.

Once the overall scope has been determined, decide what to include and what to exclude. The whole counsel of God is worth teaching, but time will limit how much you can teach in a given context. What you decide to exclude, called the *null* curriculum, can be just as important a decision as what you decide to include (see Figure 9.2).

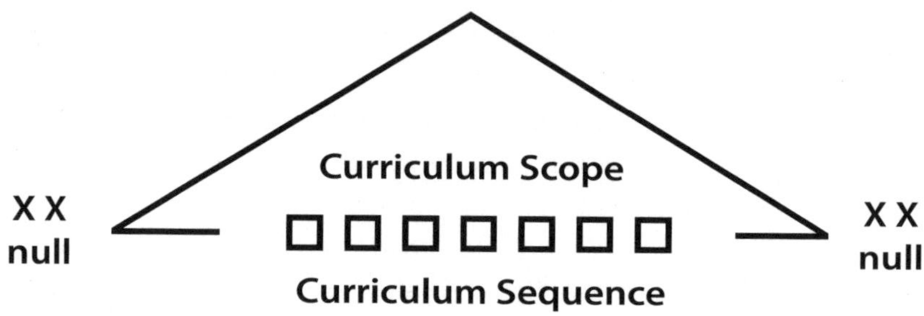

Figure 9.2: Null Curriculum

Remember, the needs assessment should provide guidance for these decisions. Our forty-eight–week Old Testament survey curriculum had two lessons covering the life of Solomon, but it did not cover many of the other kings of Judah and Israel due to time constraints.

The order in which the biblical content will be taught is called the *sequence*. When teaching a book of the Bible, the sequence will normally start at the beginning of the book and flow through it in the order presented. However, there may be a reason to jump ahead to lay a foundation for what will follow. John 20:30–31 says, "Jesus performed many other signs in the presence of his disciples, which are not recorded in this book. But these are written that you may believe that Jesus is the Messiah, the Son of God, and that by believing you may have life in his name" (NIV). The purpose of John's gospel may be worth teaching at the beginning of the study to better understand what he included and why. If the curriculum is based on a biblical character, life issue, doctrinal position, or theological topic, the sequence will be determined by the logical flow of the biblical information discovered by thorough study.

The scope-and-sequence decisions lead to the development of a curriculum plan, which is an outline of sorts. There are three main parts of the plan: the curriculum title, the unit titles, and the lesson titles. The curriculum title should be short, to the point, possibly pithy, and can be determined after the units and lessons are developed since the title will most likely be used to motivate the intended audience to show up and go through the study. The biblical content is divided into units with unique titles. The unit titles should collectively point to the curriculum title. A unit will typically have between two and five individual lessons in it. Each lesson should have a unique title that is directly related to the primary biblical passage associated with it. The lesson titles should collectively point to the unit title they fall within. The curriculum plan is hierarchical, much like an outline would be.

There are several helpful patterns of curriculum organization for sequencing the units and lessons, three of which are the anchor pattern, the linear pattern, and the wheel pattern.[12] Using the anchor pattern, the first unit introduces the biblical principle or concept. Subsequent units logically develop related aspects of the biblical principle or concept and may highlight the different ways it can be applied to life concerns.

Course Title: The Future Is Known

Unit 1: Bible Prophecy
Unit 2: Prophecy Related to Israel
Unit 3: Prophecy Related to the Church
Unit 4: Prophecy Related to Christ's First and Second Comings
Unit 5: Prophecy Related to the End Times
Unit 6: The Blessed Hope

The linear pattern has several units that follow logically in a sequence. Each subsequent unit develops the biblical principle or concept and may build on previous units.

Course Title: The Discipleship Process

Unit 1: Win the Curious
Unit 2: Build the Convinced
Unit 3: Equip the Committed
Unit 4: Send the Commissioned

12. Ford, *A Curriculum Design Manual*, 246–48. Ford credits Raymond Rigdon for these design patterns, though no citation is provided. See also Karen L. Estep, "Charting the Course," in *Mapping Out Curriculum in Your Church: Cartography for Christian Pilgrims*, ed. James R. Estep, Roger White, and Karen L. Estep (Nashville: B&H Academic, 2012), 192–94.

The wheel pattern has several units organized around a biblical principle or concept. The units can be randomly presented because they do not exhibit a logical sequence. The first unit does not serve as an anchor.

Course Title: Spiritual Disciplines

Unit 1: Prayer
Unit 2: Bible Study
Unit 3: Evangelism
Unit 4: Worship
Unit 5: Service

Most churches that develop their own curriculum do not do so in a vacuum. They should consider how each Bible curriculum integrates within the discipleship strategy of the church, keeping the needs-assessment findings in mind. Thoughtful *vertical* integration would be demonstrated by Bible study curriculum that builds from study to study, covering more involved concepts and topics as the disciple matures. A new convert may sign up for a new believers' Bible study that covers the basic spiritual disciplines of a Christ follower. Upon completion, he or she could join a study of the gospel of Luke that chronologically presents the life and claims of Christ. Next in line could be a concentrated look at the character qualities of the "fruit of the Spirit" in Galatians 5. Each Bible study builds upon the last one and takes the disciple deeper into the faith.

Purposeful *horizontal* integration is evident when Bible study curriculum studies are interrelated based on some organizing factor, like age or life stage.[13] A curriculum on biblical stewardship, a curriculum on biblical parenting, and a curriculum on biblical marriage could all be taught coincidentally for a group of young married couples with children in the same life stage within the church.

A generic curriculum plan would look something like the following:

13. Ornstein and Hunkins, *Curriculum*, 243–44.

Course Title

Scripture Passage for the Course

Unit 1: Unit Title

Lesson 1: Title (focal Scripture passage)
Lesson 2: Title (focal Scripture passage)
Lesson 3: Title (focal Scripture passage)

Unit 2: Unit Title

Lesson 4: Title (focal Scripture passage)
Lesson 5: Title (focal Scripture passage)
Lesson 6: Title (focal Scripture passage)
Lesson 7: Title (focal Scripture passage)

Unit 3: Unit Title

Lesson 8: Title (focal Scripture passage)
Lesson 9: Title (focal Scripture passage)
Lesson 10: Title (focal Scripture passage)

Unit 4: Unit Title

Lesson 11: Title (focal Scripture passage)
Lesson 12: Title (focal Scripture passage)
Lesson 13: Title (focal Scripture passage)

Step 4: Formulate Goals and Objectives

One reason for reordering Taba's seven steps (see above) is the special nature of our task. When writing curriculum for a public school or institution, once the needs assessment is complete, the objectives are then built on the findings, then the subject matter is built on the objectives. In contrast, when writing Bible study curriculum for a church or ministry, once the needs assessment is complete, the subject matter, which is God's Word, is engaged. The objectives are then formulated based on what Scripture says, not on what the teacher wants to say or the church decides to say. This makes selecting the Bible content to address issues raised by the needs assessment even more dependent on the curriculum designers' knowledge and understanding of Scripture. It is imperative that designers thoroughly study the biblical passage(s). The central truth (see chapter 3) of the passage(s) can then be discovered, which the objectives must be built upon.

Formulating instructional goals and objectives is the hardest part of curriculum development. It takes time and practice to learn the process and to do it consistently well. In addition to the detailed description of the process in chapter 8, consider the following embellishments and reinforcements.

The literature on goals and objectives can be confusing since the two terms are flipped depending on the author or field of use. For our purposes, instructional goals are broad statements of what the student will learn. Goals focus on outcomes, not methods. Goals specify the kind of learning to be achieved in the cognitive, affective, or psychomotor domains. Goals indicate the topic to be learned. The language of a goal statement should be precise and concise. Does it say exactly what it needs to say (precision) as efficiently as possible (concision)? One way to ensure the goals stay focused on what the students will do is to begin each goal statement with, "The students will . . ." Goals should first be written for the curriculum course as a whole and then for each unit of the curriculum plan.

Each lesson in each unit will have at least one instructional objective that derives directly from the central truth of the biblical passage(s) for that lesson, but there could be up to three per lesson (one per learning domain). Like goals, objectives specify the kind of learning to be achieved in the cognitive, affective, or psychomotor domains. There should be a cognitive objective, an affective objective directly tied to the cognitive objective, and occasionally a psychomotor objective. The instructional objective(s) will be more specific than the unit goal it is hierarchically related to. Objectives are stated in behavioral terms and indicate what the learner will specifically do to demonstrate achievement of the intended learning outcome. Objectives specify conditions under which desired learning will be demonstrated or a degree of competence considered satisfactory; in other words, they must be measurable. This is a significant difference from a goal. The same guidelines for writing goals apply here. Objectives should be precise, concise, and begin with, "The students will . . ." There should be one cognitive and one affective objective for each lesson. Adding to the generic curriculum plan above, the following illustrates this step:

Course Title

Scripture Passage for the Course

Course Goal(s)

Unit 1: Unit Title

- Unit 1 Goal(s)

Lesson 1: Title (focal Scripture passage)
- Instructional Objective(s)

Lesson 2: Title (focal Scripture passage)
- Instructional Objective(s)

Lesson 3: Title (focal Scripture passage)
- Instructional Objective(s)

Unit 2: Unit Title

- Unit 2 Goal(s)

Lesson 4: Title (focal Scripture passage)
- Instructional Objective(s)

Lesson 5: Title (focal Scripture passage)
- Instructional Objective(s)

Lesson 6: Title (focal Scripture passage)
- Instructional Objective(s)

Lesson 7: Title (focal Scripture passage)
- Instructional Objective(s)

The curriculum plan, with a course title, course goal(s), unit titles, unit goal(s), lesson titles, and instructional objective(s) as presented, demonstrates the hierarchical organization. The unit goals are related to the course goal(s). The instructional objectives are related to the unit goal under which they are listed.

Step 5: Create Lesson Plans

Once the instructional objectives have been written for a lesson, the lesson plan must be created. A thorough discussion and explanation of the process of lesson plan development is presented in chapter 8. Once again, consider the following embellishments and reinforcements.

The instructional objectives form the target for the lesson. The entire lesson plan should focus on fulfilling the instructional objectives. Several lesson-plan templates exist. The most basic is the intro-explore-apply format. Larry Richards's hook-book-look-took format is similar but divides the apply section into two more specific sections (see Figure 8.1). The hook (intro) section is the introduction where the teacher gets the students excited, motivated, and interested in learning the material to be presented. The book (explore) takes the students to the biblical text(s) and guides them to know and understand the meaning of the passage(s). The cognitive objective *must* be fulfilled during the book section. The look (apply 1) section is where the universal biblical principle or concept is discovered, which applies to all people, at all times, and in all places. The took (apply 2) section provides the students an opportunity to decide how the lesson can be specifically applied in their personal lives that day, that week, or for the future. The affective objective *must* be fulfilled in either the look or the took section.

The teacher will need to craft transition statements to signal a shift from one section to the next. A transition statement should be short enough to memorize, and it should directly tie the previous section to the next. A transition statement is not just a summary of what the teacher just said, nor is it just an introduction of what the teacher is about to say. It should establish a content connection between the sections.

The teacher will need to select learning activities that are directly tied to the lesson objective(s). Whatever the instructional objectives say the students are going to do, they must do it during the lesson through participation in various learning activities. Dan Lambert has developed the world's longest list of teaching methods (learning activities).[14] The teacher should use a variety of learning methods that

14. Dan Lambert, *Teaching That Makes a Difference: How to Teach for Holistic Impact* (Grand Rapids: Zondervan, 2004), 147–63.

fit the lesson objective(s) to keep students interested and motivated to participate.

To make the lesson plan work better, remember that the lesson plan is a *guide* and not a *crutch* for teaching. The teacher's preparation ought to be robust enough that the lesson plan is only used to prompt the teacher to continue making progress and stay on track. Teachers should not be reading directly from the lesson plan.

Try to keep the lesson plan to a single sheet of paper, preferably on one side only. Use legal size paper to gain an extra three inches of space if needed. It would be quite embarrassing to shuffle multiple pages of the lesson plan, get them out of order, and then be completely lost and confused. Regaining control of the lesson at that point will be a challenge.

List all the materials needed for each learning activity to teach the lesson. Some learning activities require art supplies, technological equipment, or writing instruments and paper. Planning far enough ahead to make sure these things are available and accessible could make or break the lesson.

There should be enough detail in the lesson plan so a substitute teacher could teach the lesson if the regular teacher is sick or unexpectedly absent. Have someone unfamiliar with the curriculum examine the lesson plans and provide feedback on the lesson objective(s), specific directions, learning activities, and overall flow to see if it is feasible to teach with little forewarning. A substitute teacher would not be expected to teach the lesson as well as the one who developed the lesson, but he or she should do a reasonable job with the directions and guidance in the lesson plans. If the curriculum is being produced for others to teach, this consideration is critical, especially if no teacher preparation and training are involved.

File every lesson developed so if there is a need to teach on the passage again, and there will be, the teacher does not have to start from scratch. Enough detail needs to be in the lesson plan so that in two years when the plan is pulled from the file, the teacher will understand what is meant by what is written. For example, if the lesson includes showing a movie clip from a *Superman* movie (there are seven as of this writing), identify which one and the exact location of the clip in the film, or expect to be very frustrated when the clip cannot be located and/or the technology required to display the video is not available, and that clip is critical to the lesson objective(s).

Step 6: Teach the Curriculum

Take into consideration everything that happens from the moment the first student arrives until the last student leaves. This is called the "total period teaching" approach. The lesson plan is the heart and soul of each teaching session, but there is more to the process. The formal start to the lesson plan is the hook. The formal end to the lesson plan is the "took." But consider the things that happen before the lesson formally begins and after the lesson formally ends to make the learning experience the best it can be.

The teacher should plan to arrive early and stay late. Arrive early enough to get everything ready so the focus can be on the arriving students and building relationships with them. The room should be preset for the planned learning activities. Check the lighting, temperature, seating arrangements, access to Bibles and pens, and technology. Greet each student and engage in conversation as they arrive. Teach the lesson. Once the lesson concludes, be available for individual discussion and interaction the lesson may provoke. Do not start cleaning up, rearranging, and gathering up all the materials until the last student leaves. Prioritize the *students*.

Be flexible with the lesson plan. There will be times when the lesson does not go as planned, especially if the students want to talk about a pressing matter or a current event. The discussion may not fit your lesson objective(s), but plodding through the lesson plan at all costs may alienate the students who are displaying a felt need that should be addressed. This requires sensitivity to and dependence on the Holy Spirit and truly caring for the students.

The basis for life transformation is built on relationships (to be developed further in chapters 15 and 17). Learn students' names as a bare minimum. Be intentional about getting to know the students and their specific life contexts. There should be correlation between the information surfaced in the needs assessment, if done well, and what the teacher encounters through direct interaction with the students. A skilled teacher will learn through the weekly experiences of teaching the curriculum to adapt the lesson plans to better meet the needs of the students.

Pay close attention to the interactions and responses of the students throughout the curriculum implementation. The next section will explore the need for evaluation from several different perspectives, which includes weekly observations on the part of the teacher after each lesson is taught.

Step 7: Evaluate the Curriculum

Evaluation is a necessary step in the design process to help the curriculum developer(s) know if all the time and energy invested was worth the effort.[15] There is tremendous satisfaction in knowing the students have been transformed by the curriculum they completed. Remember, the first step in the curriculum design process was to conduct a needs assessment to find out the gaps between "what is" and "what should be." Evaluation is a retrospective concern with the gaps between what has been achieved through the curriculum and the intended outcomes previously determined. It is a process used to gather and interpret data to make decisions about whether to accept the current situation.[16] The terms *evaluation* and *assessment* are commonly used interchangeably.

There are two broad types of evaluation, *formative* and *summative*.[17] "Formative assessment provides ongoing, occasional feedback that informs ongoing changes during the process of curriculum evaluation on the level of the congregation, ministry, program, or even individual."[18] Those involved in designing, administering, and teaching the curriculum should be included in the process of evaluation throughout its implementation by gathering feedback in a variety of ways. The goal of formative evaluation is to make course corrections if the feedback identifies problems that can be immediately addressed. Alterations can be made that reflect sensitivity to the learning situation and should demonstrate a flexibility to change to better accomplish the instructional objectives and course goals. The ultimate purpose is to maximize life transformation. If lives are not being transformed, then make the changes necessary to make transformation more likely.

Summative evaluation is more commonly thought of when discussing this topic. "Summative assessment provides end-product feedback and is most useful for continuous improvements. It provides the information to

15. Ornstein and Hunkins, *Curriculum*, 335.
16. Ornstein and Hunkins, *Curriculum*, 334.
17. See additional discussion of formative and summative evaluation, also referred to as assessment, in chapter 8.
18. Karen L. Estep and James R. Estep Jr., "Checking the Legend and Assessing the Journey," in Estep, White, and Estep, *Mapping Out Curriculum in Your Church*, 217; Gordon, Taylor, and Oliva, *Developing the Curriculum*, 223–24.

tell us if we have met our objectives and provides a measure of their quality and relevance."[19] Once the Bible study curriculum has been taught and experienced, summative evaluation aims to determine its effectiveness. Quality feedback at the end of the course should help in determining if lives were transformed. If not, then why not? If so, then why so? Based on the feedback, decisions should be made to strengthen the aspects determined to work well, correct the aspects that created difficulty or unnecessary challenge, develop the unforeseen aspects as new possibilities, and eliminate aspects that seemed to fail.

There are three main areas of the curriculum design process to evaluate: the design itself, the teacher and process of teaching, and student learning success or life transformation.

Evaluation of the Curriculum Design

Four areas to evaluate in the curriculum design are the *content* (what does it say?), the *philosophy* (how is it designed?), the *methods* used (how does it help?), and the *mechanical features* (what does it look like?).[20]

Content: Is the content strongly oriented to the Bible with demonstrated respect for the text? Are proper interpretations evident based on sound hermeneutics? Are distinctly Christian values presented with opportunities for students to internalize them? Are the issues addressed relevant to the lives of the learners with sensitivity and insight? Is there an acknowledgment of developmental considerations?

Philosophy: Is the goal of life transformation evident as the intended overall outcome? How much time is devoted to application in the lesson plans? Are students led to individualized and active response to the biblical content? Does the curriculum emphasize the home, family needs, strengthening family relationships, and church and community health? Is there an organizing principle evident throughout the materials?

Methods: Are there a variety of developmentally appropriate teaching techniques? Are there sufficient teaching aids provided or suggested with instructions on how to use them? Does the curriculum provide

19. Estep, White, and Estep, 217.
20. Adapted from George M. Hillman Jr. "Putting It All Together: The Education Cycle," in *Invitation to Educational Ministry: Foundations of Transformative Christian Education*, ed. George M. Hillman Jr., and Sue G. Edwards, Invitation to Theological Studies (Grand Rapids: Kregel Academic, 2018), 483–87.

additional help for teacher preparation? Is the curriculum flexible enough to be used in a variety of contexts? Does the material consider various levels of teacher and learner ability?

Mechanical features: Is the layout easy to read? Is color used advantageously? Are pictures and artwork helpful, contemporary, and relevant to the learners' interests? Are the supplies of high quality? Is the material durable and reusable? Are there references to events and people that date the material?

Evaluation of Teaching the Curriculum

While I was serving in the role of minister of education, a group of Sunday school teachers approached me to complain about the poor quality of the materials our church used, which were purchased from the denominational curriculum house. I listened to their concerns and switched to a different publisher. A few months later, the same group of teachers complained about the poor quality of the new materials. Another publisher was selected after proper consideration. Several months later, the same group of teachers complained about the poor quality of the new materials. It became apparent that the issue was not the quality of the materials. The teachers' abilities were suspect.

Poorly designed curriculum will amplify what is lacking in teacher ability. In contrast, the curriculum can be of high quality, but if the teacher is not skilled, the result often can still be a poor Bible teaching session. Teacher training and mentoring should be a high priority in the church (see chapter 16 for more on how to foster good teaching).

Teachers must evaluate the curriculum as they teach the lessons.[21] The lesson plan format presented in chapter 8 (Figures 8.1 and 8.2) has a box at the bottom with "Evaluation" as the heading. At the end of each lesson, the teacher should take five minutes to reflect on the lesson. What went well? What did not go so well? What should be changed? What should be amplified or strengthened? What should be cut? Were any design flaws identified during the execution of the lesson? This kind of evaluation assumes the lesson will be taught again. Unfortunately, many lessons are "one-and-done." The teacher will never teach the lesson again. For our purposes, the curriculum you spent so much

21. Michael S. Lawson, *The Professor's Puzzle: Teaching in Christian Academics* (Nashville: B&H Academic, 2015), 149.

time writing should be used multiple times with different learner groups, each time taught better than the time before.

Teachers should also be evaluated on how they use the curriculum.[22] How well prepared was the teacher for the session(s)? Did the teacher stay on track with the lesson plan? How well did the teacher manage the teaching environment? Was the teacher properly organized? Did the teacher use a variety of the suggested methods? Was there evidence the teacher internalized the lesson personally? Did the teacher manage learner participation and not dominate discussions? Was there evidence of creativity in the execution of the lesson? Does the teacher's personality help or hinder the learning process? These and other questions can be helpful to determine the effectiveness of the curriculum. If there is no life transformation evident in the learners, it is quite possible the issue is with the teacher and his or her abilities and willingness to follow the guidance provided by the curriculum.

Evaluation of Student Learning

The final step in evaluating the curriculum is the most important. Did the students learn anything? Did they develop cognitively and affectively according to the instructional goals and objectives? Were any of the identifiable needs surfaced in the needs assessment effectively addressed and met? Ultimately, was there any discernible life transformation? Paul writes, "He is the one we proclaim, admonishing and teaching everyone with all wisdom, so that we may present everyone fully mature in Christ" (Col. 1:28 NIV).

Various formative and summative techniques can be used to evaluate learner achievement. Most resources suggest tests to ascertain the level of competence and accomplishment. Most Sunday school or small group teachers react negatively to the idea, but the use of pop quizzes, for example, can be fun and engaging. A Bible knowledge quiz at the beginning of a lesson could serve as an effective hook to motivate the learner to better participate. The same quiz could be given at the end of the lesson to quickly see if any progress has been made. If your needs assessment incorporated a pretest to gauge the learners' understanding of what would become the course content, then a posttest could be given to indicate any change as a result of experiencing the curriculum.

22. Ornstein and Hunkins, *Curriculum*, 336.

Opinion questionnaires can be used to gather information on a variety of levels. Both cognitive and affective course goals can be measured this way as students share what they think about what they have learned. Open- and close-ended questions, rank-ordering questions, Likert-scale questions, multiple-choice questions, matching questions, true-false questions, and fill-in-the-blank questions can all be appropriately used to discover learner transformation.

One of the best ways to evaluate affective change is by using case studies. As students think through the case study, they have to apply what they learned to understand the situation, to solve a problem, to make a decision about the best way forward, or to distinguish between possible outcomes. Case studies can reveal maturity of thinking and processing, moral development, and spiritual sensitivity.

Learners can be personally interviewed to evaluate their progress. Just like the needs-assessment interview process, an evaluation interview needs to follow a set protocol so that information can be compared between students to look for trends and the collective effectiveness of the curriculum.

Focus groups can also be used to evaluate learner transformation. The focus group leader should be properly trained to guide the group through carefully planned questions with consistency, allowing for the subjective direction of the discussion to unfold.

Journaling is a helpful evaluation technique to discover affective change, though it is more personal and normally not shared with those conducting evaluation. If there is a high level of trust between the learners and the teacher, learners may be willing to let the teacher read through their private thoughts.

CONCLUSION

Writing quality and effective curriculum for the local church or ministry group is time-intensive and difficult work. Only those committed to designing and producing excellent curriculum materials should attempt to complete the task. Following the seven steps outlined in this chapter will greatly assist the curriculum writer or writing team to construct a Bible study course that results in life transformation, which is the goal of biblical instruction. Howards Hendricks was known to say, “Our goal is not information transfer but life transformation.”

REFLECTION QUESTIONS

1. Which one of the seven steps of the curriculum design process would be hardest for you to complete, and why?
2. How would using proper scope-and-sequence planning help you better organize your church's curriculum?
3. Why is it so important to discover the needs of your intended audience before you design your curriculum?
4. Explain the difference between formative and summative evaluation and how you should use each in your curriculum design process.

RECOMMENDED READING

Estep, James R., Roger White, and Karen L. Estep, eds. *Mapping Out Curriculum in Your Church: Cartography for Christian Pilgrims*. Nashville: B&H Academic, 2012.

Gordan, William R., II, Rosemarye T. Taylor, and Peter F. Oliva. *Developing the Curriculum: Improved Outcomes Through Systems Approaches*. 9th ed. Pearson Educational Leadership. New York: Pearson Education, 2019.

Ornstein, Allan C., and Francis Hunkins. *Curriculum: Foundations, Principles, and Issues*. 4th ed. New York: Pearson Education, 2004.

Taba, Hilda. *Curriculum Development: Theory and Practice*. New York: Harcourt, Brace and World, 1962.

Tyler, Ralph. *Basic Principles of Curriculum and Instruction*. Chicago: University of Chicago Press, 1949.

CHAPTER 10

THE TEACHING-LEARNING PROCESS: A LOOK AT LEARNING STYLES

Jim Thames

My experience over the years is that most teachers are more concerned about how they teach than they are with how their students learn. An emphasis in this book is the importance of being learner-focused teachers. This should lead us as teachers to ask a related question. If we want our students to learn, do we ever ask, "How do they learn?" This chapter will seek to answer that question.

Whole books have been written on learning style, and one can descend into the theoretical quickly. This chapter focuses less on the research and theory behind learning styles and more on the practical implications for teachers. If our goal in teaching God's Word faithfully is to help our learners not only understand God's intent and meaning but also put it into practice as a settled way of life, then we ought to do all we can to facilitate learning in the ways best suited to their learning styles.

DEPENDING TOO MUCH ON LEARNING STYLES

We need to establish from the outset that learning can and does take place regardless of attention to learning styles. In short, one cannot say that learning will not take place unless each student's preferred learning style is identified and addressed. Many factors impact human learning (aptitude, commitment, focus, desire to learn, etc.). It is also inaccurate to say that people simply cannot learn well unless they are taught in ways that accommodate their learning style. An article on whether learning-style theories are valid indicates that while determining your learning style "might help you learn about yourself, it might not help you learn."[1] Khazan's article addressed the work of Neil Fleming, who pioneered the VARK (visual, aural, read/write, kinesthetic) theory of learning styles,[2] which became one of the more popular ways of categorizing learning styles and is similar to the categories of learning styles later presented in the chapter. Khazan states that even Fleming in later years cautioned against putting too much stock in learning styles.

Julie Dirksen likewise cautions against depending too much on learning styles.[3] Depending too much on learning styles is difficult, she notes, because it is hard to measure learning styles, and there really are no practical ways to adapt learning to styles. Dirksen also notes that some benefit can be gleaned by recognizing that not everyone learns in exactly the same way.

These are wise cautions. Accepting the validity of learning styles will not necessarily mean students will learn better. A good teacher will likely be able to facilitate student learning regardless of a student's learning style. At the same time, a bad or careless teacher might not facilitate learning even if cognizant of and attentive to an individual student's preferred style of learning. There is risk in focusing too much on a person's style of learning because it may unnecessarily focus on learning style instead of actual learning.

So if understanding the learning styles of our students does not guarantee they will learn any better, then why spend a chapter of a book on "teaching" to focus on the learning process and learning styles? Because being aware of the different ways people learn is a tool that will help teachers focus less on what *they will do* and more on what the *student will learn*.

1. Olga Khazan, "The Myth of 'Learning Styles,'" *The Atlantic*, April 11, 2018, https://www.theatlantic.com/science/archive/2018/04/the-myth-of-learning-styles/557687.
2. Neil Fleming and David Baume, "Learning Styles Again: VARKing Up the Right Tree!," *Educational Developments*, SEDA Ltd. 7, no. 4 (Nov. 2006): 4–7.
3. Julie Dirksen, *Design for How People Learn*, 2nd ed. (San Francisco: New Riders, 2015), 53–54.

LEARNING PROCESS AND LEARNING STYLES

It is obvious that God designed human beings to learn. We start out life as a blank slate, Locke's *tabula rasa* (at least most of us believe we are blank slates; we were not aware of what we were like when we were born). Since we are all created by God in his image, we can safely say that all human beings learn similarly. But even though we are similar in design and function, God obviously created us to be different from each other. Just as we have different personality styles and tendencies, we also process new material differently and learn differently.

Examine the learning process in general. In other words, what is the typical process learners go through in acquiring and implementing new learning? Much of this discussion owes credit to Bernice McCarthy, a well-known educator who developed the 4MAT Learning System[4] based on David Kolb's theory of experiential learning.[5]

Learning is cyclical and ongoing throughout a person's life. We learn based on our experiences. Our perception of what we learn is colored by our experiences and preconceptions. The goal of education is that this new learning, however the learner perceives it, is put into practice. One hopes that over time this "practice" will become a habit and eventually become the learner's new experience, which restarts the process.

Because experience impacts learning, good teachers must take into consideration the experiences a student brings to the learning environment. Let's look at an example. You are teaching Colossians 3:13, which focuses on forgiving those who have harmed us, just as Christ has forgiven us. If your student has grown up in a family where forgiveness was routinely asked for and granted, this is an easy concept to grasp (I should add, however, not necessarily easy to do). But what if your student grew up in a home that didn't practice forgiveness but regularly encountered manipulation, grudge-holding, and prolonged anger? How will that student process forgiveness?

There is a story about an old gentleman who came up to a pastor who had just preached a sermon on forgiveness, with special attention

4. Bernice McCarthy, *The 4MAT System: Teaching to Learning Styles with Right/Left Mode Techniques* (Barrington, IL: EXCEL Inc., 1987).
5. David Kolb, *Experiential Learning: Experience as the Source of Learning and Development* (Englewood Cliffs, NJ: Prentice Hall, 1983).

on the forgiveness graciously available to anyone who has put his or her faith and trust in the finished work of Christ on the cross. The pastor had emphasized that this forgiveness is extended to anyone, no matter how heinous their sins and offenses may have been. The message was clear, so the old man asked the pastor if he believed God would have forgiven Adolph Hitler had he repented and turned to Christ in faith. The pastor, acting on sound theology, said that if Adolph Hitler had recognized his sin, repented, and turned to Christ in faith, yes, God would forgive Adolph Hitler. To this, the old man pointed his finger in the pastor's face and vehemently said, "I would *never* believe in a God who would forgive that man!" What the pastor did not know was that this man was Jewish and had experienced the Holocaust. He had also lost family in the Holocaust. The pastor's answer was biblically and theologically sound, but that old man's experience colored his understanding of forgiveness. The experiences of our students do make a difference in the learning process. The wise teacher takes this into consideration when he or she teaches.

The role of experience as students process new learning, especially from the Bible, will impact how they perceive and accept the truth of what they have learned. It may take some students much longer to get to the point of putting new truth into practice, but by depending on the Holy Spirit to facilitate life change, a student will eventually see the need to put biblical truth into practice. Constant practice is habit forming, and once habits are formed, the student's experience becomes a new normal.

In short, a good teacher understands the role of experience in the learning process. As students process truth in light of their experience and begin to see relevant ways to put that truth into practice, life experiences are transformed and in turn impact new learning. The process continues throughout the student's life.

LEARNING STYLES

We have seen how human beings learn in general and how experience impacts learning and life change. But what about learning styles? Do people really learn differently from one another? Does understanding the student's learning style help ensure better learning? As mentioned earlier, teaching to a student's learning style alone is not a guarantee the student will learn. However, I believe understanding learning styles will help us become better teachers because it will help us understand our students better and how they process new learning, experience notwithstanding.[6]

While the teaching process itself as discussed above is true of all learning, how we process new learning is largely related to style. Just as people have different personality traits, they also have different ways of learning, that is, different ways of perceiving the world and processing what is perceived. This is what is meant by *learning styles*. It is reasonable to assume that recognizing students' learning styles will help the teacher present material in a way that best enables students to learn.

LeFever has adopted the four primary learning styles identified by Bernice McCarthy—innovative or imaginative learners, analytic learners, common sense learners, and dynamic learners (see Figure 10.1 below).

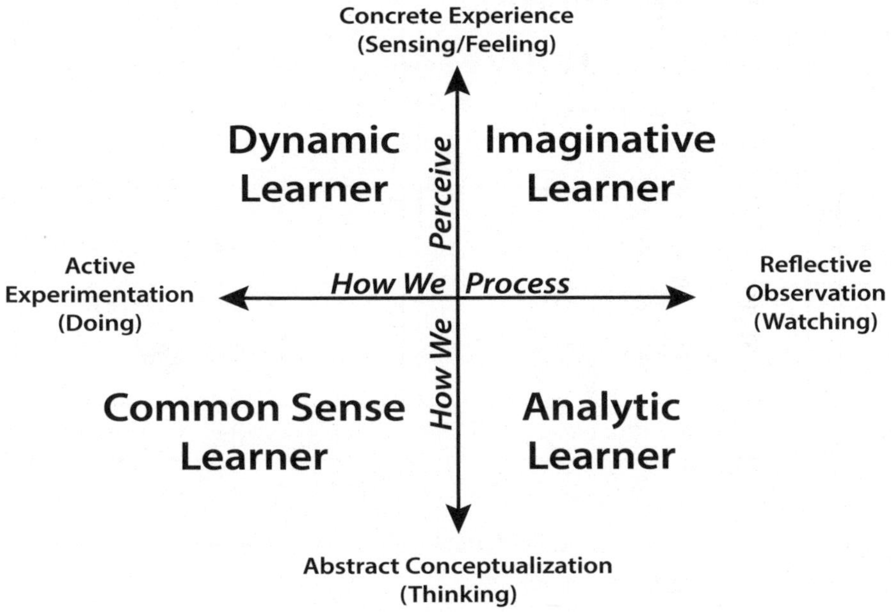

Figure 10.1: Learning Styles Based on David Kolb and Bernice McCarthy

6. I am indebted to the work of Marlene D. LeFever, *Learning Styles: Reaching Everyone God Gave You to Teach* (Colorado Springs: David C. Cook, 2004). LeFever is widely acknowledged in Christian education circles as the premier voice in understanding how people learn and finding ways to adapt their teaching to each student's learning style. Her work in learning styles was a creative blend of her own understanding of learning styles with the 4MAT system of learning styles.

A closer look at LeFever's categories reveals two constructs—people orientation and kinesthetic orientation.[7] On the people-orientation scale, innovative/imaginative learners and dynamic learners tend to learn better in community. They learn with and from others. Analytic and common sense learners tend to learn better on their own. On the kinesthetic scale, innovative/imaginative learners and analytic learners are mental learners, while common sense and dynamic learners are actively, physically involved in the learning process. With these two constructs in mind, I would chart the same four learning styles as in Figure 10.2 below, which differs from the order of the quadrants in Figure 10.1.

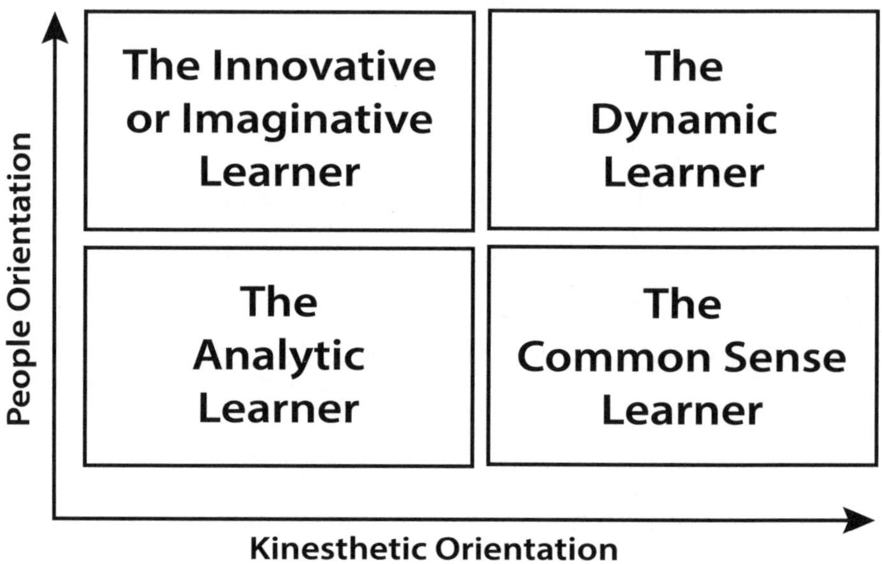

Figure 10.2: Based on Bernice McCarthy and Marlene LeFever

When teaching about learning styles to those who are considering a ministry that includes teaching God's word, one could begin class by asking students to pick the learning style that best reflects

7. "Kinesthetic" in this context describes physical movement in the learning process. Kinesthetic learners are physically involved in the learning process. They are "hands-on" learners.

how they see themselves in light of the two constructs. If they tend to be thoughtful, thinking individuals and like interacting and learning with others, they will likely select the innovative or imaginative learning style. If they are thinking people who like processing their thoughts alone, they usually choose the analytic learning style. If they like to work and learn alone but are hands-on in the learning process, they typically identify with common sense learners. If they tend to be actively engaged in the learning process but in community with others, they will opt for the dynamic learning style. Let's describe each of these four learning styles to help clarify how each is unique.

Innovative or Imaginative Learners

Innovative/imaginative learners are high on the people-orientation scale but low on the kinesthetic-orientation scale. Imaginative learners listen and share. They tend to be sociable and friendly. They are sensitive and in tune with their feelings and the feelings of others. They are empathetic and keen observers of human nature with a natural ability to sense in others when something is not quite right. It is hard to get away with simply saying "I'm fine" when you are not fine, especially with innovative/imaginative people. Innovative/imaginative learners value people above product. They are "idea" people and care especially about the ideas of others. An important part of their learning process is to learn from others along the way. Group work is important for teaching innovative/imaginative learners.

Analytic Learners

If innovative/imaginative learners listen and share, analytic learners listen and think. Analytic learners like logically, sequentially presented information. They are curious about ideas but value facts, figures, and theories. Analytic learners are notetakers—copious, thorough, well-organized notes. (In fact, when you were needing to cram for an exam in college and your notes were woefully inadequate for the task, the person whose notes you borrowed was likely an analytic learner.) Analytic learners often come across as impersonal. They do like people; they just prefer to work alone. Analytic learners love to set long-range plans. If you are teaching analytic learners, focus on a well-organized, systematic lecture.

> *Personal Anecdote*: A clue to the kind of learner I am may help here. When I began my seminary studies, the seminary catalog listed all the courses offered by each seminary department. I loved to read through the hundreds of course descriptions. The most wonderful thing about those course descriptions was that each included a schedule of when each of the courses would be offered. Some were offered every semester, but many of the electives followed a cycle. Some might be offered in the fall semester of even-numbered years, some the spring semester of odd-numbered years, and so on. This allowed me to plan out my full, four-year seminary degree program with all the courses I was required to take along with all the courses I wanted to take. I had my entire seminary career mapped out! Only one problem: the seminary did not follow the catalog! Another thing about analytic learners: lack of order and detail can be very frustrating to them.

Common Sense Learners

Innovative/imaginative learners *listen and share.* Analytic learners *listen and think*. Common sense learners *listen and do*. They are physically active in the learning process, constantly in motion. They cannot help it; they tend to fidget. Common sense learners value action, and they are goal oriented. They want to be shown something and then left alone to try it themselves. Common sense learners learn through demonstration and practice. They do not particularly enjoy lectures except to be instructed on how they should do things themselves. Like analytic learners, common sense learners can tend to be impersonal because they want to work alone. If a common sense learner learns by doing, he or she generally wants to be involved in the entire learning process, not just part of it. Otherwise, they may feel is if they have missed out on learning an important part of the process, the part someone else was a part of.

Years ago, I bought an old motorcycle that didn't run very well. Also, I tend to be a common-sense learner, as well as an analytic learner (the common denominator is I tend to be low on the people-orientation scale). I determined to completely dismantle my motorcycle and rebuild it. It was important that I be involved in the entire process. Had someone else helped me with the transmission, for example, I would not have learned much about motorcycle transmissions. I like people and enjoy working with them, but as a common sense learner, I tend to want to do things myself so I can see and understand the whole, not just parts of the whole.

Dynamic Learners

If innovative/imaginative learners *listen and share*, if analytic learners *listen and think*, and if common sense learners *listen and do*, what is left for dynamic learners? It is quite simple: dynamic learners do not listen; you just turn them loose! Dynamic learners tend to be leaders. They work well with people and enjoy working with people on projects. Dynamic learners are experimenters. They like student-directed learning. They are future-oriented, always thinking ahead to the opportunities and potential drawbacks to a course of action. Dynamic learners are strongly intuitive. And most importantly, they demand flexibility. A teacher should avoid telling a dynamic learner there is only one way to do something or "we've always done it that way." How does a teacher work with a dynamic learner? Provide options along with the pros and cons of those options, and then let the student decide on the best course of action. Students will flourish under that kind of learning environment.

As previously mentioned, a teacher could start a discussion on learning styles by asking students to choose their learning style based on whether they consider themselves people-oriented or kinesthetically oriented. Once that is done, the instructor could describe the characteristics of each style and then ask if the additional information made a difference in the students' first choices. Some would stick with their first choice, others would change, and still others would be unsure because they found themselves with characteristics of more than one. They might be able to place themselves fairly high on the people-orientation scale but would be unsure if they were more innovative or more dynamic; or they might not be sure if they were analytic or common sense, but they definitely considered themselves lower on the people-orientation scale. Confusion might occur between the innovative style and the analytic style, but both are primarily thinking, mentally processing learners. Highly kinesthetic learners might see common traits between common sense learners and dynamic learners; some actually see in themselves elements of all four. The point of the activity is to get students to recognize the characteristics of different types of learners and to recognize their own preferences in learning styles.

Statistics might help here. Anyone familiar with social science or behavioral research will be familiar with the normal curve or normal distribution (see Figure 10.3).

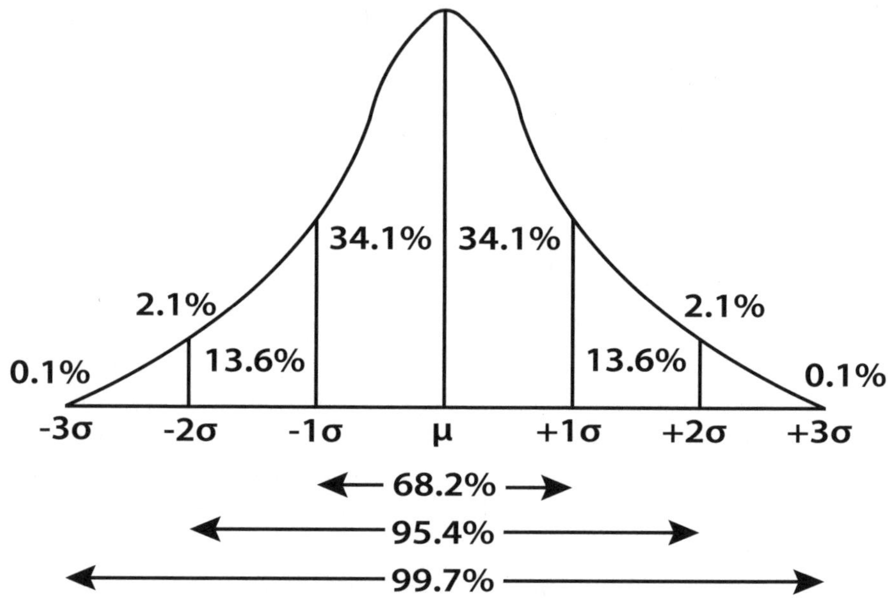

Figure 10.3: The Normal Distribution

The normal curve graphs the distribution of human characteristics or traits across a population. Learning styles would be considered traits and would be distributed normally across all human beings. The normal curve indicates that a majority of people (68 percent) tend toward the middle, or the "norm." Another 27 percent are further from the norm. Another 4 percent even further from the norm, and a small percentage of people (less than 1 percent) are outliers. What does this mean for learning styles?

Figure 10.4 shows how the normal distribution impacts learning styles.

The dotted circles roughly represent the normal distribution and illustrate that 68 percent of people have a learning style that tends toward the middle of the chart. Another 27 percent are farther from the middle, and another 4 percent even farther from the middle. The last 1 percent are nearly off the chart. You could say that learners in this last group almost define the categories!

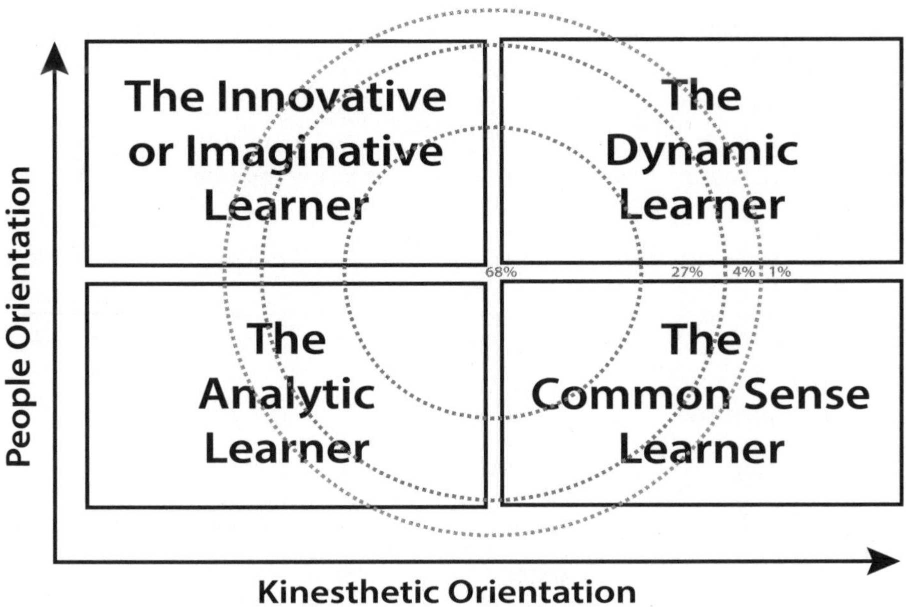

Figure 10.4: Learning Styles Adapted from Bernice McCarthy and Marlene LeFever

So how does the normal curve help us when considering learning styles? Simply this: while statistics would indicate that there is a perfectly average human being, in reality, the vast majority of people are not "normal" (statistically speaking, of course). Humans are different, and while roughly two-thirds may cluster toward the norm, they are still different. Practically, this means for the majority of learners, an imaginative learning style is not that different from a dynamic, common sense, or analytic learning style. In other words, the closer one gets to the middle, or the "norm," the closer he or she gets to others with different predominant learning styles, but differences still exist. It also makes it more difficult to determine the predominant learning style of a student and indicates that the majority of students may have characteristics of other learning styles. No wonder focusing on learning styles can be difficult for the teacher, but that does not mean it does not have value when considering how students are likely to learn.

LEARNING STYLES AND LEARNING TAXONOMIES

Students who have had any formal education classes may be familiar with the work of Benjamin Bloom and others in developing what are called the taxonomies of the cognitive, affective, and psychomotor domains.[8] For now, a brief overview may help.

The cognitive domain is the thinking/intellectual domain. The affective domain is the domain of the heart, emphasizing feelings, beliefs, and values. The psychomotor domain is the behavioral domain, the emphasis being on activity in learning. If one were to impose the domains over learning styles, it might look something like Figure 10.5.

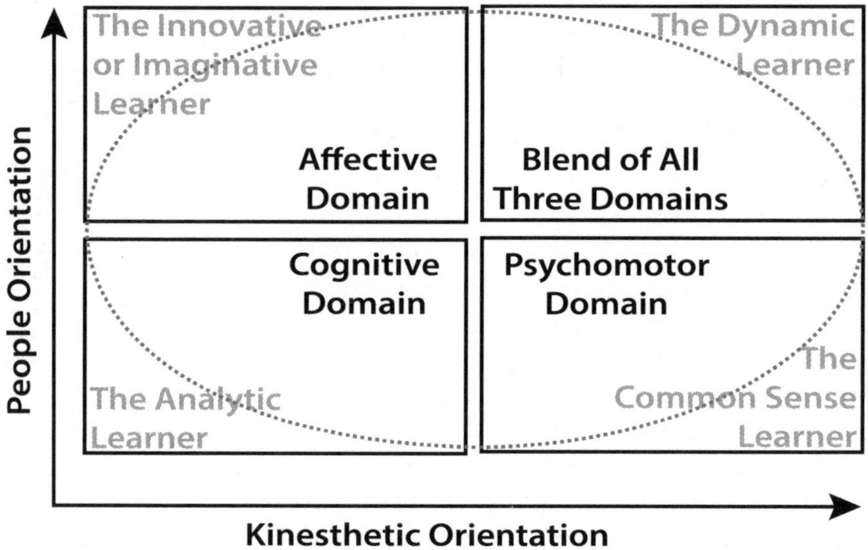

Figure 10.5: Learning Styles and Domains

When one overlays learning styles with learning domains, we see correlations between the cognitive domain and analytic learning style. We also see a connection between the affective domain and the innovative/imaginative learning style. Common sense learners correlate with the psychomotor domain. One might consider the dynamic learning style to be a more balanced reflection of all three domains.

All human beings are a mix of all learning domains. We often refer to these as knowledge, attitudes, and actions; as head, heart, and hands;

8. See Benjamin S. Bloom et al., eds., *Taxonomy of Educational Objectives: Handbook I, Cognitive Domain* (Harlow, UK: Longman, 1956); Lorin W. Anderson and David Krathwohl, eds., *A Taxonomy for Learning, Teaching, and Assessing: A Revision of Bloom's Taxonomy of Educational Objectives* (Harlow, UK: Longman, 2001); and Anita J. Harrow, *A Taxonomy of the Psychomotor Domain* (New York: David McKay, 1972).

or as thinking, feeling, and doing. We all learn things cognitively using the minds God has blessed us with. Through the work of the Holy Spirit, the things we know become important to us; they begin to shape our values. Once we begin to value something, the logical result is action. In short, we will always do what is most important to us.

Just as with learning styles, each person reflects a different balance of the three learning domains. Many people tend to function more in the cognitive domain, some more in the affective, and some more in the psychomotor. Rick Yount illustrates these domains using an all-time favorite TV series and the related movie spin-offs, *Star Trek*.[9] Whether you are a fan of the original series from the 1960s or familiar with one of its many spin-offs in recent years, certain characters are familiar to most of us. These characters also perfectly illustrate the differences in the learning domains and learning styles.

If one is familiar with *Star Trek*, one can begin to guess which characters illustrate certain learning domains and styles. The character that best illustrates the cognitive domain and analytic learning style is the first officer of the starship *Enterprise*, Mr. Spock, the Vulcan who relies purely on logic. He is analytical in the extreme and values logic far above emotion. In fact, he avoids emotion at every turn.

The character who best illustrates the innovative/imaginative learning style or the affective domain is Dr. Leonard McCoy, the medical doctor in the series. He feels deeply about everything, strives to build relationships, and when he is upset or frustrated, it is usually with Mr. Spock.

The character who illustrates the common sense learner best or the psychomotor domain is Mr. Scott, the chief engineer of the *Enterprise*. He can take the facts, theories, and logic of Spock and put them into practice. He is the one who can fix the *Enterprise*, seemingly with a rubber band and duct tape at just the last second before the ship is annihilated by an enemy alien species.

But of all the characters, the one who appears to be the balance of all three learning domains, the one who best illustrates the dynamic learning style, is Captain James T. Kirk. Depending on the episode, he can out-logic Mr. Spock, out-feel Dr. McCoy, and come up with a miracle engineering fix at the last moment just like Scotty.

9. William (Rick) Yount, *Created to Learn: A Christian Teacher's Introduction to Educational Psychology*, 2nd ed. (Nashville: B&H Academic, 2010), 399–400.

These characters illustrate the variety of learning styles a teacher is likely to face in the classroom. Take a moment right now to think of people you know who would illustrate the overlapping learning domains and learning styles. But as we have already discussed, for every student whose learning style is obvious, there are many more whose styles are less obvious, largely because the majority of people are not significantly different from one another. If that is true, why bother focusing on learning styles at all? Because understanding how people learn will help us think of better ways to teach with respect for the variety of learning styles and therefore better help all our students grasp the truths of God's Word as we teach, providing them with greater joy and fulfillment in the process.

WHY CONSIDERING LEARNING STYLES IS IMPORTANT

What is the point of all this? Why is this important for teachers? The following observations will help bring this all together.

Most People Do Not Enjoy Learning the Way You Do

If human characteristics and learning styles are distributed somewhat equally across the entire human population, then you could argue that each of the four learning styles would represent about 25 percent of the population. So if you consider yourself an analytic learner, you are like 25 percent of people. But this means that 75 percent of people will enjoy the learning process in ways different from the way you prefer. Be cognizant that all four learning styles are present in your classes. All of your students may learn something from your teaching regardless of how you teach, but if you develop teaching strategies that address the learning styles of all your learners, they will better appreciate the learning process and enjoy learning more. And when students enjoy learning, they will learn better.

You Will Tend to Teach the Way You Learn

This should be obvious. If the teacher is an analytic learner, he or she will tend to teach by well-organized and developed lectures and will focus on the transmission of facts and figures. The analytic teacher will value detailed exegesis and exposition of Bible passages and will focus on those in the class presentation. Analytic learners in the class will be fully engaged, but the innovative, common sense, and dynamic learners less so.

Most Students Will Not Respond as Well to Your Teaching Style

For those few people who are learning-style neutral (those would be in the middle of the normal curve), whether teachers or students, it would be true that teaching style and learning style overlap nicely. But if the majority of the students in the class do not process information like the teacher does—and teachers naturally tend to teach the way they learn—it is likely many of the students in their classes will not enjoy or engage learning as much as we would like. Worse, many students may become discouraged with the learning process and withdraw, assuming they are somehow less capable of learning. While that assumption is rarely the case, the problem lies with teachers failing to recognize that all students benefit from being taught in ways that fully engage their learning styles.

UTILIZING LEARNING STYLES IN TEACHING

How do teachers adapt their natural teaching styles to the learning styles of their students? They do this by focusing on using a variety of methods in their teaching. Numerous teaching methods that can be employed in our classes, but some examples here might be helpful.

Innovative/imaginative learners will likely respond better to methods that involve them with other students. They enjoy group work and discussion. They enjoy learning activities that allow them to engage with others in the learning process. Drama, skits, and role-playing activities interest them. Innovative learners do not particularly care for nonstop lectures, tests, working by themselves on a project, asynchronous online learning, or other activities that do not allow interaction with others. Neither are they particularly responsive to teachers who approach learning analytically or to common sense teachers. In other words, give your innovative and imaginative learners the opportunity to engage others in the learning process.

Analytic learners love clearly presented, well-organized lectures that focus on facts and theories. They enjoy learning activities that allow them to work alone. They actually like pop quizzes or Bible trivia games because it gives them an opportunity to prove that they have learned. On the other hand, analytic learners do not like group activities. They are not as impressed with what others know, except for maybe the teacher. They will participate in discussion as long as they have an opportunity to present material they have learned, which makes group discussion with analytic learners fairly one-sided. Analytic learners respond better to teachers who stay on task and seek to involve students in learning activities.

Common sense learners respond well to demonstration and then being left alone to work on their own. They like experimentation. They enjoy problem-solving. They do not like long, fact-filled lectures. They do not respond well to lots of required reading or test-taking. Because they tend to prefer working alone, group projects, even activities, are not as engaging for them. If you teach common sense learners, give them latitude to work on projects to learn by doing, not listening. And just like analytic learners, they do not respond as well to innovative/imaginative learner-style teachers.

Dynamic learners enjoy things like case studies, creative projects, dramatics, and assignments requiring originality. They like working in groups and tend to rise to the surface as natural leaders in the learning process. They want to have options in the learning process, to decide what they need to know rather than being told what they need to know. Dynamic learners do not respond well to analytic-style teachers, especially rigid and inflexible ones.

Being aware of the preferences of learners based on their learning styles can help teachers begin thinking of ways to address the needs of all their students. Being more flexible in your teaching methods and approaches will ensure that you will be engaging all your students meaningfully. Remember, students do not expect the learning environment to accommodate their style. But even if they do not know they have a learning style, they will appreciate the opportunities given them to thrive in the learning process.

CONCLUSION

It may be true that a teacher's understanding of learning styles will not make everyone a successful learner. It may also be true that too much emphasis on understanding individual student learning styles may keep us from thinking of better ways to teach. While students may still learn even if we are not cognizant of their learning styles, how much more fulfilling and engaging might their educational experience be if attention is given to the fact that people do not all learn in the same way. As teachers of God's Word, it should be our passion to understand the variety of ways our students process knowledge and engage truth so that we might better help them grow in their knowledge of their Creator who made them as unique as a fingerprint or a snowflake. And in so doing, they might grow and become more like their Savior.

May God give us the wisdom and passion to understand how our students prefer to learn best and to tailor our teaching to make learning as effective and engaging for each of them as we can.

REFLECTION QUESTIONS

1. What might be some ways that you could adapt your teaching style to address the preferred learning style of many of your students?
2. List at least two different teaching methods that might resonate with imaginative learners; with common sense learners; with analytic learners; and with dynamic learners.
3. Can you think of other factors that impact learning other than learning styles? How might you employ those in your teaching?
4. Why do you think there might be a predominant learning style in your classes or in the classes of other teachers you know?

RECOMMENDED READING

Dirksen, Julie. *Design for How People Learn.* 2nd ed. San Francisco: New Riders, 2015.

Khazan, Olga. "The Myth of 'Learning Styles.'" *The Atlantic,* April 11, 2018.

LeFever, Marlene D. *Learning Styles: Reaching Everyone God Gave You to Teach.* Colorado Springs: David C. Cook. 2004.

McCarthy, Bernice. *The 4MAT System: Teaching to Learning Styles with Right/Left Mode Techniques.* Barrington, IL: EXCEL, Inc. 1987

McCarthy, Bernice. *The Learning Cycle, The 21st Century and Millennial Learners.* Wauconda, IL: About Learning, Inc., 2012.

Yount, William R. *Created to Learn: A Christian Teacher's Introduction to Educational Psychology.* 2nd ed. Nashville: B&H Academic, 2010.

CHAPTER 11

TEACHING FOR CHRIST-CENTERED CRITICAL THINKING

James Riley Estep Jr.

All too often Christian education is limited to *indoctrination*, which calls for people or groups to *uncritically* affirm something, even without fully understanding it.[1] *All* education may start out with indoctrination, such as knowing our ABCs in the established order, recognizing the meaning of mathematical symbols (+ - x ÷ < >), or even memorizing the books of the Bible in their canonical order. But if Christian education fails to proceed *beyond* indoctrination, it is doing a disservice to the student and the church.[2]

Everyone has assumptions, preformed opinions, prejudgments, even unquestioned affirmations, all of which are unknown or unacknowledged. Yet critical reflection makes students begin thinking, reassessing, reconsidering, and thus opening their minds to not only acknowledge but further develop and articulate their assumptions, opinions, judgments, and affirmations. *This is critical thinking*: knowing not only what you believe but why you believe it and with an awareness of your epistemology, how you know what you know. This chapter

1. Terence Copley, *Indoctrination, Education, and God: The Struggle for the Mind* (London: SPCK, 2005).
2. Stephen Snyder, "More Than Content," *Christian Education Journal* 15 (1994): 21–32.

will explore how to use critical thinking as a teaching strategy and how such strategies produce critical thinking, i.e., teaching with and for critical thinking.

DEFINING CRITICAL THINKING

Some Christian educators are reluctant to embrace critical thinking for numerous reasons. They may regard critical thinking as a mask for skepticism and cynicism. Likewise, Christian educators are often skeptical of critical thinking due to the logical fallacy of guilt by association. While critical thought existed prior to John Dewey,[3] he coined and popularized the phrase in his book *How We Think*,[4] which can be problematic for some Christian educators. Similarly, it has been linked to transformative learning theory, such as that of Jack Mezirow.[5] Carl Sagan described critical thinking as a "bologna detector," often illustrating it by finding fault with religious claims.[6] In the company of such individuals, critical thinking is often perceived as a threat to faith.

However, critical thinking is perhaps best recognized when it is *not* practiced. It is easy to identify noncritical thinking. It is like the meme where a student searches online for "What I want to be true," simply searching for affirmation rather than analysis. Consider that in the absence of critical thinking, a student would have no filter by which to assess the truth claims of any statement. We would have no intellectual brakes by which to call into question internet memes, the claims of a website, or even the beliefs of another religion. It would be like serving on a jury wherein the testimony of all the witnesses and the presentation of the prosecution and defense attorneys were accepted at face value, without cross-examination or serious examination of their statements.

Critical thinking focuses on challenging assumptions, or as Stephen Brookfield calls it, "hunting assumptions," determining their source, and then "checking assumptions" by assessing their validity.[7] As Hous-

3. Jonathan Haber, *Critical Thinking* (Cambridge, MA: MIT Press, 2020), 1–20.
4. John Dewey, *How We Think* (1933; repr., New York: Barnes & Noble, 2013).
5. Sue Marks, "Transformative Learning and Pedagogy: A Model for Christian English Teachers," *Journal of Christian Education*, 49 (2006): 7–22.
6. Carl Sagan, *The Demon-Haunted World: Science as a Candle in the Dark* (New York: Ballantine, 1995), 209–17.
7. Stephen D. Brookfield, *Teaching for Critical Thinking: Tools and Techniques to Help Students Question Their Assumptions* (San Francisco: Jossey-Bass, 2011), chapter 2, Kindle.

ton Heflin wrote, critical thinking "is the ability to challenge ideas we consider to be true. We may be entering a teaching experience with assumptions about our students, but to really know them we have to suspend judgment long enough to listen and learn."[8] Essentially, critical thinking moves the student from a know-it-all with knee-jerk reactions to new information toward a posture of clarifying, honing, and re-articulating their thoughts and ideals.

Robert von Oech, an American creativity theorist, classifies thinkers into four categories, depending on the purpose of their thinking:[9]

- *Explorer:* When you're *searching* for new information
- *Artist:* When you're turning resources into new *ideas*
- *Judge:* When you're *evaluating* the merits of an idea
- *Warrior:* When you're carrying your idea into *action*

Critical thinking belongs in each of the four categories to some degree but is indeed most prevalent in the person's role as "judge," wherein an idea must stand on its own merit and remain intact when challenged. The judge likewise must determine how new information relates to existing information, that is, how new learning relates to old learning.

Richard Paul and Linda Elder, founders of the Foundation for Critical Thinking, have defined critical thinking as "the ability and disposition to improve one's thinking by systematically subjecting it to intellectual self-assessment."[10] According to their theory, learners assimilate information in three ways:[11]

- *Inert Information:* Taking into the mind information that, though memorized, we do not understand, despite thinking we do
- *Activated Ignorance:* Taking into the mind and actively using information that is false, though we mistakenly think it is true

8. Houston Heflin, *Teaching Eutychus: Engaging Today's Learners with Passion and Creativity* (Abilene, TX: Abilene Christian University Press, 2012), 494.
9. Roger von Oech, *A Kick in the Seat of the Pants: Using Your Explorer, Artist, Judge, and Warrior to Be More Creative* (New York: Harper Perennial, 1986), 12–13.
10. Richard Paul and Linda Elder, "Critical Thinking: Implications for Instruction of the Stage Theory," *Journal of Developmental Education* 20, no. 3 (1997), 34.
11. Paul and Elder, "Critical Thinking: Implications for Instructions of the Stage Theory," 46.

- *Activated Knowledge:* Taking into the mind and actively using information that is not only true but that, when insightfully understood, leads us by implication to more and more knowledge

Critical thinking is essentially the process of moving from inert information through activated ignorance toward activated knowledge. The process is characterized by thinking that habitually practices reflection, self-examination, clarification, refining, and rearticulation of one's beliefs and convictions in light of new information.

IS CRITICAL THINKING CHRISTIAN? CAN IT BE?

Christian educators have often shied away from critical thinking because of its association with non-Christian theorists. However, critical thinking does *not* necessarily lead to skepticism, a cynical mindset, or nihilism. In fact, *most* advocates of critical thinking as a tool of education likewise advocate limits or guidelines to curb the unbridled slide toward nihilism. For example, one article posed the question: Are we teaching "critical thinking or just [being] critical?'" suggesting that humility can prevent critical thinking from degenerating into skepticism.[12] Others note that perhaps a more positive approach to critical thinking is to make it more about the community than the individual and hence foster more constructive thinking.[13] Advocates of critical thinking acknowledge it has limits and that its intent is to construct ideas, not deconstruct reality. Critical thinking is not the problem. The problem is why and to what end it is applied. But is it Christian?

Critical thinking is required of Christians studying Scripture in Bible college or university and seminary because of the very nature of the Bible and the student.[14] For example, Donald Sanders suggests that critical thinking can facilitate Christian spiritual formation when applied in a context that affirms God's revelations, both general and natural, as well as the work of the Holy Spirit to achieve conclusions

12. Heidi Oberholtzer Lee, "Critical Thinking or Just Critical?: Reintroducing Humility to the Literature Classroom," *Christian Scholar Review* 39, no. 4 (2010): 421–37.
13. Perry Shaw, "Moving from Critical to Constructive Thinking," *Evangelical Review of Theology* 45, no. 2 (2021): 128–40.
14. Elna K. Solvang, "Thinking Developmentally: The Bible, the First-Year College Student, and Diversity," *Teaching Theology and Religion* 7, no. 4 (2004): 223–29.

that are more than temporal relativistic pragmatics.[15] Similarly, developing one's ability to think critically can aid in apologetics, both in the mind of the believer and unbeliever.[16]

JESUS'S TEACHING AS FOSTERING CRITICAL THINKING

Chapter 1 introduced us to Jesus as a teacher, one employing a variety of methods. Now we look at how Jesus was often critical of *noncritical* thinkers, especially when noncritical thinking led individuals toward blind obedience to religious leaders.[17] While present in all the Synoptic Gospels, such instances of challenging critical thinking are most often depicted in Matthew's gospel, e.g., healing a crippled man on the Sabbath (Matt. 12:12–14), breaking the traditions of the elders (Matt. 15:1–67), and his dialogue with Pharisees and religious leaders about divorce and remarriage (Matt. 19). Jesus's classic response to a binary question (yes/no) by asking a more probative question was not a way of avoiding the question at all but a way of facilitating critical thinking in the questioner's mind.

More directly, Jesus engaged his opponents in critical thinking, particularly in a situation of conflict. When Jesus was in conflict with religious authorities, he used critical thinking to challenge their assumptions and conclusion. Hence, Kingsbury describes Jesus as actually provoking, triggering, or inciting conflict with the religious authorities to create a more conducive learning environment.[18] Jesus's relationship with the religious authorities was weak, but his frequent contact with them led to the challenge approach to critical thinking. He challenged their assumptions (Matt. 22:23–33; Mark 12:18–27; Luke 20:27–40), their allegations (Matt. 12:22–28; Mark 3:20–30, and their hypocrisy (Matt. 9:1–8; Mark 2:1–12; Luke 5:17–26). He was forcing them to critique themselves before critiquing him, which is essential to

15. Don Sanders, "From Critical Thinking to Spiritual Maturity: Connecting the Apostle Paul and John Dewey," *Christian Education Journal* 15, no. 1 (2018): 96–98.
16. Gregory Koukl and Lee Strobel, *Tactics: A Game Plan for Discussing Your Christian Convictions* (Grand Rapids: Zondervan, 2009). Cf. William R. Osborne, "Thinking Critically, Reading Faithfully: Critical Biblical Scholarship in the Christian College Classroom," *Criswell Theological Review* 11, no. 2 (2014): 79–89.
17. Lawrence O. Richards, "Critical Thinking and Christian Perspective," *Christian Education Journal* 15, no. 1 (1994): 17–19.
18. Jack Dean Kingsbury, *Conflict in Mark: Jesus, Authorities, Disciples* (Minneapolis: Augsburg Fortress, 1991), 85–96.

critical thinking spiritual growth; the closed mindset of the noncritical thinker must be overcome.

PAUL'S USE OF CRITICAL THINKING

Paul demonstrated critical thinking not only in Romans but even more so in 1 Corinthians. Paul rises to the challenge of facilitating critical thinking in the Corinthian believers. He uses what New Testament scholars call an A^1–B–A^2 format, wherein he raises a subject of controversy (A^1), then shifts subject matter to a point of agreement (B), and then returns to the original point of controversy using the agreed-upon principle to inform their thinking (A^2). This literary pattern is employed to change their minds by assessing their previously held conclusion in light of a new perspective.

We can see several of these cycles throughout 1 Corinthians, but see, for example, 1 Corinthians 5–7. Paul opens the section with an accusation again the Corinthians as to how they have addressed a case of incest in the church (5:1–13), to which he expects resistance because they do not recognize the wrong (5:2) and because of their seeming unwillingness to pronounce judgment on those involved (A^1). However, Paul suddenly turns his attention to a matter on which the Corinthians and he agree (B) in chapter 6, which describes how to address disputes between believers without involving the civil, pagan authorities, noting that we can do this since in the last days "we will judge angels" (6:3a NIV), so surely temporal matters are far easier for us. Then Paul *returns* to the original subject (A^2), the matter of incest and their unwillingness to correctly address it, using what he just affirmed regarding their abilities to make godly and sound judgments on such matters. Now he encourages them to apply the same logic to this circumstance and render a judgment on it, since they are already in the practice of rendering similar judgments (6:9–20). Paul facilitates critical thinking in the mind of the Corinthians to correct their errors.

CRITICAL THINKING AND SPIRITUAL FORMATION

Paul in Romans 12:1–2 (NASB 1995) writes, "Therefore I urge you, brethren, by the mercies of God, to present your bodies a living and holy sacrifice, acceptable to God, which is your spiritual service of worship. And do not be conformed to this world, but be *transformed by the renewing of your mind*, so that you may *prove what the will of God is*, that which is good and acceptable and perfect" (emphasis added). Sanders concludes, "Paul commanded Christians to engage in critical thinking regarding their faith and conduct. While both verses are full of meaning and application, v. 2 states the purpose of critical thinking for the Christian is to pursue the will of God and the goal is to live in accordance with that revealed will."[19]

The Search Institute, led by Eugene Roehlkepartain, has continuously demonstrated the correlation (though not causation) of a "higher thinking climate" and spiritual growth.[20] Christian educators are deeply concerned with the spiritual formation of all age groups. More specifically, the idea of intergenerational education, as an integral part of Christian education, and "passing the baton" from one generation to the next are perhaps more immediate concerns to us than to others. Yet we often rely on catechesis, Christianity 101 classes, or new member classes, for instance, approaches that are typically dependent on indoctrination as their sole approach to instruction. While it may be suitable for new believers, helping them critically reflect on their pre-Christian beliefs and convictions would likewise benefit their continued spiritual growth.

Critical thinking, whether individual or corporate, creates an environment that is conducive to Christian spiritual formation. Steve Fortosis comments about the factors contributing to spiritual formation in his model of spiritual formation:

> As in other structural theories, Christian growth takes place most readily when it is spurred by dissonance. That is, in our encounters with new information and situations that throw us off balance, we attempt to understand and adjust to them and, thus, resolve the dissonance (Steele, 1990). Piaget (1970) terms this process disequilibration; Erikson (1980) describes it as growth crises. These dissonant situations may not be upsetting or tragic—even a job promotion or a birth in the family produces stress. Erikson claims that these are simply turning

19. Sanders, "From Critical Thinking to Spiritual Maturity," 98.
20. Eugene Roehlkepartain, *The Teaching Church: Moving Christian Education to Center Stage* (Nashville: Abingdon Press, 1993).

points or points of decision that can result in either growth or stagnation, depending upon one's response.[21]

Critical thinking is *not* an end but rather a means. When engaged without a specific purpose, without inherent limitations, critical thinking can be counterproductive and even destructive. However, it is indeed possible to use critical thinking to facilitate the process of spiritual formation, as well as beneficial for educational administration in Christian education.

THE THEORY AND PROCESS OF CRITICAL THINKING

Critical thinking does not occur instantaneously; it develops over time. For this reason, critical thinking can be described as developing in stages. The formation of critical thinking parallels taxonomies of cognitive development (see chapter 5). The following is a summation of the stage theory of the development of critical thinking proposed by Stephen Greenlaw, Professor Emeritus of Economics at the University of Mary Washington, and Stephen DeLoach, Professor of Economics at Elon University.[22]

- Level 1—One-Dimensional Descriptions: Students can define terms, paraphrase information, and restate a question but add little or nothing new to the issue or question. Thinking is underdeveloped, with words, concepts, and phrases all having a singular meaning without any alternatives. Similarly, questions require a singular response, only one correct response. Thinking is virtually binary: yes/no, right/wrong.
- Level 2—Simplistic Selections: Students are aware of alternative responses to a situation or question but are quick to select one option without fully exploring other alternatives. They tend to make unsupported assertions or simplistic arguments to affirm their chosen option. Thinking is still somewhat binary, but students realize that others may not choose as they did.
- Level 3—Basic Analysis/Reasoning: At this stage, students begin to move beyond binary thinking. Students make a signif-

21. Steve Fortosis, "A Developmental Model for Stages of Growth in Christian Formation," *Religious Education* 87, no. 2 (1992): 295–96.
22. Stephen A. Greenlaw and Stephen B. DeLoach, "Teaching Critical Thinking with Electronic Discussion," *Journal of Economic Education* 34, no. 1 (2003): 36–52.

icant effort to construct an argument or to analyze multiple arguments by appealing to simple evidence for support.

- Level 4—Theoretical Inference: Students use hermeneutics and theology to make a cohesive argument, i.e., they connect the dots.
- Level 5—Empirical Inference: Students introduce empirical evidence to strengthen their theological argument; they examine appropriate biblical passages and theological insights to evaluate the validity of an argument and draw a conclusion based upon these results.
- Level 6—Merging Values with Analysis: Students move beyond objective analysis to incorporate subjective interest.

As with any teaching method, our approach to teaching critical thinking must facilitate the process of developing critical thinking, changing the characteristics of the learners as they develop their critical thinking skills.

THE CHARACTER OF CRITICAL THINKERS

What does character have to do with critical thinking? Critical thinking is more than a cognitive exercise. It includes one's attitude and integrity. Elder and Paul speak of three kinds of critical thinkers: (1) The uncritical person, who is "good hearted but self-deceived"; (2) the self-serving critical person, who is "unethical, self-righteous, and self-deceived"; and (3) the fair-minded critical person, who exhibits an "ethical, empathetic and just" character.[23] Similarly, Robert Ennis, researcher and professor emeritus at the University of Illinois and is considered an expert in the field of critical thinking, speaks of three "dispositions" of critical thinkers:

1. "Care about 'getting it right' or, more broadly, to care about coming up with the best, most unbiased answer."
2. "Care to be honest and clear about what is written, thought, and said."
3. "Care about worth and dignity of every person."[24]

23. Richard Paul and Linda Elder, *The Miniature Guide to Critical Thinking: Concepts and Tools* (New York: Rowman and Littlefield, 2020), 12–13.
24. Robert Ennis, *Critical Thinking* (London: Pearson, 1995), xviii.

4. Critical thinking, if it is to be constructive, requires the student to possess a character that reflects intellectual humility, courage, empathy, autonomy, integrity, perseverance, confidence in reason, and fair mindedness. Paul and Elder tie the process of the formation of critical thinking to the shifts in character within the student, as depicted in Figure 11.1.[25]

UNCRITICAL		**CRITICAL**
Egocentric		Altruistic
Sociocultural Specific		Universal Principles
Egocentric Defenses	→	Fair-Mindedness
Intellectual Arrogance		Intellectual Humility
Rationalizations		Integrity
A priori Assumptions		*Challenged* Assumptions

1. Unreflective	**2. Challenged**	**3. Beginning**	**4. Practicing**	**5. Advanced**	**6. Master**
We are unaware of significant problems with our thinking.	We become aware of problems in our thinking.	We try to improve our thinking, but without regular practice.	We recognize the necessity of regular practice to improve our thinking.	We advance in accordance with our routine practices.	We become skilled and insightful thinking people; it is second nature!
I do not see the need to challenge my thinking or perceptions.	Am I *willing* to take active steps to take command of my thinking?	What am I doing to take command of my thinking?	What am I doing on a daily basis to take command of my thinking . . . implement Stage 3 thinking	Am I developing depth of understanding, deeper levels of problem-solving?	Am I living my basic values? Do I have an integrated worldview?

Figure 11.1: Formation of Critical Thinking

Figure 11.1 shows the transition from more self-centered, self-serving, and self-vindicating kind of thinkers, unaware of their epistemological assumptions, toward those who are less dependent on themselves and more reflective of objective, assessed information, precise

25. Based on Richard Paul and Linda Elder, "Critical Thinking: A Stage Thinking of Critical Thinking: Part 2," *Journal of Developmental Education* 20, no. 2 (1996): 34–35; Richard Paul and Linda Elder, *Critical Thinking: Tools for Taking Charge of Your Learning and Your Life* (Upper Saddle River, NJ: Prentice-Hall, 2001).

thinkers aware of their epistemological assumptions and capable of objectively justifying them. How does one respond to the query, "Do you think the whole universe revolves around you?" Figure 11.2 illustrates the two kinds of thinkers' responses to this question.

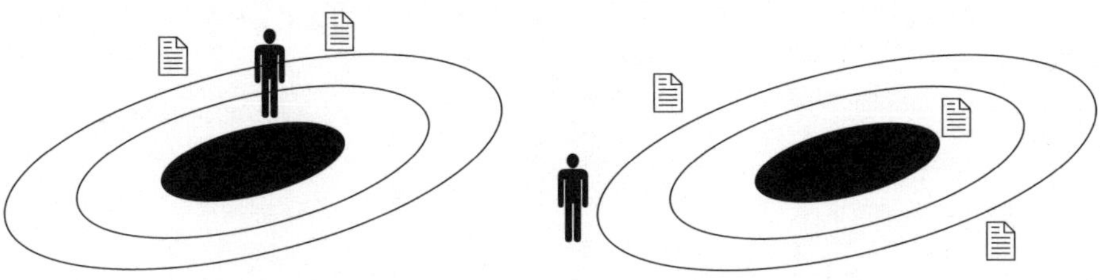

Figure 11.2: Uncritical vs. Critical Thinking

In the first illustration, the thinker is in the middle of his or her own personal universe, and hence opinions are held close to their self-perception. Since they are in the center, they cannot objectively or critically assess their thinking; in other words, they think the universes does indeed revolve around them. However, in the second illustration the thinker has transitioned out of the center to a position that provides a more comprehensive and objective perception of the universe and hence that person forms opinions based on the facts, not heavily influenced by personal biases. Thus, when asked, "Do you think the whole universe revolves around you?" the person responds, "Well, no; my thoughts are verifiable via facts, not personal biases." The character of critical thinkers requires them to be less self-centered and recognize that truth exists regardless of their opinions.

BEYOND JUST CRITICAL THINKING: CHRIST-CENTERED CRITICAL THINKING

As previously noted, specific applications of critical thinking in specific contexts can be used constructively, but without limitations it could potentially degenerate into skepticism and cynicism. Likewise, the character of critical thinkers demonstrates the connection between the cognitive and affective environment created by critical thinking. Such contexts and connections are conducive to facilitating the process of spiritual formation. For example, Stephen Fortosis describes spiritual formation in a three-stage progression (Figure 11.3).

Stage 1 Formative Integration (New or Delayed Christians)	Stage 2 Responsible Consistency (Growing Christians)	Step 3: Self-Transcendent Wholeness (Mature Christians)
• Egocentrism • Little Bible knowledge • Dualistic moral outlook • Conditional love • Feeling orientation • Juxtaposed motives/attitudes • Theological instability • Fluid convictions • Idealized (unreal) relationship with God	• Pragmatic relationship with God • Solidifying convictions • Theological balance: Dogmatism vs. openness • Purer motives/attitudes • Faith orientation • Less conditional love • Discriminating moral outlook • Greater biblical knowledge/discernment • Others-centered reasoning	• Self-transcendence • Thorough knowledge • Universalized outlook • Compassion toward others • Unwavering faith • Little public/private duplicity • Secure/flexible theology • Internalized convictions • Intimate (real) relationship with God

Figure 11.3: Fortosis's Characteristics and Stages of Spiritual Formation[26]

As one reviews the progressions of a student toward developing critical thinking, the characteristics of the students begin to align with items in Fortosis's spiritual formation progression, highlighting the potential connection between the development of critical thinking and its contribution to spiritual formation.

1. *Loss of self-centeredness:* lowering of the self/ego
2. *Broader perspective on life and living:* "universal" tendency, asking the big questions
3. *Beyond mere content mastery toward a Christian worldview perspective on life:* an integration of the gospel into all of life, not only intellectually but in terms of values and the will
4. *Ability to regularly assess situations and respond accordingly*
5. *Growth only occurs when the process becomes habitual*[27]
6. *Openness to growth and change:* no longer satisfied with status quo

26. Based on Steve Fortosis, "Theological Foundations for a Stage Theory of Spiritual Formation," *Religious Education* 96, no. 1 (2001): 49–63; Steve Fortosis, "A Developmental Model for Stages of Growth in Christian Formation," *Religious Education* 87, no. 2 (1992): 283–98.
27. George W. Stickel, "The Definition of Critical Thought and Its Implications for Christian Education," *Christian Education Journal* 15, no. 1 (1994): 38–39.

All of this is also contingent on a more mature person leading and guiding the individual.

Larry Richards observes that *many* evangelical Christians believe that since the Bible is God's word, then authoritative or transmissive approaches to teaching it are all that are required, However, while the Bible is God's word and we should teach it aurhotitatively, we likewise should use methods beyond indoctrination, including those that engage critical thinking.[28] Belief must become habitual. Rote memorization and repetition must move beyond a habit in order to transform life.[29]

Michael Warren speaks of a congregation—not just a classroom—as a comprehensive context of critical thinking, providing permission for the "free discussion of complex issues." In the absence of such an environment, "The role of the laity is to be consumers of the religious insights of others. They are invited to reproduce religious speech, instead of engaging in the original coproduction of religious insight."[30] Eugene Roehlkepartain, Director of the Search Institute, and Eboo Patel, founder of Interfaith America, likewise affirm that "congregations merit exploration as critical ecological contexts for spiritual development."[31] In an earlier publication, Roehlkepartain outlined how congregations could be the context for critical thinking for spiritual formation:[32]

- Are questions encouraged or discouraged?
- How does the congregation deal with diverse opinions?
- Are members challenged to examine their faith and everyday lives?
- How do leaders model a thinking faith?
- Are youth given answers, or are they led to discover answers?

The church, the people of faith, form a context wherein critical thinking can be engaged for the purpose of spiritual formation.

28. Richards, "Critical Thinking and Christian Perspective," 15.
29. Cf. Stickel, "The Definition of Critical Thought," 33–41.
30. Michael Warren, "The Sacramentality of Critique and Its Challenge for Christian Educators," *Christian Education Journal* 15, no. 1 (1994): 49.
31. Eugene C. Roehlkepartain and Eboo Patel, "Congregations: Unexamined Crucibles for Spiritual Development," in *The Handbook of Spiritual Development in Childhood and Adolescence*, ed. Eugene C. Roehlkepartain et al. (Thousand Oaks, CA: Sage, 2009), 325.
32. Eugene C. Roehlkepartain, "The Thinking Climate: A Missing Ingredient in Youth Ministry," *Christian Education Journal* 15, no. 1 (1994): 61–62.

Candidly, what better context than the church to address or confront faith challenges, or refine and rearticulate an individual's faith? What would be the result of facing these faith challenges in a context other than a Christian one?

TEACHING FOR CHRIST-CENTERED CRITICAL THINKING

Robert H. Ennis identifies four strategies for teaching critical thinking, overarching approaches describing and designing the presence of critical thinking in the curriculum. The strategies are as follows:[33]

- *General:* Teach critical thinking as a discrete subject from other subjects;
- *Infusion:* Integrate critical thinking into other subjects;
- *Immersion:* Utilize critical thinking as one studies other topics; and
- *Mixed:* Combine general with infusion or immersion.

However, to move from the strategic level to a more tactical level requires a step-by-step approach to instruction. Susanna Hookway outlines a five-step process of teaching critical thinking or using it when teaching other subjects.[34]

- *Problematizing:* Development of "key questions" that will be used to assess truth claims;
- *Mirrors:* Self-assessment of one's own articulated truth claims;
- *Windows:* Viewing the truth claims made by others;
- *Microscopes:* Examination of all the truth claims against the key questions, for instance, using agreed upon criteria to assess all claims fairly.
- *Reflection:* Actually a part of each of the previous four steps, a cycle of reflection throughout the process, now concluding with a reexamination of the individual's original articulation so as to form an assessed rearticulation of it.

---

33. Robert Hugh Ennis, "Critical Thinking Across the Curriculum," *OSSA Conference Archive* 44 (2013), https://scholar.uwindsor.ca/ossaarchive/OSSA10/papersandcommentaries/44.
34. Susanna R. Hookway, *Questions of Truth: Developing Critical Thinking Skills in Secondary Religious Education* (Norwich, UK: Religious and Moral Education, 2004), 5.

Perhaps the one universal factor in developing critical thinking in students is to facilitate *routine* practices, not singular or occasional ones. Critical thinking is not a one-time exercise but must become a common pattern of cognitive engagement. Elder and Paul affirm this, illustrating it with a simple diagram (Figure 11.4).[35]

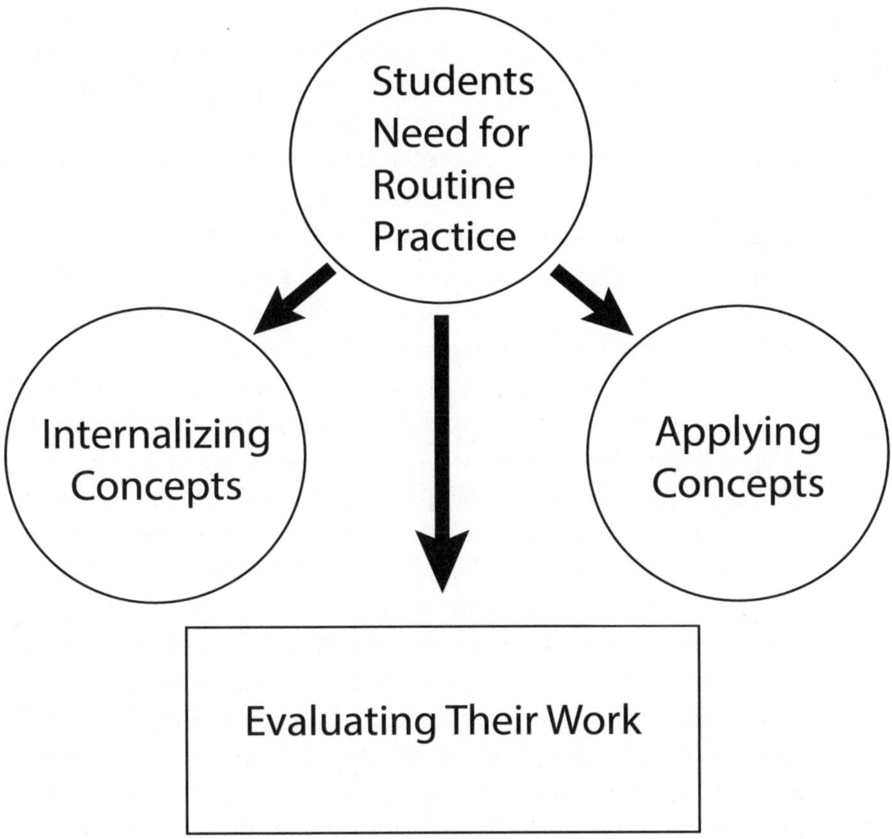

Figure 11.4: Routine Practices

How does one facilitate these routine practices or use the strategies and patterns of instruction outlined above? Students learn new ideas best when they apply to a real-life situation with the instructor provid-

35. Linda Elder and Richard Paul, "Critical Thinking: Strategies for Improving Student Learning, Part I," *Journal of Developmental Education* 32, no. 1 (2008): 32–33.

ing critical feedback to their application. Classroom strategies that give students time to practice critical thinking and connect concepts/ideas to one another are more beneficial than those that merely explain concepts or have students memorize them. Numerous means and methods have been identified as being most advantageous for facilitating critical thinking.[36]

- *Model It:* Students learn the process of critical thinking by watching the instructor engage in critical thinking while providing narration to explain the process.
- *Mentor:* Students receive feedback on their own ideas provided by a more experienced critical thinker. This sharpens their abilities to think through correction, challenge, or conversation.
- *Opposing Vantage Points:* Students read position papers that are diametrically opposite and must analyze the evidence, lines of argument, and conclusions.
- *Questions/Discussions:* Employ the Socratic method with students to help them raise critical questions to further sharpen their answers to open-ended questions.
- *Small Groups:* "By giving people specific instructions and giving everyone in the group the opportunity to be heard, it is more likely the group time will result in communal wisdom and critical thinking" as opposed to "groupthink."[37]
- *Habits:* As Elder and Paul emphasize, becoming a critical thinker is neither instantaneous nor solo. If students are to become critical thinkers, critical thinking must become habitual.
- *Finding Focus:* One practice of critical thinking is to avoid the mental fog and "rabbit trails" that often distract students from engaging a topic's core issue. Teachers could assess a student's ability to identify and engage the core topic of a certain subject, providing guidance when required.
- *Decision-Making Tree:* While decisions are not always binary, stringing enough "yes/no" responses together can indeed lead to critical thinking. Like the binary code of computers (a series

36. Paul and Elder, "Critical Thinking: Implications for Instruction of the Stage Theory," 34–35; Richard W. Paul, *Critical Thinking: How to Prepare Students for a Rapidly Changing World* (Santa Rosa, CA: Foundations for Critical Thinking, 1993), 273–396.
37. Heflin, *Teaching Eutychus*, chapter 3.

of ones and zeroes) and elementary inferential statistics coin flips, leading students through a series of yes/no questions can catalyze critical thinking.

- *Debate the Opposite:* Students have opinions, whether uncritically or critically derived, but what if they had to argue the opposite view? One way to facilitate critical thinking is to require students to research and argue the case for the opposite opinion. This often results in a refinement and more accurate articulation of their own opinion.
- *Case Studies:* Situations require analysis, even exegesis. Like a puzzle to be solved, case studies can challenge assumptions and prejudices, test hypothetical solutions, and provide an artificial environment in which to work through real-life circumstances, which will require the use of critical thinking to address not simply an academic problem but a life situation.
- *Silence:* Silence can be deafening, especially when a class full of students is waiting for you to provide the appropriate response to a question. Don't give them the answer. Their silence is their thinking, processing; don't take that away from them.
- *Scaffolding:* As will be described in chapter 16, a scaffold provides temporary support as a construction project is in process but is removed as the building is completed, the instructor can use questions to guide and direct a student through the process of critical thinking.[38] The instructor is *not* answering the question for the student but asking a series of questions to appropriately direct a student's thought processes.

Teaching to facilitate critical thinking is not a matter of simply lecturing or overuse of a single preferred method of instruction. The Christian educator has a plethora of methods from which to choose. Each method provides its own distinctive advantage depending on the students, purpose of the study, and even the context in which students are being taught.

38. Paul S. Baeder, "Scaffolding: A Critical Thinking Technique," in *FACT Focus 2010*, ed. Jared Anthony and Paul Baeder (Lakewood, WA: Faculty Association of Community and Technical Colleges, 2010), 5–6.

TEACHING FORMATS

Just as there is a need for more than one method of instruction, there is a need for more than one teaching format. Facilitating the formation of a critical thinker requires a multi-phased approach to teaching that moves students through the process of developing critical thinking practices. This likewise changes the way in which one teaches the course, relates to the student, and the selection of favored methods for instruction.

Figure 11.5 contains the four essential teaching formats necessary for facilitating critical thinking in the classroom.

Indoctrination	Exposition	Conversation	Exploration
"Do you know the information?" • *Teacher-directed high* • *Teacher-student interaction low*	**"Can you explain the information?"** *Teacher-directed high to moderate* *Teacher-student interaction moderate to high*	**"Can you converse on the information?"** *Teacher-student interaction high to moderate* *Teacher-directed moderate to low*	**"Can you think for yourself?"** *Teacher-student interaction low* *Teacher-directed low*
Critical			
• Aim: control • Teacher: authority figure • Teaching: unidirectional, pre-structured material • Learner: subservient (sponge) • Knowledge: content deposit • Questioning: threat, ignorance • Method: lecture • Assessment: objective testing • Classroom Structure: hierarchy	• Aim: personal affirmation • Teacher: expert • Teaching: content explanation • Learner: client • Knowledge: content comprehension • Questioning: clarification • Method: discourse • Assessment: essay testing • Classroom Structure: consultive	• Aim: joint conclusion • Teacher: facilitator • Teaching: interactive discourse • Learner: communal participant • Knowledge: communal • Questioning: basis for dialogue • Method: guided discussion • Assessment: participation in teacher-led dialogue • Classroom Structure: network	• Aim: wisdom • Teacher: mentor • Teaching: do theology • Learner: independent • Knowledge: not yet determined • Questioning: essential; valued more than an answer • Method: research • Assessment: participation in student-led dialogue • Classroom Structure: collegiality

Figure 11.5: Four Teaching Formats

Each of the four formats represent four classroom dynamics, such as the relationship between and role of the teacher and students, the treatment of the content, and even the purpose of instruction. What is important in this discussion is how critical thinking is facilitated. Notice that the role of the teacher and expectations for the student change as one moves from left to right, from a more teacher-directed approach toward a more student-focused approach. Critical thinking develops as the students move from the more teacher-centered learning environments (indoctrination and exposition), where the teacher is the proverbial "sage on the stage," to a different instructional posture, the "guide at the side" as a means of facilitating the formation of critical thinking (conversation and exploration). For example, consider the "owner" of the content. In the first two formats, the teacher is the purveyor of information, the transmitter, and the students are receivers. However, in the latter two formats, the content is "owned" by the students, with the teacher simply facilitating the processing of the content.

The key consideration is that no *single* format can facilitate critical thinking. One cannot grow to become a critical thinker in a context of indoctrination or even exposition, but these can form the bases upon which critical thinking is formed. Developing the appropriate environments for this to occur is the responsibility of Christian educators.

CONCLUSION

Critical thinking is not just for universities and seminaries but also for congregations and adult education in the church. Failure to engage critical thinking makes faith remain at arm's length, something we rent rather than own, and unrealistic. If we want to pass faith to members of the next generation, then it has to be more than an inherited heirloom; it has to be something to which they add their distinctive mark. If the church becomes an institution wherein critical thinking is not welcome or facilitated, they will simply find another outlet for their thoughts, feelings, and faith. But if the church can become a place of critical thinking within an atmosphere of faith, it can be a seedbed for thought, feelings, and faith.

REFLECTION QUESTIONS

1. How would you describe the value of critical thinking as both a practice and a method of teaching?
2. On the scale of critical thinking in this chapter, where would you assess your current level? Why?

3. What is one practice you could adopt that would improve your critical thinking abilities?
4. Where in your congregation is critical thinking promoted?

RECOMMENDED READING

Brookfield, Stephen D. *Developing Critical Thinking: Challenging Adults to Explore Alternative Ways of Thinking and Acting*. San Francisco: Jossey-Bass, 1987.

Cohen, Martin. *Critical Thinking Skills for Dummies*. For Dummies: Learning Made Easy. Chichester, UK: John Wiley and Sons, 2015.

Heflin, Houston. *Teaching Eutychus: Engaging Today's Learners with Passion and Creativity*. Abilene, TX: Abilene University Press, 2012.

Paul, Richard, and Linda Elder. *The Miniature Guide to Critical Thinking: Concepts and Tools*. New York: Rowman and Littlefield, 2020.

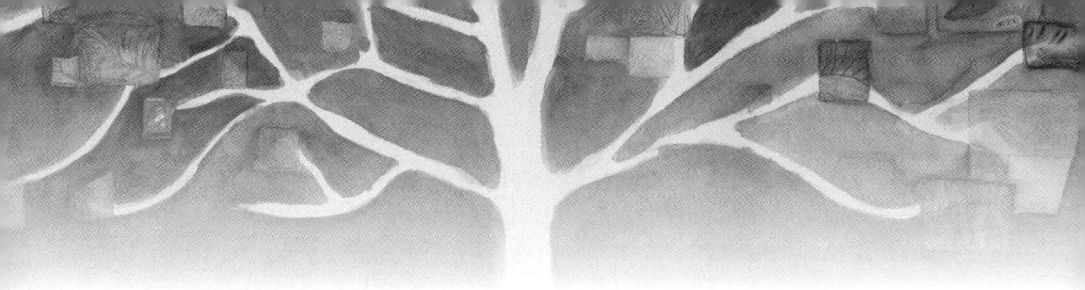

CHAPTER 12

TEACHING FOR FAITH-LEARNING INTEGRATION

James Riley Estep Jr.

One of the fundamental distinctions of Christian education is its commitment to faith-learning integration.[1] While this may have been recently questioned and challenged even by some evangelicals, it persists as a distinctive characteristic of congregations and campuses. It has often been expressed with the statement: We teach from a Christian perspective. However, in spite of Christian education's commitment to faith-learning integration, it remains somewhat *enigmatic*. It has degenerated from a substantial engagement on the part of evangelical academics, professors, and practitioners into a mere "slogan," lacking substance,[2] or as Kenneth Gangel prefers, a "symbol, a shibboleth to utter *but not demonstrated*,"[3] a

1. Cf. Arthur F. Holmes, *The Idea of the Christian College* (Grand Rapids: Eerdmans, 1975), 6; Robert T. Sadin, *The Search for Excellence: The Christian College in an Age of Educational Competition* (Macon, GA: Mercer University Press, 1982), 15; David L. Wolfe, "The Line of Demarcation between Integration and Pseudointegration," in *The Reality of Christian Learning: Strategies for Faith-Discipline Integration*, ed. Harold Heie and David Wolfe (St. Paul, MN: Christian University Press, 1987), 11.
2. Kenneth Badley, "The Faith/Learning Integration Movement in Christian Higher Education: Slogan or Substance?" *Journal of Research on Christian Education* 3, no. 1 (1994): 27.
3. Kenneth O. Gangel, "Integrating Faith and Learning: Principles and Process," *Bibliotheca Sacra* 135 (June/July 1978): 99, emphasis added; cf. Clarence W. Joldersma, "Faith /Learning Integration: A Substantive Example That Transcends Sloganeering," *Journal of Research in Christian Education* 5, no. 1 (1996): 67–87.

meaningless mantra chanted but rarely achieved.[4] We often relegate the idea of faith-learning integration to institutions of Christian higher education, but this does *not* mean congregations should avoid the topic. Rather, *every* believer, particularly adolescents and adults, would benefit by learning how to integrate their faith and what they are learning.

This chapter will first define faith-learning integration as a feasible practice for the Christian educator. Second, more than providing pre-integrated content, it will explore the process of integration that, finally, requires a strategy that facilitates the process, with a particular set of teaching methods that facilitate integrative thinking. Ultimately, teaching to facilitate faith-learning integration achieves a believer who *consistently* thinks as a *Christian.*

IS FAITH-LEARNING INTEGRATION CHRISTIAN?

Perhaps the quintessential passage cited as the mandate for faith-learning integration in is Paul's injunction to the Corinthians to "take every thought captive to obey Christ" (2 Cor. 10:5 ESV).[5] In a context that uses images of a military campaign, Paul explains that the Christian must not only destroy falsehood but take prisoner, for instance, thoughts and center them on Christ.[6] Paul cautioned the Corinthians in his first letter about the educational elite of the ancient world (1 Cor. 1:20)[7] and warns in Colossians 2:8 (NIV) to "see to it that no one takes you captive through hollow and deceptive philosophy, which depends on human tradition and the basic principles of this world rather than on Christ." Both passages use military imagery. Paul's injunction is clear: we must integrate every thought with a Christian worldview!

Paul further asserts the value of faith-learning integration when he critiques those who are "always learning and never able to arrive at a knowledge of the truth" (2 Tim. 3:7 ESV), indicating that the mere acquisition of information is not enough but learning must be centered

4. Badley, "Faith/Learning Integration," 23, 28–29.
5. Richard Knopp and John Castelein, *Every Thought Captive: Essays in Honor of James D. Strauss* (Joplin, MO: College Press, 1997).
6. Victor Paul Furnish, *II Corinthians*, Anchor Bible (Garden City, NY: Doubleday, 1984), 462–63.
7. James Riley Estep Jr., "Philosophers, Scribes, Rhetors, and . . . Paul?: The Educational Background of the New Testament," *Christian Education Journal* 2, no. 1, NS1 (2005): 30–47.

on Christ.[8] The Bible not only calls for the integration of faith-learning, but demonstrates its practice on numerous occasions.[9]

Theologically, the practice of faith-learning integration affirms that God is both the Creator (Gen. 1:1; John 1:1–3) and the ultimate Author of Scripture (2 Tim. 3:15–16; 2 Peter 1:20–21), which leads to the conviction of the unity of truth based on God's natural/general revelation and his supernatural/special revelation (Ps. 19:1–11; Rom. 1–3). Likewise, the innate curiosity, or desire to search for knowledge, that is part of being human compels us to inquire of God's revelation and seek the unity it offers. Edward Curtis observes, "The presence of level one wisdom [natural/general revelation] embedded in the level two wisdom of Scripture [special revelation] provides a model for the effective search for truth in God's general revelation."[10] Faith-learning integration affirms and facilitates this theological conviction.

DEFINING FAITH-LEARNING INTEGRATION

One of the reasons faith-learning integration remains an enigma is because it escapes definition. We think of it conceptually but not practically. Even secular educators affirm the benefits of integration as a teaching method, in the absence of faith of course. One educator described it as the "process of examining similarities and differences among related concepts."[11] Hellmut Lang, professor at University of the Cumberlands (Kentucky) and Lang Evans, professor at Liberty University, and are regarded as experts in the field of faith-learning integration in higher education. They describe faith-learning integration as "thematic instruction [that] occurs when instruction is organized around macro 'themes.'"[12]

Christian educators have articulated a plethora of approaches to faith-learning integration, accompanied by a plethora of alternative

8. Cf. Martin Dibelius and Hans Conzelmann, *The Pastoral Epistles*, Hermeneutica (Philadelphia: Fortress, 1972), 116.
9. James Riley Estep Jr., "'As Some of Their Own Poets Have Written . . .': A Biblical Affirmation of Faith-Learning Integration," *Journal of Faith and the Academy* 12, no. 1 (2019): 5–17.
10. Edward M. Curtis, "Old Testament Wisdom: A Model for Faith-Learning Integration," *Christian Scholar's Review* 15, no. 3 (1986): 217.
11. Donald C. Orlich et al., *Teaching Strategies: A Guide to Better Instruction* (Lexington, MA: D. C. Heath, 1998), 180.
12. Hellmut R. Lang and David N. Evans, *Models, Strategies and Methods for Effective Teaching* (London: Pearson, 2005), 231.

definitions and processes.[13] Essentially, in a Christian context, faith-learning integration is the assimilation of Word and world in the mind of the Christian into a unified perspective and approach to all of life. It challenges the believer to think Christianly about subjects that are not essentially or exclusively Christian. It is one thing to study theology, which is innately Christian, and quite another thing to study business administration. The believer whose career is in a corporation would benefit by approaching business administration from the perspective of Christian faith. But how?

Kenneth Badley, Professor at Biola University in La Mirada, California and regular contributor to scholarship in the field of faith-learning integration, surveys the five main approaches to faith-learning integration, affirming the final one.[14]

1. *Fusion:* Creation of a new entity or hybrid by combining faith and learning (e.g. A + B = C or A + B = AB).
2. *Incorporation:* One element disappears into, dissolves in, or filters the other.
3. *Correlation:* "Points of intersection or common interest." This turns the faith-learning integration process into a search for the lowest common denominator between academic disciplines and matters of faith.[15]
4. *Dialogical:* "High and continuous degree of correlation . . . a conversation." This approach leads to no *decisive* conclusions.[16]
5. *Perspective:* This approach seeks to transform students' understanding of knowledge by undergirding it with faith-based assumptions and framing it within a faith context, encouraging students to see their studies as interconnected with their beliefs, not separate from them.

13. Ronald R. Nelson, "Faith-Discipline Integration: Compatibilist, Reconstructionist, and Transformationalist Strategies," in Heie and Wolfe, *The Reality of Christian Learning*, 317–39; Michael S. Hamilton and James A. Mathisen, "Faith and Learning at Wheaton College," in *Models of Christian Higher Education: Strategies for Success in the Twenty-First Century*, ed. Richard T. Hughes and William B. Adrian (Grand Rapids: Eerdmans, 1997), 268–71; and Robert A. Harris, *The Integration of Faith and Learning: A Worldview Approach* (Eugene, OR: Cascade, 2004), 221–47.
14. Badley, "Faith/Learning Integration," 13–33.
15. Badley, "Faith/Learning Integration," 24.
16. Badley, "Faith/Learning Integration," 25.

The transformational approach (called *perspective* above) is the most commonly held means of faith-learning integration used in Christian scholarship. Without oversimplifying this paradigm, it asks the simple yet profound question: "*Where is God in . . .?*" Wayne McCown, a professor in Liberty University's School of Education and specialist in faith-learning integration, argues that using a biblical-theological framework provides Christian scholarship with (1) perspective, (2) philosophical assumptions, (3) a means of assigning meaning and interpretation, and (4) evaluation of other disciplines.[17] In this method of faith-learning integration "a worldview supplies the coherence" between the disciplines and faith.[18]

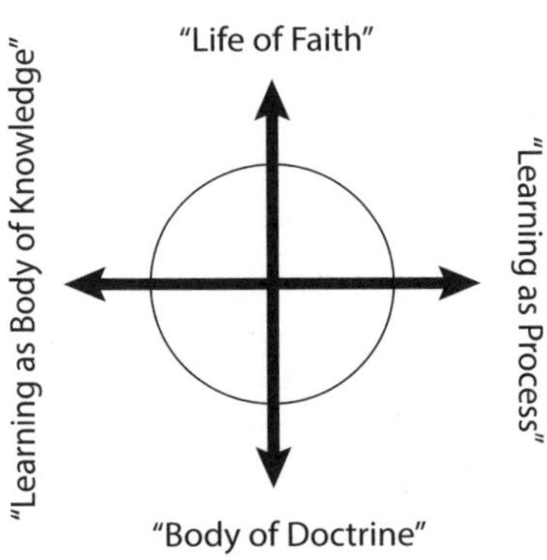

Figure 12.1: Badley's Paradigm for Faith-Learning Integration

What is needed for the congregation to practice faith-learning integration is a model that includes a practical dimension that focuses on the faith and life of the believer. Badley's transformational approach is illustrated in Figure 12.1. Faith-learning integration exists along two axes: (1) *faith* as the "life of faith" and/or "body of doctrine," and (2) *learning* as the "process of learning" and/or "body of knowledge." These two axes create a matrix in which to describe faith-learning integration as a combination of some or all of these four quadrants along the two axes.[19]

When students from your congregation go to university, how do they integrate what they are learning into their faith? For example, the four dimensions of Badley's model would relate to the study of history in this way: learning as process, the process of doing and learning history is *historiography*; the body of knowledge would consist of the

17. Wayne McCown, "The Use of the Bible in the Integration of Faith and Learning," *Kerygma and Praxis: Essays in Honor of Stanley R. Magill*, ed. Wesley Vanderhoof and David Basinger (Rochester, NY: Roberts Wesleyan College Press, 1984), 29–31.
18. Badley, "Faith/Learning Integration," 25
19. Badley, "Faith/Learning Integration," 28.

historical content of the time period or culture in question; the faith dimension would be the body of doctrine explaining the involvement of *God in history*, (sovereignty, providence, theocracy); and the personal implications that arise from the study would be the life of faith. Faith-learning integration can begin in any of the four quadrants, but ideally the results are centered in the middle and include the practical dimension of how this influences Christian living. How does having a Christian perspective on history inform my walk with Christ? As one person put it, "A Christian understands history as *His*-story!"[20] However valuable this paradigm may be, it focuses on content, but not the educational process by which a teacher can assist students to think Christianly.

Describing Faith-Learning Integration

Faith-learning integration has been described in a variety of ways: as a biblical reality;[21] a theological necessity;[22] and even a Christian quality of character and spiritual formation,[23] which is most relevant to Christian education in congregations. Faith-learning integration has also been described theoretically as a model of integration.[24] Perhaps most

20. Dr. Reuben G. Bullard, "Introductory Lectures," Ancient History 2, Cincinnati Christian University (Cincinnati, OH), January 1982.
21. Cf. John Wesley Taylor V, "A Biblica*l Foundation for the Integration of Faith and Learning,*" Asia Adventist Seminary Studies 4 (2001): 19–34, https://journals.aiias.edu/jaas/issue/view/58/10; Curtis, "Old Testament Wisdom," 213–17; John W. Hilber, "Old Testament Wisdom and the Integration Debate in Christian Counseling," *Bibliotheca Sacra* 155:620 (1998): 411.
22. Cf. William Hasker, "Faith-Learning Integration: An Overview," *Christian Scholar's Review* 21, no. 3 (1992): 234–48; Harris, *Integration of Faith and Learning*, 23–56; Brad Green, "Theological and Philosophical Foundations," in *Shaping a Christian Worldview: The Foundations of Christian Higher Education*, ed. David S. Dockery and Gregory Alan Thornbury (Nashville: B&H Academic, 2002), 62–91.
23. William E. Hull, "Christian Higher Education at the Crossroads," *Perspectives in Religious Studies* 19, no. 4 (1992): 441–42.
24. Cf. Nelson, "Faith-Discipline Integration," 317–39; Hamilton and Mathisen, "Faith and Learning at Wheaton College," 261–83; cf. James Riley Estep Jr., "Developmental Theories: Foe, Friend, or Folly?" in *Christian Formation: Integrating Theology and Human Development*, ed. James Riley Estep Jr. and Jonathan H. Kim (Nashville: B&H Academic, 2010), 37–62; James Riley Estep Jr., "What Makes Education Christian?" in *A Theology for Christian Education*, ed. James Riley Estep Jr., Michael Anthony, and Gregg Allison (Nashville: B&H Academic, 2008), 25–43; James Riley Estep Jr., "How Christian Is Christian Education? The Relation of Theology and Education in the Church," *Stone-Campbell Journal* 10, no. 1 (2006): 63–76; James Riley Estep Jr., "Faith as the Transformer of Learning," *Christian Education Journal* 2NS, no. 2 (1998): 60–76.

commonly is the worldview or perspective approach to faith-learning integration in Christian higher education.[25]

However, rarely if ever has faith-learning integration been described educationally. There is no doubt that an educational agenda for faith-learning integration could *not* exist without first describing it. However, it is equally true that without the educational agenda for faith-learning integration, the previous five ways are incomplete and wholly hypothetical, lacking in any tangible or recognizable subsistence. In spite of the many benefits of all the previous depictions, faith-learning integration has simply *not* been effectively translated into the classroom.

Levels of Faith-Learning Integration

A common paradigm for assessing and practicing faith-learning integration contains five levels ranging from disintegration through a paradigmatic level of integration. The five levels are as follows:[26]

1. *Disintegration:* A level of non-integration due to being unaware of anything to integrate. It is literally a state of ignorance, not stupidity, wherein individuals simply lack the knowledge of *other* information, such as adult learners who do not see the relevance of Christian faith to their careers and instead base their careers solely on organizational culture and contemporary business theory.
2. *Segregation:* A level of awareness of other information or perspectives that may be different from Scripture or theology, but it is not regarded as relevant or important. This is a level of intentional rejection of information from other sources as irrelevant. For example, the adult learner is aware of Scripture and theology as well as business theory and organizational culture but does not see how the two relate to one another and uses them independently from each other.
3. *Paradoxical:* A level of integration wherein value is given to both Christian Scripture and theology as well as other sources

25. David S. Dockery, "Shaping a Christian Worldview," in Dockery and Thornbury, *Shaping a Christian Worldview*, 1–18; David S. Dockery, *Renewing Minds: Serving Church and Society Through Christian Higher Education* (Nashville: B&H Academic, 2007).
26. Estep, "What Makes Education Christian?," 33–37; Estep, "Developmental Theories," 48–50.

of information and both are regarded as relevant to the subject, but the two are intentionally kept separate, with the learner living in the tension between the two. For example, as in level 2 (segregation) there is awareness on the part of the learner, but now *value* is placed on both and a basic dialogue between the two sources of information occurs—between Christian theology and business theory—but the sources are used one at a time, not simultaneously. Thus, the level of integration is nominal.

4. *Synthetic:* A level of integration that values not only the sources of information but also the idea of integrating the two into a singular perspective, avoiding the duality of previous levels, but all too often it is the non-Christian source that receives primacy. For example, Christian theological themes are applied to business theory, renaming and reframing it; however, the theory is essentially unchanged or unchallenged. Christian theology is added but at a noncritical level.
5. *Paradigmatic:* The final level of integration is achieved when both sources of information, Christian theology/Scripture and the other source, are jointly, simultaneously used in response to common questions and concerns with primacy given to Scripture as God's Word over any other source. For example, the Christian business person values their employees not as mere assets to the firm but as individuals who possess innate value and deserve respect as the *imago dei*.

These five levels build upon one another until an individual thinks simultaneously from a Christian perspective and contemporary relevance.

Delineating the Instructional Description

When discussed in an instructional context, the idea of *faith* had two dimensions, one more like the "life of faith" dimension of Badley's paradigm (see Figure 12.1) rather than the second dimension, intellectual integration of a unified truth between worldview and subject matter.[27]

27. Cf. Mark R. McMinn, Gary W. Moon, and Angela G. McCormick, "Integration: Ten Teaching Strategies," *Journal of Psychology and Theology* 37, no. 1 (2009): 39–47. Cf. Arthur Holmes, "What About Student Integration?," *Journal of Research on Christian Education* 3, no. 1 (1994): 3–5.

Such treatments are indeed insightful and beneficial for the practical "life of faith" dimension but may not give adequate attention to the cognitive process of integrating theology and theory into a consistent perspective on a field of study or vocational career/calling.

One critical issue that requires attention is *who is doing the integrating*. Is it the teacher, providing *pre*-integrated content to the student? Or is it teaching students to be integrative thinkers? Many studies indicate that it is the former rather than the latter that usually occurs, with integrative behavior primarily attributed to the teacher and not the students.[28] Students can receive previously integrated material and understand how the instructor can make connections, but they are not able to actually engage the integrative process themselves (Figure 12.2).

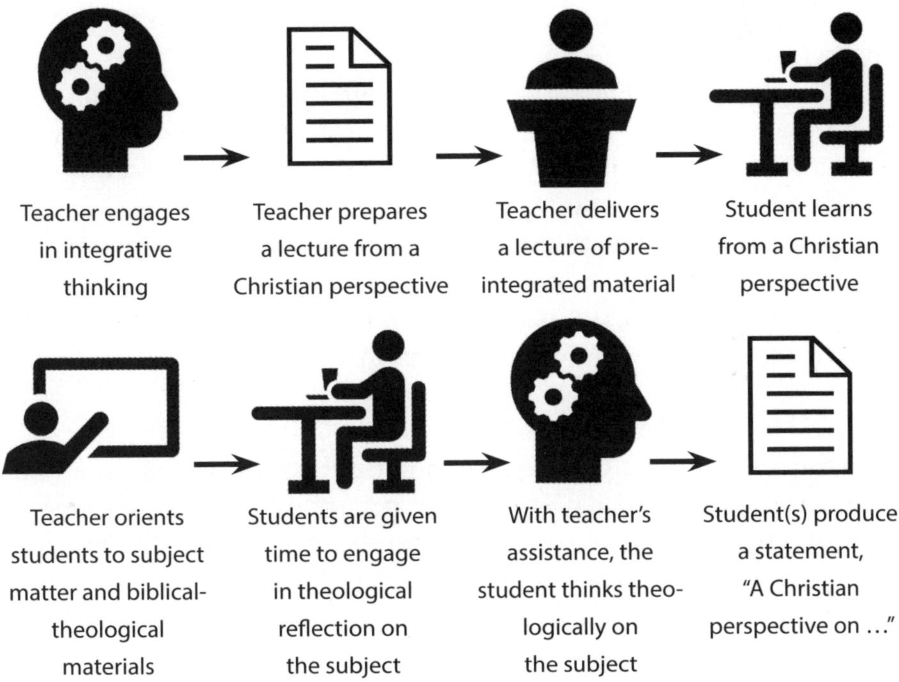

Figure 12.2: Pre-Integrated Materials vs. Integrative Process

28. Terry Anne Lawrence, Larry D. Burton, and Constance C. Nwosu, "Refocusing on the Learning in Integration of Faith and Learning," *Journal of Research on Christian Education* 14, no. 1 (2005): 41–42; Larry D. Burton and Constance C. Nwosu, "Student Perceptions of the Integration of Faith, Learning, and Practice in an Educational Methods Course," *Journal of Research on Christian Education* 12, no. 2 (2003): 101–35.

Christian teachers are more than capable of integrative thinking, producing theologically informed content, and delivering already integrated content, who simply learn the subject matter and make application from the instruction. This approach will *not* enable students to integrate content on their own but only reinforce reliance on the instructor to engage in faith-learning integration *for* them.[29] Only a strategy of the instructor engaging the students directly to lead them through the process of faith-learning integration on their own can facilitate students producing integrative content for themselves. In fact, in a recent study students identified three classroom factors that contributed to faith-learning integration: the classroom learning process, making connections between the content of faith and the content of the subject matter, and a positive and interpersonal classroom atmosphere.[30] To employ an old idiom: you can give your students a fish, or you can teach them how to fish.

How do we facilitate theologically informed integrated thinking within the minds and lives of our students? More specifically, how do we enable students to integrate faith and learning for themselves? The process of faith-learning integration will be addressed in two sections: (1) a general orientation to the integration-friendly classroom environment, intending to provide an overview of the classroom issues, and (2) specific teaching methods that are conducive to facilitating faith-learning integration within a congregation's classrooms.

THE PROCESS OF FAITH-LEARNING INTEGRATION

A method or process of integration faithful to the transformational approach to faith-learning integration occurs in three phases: dualistic, synthetic, and integrative. It utilizes the strengths of the previous methods and approaches while minimizing their deficits by using them in conjunction with one another. Figure 12.3 describes and illustrates this process.

---

29. Cf. Loren T. Gustafson, Gary L. Karns, and Lisa Klein Surdyk, "Teaching Through the Eyes of Faith: An Investigation of Faith-Learning Integration in the Business Classroom," *Research on Christian Higher Education* 7 (2000): 1–21, who focus their entire treatment of the subject on the faculty member's ability to do integrative thinking but give little to the students' engagement of faith-learning integration.
30. Cf. Burton and Nwosu, "Student Perceptions of the Integration of Faith."

Dualistic	Synthetic	Integrative
Faith ○ ○ Learning	**Faith ◯◯ Learning**	**Faith ◎ Learning**
Faith and learning begin in dialogue, but with tension existing between the relative authorities, e.g., theological vs. cultural. However, areas of agreement and disagreement are being mapped and acknowledged. This stage of integration would utilize methodologies consistent with Badley's first two paradigms (i.e., fusion and incorporation).	Faith and learning begin a merger of those areas in which the authorities agree, similar to Badley's correlation and dialogical paradigms. However, areas of disagreement remain outside the integrative process. Hence, the dualistic tension remains, but is significantly weakened.	Faith and learning become (theoretically) a single entity as the process continues, since the areas of agreement are already adopted, and the areas of disagreement are assessed theologically and addressed by either adaptation or critical rejection. This, of course, parallels Badley's perspective methodology.

Figure 12.3: The Process of Faith-Learning Integration

Parents often face an onslaught of opinions regarding the art of child-rearing. They are inundated with information often fraught with internal contradiction. How does one parent as a Christian in today's world? Perhaps more specifically, how do Christians discipline their children? As Figure 12.4 shows, we become familiar with the contemporary sources of the day, but we must also become familiar with what Scripture says about parenting, and perhaps even an evangelical theology of the family.

More than a *blending* of sources, the final step of faith-learning integration is to think theologically about the topic at hand. It is not simply the merger of scriptural and theological content with contemporary literature or sociological studies, as if one were merely shuffling two decks of cards into one pile. Rather, it is using a scripturally based theological lens to frame an answer to the pertinent issues about disciplining children from a godly perspective, undergirded with contemporary wisdom and insights when they are consistent. One will also recognize that some material simply cannot be reconciled, that irreconcilable differences do exist, where Scripture asserts a principle that is contradictory to conventional wisdom. From this final phase, the parent can capture a Christian perspective on child discipline relevant to today, perhaps writing down what they have learned or sharing it with other parents. A strategy for teaching that facilitates this process is needed to turn the theory into practice, the intention into an instructional method.

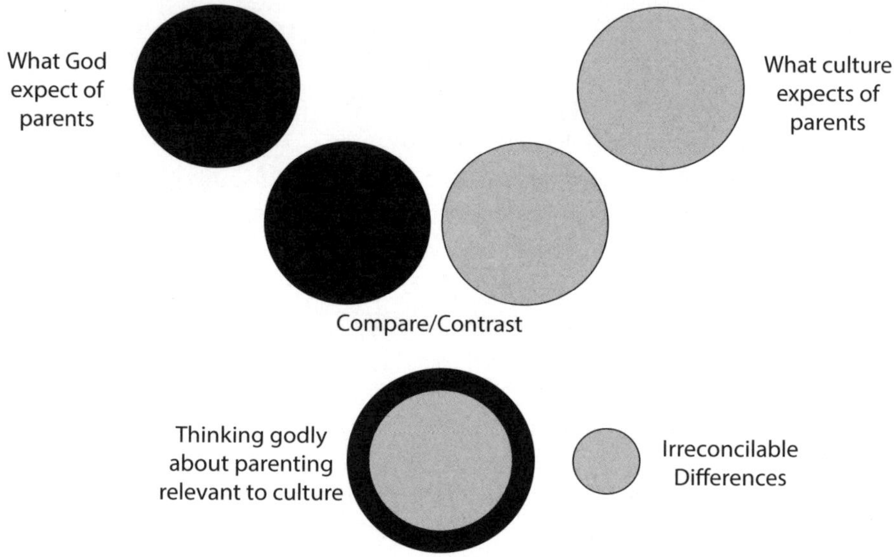

Figure 12.4: What Scripture Says About Parenting

TEACHING FOR FAITH-LEARNING INTEGRATION

Figure 12.5 summarizes a study conducted by Michael E. Sherr and George E. Huff, professors in social work at Cedarville University (Ohio) in conjunction with Mary A. Curran of the University of Washington, outside of Seattle.[31] The qualitative study interviewed eighty-nine undergraduate social work students from seven schools accredited by the Council on Social Work Education and the Council of Christian Colleges and Universities regarding how the classroom aided their faith-learning integration. The study concluded that the two most important factors for students actually attaining a tangible level of faith-learning integration about their Christian vocation were (1) the instructor's "relationships with God and with

31. Michael E. Sherr, George E. Huff, and Mary A. Curran, "BSW Student Perceptions of Salient Integration of Faith and Learning Indicators," *Social Work and Christianity* 33, no. 1 (2006): 69.

students" and (2) the instructor's "competence providing specific IFL [integration of faith and learning] curriculum coverage [i.e., content] and providing safe classroom settings [i.e., as a context for processing]."[32] The classroom context for faith-learning integration is illustrated in Figure 12.5.

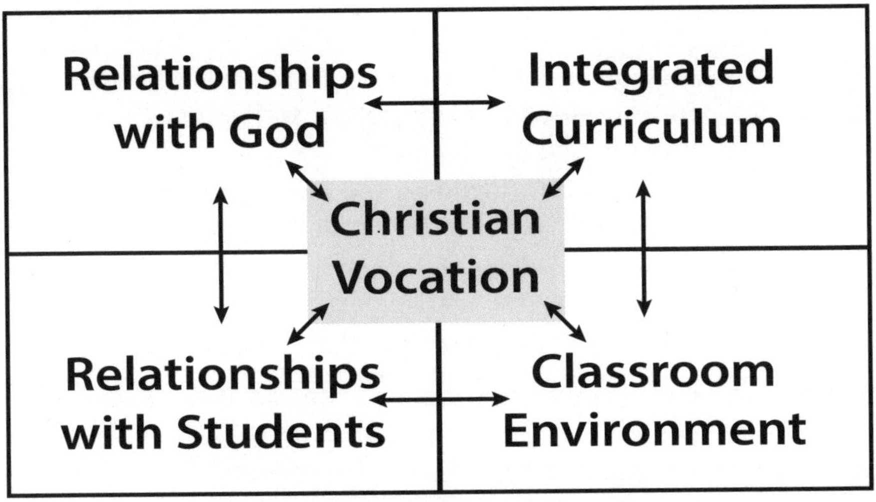

Figure 12.5: Teaching for Faith-Learning Integration

Any classroom in the church that intends to intentionally engage the process of faith-learning integration must openly acknowledge that barriers to faith-learning integration are real. Some are out of the teacher's hands, but Sherr, Huff, and Curran's research seems to minimize some of these barriers and contributes more fully toward having a classroom conducive to faith-learning integration.

Teaching for faith-learning integration involves four phases wherein the teacher facilitates and assists the students to move through the integrative process mentioned in the prior section, Process of Faith-Learning Integration:

- *Phase 1: Study*—Teacher orients the students to the subject matter, raises initial questions, provides relevant material from both a Christian and a secular source, and gives some guidance as to the desired outcome.

32. Sherr, Huff, and Curran, "BSW Student Perceptions," 58.

- *Phase 2: Theologizing/Theorizing*—Students, either as individuals or in teams, work together to first compare/contrast the source materials in light of the teacher's instructions. Likewise, they begin to view the content jointly through the lens of Scripture and theological rubric. A Christian perspective emerges through this process.
- *Phase 3: Application*—Students then use their Christian perspective on the subject matter to address a practical situation, drawing points of application to live out the Christian perspective previously formulated.
- *Phase 4: Integration*—Blending the theological, theoretical, and practical into what is commonly called a "Christian perspective toward . . ." a given subject or "What life changes are necessary . . ." as a result of having the Christian perspective. The model indicates an interactive process, illustrated in Figure 12.6.

LECTURE	**CASE STUDY**	**DIALOGUE**	**BRIEF/PAPER**	**ASSESSMENT**
Orientation & identification of issues	Individual or group work	Open, guided discussion	Articulation of Christian idea	Feedback from instructor

Study	**Theologizing/ Theorizing**	**Application**	**Integration**

Figure 12.6: Course Process of Integration

Hence, faith-learning integration is *not* accomplished in a lecture or an assignment or even in one class session but throughout a course of study and the entire curriculum.

CLASSROOM METHODS TO CONSIDER

No teaching methods are distinctively or automatically integrative in nature. Faith-learning integration in the classroom does not naturally occur; it must be intentional. Students do not automatically think Christianly about fields of study or vocation, nor can a teacher *force* students to integrate their thinking. However, there are classroom methods that can be readily modified to facilitate, encourage, and nurture faith-learning integration, turning students from recipients into participants. As with any teaching method, not all of these will apply to every subject or classroom environment, but some can be used as part of the teaching/classroom process described in Figure 12.6.

Selection and use of class readings: The selection and use of class readings or videos could aid in the integrative process. We all have a pedagogical rationale for the use of course materials. If the readings are already written from a Christian perspective, then provide student exercises that aid in personalizing and contextualizing them to life, family, ministry, or work. If not written from a Christian perspective or even if it is written from a Christian perspective, ask students to read them and critique the content. This will facilitate their processing of the materials for themselves rather than simply accepting them as stated in the text. Simply assigning a reading will not necessarily lead to integrative thought, but it is far more likely to occur when a teacher uses the classroom to analyze, not merely lecture.

Moving beyond lecture: A Christian teacher is perfectly able to deliver previously integrated materials to a classroom full of students. But a simple lecture alone will not do for faith-learning integration.

Methods beyond lecture, such as case studies, dialogue and debate, and simulation games encourage integrative thinking. Integration only happens in the higher levels of Bloom's taxonomy of cognitive development (chapter 5), and these levels of cognition are only attainable when students actively participate in their learning. Case studies could pose issues that involve more than biblical exegesis or pastoral practice but engage students in a practical decision-making situation that requires them to assess the situation and apply wisdom to it. This can occur in class, as individual homework, or in duos/triads, or even as a cocurricular activity.

Teaching on faith-learning integration itself: Oftentimes in the classroom, faith-learning integration is treated as part of the null, or hidden, curriculum. We assume or expect it of our students, but we do not actually teach about it. Providing students with patterns and paradigms for the integrative process is the first step in facilitating integrative thinking. *Why not make use of these theories to inform, explain, and guide students as they venture into the integrative process?* This may avoid some of the confusion students have reported when asked to define faith-learning integration.

Dialogue and instructional technology: The opportunity for discussion of ideas is essential in facilitating faith-learning integration.[33] Integrative thinking does not occur instantaneously; it is a process that requires ongoing instruction. Open discussion in a supportive environment with soft guidance from a teacher can be most conducive to theorizing a faith perspective on any subject. The process of theological integration into subjects is not merely a matter of feedback or critique but a cooperative engagement on a given issue. The use of *instructional technology* is beneficial in this regard. Contemporary digital technology makes the task and process of integration somewhat easier, in terms of both accessing and processing information. For example, a teacher might stream a video about another faith produced by an adherent to that belief system. Rather than lecturing on what students have watched, the teacher could raise critical questions, asking the class to discuss their responses. The teacher could provide a set of Scriptures to add a compare/contrast element to the discussion. If digital tablets are made available, perhaps a class could be put into groups with each watching a different video on the same topic, and then the dialogue would be informed from multiple perspectives as the class assessed them from a scriptural perspective.

Cultural/event analysis: What is a Christian perspective on art? Literature? Music? Cinema? Math? This moves beyond just seeing where music is in the Scriptures but to ask, "Where is God in it?" This kind of question requires a theology of these cultural elements and an analysis of these elements through the lens of theology. One need only visit a bookstore to see titles that explore Christian theological perspectives on science fiction or fantasy series. One way of facilitating the Christian perspective on culture would be to visit a museum, ask students to write a worldview assessment on a particular artifact, and then compare it to a Christian worldview. If a student wrote on the mummified remains of an Egyptian pharaoh, what worldview did the ancient Egyptians have? How is it reflected in the practice of mummification? As Christians, how would our beliefs be similar or different from this view?

Likewise, while it may sound like it belongs to a philosophy class, the problem of evil is relevant for everyone. Oftentimes, it is discussed

33. Sherr, Huff, and Curran, "BSW Student Perceptions," 58. Cf. Burton and Nwosu, "Student Perceptions of the Integration of Faith," 119–20 and Lawrence, Burton, and Nwosu, "Refocusing on the Learning," 38–39.

as an isolated subject, a chapter in a book, a theoretical event. But to better facilitate faith-learning integration, a teacher could engage a more immediately relevant topic, such as a natural disaster or horrific incident. How do Christians respond to the question of "Why did God let this happen? Did he cause it? Where is God when we need him?" Similarly, an element of culture, current or historical, can facilitate discussions that may require time to process and analyze, such as the Christian perspective on "civil unrest in the Middle East" or "racial tension in the United States."

Theology of vocation/career: Raising critical questions about being a Christian in a chosen career field is yet another means of engaging students in the process of faith-learning integration. Such dialogues encourage students to move beyond the reflexive responses of Christian ethics and being a witness in the workplace, toward a more substantial response to the question, "What is *Christian* about being . . . ? How do I glorify God through my vocation?" While this may seem essential for secular vocations, it is perhaps even more necessary for those entering pastoral service.

Ritual: Joyce Hardin, dean at Lubbock Christian University (Texas) and executive director of the Texas Association of Colleges for Teacher Education, along with her two coresearchers John Sweeney and Jerry Whitworth, observed that including an element of routine practice or ritual adds a faith element to an otherwise generic study or activity.[34] Perhaps before reading a book or engaging in a dialogue on a difficult matter, offering a prayer or reciting the Prayer for Students by St. Thomas Aquinas would focus everyone's attention and provide some perspective.

Learning assessments: Assessing a student's ability to engage in integrative thought cannot be accomplished by a simple objective test or trivia game. Rather, faith-learning integration always involves content beyond Scripture and Christian theology; without it there is nothing to integrate. A student's attitude and approach to integration could be assessed by adapting the five levels of integration previously discussed into an assessment rubric.

34. Joyce Hardin, John Sweeney, and Jerry Whitworth, "Integrating Faith and Learning in Teacher Education," paper presented at the Extended Annual Meeting of the Association of Independent Liberal Arts Colleges for Teacher Education, February 24, 1999, 8–9.

CONCLUSION

Achieving faith-learning integration in the church or ministry classroom is predicated on an instructor who can do faith-learning integration, is committed to seeing students independently engage in faith-learning integration, and is likewise committed to the process as well as the product of faith-learning integration. However, ultimately, it depends on willing students. This is the one factor that is beyond our immediate control as teachers. Regardless, we can still make every effort to help our students "take every thought captive to obey Christ" (2 Cor. 10:5 ESV) that we might "win as many as possible" (1 Cor. 9:19 NIV).

REFLECTION QUESTIONS

1. How do you define faith-learning integration?
2. What topics are most relevant for your church or campus to address from a Christian perspective?
3. What part of teaching for faith-learning integration most concerns you? Why?
4. How does faith-learning integration apply to Christian higher education? To a congregation?

RECOMMENDED READING

Cosgrove, Mark P. *Foundation of Christian Thought: Faith, Learning, and the Christian Worldview*. Grand Rapids: Kregel, 2006.

Harris, Robert A. *The Integration of Faith and Learning: A Worldview Approach*. Eugene, OR: Cascade, 2004.

Heie, Howard, and David Wolfe, eds. *The Reality of Christian Learning: Strategies for Faith-Discipline Integration*. St. Paul, MN: Christian University Press, 1987.

Plantinga, Cornelius. *Engaging God's World: A Christian Vision of Faith, Learning, and Living*. Grand Rapids: Eerdmans, 2002.

CHAPTER 13

INTERCULTURAL TEACHING: BECOMING AWARE TO BE EFFECTIVE

Michael A. Ortiz

I had recently graduated from seminary and was eager to share the depth of knowledge I had collected as a ThM New Testament student. I spent weeks poring through Romans, examining the Greek text and all my class notes. Months were invested to review all major commentaries, recent articles, and the most important books on Romans to develop my own teaching outline that exceeded 140 pages. The lesson plans for each day were calculated to the minute. I reviewed and corrected and reviewed and corrected time and again. I was not leaving anything to chance. At least, I thought I was not.

A seminary in Latin America had asked me to teach Romans to their students. The dean introduced me as the Romans professor for the week to twenty-eight students from across the country. Class began, and I proceeded with my extensive outline and lesson plans, sharing all the insights I thought were significant for these students to grasp and apply in their lives and ministries. As usual, the first day was mostly getting a feel for the students and how my material would be received. It did not take long for me to realize I was not as ready as my preparation suggested.

As I interacted with the class, a consistent theme surfaced. The students regularly asked about my own context. They wanted to know about what it was like to live in the United States. They were asking questions about education, finances, work opportunities, and even politics. I would address their questions in brief fashion and quickly press forward through my outline and lesson plans. Still, their curiosity about my own context continued. As I asked other professors and seminary leaders about this persistent curiosity, I realized something vitally important about my students.

Within their context, there is a cultural rhythm from an early age toward migrating out of their homeland. It is a regular topic of conversation and reflection in their homes and with family, in their workplaces, and within their churches. Their personal circumstances have been so harsh for so long that figuring a way out is a daily preoccupation. And one way to migrate out of their context is earning a seminary degree.

My students were in my course to continue their journey through seminary hoping it would open another journey—ministry work in another country. They viewed seminary preparation as a vital step to open pastoral and ministry leadership positions in another land. I could not have prepared any better to teach Romans, except that I had done little to understand the context of my students. As the week moved forward, I realized that although my outline and lesson plans were useful tools for me as a teacher, I needed to loosen my grip on that material, listen and learn, and grow as a cultural learner for the sake of my students during our short time together.

As teachers, we may come to cultural realizations at inopportune times if we have not done our background work to understand contexts and their influences on those we will teach. Especially as teachers engaging intercultural learners, we must be more aware in order to be more effective. Regardless of their preparation, teachers can be taken off guard by how students' context influenced them. Effective teachers take the students' culture into account as they prepare to teach.

Many of us have been well trained and over time are able to develop sound content for our teaching. This chapter addresses teachers' preparations to teach that content effectively to students from settings other than theirs. The focus is on awareness that leads to effectiveness in intercultural teaching and reminds Christian educators that they will continue to have increasing opportunities to teach interculturally. For that reason and others, intercultural teaching is especially important for you today.

INTERCULTURAL TEACHING TERMINOLOGY

A principal term is *students' contexts*, referring to the cultural setting most associated with a student. The phrase encompasses more than traveling to another country to teach; it includes students who might be in the teacher's own cultural setting. Most of our communities and churches have a growing number of people from different parts of the world who could end up being your students. Additionally, at times you might have students in your class who join via remote video. In today's world, those students could be in their home context but wanting to receive your teaching. Today's global mobility and technology tools allow for this more than in years past.

Along these lines, when students' contexts differ from that of the teacher's, these are then called *intercultural students*, regardless of how students might be gaining access to the class; in turn, the phrases *intercultural teacher* and *intercultural teaching* are likewise relevant to this chapter. They do not just refer to a teacher traveling to another context to teach, but one having intercultural students in the classroom, no matter the teaching modality. Due to the widened ways in which we offer courses and the global breadth of our student pools, it behooves us to interpret intercultural teaching in its broadest sense possible. With broader understanding of what an intercultural teacher is and who intercultural students are, you will more likely be aware of the cultural differences represented in your courses and be better positioned to increase your teaching effectiveness.

INTERCULTURAL TEACHING MATTERS TODAY

No matter how well prepared you are with your content, an awareness of and preparation for students' cultural realities will undoubtedly improve your teaching effectiveness. This is most significant when discussing intercultural teachers who are doing intercultural teaching. Considering today's global environment and the diaspora of peoples, being in tune as an intercultural teacher, perhaps more than you have been in the past, is even more crucial. This chapter explores a few ways in which intercultural teaching matters for teachers today.

As a starting point, there is a central biblical reason why intercultural teaching matters. Teachers cannot look at any form of Christian education as being in a silo removed from its larger function within God's plan as revealed within the fullness of the Scriptures. As Christ followers, our education endeavors should always be set within a biblical missiological framework. The whole of the Scriptures speaks to the ongoing redemptive plan of God for every nation, every tribe, every language, and all peoples. Noted missiologist and educator Christopher Wright puts it in these words: "The writings that now comprise our Bible are themselves the product of and witness to the ultimate mission of God. . . . The Bible renders to us the story of God's mission through God's world for the sake of the whole of God's creation."[1] Wright seeks to have us more fully grasp the whole of God's biblical redemptive plan and live motivated by it. Mark Young, president of Denver Seminary, recently explained in his book *The Hope of the Gospel*, "A school's mission and vision must be formulated on the basis of shared theological convictions about the nature of God's mission in the world, the role of God's people in that mission, and the unique contribution theological education can make to that mission."[2] The same could be said of any Christian education program.

If we are truly people of the Word, then we must consistently view teaching as an instrument contributing to God's mission through our and our students' lives. As we embrace this perspective and model a heightened intercultural awareness in our teaching, we will cultivate learning experiences that cast a widened global vision and greater alignment with God's mission. For this reason, good intercultural teaching practices that intentionally reflect and contribute to God's mission in the world matter for today and into the future.

GLOBAL EDUCATION PERSPECTIVE

Over the last few years there has been a recognition that we can no longer think of missions as from the West to the rest. The global landscape for intercultural missions has been drastically reshaped. One way to speak of these substantial changes is through "polycentric" terminology. Polycentric missiology contends that there is no longer one major

1. Christopher J. H. Wright, *The Mission of God: Unlocking the Bible's Grand Narrative* (Downers Grove, IL: IVP Academic, 2006), 48, 51.
2. Mark S. Young, *The Hope of the Gospel: Theological Education and the Next Evangelicalism* (Grand Rapids: Eerdmans, 2022), 1. On 77–78, Young also makes these claims worth noting: "Not seeing the Bible as that one true story creates the tragic inevitability that we will live by another story. . . . Theological education for the next evangelicalism must be conceived and imbued with the startling claim that the Bible is cosmic history, that Jesus is the centerpiece of that history, and that our faith is a unique telling of it."

center for missions (formerly the West) but that there are now various centers, especially within Majority World contexts.

The Mission Commission of the World Evangelical Alliance (WEA) further promulgated this updated perspective of missions through their gathering in Panama in 2016, which has resulted in publications and inclusion of polycentric language among various global ministries.[3] The International Council for Evangelical Theological Education (ICETE) has likewise contributed to polycentric reflections about Christian education. For instance, the ICETE Manifesto II is a global declaration for renewal in education, and states that "in an increasingly globalized and polycentric world, partnerships in theological education will become more and more important and significant." [4] The Manifesto II further states:

> In order to be relevant for the church in mission in various contexts and situations, theological education is to be offered in many formats serving multiple needs. In addition, theological education must be accessible to all God's people. Special attention must be given to groups of people who have traditionally had and still have limited access to education: Neither gender nor social status, neither skin colour nor nationality, neither geographic location nor lack of personal connections should exclude people from theological education.[5]

Globally, education leaders are embracing a more polycentric, reciprocal, and inclusive outlook; we must allow the new global posture growing among educators to shape how we teach.

Holding a more polycentric posture will widen teachers' mindsets and global relevance for their own sake, for their churches and ministries, and for their students. It is not just about the West any longer. Teaching should not only draw instructors and students closer to God's

3. WEA Mission Commission, "The Panama Statement," accessed May 4, 2023, https://weamc.global/the-panama-statement/. See also Joseph W. Handley Jr., *Polycentric Mission Leadership: Toward a New Theoretical Model for Global Leadership* (Oxford: Regnum, 2022); and Allen Yeh, *Polycentric Missiology: Twenty-First Century Mission from Everyone to Everywhere* (Downers Grove, IL: IVP Academic, 2016).
4. The International Council for Evangelical Theological Education, "The ICETE Manifesto," 13, accessed February 19, 2023, https://icete.info/resources/manifesto/.
5. ICETE, "The ICETE Manifesto," 11.

mission, but it should also include a sense of connectedness to the richness of what God is doing outside the West. Your intercultural students themselves could play essential roles to help raise global awareness of God's work as part of the classroom experience. But should teachers in the West fail to embrace a broadened, more polycentric perspective, they will grow increasingly siloed, and their teaching will become decreasingly pertinent to those from other cultures. Intercultural teaching matters to keep you and your students relevant for a variety of life settings.

Expanding Global Opportunities

Through today's ever-expanding globalization, there are numerous opportunities to teach interculturally. For example, many higher education institutions have become more intentional in exploring ways to extend their programs outside of North America, and especially into Majority World contexts such as Latin America, Africa, and Asia. Colorado Christian University, Oklahoma Christian University, and Taylor University, along with Asbury Theological Seminary and Dallas Theological Seminary through its relatively new Global Ministries Division are just a few institutions with substantial and increasing global work.

Additionally, many teachers desire to do missions through teaching overseas apart from their regular home teaching work. Often, this is done through training ministries based in North America that serve in various parts of the world, through a teacher's own church, or simply through an invitation extended by teaching ministries and churches overseas. Theologians Without Borders facilitates these types of arrangements through its database of institutions looking for short-term Western teachers. Further, as the church in Majority World contexts continues to grow, the chances for teaching overseas will only continue to enlarge.[6] There are bountiful opportunities to come alongside churches right in their contexts and help elevate the training of their leaders and lay people alike.

6. Center for the Study of Global Christianity at Gordon-Conwell Theological Seminary, "What Percentage of Pastors Worldwide Have Theological Training?," accessed November 3, 2022, https://www.gordonconwell.edu/center-for-global-christianity/research/quick-facts/. This report indicates that pastoral leaders total about 5 million worldwide (including bi-vocational servants), but only 5 percent have any formal theological training (undergrad or graduate level).

Increased Distance Learning

There is little doubt that COVID-19 accelerated online teaching opportunities. The pandemic was a tenuous time for many churches and teaching programs, but those best suited to pivot toward online remote video teaching were more likely to not only survive but thrive. The trajectory toward more online teaching offerings will only continue to grow (see chapter 14 on technology and education).

In addition, this growth will increase through asynchronous teachings. Numerous platforms like YouTube and Vimeo make teaching available when and how our students desire. This type of teaching will only multiply through the growing use of mobile devices and tablets worldwide. Today more than ever educational professionals have a larger potential scope of students through technology. At times, our teaching is recorded and later delivered to users. Such delivery takes place without us having any direct interaction with those "students" receiving our content. Platforms may disburse our teaching to students from diverse cultural backgrounds and distant parts of the world. If you have opportunities to have your teaching be recorded, it would be advisable to be more sensitive to how intercultural students might receive your content, particularly with illustrations and teaching moments intended to drive home core teaching points. Since you might not ever have the advantage of direct contact with students who study your material through an online platform, you could improve your teaching by embedding more context-neutral content. As you do so, this will increase your intercultural teaching awareness and effectiveness.

PREPARING TO TEACH INTERCULTURALLY

What should a Christian educator consider when preparing to teach interculturally? The tools and suggestions in this section will assist teachers to be contextually better prepared so as to make them more aware and effective in intercultural teaching.

Gaining Insight into Students' Contexts

There are various ways teachers can glean valuable insight about the contexts of their students. In today's world of rapid technology information, it is not difficult to read articles and news information about students' home settings, for example, by using news apps from international sources such as the BBC (United Kingdom) or NHK (Japan).

Teachers may also have access to national press publications that will give more insight on current issues and trends. Such resources could prove highly valuable to connect and build rapport with intercultural students and potentially to adapt teaching.

Teaching Across Cultures: A Global Christian Perspective contains firsthand experiences from intercultural teachers who collectively have taught in thirty-one countries.[7] Should your intercultural students' context be one of those, this book will give you solid insights for your preparation. Also consider *Global Christianity: A Guide to the World's Largest Religion from Afghanistan to Zimbabwe*.[8] In this book, Gina Zurlo, codirector of the Center for the Study of Global Christianity at Gordon-Conwell Theological Seminary, offers Christian profiles for 233 countries, including substantial data and keen summaries. A quick glance will give you valuable insight into a student's home context.

Utilizing colleagues and friends who have traveled substantially, and perhaps even missionaries who have spent substantial time in the students' contexts, can also be beneficial. Spending a short time with them will likely yield meaningful insights, especially if they have recently been there. Digging a little deeper with them, you could also discover additional people who you might be able to contact and further glean what they know about a context. You may also consider expatriates who would be open to share about their home country. With today's global diaspora, it is not too hard to find someone within your hometown who might be from your students' contexts.

Another category of individuals are nationals still within their context. Since they are still living there, they may prove monumental in helping gain a deeper understanding of the students' contexts. Of course, there may be access challenges to nationals, but still, it is something to strive for, particularly if you intend to be in their context more than once. If possible, through repeated travels, develop "friends in context." These are nationals—perhaps no more than two, maybe three—with whom you invest to build trust and close relationships. They are valuable to further learn about students' contexts and will typically lead to you adjusting lesson plans.

7. Perry Shaw, et al., *Teaching Across Cultures: A Global Christian Perspective* (Carlisle, UK: Langham, 2021).
8. Gina A. Zurlo, *Global Christianity: A Guide to the World's Largest Religion from Afghanistan to Zimbabwe* (Grand Rapids: Zondervan Academic, 2022).

Another practical tool to assess your students' cultural setting has to do with research conducted by Geert Hofstede.[9] Hofstede's website makes it easy to look up where a country might stand on various cultural dimensions. Although he includes six cultural dimensions, the power distance and individualism dimensions are most useful to assess culture for educational purposes.[10] The individualism dimension simply measures the extent to which a culture typically prefers to function individually as opposed to more collectively in community. The power distance dimension intends to measure the culturally accepted way in which people relate to those who have some form of authority.

As an example, if a teacher has a student from a context with a large power distance, the student will likely not want to ask many questions in class, speak during your teaching, or do anything to challenge the teacher. In fact, that student might simply accept all that is said and be able to recite it back perfectly to the teacher. If the teacher is aware that the student might have this type of orientation, then the teacher can be more intentional to stimulate exchanges and foster critical reflection. Most of us are also familiar with the influence of honor-shame on individuals.[11] Students who come from a predominantly honor-shame setting will likely expect a similar learning environment as those who come from a large power distance setting. And so, beside Hofstede's tool, be cognizant of students who come from honor-shame.

On the individualism dimension, if a teacher finds that the student's context has a low individualism score, then they know it is more likely a community-based setting. In preparation for teaching students with that type of cultural dimension influence, small group conversations and perhaps even group projects might prove useful.

But there is a word of caution for using these sorts of tools. Cultures today are more dynamic and fluid than ever, and it is terribly ambitious

9. Hofstede Insights, "Country Comparison Tool," accessed May 24, 2023, https://www.stede-insights.com/country-comparison-tool.

10. James E. Plueddemann, *Teaching Across Cultures: Contextualizing Education for Global Mission* (Downers Grove, IL: IVP Academic, 2018), 62–67. Plueddemann illustrates the use of power distance and individualism versus collectivism for more effective intercultural teaching.

11. Roland Müller, *The Messenger, the Message, the Community: Three Critical Issues for the Cross-Cultural Church Planter*, 2nd ed. (Manitoba: CanBooks, 2010). Müller outlines three major cultural paradigms because of the sin that entered the world at the garden of Eden. Briefly, he argues that most cultures can be identified by either guilt-innocence, fear-power, or honor-shame.

to attempt to summarily define a culture. Educators must avoid stereotyping all individuals within the same context.[12] Plus, we know cultures are made up of various subcultures.[13] Rather, use these tools as a starting place, and then do everything possible to get to know students and individually evaluate how they might differ from that. The next section will focus on getting to know your intercultural students.

Rapport Building with Intercultural Students

Before we consider how to get to know your intercultural students, let's begin with you as the intercultural teacher. An essential element will be the disposition you assume. As teachers who have been well prepared with degrees, experiences, and accomplishments, you must be careful not to come across as too assuming. Although this could be said in relation to all your students, it is notably important with your intercultural students. As you encounter them, they will be fairly intimidated and even anxious about being taught by someone with likely greater credentials than they possess. Your position of "authority" as a teacher will be heightened with intercultural students.

It is the intercultural teacher's responsibility to welcome students, whether in person, online, or otherwise. Duane Elmer, in his book *Cross-Cultural Servanthood*, writes about the importance of having an intercultural openness based upon the ability to "welcome people into your presence and make them feel safe."[14] One simple way to do this is to listen to their stories, and perhaps tell them yours. You can do this in class or outside of class, individually or with a group of students.

Intercultural students often want to gather in groups outside of class time, especially over meals. Particularly when you are a teacher from overseas, students know they likely will only have you for a short time and will want to spend as much as possible with you. Embrace those times. By doing so, you welcome them into your presence, make

12. Craig Ott, *Teaching and Learning Across Cultures: A Guide to Theory and Practice* (Grand Rapids: Baker Academic, 2021), 36–37. Ott also rightfully warns that such national profiles may not differentiate enough between specific contexts and forms of teaching within a country (55). Additionally, Ott notes that "Western conceptions of non-Western pedagogies have historically been notoriously ethnocentric, and cross-cultural teachers will do well to familiarize themselves with those critiques" (24).
13. Plueddemann, *Teaching Across Cultures*, 43.
14. Duane Elmer, *Cross-Cultural Servanthood: Serving the World in Christlike Humility* (Downers Grove, IL: IVP Books, 2006), 39.

them feel safe, and build trust and rapport that will elevate your teaching and your students' learning experience.

Your trust and rapport building will open ways to engage your intercultural students and help practically apply your Christian education. Certainly, intercultural students want to understand what they're being taught on a cognitive level, but they are especially oriented toward real-life concerns and needs within their contexts. Globally, learners are more than ever looking for material that will help with their questions and their effectiveness in ministry.[15] In Judith and Sherwood Lingenfelter's book *Teaching Cross-Culturally,* they convey, "We propose that good teaching in any culture will include traditional learning techniques and that a teacher who wants to be a Christlike servant in a cross-cultural setting will try to make learning as context specific and real to life as possible."[16] Plueddemann puts it plainly when he suggests that effective intercultural teaching includes a "teacher who helps the learners to tie together knowledge and life."[17] As you build rapport with your intercultural students, they will increasingly believe you can offer guidance to help address their everyday ministerial needs and tie what they are learning to life.

As an illustration, I was in a particular context teaching on the Sermon on the Mount. The vast majority of my students in this context were poor, most had endured significant losses, and a number had undergone persecution for their faith. Yet they were gentle, humble people continuing in their faithful journey with Christ and trusting they would be blessed. As I spent time with them and went through my teaching, I realized I needed to slow down and guide my students through the text so that it would directly speak to them. As the

15. Perry Shaw, *Transforming Theological Education: A Practical Handbook for Integrative Learning* (Carlisle, UK: Langham, 2014), 137. Shaw adds that this is especially the case when students are more mature than in the past and have less and less spare time to give to their studies. He writes about the curriculum being designed for "context to text."

16. Judith E. Lingenfelter and Sherwood G. Lingenfelter, *Teaching Cross-Culturally: An Incarnational Model for Learning and Teaching* (Grand Rapids: Baker Academic, 2003), 40.

17. Plueddemann, *Teaching Across Cultures*, 34. The full context: "I'm convinced that the paradigm I'm suggesting has the potential of promoting effective teaching in any culture. It begins with students immersed in their cultural context and a teacher who helps the learners to tie together knowledge and life." In another section Plueddemann states, "In contrast, today most higher education takes place in a classroom separated from the context of living. Connecting subject matter with the learner's experience in a low context environment is challenging but doable" (112).

Lingenfelters suggest, my teaching and their learning needed to be as real to life as possible. Not only did the students wrestle with how the Sermon on the Mount applied to them, but as a class we had the safety to discuss how the teaching and the power of the gospel could be effectively transmitted to those they ministered to who were in similar life circumstances.[18] Fortunately, I had the rapport to move further with them so that my teaching would practically impact their lives, those they served, and their settings.[19]

This reminds us of the importance of potential social impact through your intercultural students. As has already been suggested, many of those students come from environments where there are multiple cultural layers of societal concern whether due to poverty, oppression, corruption, political stress, racism, and so on. You simply cannot disregard their constant realities. In fact, doing so runs the risk of losing any rapport you have built. Duane Elmer reminds us not only that "trust becomes the basis for deep sharing and mutual learning" but that it is fragile, and we must do all we can to maintain it.[20] Students from varied backgrounds frequently voice a lack of connectedness with teachers who show little interest with their real-life struggles. Guard against students saying this about your intercultural teaching.

Craig Ott, who has written extensively on contextualization, missions, and teaching interculturally, states, "Education is one of the most powerful agents of culture change and the cross-cultural teacher brings an added dimension to such change by exposing experiencing learners to new ideas and his own cultural 'otherness.'"[21] Of course, we do need to respect the intercultural students' home contexts and do not want to overreach. But at a minimum, consider how much your teaching could relate to their realities and walk wisely with them. If

18. R. Daniel Shaw, "Beyond Contextualization: Toward a Twenty-First Century Model for Enabling Mission," *International Bulletin of Missionary Research* 34, no. 4 (2010): 208–215. Shaw speaks of the power of the gospel in cultures to transform people. He says: "If the intent of Gospel communication is to enable people to become more like God intended them to be, that is, to display God's image, then transformation in those who bring the Gospel and in those who hear and 'receive' it will move both toward that goal."
19. In *Teaching Cross-Culturally*, the Lingenfelters also state, "To be an effective teacher cross-culturally one must learn how to apply the insights gained from cultural observation to practical issues in the classroom" (29).
20. Elmer, *Cross-Cultural Servanthood*, 82–83, 88.
21. Ott, *Teaching and Learning Across Cultures*, 33.

you have built good rapport, they will seek your wisdom beyond your lesson plans.

Good rapport with your intercultural students will moreover give you a greater passport to challenge their perspectives, especially when not in accordance with sound biblical and theological views. As an intercultural teacher, you need to discern when and how to challenge them, or even if to do so at all. But our responsibility includes correction as we deem necessary. The Lingenfelters have emphasized helping intercultural students think beyond their boundaries. Referring to Jesus as a model, they put it this way:

> Jesus began with the traditions of his people yet pushed them to think beyond the customs and boundaries of their knowledge and practices. By observing some of the techniques Jesus used we can learn to teach in a traditional context while stretching students to think and learn outside the boundaries of their contexts.[22]

The Other Side of Rapport Building

There will be two by-products from investing in relationship building with your intercultural students. Certainly, it will result in greater awareness and more effective teaching, but it will also increase your appreciation for God's mission and expand your global perspective. When teaching numerous students from different contexts, we are regularly reminded that God indeed is at work worldwide and that his redemptive plan is continuously unfolding. We see how God is uniquely at work through the lives of intercultural students by interacting with them, welcoming them, and building trust and rapport with them.

Intercultural students will expose you to cultural practices and perspectives different from yours. This may cause you to question some aspects of your own culture, become more curious about their culture, and wonder if you should lessen your hold on your culture and adopt some of their cultural practices. Within missions, this is commonly referred to as one's "bicultural development." You may have noticed that some use the phrase "cross-cultural" as opposed to the "intercultural" term used in this text. "Cross-cultural" implies going from one to another in a single direction. "Intercultural" better captures the nuance

---

22. Lingenfelter and Lingenfelter, *Teaching Cross-Culturally*, 53.

of people from different cultures informing one another. Through intercultural teaching, a sense of mutuality could unfold that will lead to growth in your bicultural development.

Along these lines, the Lingenfelters suggest intercultural teachers embrace an expanded outlook. Lingenfelter and Mayers state that "those who minister cross-culturally should seek to become 150 percent persons--75 percent birth culture and 75 percent incarnate in the culture of ministry."[23] In other words, intercultural teaching opportunities give us the space and time to become a little less ethnocentric and a little more global, gaining a more polycentric perspective as noted in the prior section. We may feel humbled by some of our intercultural students' cultural limitations, challenges, concerns, and the extent to which they must work to navigate well through their culture. Such student interactions regularly lead teachers to examine the many areas of abundance in their own lives and, at times, to contemplate adjustments that should be implemented.

Before closing out this section, there is one more item to consider. Theologically, teachers need to be prepared to be challenged as they teach intercultural learners. The teacher's greatest theological exam will be when they cross cultures. Theological categories like ecclesiology, pneumatology, eschatology, and soteriology are typically viewed differently outside the West. In *Teaching Across Cultures,* César Lopes states this point rather well: "Crossing boundaries to teach means to be inserted into an exchange with other rationalities and epistemologies which translate themselves into other categories. In other words, crossing boundaries to teach challenges the hegemony of Western theologies."[24]

Lopes goes on to explain the importance of theological humility when teaching interculturally. If you approach your intercultural

23. Lingenfelter and Lingenfelter, *Teaching Cross-Culturally*, 22–23. Sherwood G. Lingenfelter and Marvin K. Mayers, *Ministering Cross-Culturally: An Incarnational Model for Personal Relationships*, 2nd ed. (Grand Rapids: Baker Academic, 2003), 24. See also Elmer, *Cross-Cultural Servanthood,* 93, where he suggests we should be willing to learn about, from, and with those we intend to serve. See also Jane Vella, *Learning to Listen, Learning to Teach* (San Francisco: Jossey-Bass, 2002), 91, who, although not specifically addressing intercultural teaching, states: "We can never control what another person thinks. We can nurture their thinking power by affirmation and building a learning relationship."

24. César Lopes, "Theological Humility in Cross-Cultural Teaching," in Shaw et al., *Teaching Across Cultures*, 121.

opportunities humbly and develop a sound rapport with your students, your theological and even biblical perceptions will likely be broadened. Of course, this is not to say you will need to abandon your doctrinal positions, but you may have more to reflect upon and perhaps incorporate due to your experience as an intercultural teacher. You might even have some bicultural development that shapes your theological views.

Language Factors

An important area of inquiry has to do with language. When teaching students with a language other than yours, there are additional factors to consider. In the Western English-speaking world, there is a grand abundance of literature in biblical and theological studies. Other languages—even Spanish—are still rather restricted. A way of dealing with this intercultural limitation is to find articles and other shorter pieces of literature—perhaps even a textbook—in the students' language,. Teachers could compile all this to offer students comparable literature in their language.

Remarkable translation tools exist and advances are taking place, but still there needs to be the investment of personnel to assure the translations appropriately communicate biblical and theological ideas and important nuances from one language to another. Additionally, one needs to be careful with copyright restrictions that publishers and authors may have in place before using their material in a different language. As teachers consider intercultural teaching with students unable to read in English, you should account for additional time to inquire how to get literature in their language. Do not count on what you have typically used in English being available in their language.

The other language factor has to do with interpretation. There are numerous opportunities to teach overseas in English. In Africa and Asia particularly, there are many churches and training ministries that use English as their primary language. In Latin America, this is not as much the case. Still, there are many opportunities for an English speaker to teach in a different context without having to use an interpreter. If a teacher is just beginning to teach interculturally, it would be sensible to do so in English for the first several times. As one enters a different context to teach, there will already be voluminous layers of culture to become aware of and navigate to be effective. If English is your primary language, there is little reason to add language as an additional layer.

Nonetheless, if teaching interculturally in a language other than your own is inevitable, there are several inquiries to consider with regard to your interpreter. Converse with your interpreter in advance and attempt to glean their knowledge of your teaching subject area. They may have some preformed views that might not align with yours. You need to know those before you begin class. Furthermore, have your interpreter translate all your materials, including outlines, handouts, lesson plans and so on translated. This will give that person a greater chance to become familiar with your content and how you wish to deliver it.

That translation work will help you to identify strengths and weaknesses your interpreter might have. You must do all you can to make sure the interpreter understands meaningful nuances in your teaching, since often miscommunicating nuance could radically alter what your students will comprehend. Remember, in essence during class you will be teaching the interpreter, and the interpreter will be teaching the students.

Teachers should also not be shy about asking for an interpreter's experience and perhaps even following up with those who have used the interpreter before. Since the interpreter will be communicating on your behalf, ultimately you are responsible to make sure your content is accurately presented to your intercultural learners.

Additional Areas of Inquiry

One area worth your inquiry has to do with the extent to which globalization has influenced your students' lives. Today with the availability of information in virtually every part of the world—and often readily through mobile devices—people will increasingly allow their values, beliefs, and practices to be shaped through digital information. For example, if you are teaching in an extremely poor intercultural context, but one that has access to the internet, your students may have a strong awareness about Nike shoes. Although they do not possess any Nikes, the students may perceive them to have a high global value and may want to gain access to those shoes and be associated with that value. This is just one example of thousands that could illustrate the power of global economics, politics, technology, and so on in influencing otherwise isolated contexts. People in poor intercultural contexts are not as removed from the rest of the world as they once were.

Briefly, prosperity theology is a matter of concern. In my travels and regular contacts with ministry leaders, especially in Latin America and Africa, prosperity theology continues to be one of their most significant challenges. Besides trying to discern how other areas of globalization have shaped a context, try to understand how prosperity theology has become part of the church teaching, how it has manifested, and what is already being done to counter it, if anything. At times this theology is connected to more charismatic Christian expressions. Good intercultural teachers will be prepared to not only interact with students on this topic but carefully consider how their teaching content might appropriately address it.

Technology is especially relevant when your teaching takes you to a different setting. There are many contexts where internet connections are limited either due to lack of connectivity and/or lack of electricity. This is particularly the case in many African and Latin American settings. The planned lesson tools in these contexts may be restricted by a lack of internet access. Likewise, students' access to additional resources will be limited. It may be advisable to travel with flash drives to deliver resources for students. Assuming students have computers, they can simply download the content onsite without having to rely upon an internet connection. Before you journey to teach, inquire about internet connectivity, the availability of computers for students, and presentation tools such as projectors and screens.

Those teaching online may need to make technology accommodations for students who are joining the class from contexts that have regular internet limitations. In advance of starting, privately communicate with students from those potential contexts to inquire about this matter. Well-intended teachers will want their intercultural online learners to have access to everything offered during the class. Some of this may need to be done offline through email or otherwise. As a matter of practice, one should consider recording online remote video sessions since intercultural students may occasionally drop off and miss some, if not most, of a session.

A culture's educational philosophy is a particular inquiry that any intercultural teacher should research and examine. Perhaps apart from family, how people are taught within their context might shape them more than anything else in society. For example, some settings may fully embrace a neo-scholastic educational philosophy from preschool all the way through graduate studies. As you might imagine, the cultural power distance is considerable. Students likely had never critically reflected upon what had been taught to them, but simply regurgitated it back to the teacher. Reflection and critique were totally absent skills. Should learners from that educational background be in your class, it will be a crucial task to engender an interactive learning experience.

Australian educator Perry Shaw spent years as a teacher and administrator of a seminary in the Middle East. On this point he writes, "If we want to help our students to make an impact on the world for Christ, we need to cultivate more sophisticated thinking skills; we need to help them develop the ability to process and apply facts."[25] These skills are particularly vital for the global church, especially with the increasing access to digital information. People must be able to rely upon church leaders to help them wisely discern the information flood. Although this is just one illustration, it demonstrates the importance of intercultural teachers being aware of how their students have historically been educated and considering ways to adapt their styles and lesson plans to be most effective in their teaching objectives.[26]

CONCLUSION

This chapter has tried to refine and expand how we think about intercultural teaching. Its terminology has been considered in order to realize that we have more opportunities to impact students from cultures different than ours than we might at first realize. We have examined why intercultural teaching matters today. We also stepped into practical suggestions for intercultural teaching, whether through travel to another context or through the variety of means in which intercultural students have access to us.

Despite the gains from reading this chapter, we still have a lot to learn when it comes to intercultural teaching. The words of James Plueddemann are most appropriate as this chapter comes to an end: "Nobody gets it right the first time or even the second or the third time, but that's all right. Perhaps the key to successful cross-cultural teaching

25. Shaw, *Transforming Theological Education*, 74.
26. In *Teaching and Learning Across Cultures*, Ott states: "The wise cross-cultural teacher will become well acquainted with such collective preferences and expectations, then judiciously determine whether and how to adapt teaching" (55).

is the ability to be curious and flexible toward other cultures."[27] If nothing else, remain curious and flexible and keep pressing on to see how God uses you in the lives of the intercultural learners in your classes. As you do so, you will indeed grow in awareness and over time become a more effective intercultural teacher.

REFLECTION QUESTIONS

1. In your experience as a Christian teacher, when have you had someone in class from a context other than your own? How, if at all, did their presence in your class influence what and how you taught?
2. How would a widened, more global perspective within your teaching ministry help shape how you teach?
3. Listening well is often an important aspect of good teaching. With intercultural students in the past, what were some ways you listened well? What were some of the most significant items you learned about life in their settings?
4. What are some challenges you have faced when trying to get to know those from other cultures in your classes? What are some ways you could build greater rapport with intercultural students in future classes?
5. How have your intercultural teaching experiences challenged you? How have they challenged your own walk with God?

RECOMMENDED READING

Escobar, Samuel. *The New Global Mission: The Gospel from Everywhere to Everyone*. Christian Doctrine in Global Perspective. Downers Grove, IL: IVP Academic, 2003.

Greenman, Jeffrey P., and Gene L. Green, eds. *Global Theology in Evangelical Perspective: Exploring the Contextual Nature of Theology and Mission*. Wheaton Theology Conference Series. Downers Grove, IL: IVP Academic, 2012.

Moreau, A. Scott, Evvy Hay Campbell, and Susan Greener. *Effective Intercultural Communication: A Christian Perspective*. Encountering Mission. Grand Rapids: Baker Academic, 2014.

Newell, Marvin J. *Crossing Cultures in Scripture: Biblical Principles for Mission Practice*. Downers Grove, IL: InterVarsity Press, 2016.

27. Plueddemann, *Teaching Across Cultures*, 44.

CHAPTER 14

PEDAGOGICAL USES OF TECHNOLOGY

John Dyer

Today's digital technology, for all its challenges and frustrations, offers an incredible array of tools through which we can connect, guide, and enrich our students' transformative learning. The following pages will offer a few tips and tricks, best practices, and guidelines for taming and using these tools in a way that will help you connect with your students both inside and outside of the classroom.

TECHNOLOGY AND EDUCATION IN SCRIPTURE

Before we jump into digital technology, it is worthwhile to consider how the Scriptures treat the use of media and technology for education. If we go back to the book of Exodus, we find that right in the middle of the story lies one of the largest technologically enabled educational projects ever conducted.

The book of Exodus begins with Moses's remarkable birth (Exod. 1–2), continues to the liberation of God's people from Egypt (Exod. 3–18, and shows us God giving the Law and commandments to Moses (Exod. 19–30). But then in Exodus 31, the scene shifts from God speaking to Moses to working through another man, Bezalel, filling him with his Spirit and "with all kinds of skills—to make artistic designs . . . and to engage in all kinds of crafts" (Exod. 31:3–4 NIV). In this critical moment, God was giving Bezalel the task of transforming the principles and ideas that Moses heard into visual, tangible objects that the

Israelites could see, touch, and smell. Hebrew scholar John Sailhamer notes that "there is an important parallel here with God's work of Creation in Genesis 1"[1] in that both God and Bezalel do their creative work through the Spirit of God.

Though scholars note that "we know precious little of Bezalel"[2] and most treat him as a footnote in education,[3] we can draw lessons from this story. The first is that transformative education is inseparable from creative media. Educating the people of God was never just a matter of an expert transmitting data; rather, it has always been a holistic transformation that engages all the senses. As teachers and leaders, we are important—essential even—in the formation of our students. But the visual, the tangible, and the experiential are an essential part of our craft. If we are to be godly guides like Moses for our students, connecting the big ideas to their lives and vocations, we must also draw on the expertise of Bezalel.

Sometimes, like Jesus, all we need is a good story or parable to connect with our students. But even Jesus used fig trees (Matt. 21:18–21), children (Mark 10:14–16), coins (Luke 15:8–10), and spit (John 9:6) as reference points for the deep truths he was communicating. Today, we have even more tools at our disposal that can draw students in and make connections between their lives and what we are teaching.

TEACHING OUTCOMES AND TECHNOLOGICAL NOVELTY

Before we delve further into categories for using technology in education, it is important to acknowledge something about technology—sometimes technology is just fun. Trying something new with students or showing them an interesting feature can draw them in and disrupt the same old patterns they might be used to. Switching up the learning environment can stimulate curiosity and help with the stickiness of what is taught. In the Exodus story, we see God writing the Law on tablets of stone (Exod. 31:18), which communicates their importance and permanence. On the other hand, when Miriam wants to communicate the joy of the Lord, she sings, dances, and plays instruments (Exod.

1. John H. Sailhamer, *The Pentateuch as Narrative: A Biblical-Theological Commentary* (Grand Rapids: Zondervan Academic, 1992), 309.
2. Peter Enns, *Exodus*, NIV Application Commentary (Grand Rapids: Zondervan Academic, 2000), 543.
3. D. A. Carson, "A Biblical Theology of Education," *Themelios* 42, no. 6 (2021): 257–68.

15:20). Bezalel is tasked with fashioning the articles of the tabernacle which help visualize the holiness of God, the destructive nature of sin, and God's provision of redemption.

However, we must also be aware of the temptation to allow the technology itself to become the focus rather than a means or to allow technology to dictate the terms of learning. This happens when we spend more time on the question, "How can I use [Technology X] in the classroom?" and forget to ensure that our primary question is, "What do I want my students to learn, and how do I get them there?" These two questions are related to one another, but as other authors[4] in this volume point out, we must always begin with our instructional objectives. When a new educational technology comes along, it is important to investigate how it can be used, but the driver of its usefulness should not be how new it is but if it aligns with class objectives. Otherwise we can unintentionally adopt what Sonny Magana calls the "let's add technology and see what happens" mindset.[5]

One other area we must always consider with technology is understanding what message the technology itself sends. That is, what does the choice to use or not use a technology tell students about their learning? For example, in some teaching environments teachers may spend a lot of time on their presentation slides, working to ensure they clarify and augment what they intend to say. However, they may communicate the message that "teaching is mostly about talking through pretty slides." This means it is important to punctuate slide-heavy classes with times when the projector is turned off and the teacher guides the class in a different way. The activity should have a goal and a desired outcome, but it also sends a message about learning and community. This also ensures that teachers do not get into the rut of "thinking in PowerPoint" and that they allow students with different learning styles to flourish in class. These are examples of what media scholar Marshall McLuhan meant when he wrote, "The medium is the message."[6] In other words, the medium itself communicates as much or more as the message you put into it.

4. See chapters 8 and 9 for discussions of educational objectives and instructional design.
5. Sonny Magana, *Disruptive Classroom Technologies: A Framework for Innovation in Education* (Thousand Oaks, CA: Corwin, 2017), 5.
6. Marshall McLuhan, *Understanding Media: The Extensions of Man* (New York: New American Library, 1964), 7.

Class discussions offer another example of how technology can send a message that might be difficult to communicate directly. Imagine asking the people in a ministry or classroom to share some of their struggles and talk about how they really feel. In a group with a lot of established trust, people often feel free to share, but people in a new or large group might feel uncomfortable sharing even when you assure them it is a safe space. In this context, a survey tool could be used to communicate safety. For example, ask people to answer a survey on their phones with the question, "Fill in two words that describe God." In this instance students will tend to answer using positive words like "powerful, loving, father" and so on, and the survey tool will create a colorful word cloud from those terms. While that prompt often elicits "Sunday school answers" (which are of course true!), following it with a deeper question like, "What do you struggle most to believe about God?" can often surface more difficult and painful answers that feel more like, "I believe; help my unbelief" (Mark 9:24 ESV). The anonymity of the survey tool allows people to share more vulnerably and then see that their fellow classmates are also working through their salvation "with fear and trembling" (Phil. 2:12 NIV). In this case, the anonymous survey technology says, "This is a safe place to share your struggles" better than if you personally say those same words out loud. This means we need to constantly ask, "What message does this technology send?" or "What kind of environment does this technology make possible?"

One final consideration is the quality of our design and technology usage. As leaders, our job is not to spend all our time on design or try to become technology wizards. That said, we still need to be attentive to the message our design, or lack thereof, might send. Content is important and central (Moses and Miriam), but an overly flashy design with lots of animation can be distracting, and a jarring color scheme with too much text can create a negative impression. In contrast, a well-designed presentation can instill confidence, drawing students into the material like the sights and smells of the tabernacle drew in the ancient Israelites (Bezalel).

These examples are intended to show that, yes, technology can send literal messages, but that we must also be aware of the ways in which the presence or absence of a technology itself sends a message (or, better, creates an environment). Now let us move on to consider some specific technologies.

FOUR CATEGORIES OF EDUCATIONAL TECHNOLOGY (PLUS ONE BONUS CATEGORY)

One of the biggest challenges with modern technology is how fast it changes. Because of the pace of change, it would be nearly impossible to categorize and adequately explain each new tool in educational technology. And even if one could accomplish such a feat, it would quickly be outdated. To simplify this and offer some enduring practices, this chapter will categorize educational technology into four simple buckets, with one additional category to consider.

Technology Before a Session	This covers the tools to use for research and preparation for teaching. Bible apps, generative AI tools, presentation software, and even the lowly word processor, for example, all fit this category.
Technology During a Session	This refers to the things used in a room with students. The most common of these today is a projector to show slides or video clips, but this might also include printed handouts, an electronic poll, and the devices the students have with them in class.
Technology Between Sessions	This includes all the tools used to interact with students in nonsynchronous ways. Schools and universities rely on powerful tools called *learning management systems* (LMS) for content delivery and assignment collection, but any form of education in ministry can use communication technology like email, discussion boards, text messages, and other social media apps to keep their communities informed between sessions.
Technology as a Session	This moves the entire meeting time online by incorporating technologies that enable synchronous (or real-time) online learning and connection. Learning most commonly takes place over some form of video conferencing software or hardware where a group can meet online, or the teacher could use more broadcast-oriented communication tools that create a webinar or live-streaming environment.

There are some overlaps in these categories, and most educational experiences will use some combination of them. In the coming pages, we'll focus on collecting the best practices for each area so you can choose where to hone and develop your teaching skills.

TECHNOLOGY *BEFORE* A SESSION

Before teaching, whether it takes place in a family devotional, a small group Bible study, a church ministry group, a school classroom, or a large auditorium, you will most likely be using a variety of technologies to research, organize, and design the lessons. This could include pen, paper, and books (sometimes the oldest technology is the most effective), powerful Bible software, or generative artificial intelligence tools that assist you in creating content.

In the section below, presentation software will be considered in more depth, but this section will focus on other preparation materials. The primary goal at this point is to organize your ideas. Some people prefer to start fresh with paper to avoid the distractions of screens, others prefer to jot down an outline in Microsoft Word, and still others enjoy using concept-mapping tools to explore connections between ideas. The goal here is to find a technology that helps capture and organize your thoughts, ideas for lessons, and the desired outcomes before going into more detail on how to execute that vision.

Once you have an overall idea of the direction of the lesson, the next step is to find good sources. One approach is to use existing curriculum. But if you're keen on putting together your own lesson, you will want to use additional software to help you find good resources. You can use websites like theopedia.com to help you begin to understand theological concepts and bestcommentaries.com to find an appropriate commentary for the book of the Bible you plan to teach, or you can develop your own list of trusted resources. A Bible app like Logos Bible Software can provide dozens of resources, organizing them by passage of Scripture, theme, or biblical character. In fact, Bible software makers sometimes describe their products as a "time machine for pastors"[7] because they can do the initial work of finding resources much faster than a person hunting for books in a library.

---

7. See John Dyer, *People of the Screen: How Evangelicals Created the Digital Bible and How It Shapes Their Reading of Scripture* (New York: Oxford University Press, 2022), chapters 4–5.

ChatGPT launched interest in generative AI tools that can augment and accelerate your ministry. For example, you could upload a recording of you or your pastor's sermon into an AI and ask it to generate discussion questions for your congregation's small groups. If you have a general idea of something you want to teach, you could upload your outline into a generative system and ask it to fill in more details, suggest resources, or create activities based on the material. Generative image tools can also be used to create complementary illustrations that conform to a particular style (see below for additional guidance on the use and misuse of images). It can also be fun to use a generative system live with people in your ministry, incorporating its output into a discussion about how the internet, as a whole, tends to see a certain idea. But you should always be careful to track down and confirm the claims an AI makes and the sources it uses. AI apps are very powerful but still make mistakes. Educators are still learning how to best harness these tools, and new resources for educational ideas[8] and their ethical implications[9] are on the rise.

The use of generative tools and online resources brings up an important point for both ministry leaders and students regarding trust and plagiarism. Plagiarism is presenting another's work as your own, which includes copying the work of a person without citing it or passing on AI-generated content as your own. The point of education is not to merely regurgitate facts, which an AI can do better than a person, but to engage in a process of learning that reforms the mind and soul. Overusing generative systems can bypass that process and prevent the transformative part of education from taking place. Also, if people pass off AI product as their own, it can erode trust because they are presenting themselves as knowing something they do not. This is true not only of students turning in assignments, but also of teachers who do not acknowledge their sources.. This is true of a student turning in an assignment but also of a teacher who does not acknowledge their sources. We are all still learning, and we must be honest about all our sources including AI.

8. Matt Miller, *AI for Educators: Learning Strategies, Teacher Efficiencies, and a Vision for an Artificial Intelligence Future* (San Diego: Ditch That Textbook, 2023).
9. Heidi A. Campbell and Pauline Hope Cheong, *Thinking Tools for AI, Religion & Culture* (College Station, TX: Digital Religion Publications, 2023), accessed July 25, 2023, https://oaktrust.library.tamu.edu/handle/1969.1/198190.

TECHNOLOGY *IN* A SESSION

After creating a lesson, the technology used when teaching in-person with students is likely the most influential and where the majority of our focus in this chapter will be. Below, we will consider the technology and media you could use as a teacher as well as the technology students might have that can be drawn into your teaching. This will be divided into three major areas: environmental technology, presentation media, and students' technology.

Environmental Technology

Educational technology starts by considering the classroom environment. We do not often think of the places where we meet for educational ministry as a technology, but the place—whether a home, a classroom, or an auditorium—and everything in it is made up of human-made objects designed for particular purposes. This includes chairs, desks, stages, lighting, windows, whiteboards, air-conditioning, artwork, and so on. The way these technologies are arranged and used—that is, the kind of learning environment created—will communicate much to your students about what is going to happen while in the classroom.

Consider, for example, two simple rooms with the same number of chairs but a different arrangement. In the first room, the chairs are set up in rows all facing the same direction. In the second, the same chairs are arranged in a circle. What is the difference? What message does the use of the technology of chairs send to the student? Generally speaking, the first room says that the students are going to be learning from someone up front, while the second says that they will likely be asked to participate in a group discussion.

	Chairs in Rows	**Chairs in a Circle**
Meaning	This is a lecture	This is a discussion
Value	Hearing the teacher	Hearing the students
Identity	I am a learner	I am a participant

If we shift to a church auditorium, the items present there often tell the congregant what is important to that church. Some churches have a central pulpit, which says that the preaching is most important, while others include additional features such as a baptismal font or a table for communion elements. The placement of an offering plate or box also communicates what the church values, as does how many screens, speakers, or cameras a church has in view, and what kind of seating they offer for disabled persons. A pastor can say what the church values from the stage, but people will always believe what the environment tells them over the literal words someone says.

Teachers and leaders do not often get to control everything in their teaching environment, but some things that are usually within their control and can be adjusted according to the intended message and the outcomes they want to achieve. Whether just starting out or teaching the same group for a long time, rethinking the tools in the classroom, home, or auditorium can help teachers more deeply connect with their students.

Presentation Media

What is the difference between a sermon and a lesson? PowerPoint. Although this is clearly a (bad) joke, there is a ring of truth to it, because it surfaces an important consideration of when and where to use slides and other visuals in teaching. Most sermons are delivered without any visuals, so they rely on rhetorical force and the speaker's ability to create an image in the hearer's mind. Teaching lessons, on the other hand, often includes text, images, and videos on screen to show something rather than only tell about it.

There are dangers of overusing slides or doing them so poorly that they become a distraction. At the same time, a slide can make a lesson point much clearer. For example, when a teacher begins a lesson on Isaiah and Hezekiah, a slide with a simple timeline can orient a student for what is about to come. Likewise, a lesson on Ruth and Naomi with a map would make their journey much clearer. And if you are focusing on helping students understand a process (such as salvation), a slide that has a circular visual where each stage (justification, sanctification, glorification) appears successively as you explain it will help visual learners put everything together. When commenting on how the best TED talk speakers use visuals, Carmine Gallo writes, "The slides did not replace the narrative; the slides complemented the story."[10]

10. Carmine Gallo, *Talk Like TED: The 9 Public-Speaking Secrets of the World's Top Minds* (New York: St. Martin's Griffin, 2015), 217.

With this in mind, below are some best practices for creating slide decks that can maximize learning. These are generally true whether creating with the most widely used tools like Microsoft PowerPoint, Apple Keynote, and Google Slides, or exporting them to systems like ProPresenter and MediaShout.

- *Objectives:* It is tempting to open up a slide program and start adding content. However, there is a danger of getting lost in the details and missing the overall point. So start with writing out the main points and outcomes of the overall lesson, and then think through how this slide deck will help accomplish those objectives. It can also be helpful to write a simple outline of what the created slides will cover, including where breaks for questions or interaction with your class may be inserted. Once this is complete, then begin creating slides (or asking an AI for some help).
- *Consistent Design:* Choosing a beautiful, clean design template used consistently can go a long way in avoiding distractions. Today, there are many free templates online and several excellent ones at a reasonable cost. Look for templates that have a variety of slide layouts so there will be no need to stray from the design later. Tools like Microsoft PowerPoint also have features like "Design Ideas" that can customize a single slide, but be wary of overusing this because the ideas it provides are not usually related to the rest of the deck. YouTube has many excellent tutorials for those who want to try making their own slides, such as "One Skill PowerPoint." But creating traditional slides is not the only way to teach—apps like Prezi allow you to organize your visuals in a larger format that zooms in and out, which can be helpful for showing relationships between ideas.
- *Amount of Text:* We have all seen slides with so much text it is difficult to tell where the focus should be. Several good rules can help you avoid putting too much text on a slide. One is the "5/5/5 rule," which is to have no more than five (5) *words per line* of text, five (5) *lines of text* per slide, or five (5) *text-heavy slides* in a row. Another is the 10/20/30 rule (coined by Guy Kawasaki),[11]

11. Guy Kawasaki, "The 10/20/30 Rule of PowerPoint," Guy Kawasaki, December 30, 2005, accessed December 6, 2022, https://guykawasaki.com/the_102030_rule/.

which states that a presentation should have no more than ten (10) slides, be no longer than twenty (20) minutes, and use at least thirty (30) point font. These guidelines come from the world of marketing where presentations are much shorter and more direct, but they are still helpful guidelines for thinking about how to "sell" ideas to students. The following points will help put these ideas into an educational context.

- *More Slides, Less Text:* Slides should be designed to *enhance* what teachers are saying, not *be* what they are saying. For example, if someone is teaching through a process with five steps, everything the teacher knows should not be crammed into a dense slide. Instead, create an introductory slide with five bullet points and, optionally, a short (five-to-seven-word) description of each step. This allows the teacher to give the big picture first and explain it orally. Then he or she can include a more detailed slide for each step and return to the summary after those slides (remember: repetition is a powerful teaching tool). Breaking up the material this way prevents information overload, allowing the teacher to guide students through the concepts, which are reinforced along the way.
- *Quotes and Handouts:* Good teaching brings in the wisdom of others, and this often means including some lengthy quotes in your presentation. It also gives the teacher a chance to include a picture of the author and showcase the diversity of your research (hopefully, not all the pictures look like you!). However, for everyone to be able to easily read the words on a slide, the font must be at least thirty points, which limits a quote to around one hundred words. If the quote is longer than that, split it into two or three slides. If the quote still won't fit, it might be time to switch technologies. Creating a handout (digitally or in print) that students can write on may be a much more effective use of media than trying to fit everything on slides. The occasional use of handouts can also vary your teaching and engage learners who prefer something tactile and interactive.
- *Images and Illustrations:* Images and illustrations in slides should either inform or beautify. Slides often fall into two extremes: boring slides with too much text and busy slides with

too many images or distracting clip art. For example, an image of a historical figure with several bullet points about that person is informative. Likewise, if the teaching process has three main steps, using an icon or illustration with each one can clarify what is happening. But if the class is discussing "wealth" and the first image they see is a stack of cash, it will likely feel forced rather than informative or beautiful. (See below for additional guidance on images.)

- *Animation:* The final and often most overlooked recommendation for slides is to take advantage of simple animations. For example, if you have a well-designed slide with five bullet points, have each bullet appear one at a time as you talk through them. There is no need for five different slides to do this; PowerPoint, Keynote, and other apps have built-in ways to do this. In addition, an animation that makes an element enter the slide from the side or move slightly can occasionally make a concept clearer. However, in most cases, it is best to use simple animations because a lot of motion can be more distracting than informative.
- *Slide Sharing:* Most audiences will request copies of the presentation slides, so be prepared on how to respond. In fact, if the slides are well designed, someone in the audience will likely be taking photos of at least one of them. One approach is to keep the slides separate and not give them to students either because they are intellectual property or because students need to focus on the ideas, not just the slides. Another approach is to send or upload them ahead of time so students have them as they are taught. A final approach is to tell students you will get the slides to them after the session so they don't have to worry about writing down everything (or taking photos of slides). No matter which way is chosen, just be intentional about it.

Use of Images

So when should you use images? Sometimes teachers may choose to teach without any visuals, using vivid language to conjure an image in the listener's mind. If done well, teachers can build toward something that is increasingly funny or set up the listener in one direction and take a humorous turn at just the right moment, all the time intentionally using words and ideas that connect to the coming point. On the other hand, if a teacher decides to show a picture of that same event, the story is immediately told all at once. Spoken words create slightly different pictures in each listener's mind, but an image on screen ensures everyone experiences the same visual at the same time. In other words, an image stops the individual's mental creativity. Whether or not this is a good thing depends on the lesson objective.

For example, if you are telling a story about getting a flat tire and show a picture of the flat tire on screen, it may gain you some sympathy, but it mostly confirms what the audience already knows. However, if you do not show a picture but tell the story well, it draws the listeners in to remember their own experiences with roadside problems and may allow you to transition to a point with more force. On the other hand, images are often very good at conveying emotional information and drawing an audience into the same emotional state. So, if you are using a story about finding an adorable kitten on the side of the road, showing a picture of the kitten on screen will usually elicit more of an emotional reaction to its cuteness (even for non–cat lovers) than words alone.

Why this long excursus on images? The point is to not think as literally about content in our slides, images, and technology, but rather to focus on how that media will affect aspects of your audience other than their cognition, including their emotions and creativity.

Personal Devices

To close our section on technology *in* a session, one last major technology to consider is the devices students bring with them. In a church setting, it is likely that everyone teenage and up will have a smartphone of some kind with them. In a more educational setting like a school or university, many students bring laptops. For all the good we know such devices can do, many studies show students to be distracted by their devices.[12] As things come to mind, students might text a friend, open a web browser, or check their email. In most cases, this is not a major problem, but occasionally some students can become a distraction not only to themselves but to those around them. Therefore, in certain settings it may be appropriate to have a device-use policy and to openly discuss

12. Arnold Glass and Mengxue Kang, "Dividing Attention in the Classroom Reduces Exam Performance," *Educational Psychology* 39 (2018): 1–14.

your expectations with your students. Just remember that this should not be about how you feel when students are on their devices (hint: it can feel discouraging) but rather how you can shape the environment for optimal learning. One approach to eliminate distractions is to create a formal time when everyone puts their devices away together and then, at the end of the teaching, have another formal moment when everyone retrieves them, using a prayer at each juncture.[13]

Teachers can also engage students using the devices they bring with them. This could be using a live survey tool, as mentioned above, for anonymous input, gauging how much the students already know about a subject, or asking for a consensus on what to do next. You also might give students five minutes to find online as many resources on a subject as possible and then have them share what they found, or have them use Bible apps to compare Bible versions or look up words in Greek and Hebrew. In a formal learning scenario, students can pair up, trade assignments, and offer comments on one another's work digitally. Students can also take quizzes on the material covered to see how much they have learned. These don't have to be formal, graded quizzes like you would use in a school setting, just a short series of questions that help you and the people in your ministry see if they are grasping the material. If you plan your time well, you can teach, have students take a quiz or answer Bible trivia, and then go back and clarify what didn't seem to stick.

TECHNOLOGY *BETWEEN* SESSIONS

A great teaching session with excited, engaged participants is wonderful, but technology also allows us to stay connected with our ministries and classes, enabling us to reinforce what they have learned between sessions or to give them a preview of what's coming in the next session. This category of technology between sessions includes any tools used to interact with students between the regular meeting times. In a school or university setting, this will often be a learning management system like Blackboard, Moodle, or Canvas; however, for the local congregation other technologies can perform similar services. Below are several potential uses for any technology between sessions.

13. An excellent prayer example is by Kara Root, "Liturgy of the Cell Phones," Lake Nokomis Presbyterian Church, accessed October 10, 2019, https://www.lakenokomispc.org/cell-phone-liturgy.html.

- *Establish a Schedule*: One of the best uses of technology is having a place where the people in the ministry can go to find out what happened and what is coming next. Teachers might do a great job the first week explaining how their eight-week series is laid out, but students will likely forget this. If, however, they give students a clear place to find a schedule of the class, it will help those who missed a session and allow them to come prepared. A weekly email, a website, or an app can facilitate this connection; just make sure that most of your students can use it.
- *Reinforce Key Points:* Teachers can also use various media to send summaries of what the students learned the week before. This can be in the form of notes, slides, or follow-up questions. You can write these yourself, but this is also a great place to get help from an AI system that can summarize what has been prepared and create questions. Short reminders could be set up via text or an app that would give students reflection points throughout the week. These might be simple statements or questions for students to consider or investigate. Many church video curricula already include these, but feel free to customize them to your group.
- *Assess Learning:* As mentioned above in the technology *during* a session section, you can repurpose survey tools to create informal, non-graded quizzes that can help you and the people in your ministry assess what is really sticking. If you use them during the session, you can immediately adjust and clarify points that you notice multiple people are not understanding. But you can also send out short, multiple-choice quizzes during the week to see how much people remembered, which can help you plan for what to review in your next time together.
- *Provide Opportunities for Feedback:* Just as we want to assess students' learning and provide feedback, online tools invite students to give feedback on the course. Most universities employ a course evaluation at the end of a teaching term, like a Sunday school quarter, but this is often focused on the overall feeling a student has about a class and possibly what they learned from it. However, getting feedback from students immediately after a class session about what made sense, what did not, and what follow-up questions they have can help you adjust mid-course rather than just the next time you teach it.

- *Facilitate Social Interaction:* The people in your ministry are there because they want to connect, so providing them an online space to interact between sessions can be a great way to deepen community. By providing a place for people to ask questions publicly that are answered publicly, the ministry can avoid answering the same questions via email over and over. There are a range of tools that can be used for this including a Facebook group, a Discord or Slack channel, a GroupMe or WhatsApp group, and the like. Keep in mind that each app has a different feature set and security standard. But in general, as long as students know where the online space is and also know how to get in touch with you for private questions, you will be able to foster deeper relationships and more learning.[14]
- *Point to Additional Resources:* Hopefully there is more to say than can be included in a session, and an online hub provides a venue to give engaged learners more of what they want. Posting links to relevant news, articles, and videos can show students just how much there is to learn.

TECHNOLOGY *AS* A SESSION

Our final category for this chapter is technology *as* a session, or conducting the session online. Long before the 2020 pandemic, many universities held classes online with a mixture of prerecorded audio and video, online assignments, and some synchronous video sessions, but online church services and small group meetings were rarer. Since then, many have experienced the highs and lows of online meetings. A well-done online meeting can make us grateful for technology and glad we did not have to fly or drive to the session, but a poorly designed meeting can be deeply demotivating.

There are a variety of reasons why moving the group or class online might be considered. There are often specific short-term reasons, such as the teacher or someone in the class getting sick, weather issues or building construction that prevents you from meeting normally, or it may be simply a matter of convenience during a busy time. Moving or starting

14. For a deeper exploration of online community, see Stephen D. Lowe and Mary E. Lowe, *Ecologies of Faith in a Digital Age: Spiritual Growth Through Online Education* (Downers Grove, IL: IVP Academic, 2018).

a class online may also be a more long-term strategy to reach a new set of people or engage in a type of ministry that cannot practically meet in person very often. Whatever the reason, if moving online is a strong consideration, below are some tips for structuring your online time.[15]

- *Rethink the Timeframe:* The first temptation is to use the same format as an in-person class. This can work for a one-time session, but it is usually not possible to sustain over multiple sessions because most people cannot hold the same level of attention in a videoconference setting as they do in person. The distractions of home and devices are simply too much. One strategy for this is to alternate what you are doing every ten or fifteen minutes (lecture, discussion, video, individual activity, response time, lecture, questions) to keep the class moving. Overall, it is generally a good idea to keep lecturing to a minimum, stopping every ten minutes or so to ask a question of the audience or to allow them to ask questions.
- *Record and Discuss:* Another strategy for adjusting the time frame is to shorten the live session by 25 to 50 percent by purchasing or prerecording some material and asking students to watch it ahead of time. If the teaching time is normally ninety minutes long, send or record a thirty-minute teaching video and meet online for sixty minutes of activities, discussion, and follow-up points. Be prepared with icebreakers and warmups. Depending on how deep the existing relationships are, sometimes students come in cold, and starting with "So what did you think of the video?" can lead to blank stares. An activity or short review along with specific questions gets the discussion going as if meeting in person.
- *Check Everyone's Technology:* By now, one might think that everyone has a device with a camera and a microphone and knows how to use video conferencing software, but this is not always true. It is always good to write out exactly what the people in your ministry or class will need and offer a testing

15. For additional guidance, see Aaron Johnson, *Online Teaching with Zoom: A Guide for Teaching and Learning with Videoconference Platforms* (Littleton, CO: Aaron Johnson, 2020).

session a few days before the class officially starts to make sure everyone's setup works. This is especially true if you decide to use something relatively new or rare. There is a bias that older students tend to need more help, but this is not always the case, so check with everyone. For example, when working with a group that is socioeconomically diverse, teachers may also need to find a way to ask if everyone has a device and internet connection. The main point here is that you should not assume that all your students will come with everything working the first day, so plan ahead to troubleshoot.

- *Come Early, Stay Late:* Just like an in-person class, it is important to arrive (or in this case, login) early and be prepared to stay after the session. In an in-person setting, those moments before and after class can be some of the richest times of connection with your students. Setting a rhythm where students can have informal time before and after an online session can replicate some of that magic. It also gives time to do tech support with students and check your own settings. If you have a technology failure or a program wants to update and reboot, that extra ten minutes can be a lifesaver!
- *Have a Communication Backup Plan:* If you teach online much at all, something will inevitably go wrong. This is why you should designate a second person in your class as a backup, an alternative means of communication. In case something happens, he or she can start the session.
- *Establish Expectations:* Once an online session starts, one of the important things to do is establish what is expected from your students. There may be good reasons to request all the students have their cameras on or not have any distractions in the background, but it may also set many students at ease if they are told that they can turn off their cameras when they need to go to the bathroom or that you celebrate seeing their children, pets, or friends come into view. While most participants know they should mute their mics when not speaking, everyone forgets sometimes, so it is helpful to know the software well enough to mute mics without needing to ask students to mute them.
- *Learn All the Features:* Whatever video software is in use, take some additional time to make sure you know all the features

and can utilize them in class. Features like chat and polls built into many apps can be a great way to engage students, and other tools like muting users, copresenting, and closed captioning can go a long way to improve the experience.

CONCLUSION

This chapter discussed how in Christian education and technology, both the medium *and* the message matter. In fact, sometimes the medium itself communicates more strongly than the message. When it comes to the things of God, this is especially true. God spoke through the prophets for hundreds of years, but his people never seemed to quite get the message. So God became the medium by sending his own Son to take on human flesh. Jesus's words and teaching matter, but it was his flesh and blood, the fullness of his humanity, that served as the ultimate medium for God's message of love (Gal. 4:1–4).

As teachers today, we do not have to be experts in any technology, but we need to do some basic preparation, love our people, learn our tools well, rely on the Spirit, and continually adjust. Ultimately, you and your life, transformed by the work of Jesus, become the message the world—and your students—need to hear.

REFLECTION QUESTIONS

1. What are your educational objectives and how will technology help you accomplish those? How will the medium you are using help reinforce the message you are sending?
2. How does your in-person or online environment shape the way your ministry will be perceived?
3. What are the technological expectations, and the technological competencies, of your audience?
4. How much AI usage is acceptable in lesson preparation, and how much is acceptable for your students to use in their learning?

RECOMMENDED READING

Gallo, Carmine. *Talk Like TED: The 9 Public-Speaking Secrets of the World's Top Minds*. New York: St. Martin's Griffin, 2015.

Johnson, Aaron. *Online Teaching with Zoom: A Guide for Teaching and Learning with Videoconference Platforms*. Littleton, CO: Aaron Johnson, 2020.

Lowe, Stephen D., and Mary E. Lowe. *Ecologies of Faith in a Digital Age: Spiritual Growth Through Online Education*. Downers Grove, IL: IVP Academic, 2018.

Magana, Sonny. *Disruptive Classroom Technologies: A Framework for Innovation in Education*. Thousand Oaks, CA: Corwin, 2017.

Miller, Matt. *AI for Educators: Learning Strategies, Teacher Efficiencies, and a Vision for an Artificial Intelligence Future*. San Diego: Ditch That Textbook, 2023.

CHAPTER 15

THE EMOTIONALLY INTELLIGENT TEACHER

Phil Humphries

The recognition of emotional intelligence as a key factor in professional success and high-functioning relationships is relatively new. Thanks to the research and publications from individuals like Peter Salovey and John D. Mayer,[1] Daniel Goleman,[2] and Reuven Bar-On,[3] emotional intelligence has been proven to be more effective than IQ for professionals in their respective fields. In fact, Goleman concluded, "When I calculated the ratio of technical skills, IQ and emotional intelligence as ingredients of excellent performance, emotional intelligence proved to be twice as important as the others for jobs at all levels."[4] Much of the research led to subsequent books and articles that formed the foundation of emotionally intelligent leadership and success in the secular world.

Thankfully, emotional intelligence has been embraced by the evangelical community, but the application of emotional intelligence in the

1. Peter Salovey and John D. Mayer, "Emotional Intelligence," *Imagination, Cognition and Personality* 9, no. 3 (1990): 185–211.
2. Daniel Goleman, *Emotional Intelligence: Why It Can Matter More Than IQ* (New York: Bantam, 2006).
3. Reuven Bar-On, Kobus Maree, and Maurice Jesse Elias, *Educating People to Be Emotionally Intelligent* (Westport, CT: Praeger, 2007).
4. Daniel Goleman, "What Makes a Leader?" in *HBR's 10 Must Reads on Emotional Intelligence*, 1st ed. (Boston: Harvard Business Review Press, 2015), 3.

teaching process is limited. The purpose of this chapter is to provide teachers with emotional intelligence skills designed to strengthen the teacher-student relationship, which will enhance learning outcomes. And, of course, those learning outcomes are the application of God's Word to the student's life.

WHAT IS EMOTIONAL INTELLIGENCE?

The starting point for implementing emotional intelligence in the educational program must begin with understanding what it is. Despite the variety of definitions in the literature on emotional intelligence, these definitions share several common elements. The following definition will be used as the basis for this chapter.

> *Emotional intelligence is an awareness of one's own emotions, the ability to manage one's emotions, an awareness of others' emotions (empathy), and the ability to help others manage their emotions to achieve desired results.*

Four skills emerge that are instrumental to teachers for achieving positive learning outcomes in their teacher-student relationships:

1. The teacher's emotional self-awareness
2. The teacher's emotional self-management
3. Awareness of students' emotions (empathy)
4. Managing emotions in students

Understanding and implementing these four skills of emotional intelligence will benefit and enhance both the teacher and student, which will strengthen the learning process.

CAN EMOTIONAL INTELLIGENCE BE LEARNED?

The teaching process faces obstacles and challenges in achieving the desired educational outcome. Some of the obstacles are motivational, socioeconomic, and cognitive; others derive from biblical illiteracy, family of origin, and peer pressure. However, when students are taught emotional intelligence skills, the results can be dramatic. Marc Brackett states, "Research indicates that social and emotional skills are associated with success in many areas of life, including effective teaching, student learning, quality relationships, and academic performance."[5] Another recent study stated:

> So you might be wondering if emotional intelligence is so important, can it be taught or strengthened? According to one meta-analysis that looked at the results of social and emotional learning programs (SELs), the answer to that question is an unequivocal yes. The study found that approximately 50 percent of kids enrolled in SEL programs had better achievement scores and almost 40 percent showed improved grade-point-averages. These programs were also linked to lowered suspension rates, increased school attendance, and reduced disciplinary problems.[6]

If students are capable of learning emotional intelligence skills, then teachers can as well. When this occurs, the classroom can become an amazing learning lab.

SKILL #1: THE TEACHER'S EMOTIONAL SELF-AWARENESS

Becoming an emotionally intelligent teacher begins with an awareness of one's own emotions. Unfortunately, according to Bradberry and Greaves only a small percentage of individuals are in tune with their emotions on a daily basis: "Over the last decade we've tested more than 500,000 people to explore the role emotions play in daily living. We've learned how people see themselves versus what others see, and we've observed how various choices affect personal and professional success. Despite the growing focus on EQ, a global deficit in understanding and managing emotions remains. Only 36 percent of the people we tested are able to accurately identify their emotions as they happen. This means that two thirds of us are typically controlled by our emotions and are not yet skilled at spotting them and using them to our benefit."[7] If such research is accurate and broadly representative of teachers, this means that six out of ten teachers are not aware of their emotions in the

5. M. A. Brackett and N. A. Katulak, "Emotional Intelligence in the Classroom: Skill-Based Training for Teachers and Students," in *Applying Emotional Intelligence: A Practitioner's Guide*, ed. Joseph Ciarrochi and John D. Mayer (New York: Psychology Press, 2007), 1.
6. "IQ vs. EQ: How Are They Different?" accessed December 12, 2024, https://www.verywellmind.com/iq-or-eq-which-one-is-more-important-2795287
7. Travis Bradberry and Jean Greaves, *Emotional Intelligence 2.0* (San Diego: TalentSmart, 2009), 13.

classroom. Such lack of awareness is neither beneficial to instructional effectiveness nor teacher-student relationships.

So, what is emotional self-awareness? Fundamentally, it is the ability to recognize an emotion as it occurs. Simple, right? Not so much, especially if the above research is correct.

Malphurs defines emotional self-awareness as "an accurate awareness of where you are emotionally."[8] Goleman defines emotional self-awareness as "the ability to understand your own emotions and their effects on your performance."[9] The key word in Goleman's definition is *performance*. The implementation of effective emotional intelligence in the classroom begins with the teacher's emotional self-awareness.

How does one become self-aware? Although it is a lifelong process, there are some strategies which can be applied immediately.

Journaling

The teacher should intentionally and intently self-observe and record emotions. This self-observation should include time in the classroom as well as during daily activities. The journal entries should include the following questions: (1) What was the emotion? (2) What caused the emotion? (3) Was the emotion "positive" or "negative"? (4) How did the emotion impact or influence those around me? (5) Did the emotion contribute to or distract from the teaching process? (6) What should be the emotional response to the same situation in the future? (This point will be discussed in greater detail in the skill #2 section.) The journaling process encourages the teacher to become self-aware of his or her emotions. The impact of emotions on the ability to effectively communicate and teach God's Word in a productive and life-changing manner cannot be overstated. Before one can manage emotions, one must first be aware of them.

Assessments

Although assessments are not foolproof for measuring emotional intelligence, they are excellent indicators of one's emotional quotient (EQ). The EQ is a score that runs from emotionally immature to emotionally mature. For example, Peter Scazzero's Emotionally Healthy Spiritual-

8. Aubrey Malphurs, *Developing Emotionally Mature Leaders: How Emotional Intelligence Can Help Transform Your Ministry* (Grand Rapids: Baker Books, 2018), 110.
9. Daniel Goleman et al., *Emotional Self-Awareness: A Primer* (Florence, MA: Key Step Media/More Than Sound, 2017), 6.

ity (EHS) Personal Assessment scores the test-taker from an emotional infant to an emotional adult.[10] Other valuable assessments are the EQ-i 2.0 from Multi-Health Systems (based on the BarOn EQ-i) and BlueEQ in *Emotional Intelligence 2.0* by Bradberry and Greaves, as well as a plethora of others.

Trusted Feedback

One of the most accurate ways of becoming emotionally self-aware is to enlist trusted coworkers, fellow teachers, friends, and family members to give honest feedback on emotions they have observed in you. Also, if you seek to have emotional self-awareness in the classroom, then search out feedback from students. All people have blind spots. This is certainly true for emotional blind spots.

The way others see you is an important source of self-awareness; in fact, one of the most important principles of personal leadership development is assessment. The Center for Creative Leadership discovered that experiencing assessment from others enables a developing leader to fill the gap between where the leader is and where the leader needs to be.[11] The same could be said of becoming a more emotionally self-aware teacher as the result of input from others.

Emotional self-awareness is the first and most essential step in developing emotional intelligence as a teacher. If one is not self-aware of emotions, then managing them appropriately becomes difficult.

SKILL #2: THE TEACHER'S EMOTIONAL SELF-MANAGEMENT

Emotional self-management is important in personal relationships but is essential for creating a classroom environment conducive to positive instruction and interaction.

Emotions influence how teachers handle students and situations. The management of those emotions, or the lack thereof, can impact the learning outcome. Imagine a scenario in which a teacher exhibits unmanaged emotions. Would that be conducive to a positive and enhanced learning environment, or would it create a distracting barrier

10. Peter Scazzero and Warren Bird, *The Emotionally Healthy Church: A Strategy for Discipleship That Actually Changes Lives* (Grand Rapids: Zondervan, 2010), 60–67.
11. Ellen Van Velsor, Cynthia D. McCauley, and Marian N. Ruderman, eds., *The Center for Creative Leadership Handbook of Leadership Development*, 3rd ed. (San Francisco: Jossey-Bass, 2010), 4–8.

between the teacher and the students? The answer seems obvious. On the other hand, if a student observes an emotionally healthy teacher, the opportunities for positive learning outcomes are greatly enhanced. Brackett and Katulak found that "teachers who can manage their own and students' emotions while teaching can create a more open and effective teaching and learning environment with fewer distractions. Similarly, those who can control their emotional reactions and effectively influence how others feel can deal better with difficult conversations."[12]

What are some strategies for a teacher's emotional self-management for classroom or small group effectiveness?

Journaling

Again, journaling can be a great asset in emotional self-management, just as it is for emotional self-awareness. Brackett and Katulak recommend that "teachers write about a negative emotion they experience at work, what triggers that emotion, the strategies they have used to deal with that emotion, and how effective each strategy has been. Then, they brainstorm about and record other possible strategies they could implement to manage their negative emotions."[13]

Accountability

Accountability is different from feedback. Once feedback is received concerning an emotion that could be detrimental to the classroom/group environment, accountability provides the motivation to manage the emotion in a healthy and productive way.

Smiling More

Yes, smiling more can facilitate the management of your emotions. The physiological action of smiling sends signals to the brain that you are happy. "Your brain literally responds to the nerves and muscles in your face to determine your emotional state."[14] One study found that participants who viewed cartoons while holding a pen in their mouth in a manner that elicited smiling (pen held in teeth) as opposed to holding a pen that prevented smiling (pen held by lips) reported feeling more

12. Brackett and Katulak, "Emotional Intelligence in the Classroom," 11.
13. Brackett and Katulak, "Emotional Intelligence in the Classroom," 11.
14. Bradberry and Greaves, *Emotional Intelligence 2.0*, 114.

amused by the cartoons.[15] When facing challenging days in the classroom, try smiling more. Your brain and emotions just might respond.

Self-Talk

There is a difference between thinking the best about someone and thinking the worst. In either case, such thinking can result in self-talk: mental talking about someone or something. If self-talk concerning an individual is positive, then the result can be a positive and productive interaction; if the self-talk is negative, then the result likely will be negative. According to Bradberry and Greaves, negative self-talk damages one's ability to self-manage emotions.[16]

Controlling self-talk is emotional self-management. In fact, the apostle Paul had something to say about this: "Finally, brothers and sisters, whatever is true, whatever is noble, whatever is right, whatever is pure, whatever is lovely, whatever is admirable—if anything is excellent or praiseworthy—think about such things" (Phil. 4:8 NIV).

At this point in developing emotional intelligence skills, a transition occurs. One of the essential components of the teacher's emotional intelligence in the classroom/group is building a connection between the teacher and the student. An emotionally intelligent teacher has a great opportunity to build emotional intelligence into the life of a student that, according to previously cited research, will result in enhanced learning outcomes.

SKILL #3: AWARENESS OF STUDENTS' EMOTIONS (EMPATHY)

One of the challenges for teachers is understanding the issues that may be affecting the spiritual growth of students. A "clinical" approach to teaching is primarily concerned with the transmission of information without accounting for learning styles, teaching methodology, appropriate lesson plans, and so on. Each of these is an important component to classroom instruction, but what could be the missing piece is an awareness of the students' emotions and expressing compassionate empathy. Dr. Brené Brown says, "Empathy fuels connection; sympathy drives disconnection."[17]

15. Nicholas A. Coles et al., "A Multi-Lab Test of the Facial Feedback Hypothesis by the Many Smiles Collaboration," *Nature Human Behaviour* 6, no. 12 (2022): 1731–42.
16. Bradberry and Greaves, *Emotional Intelligence 2.0*, 118.
17. RSA, "Brené Brown on Empathy," December 10, 2013, YouTube video, 00:09, accessed August 16, 2023, https://www.youtube.com/watch?v=1Evwgu369Jw.

Empathy is "I'm feeling with you." Sympathy, "I'm feeling for you." To understand the emotions of students and exhibit an empathic response may open the door to new instructional opportunities.

Malphurs defines awareness of others' emotions as "The ability to 'read people' emotionally—accurately pick up on their feelings and emotions and understand what's really going on with them."[18] Goleman takes it a step further: "Empathy is our social radar. It requires being able to read another's emotions; at a higher level, it entails sensing and responding to a person's unspoken concerns or feelings. At the highest levels, empathy is understanding the issues or concerns that lie behind another's feelings."[19]

There are countless stories of students whose lives were positively impacted by teachers who viewed them as unique individuals "fearfully and wonderfully made" (Ps. 139:14 NIV), with emotions and feelings. An empathetic approach in teaching philosophy and methodology will create a connection with students that leads to enhanced learning outcomes. Once the connection is made, the students will learn to trust the teacher in the learning process. Seek to become aware of your student's emotions, become empathetic toward them, and build a connection with them. Ask yourself: What are some ways to become aware of students' emotions in the classroom and demonstrate empathy?

Knowing Your Students' Names

Bradberry and Greaves state that "greeting someone by name is one of the most basic and influential social awareness strategies you can adopt. Whatever the story is behind your name, it's an essential part of your identity. It feels so good when people use your name and remember it."[20]

Students will realize their teacher seeks to know them as individuals, and that will enable a connection that enhances the teacher's understanding of the students.

Active Listening

Too many teachers enjoy the sound of their own voices over the voices of their students. Many believe if they speak long enough and loud

18. Malphurs, *Developing Emotionally Mature Leaders*, 130.
19. Daniel Goleman, *Working with Emotional Intelligence* (New York: Bantam, 1998), 4.
20. Bradberry and Greaves, *Emotional Intelligence 2.0*, 139.

enough then students will learn and possibly stay awake in the process. However, when a teacher seeks to understand students' emotions in the classroom, listening comes before speaking.

Much has been written on active listening but little with respect to the teacher-student relationship.[21] For instance, if a teacher employs the Socratic method, then listening is essential to achieving the desired result of critical thinking. The same would be true for understanding the emotions of students in order to enhance the learning process. Active listening is an essential component of an emotionally intelligent teacher. What does it look like?

Verbal Communication (What Do You Hear?)

What are your students saying? What do you hear when you are around your students? What they say and how they say it can reflect their emotions. Hearing properly is a three-step process. First, listen to and observe the content and emotions of what a student says. Second, reflect on the content and emotion behind what the student said. "What I hear you saying about [the biblical passage, others in the class, the application, etc.] is . . ." "You seem to be upset about . . ." "It sounds like you are [angry, sad, afraid, joyful, etc.] about . . ." "It seems you feel this way because . . ." Third, confirm with the student what you heard them say.

Another option for the above process is the use of role-play to observe how students respond hypothetically to certain situations. Often role-play indicates true emotions and can enable the teacher to begin understanding the emotions of the students.

Nonverbal Looking (What Do You See?)

Be observant of nonverbal cues that could reveal the emotions students may be experiencing. Nonverbal cues are often a physiological response to an emotion. The challenge is to identify the emotion from the nonverbal cue. Nonverbal cues may be both positive and negative. Examples include tears, perspiration, lack of eye contact, good eye contact, smiling, head nodding, firm handshakes, folded arms, upright posture, flaring nostrils, lip quivering, constant squirming, open palms, and various other forms of body language.

21. Marnie Reed, "Listening in the Classroom," TESOL, 2021, accessed December 16, 2024, https://www.educationcorner.com/active-listening-skills-education/.

Compassionate Empathy

The "Skills You Need" website states that empathy is "at its simplest, awareness of the feelings and emotions of other people. It is a key element of Emotional Intelligence, the link between self and others, because it is how we as individuals understand what others are experiencing as if we were feeling it ourselves."[22]

Carolyn Saarni defines empathy as "an immediate emotional response that the observer experiences on witnessing another's emotional state. With empathy, we vicariously experience a similar emotional reaction as the target."[23] When this occurs, a connection is made.

The term *empathy* was first introduced in 1909 by psychologist Edward B. Titchener as a translation of the German term *einfühlung* (meaning "feeling into").[24] There are several forms of empathy (including cognitive, emotional, and somatic), but compassionate empathy is most important in understanding student emotions in order to achieve positive learning outcomes.

What is compassionate empathy? It is feeling the pain and emotions of another (connection) and taking action to alleviate the challenge or problem the other is facing. In Mark 1:40–42 Jesus came face-to-face with a leper. The text says, "A man with leprosy came to him and begged him on his knees, 'If you are willing, you can make me clean.' Jesus was filled with compassion. He reached out his hand and touched the man. 'I am willing,' he said. 'Be clean!' Immediately the leprosy left him and he was cleansed" (NIV). Jesus felt compassionate empathy toward the leper and was moved to take action to help. And do not miss what the text says: Jesus "touched the man." A connection was made, compassionate empathy occurred, and the man's life was changed.

The classroom is a petri dish for compassionate empathy. Teachers have countless opportunities for awareness of their students' emotions, and by taking advantage of such opportunities they can connect with their students to facilitate learning outcomes that may not be otherwise available.

---

22. "Types of Empathy," SkillsYouNeed.com, accessed August 16, 2023, https://www.skillsyouneed.com/ips/empathy.html.
23. C. Saarni, "The Development of Emotional Competence: Pathways for Helping Children to Become Emotionally Intelligent," in *Educating People to Be Emotionally Intelligent*, ed. Reuven Bar-On, J. G. Maree, and Maurice Jesse Elias (Westport, CT: Praeger, 2007), 25.
24. Kendra Cherry, "What Is Empathy?" Verywellmind.com, accessed December 16, 2024, https://www.verywellmind.com/what-is-empathy-2795562.

SKILL #4: MANAGING EMOTIONS IN STUDENTS

This skill is not about manipulation or control, but rather influence, change, and positive learning outcomes.

Teacher to Student

Once teachers have learned and implemented the first three skills, they can assist students in their emotional intelligence development. Salovey and Mayer's research discovered that

> emotional intelligence includes the ability to regulate and alter the affective reactions of others. Emotionally intelligent individuals, however, should be especially adept at this process and do so to meet specific goals. On the positive side, they may enhance their own and others' moods and even manage emotions so as to motivate others charismatically toward a worthwhile end.[25]

The key phrase in the above quotation is "worthwhile end." For the teacher the worthwhile end is twofold: the student's emotional intelligence development and improved learning outcomes. Combined, these cause life change.

Patti and Tobin observe that "in schools whose purpose extends beyond academic achievement to include the social and emotional development of children, it is just as important for children to learn to read, compute, and problem solve as it is to treat themselves and others with respect."[26]As students are influenced by their teachers and grow in their emotional intelligence, they will be able to understand and manage their own emotions, which will result in greater spiritual learning outcomes. The results of social and emotional learning (SEL) initiatives contribute to such success.

Luke 6:40 says, "The student is not above the teacher, but everyone who is fully trained will be like their teacher" (NIV). An emotionally intelligent teacher who produces students with strong emotional intelligence skills gives them a greater chance of both emotional and spiritual success. However, there is another aspect of emotional intelligence

25. Salovey and Mayer, "Emotional Intelligence," 197–98.
26. Janet Patti and James Tobin, *Smart School Leaders: Leading with Emotional Intelligence* (Dubuque, IA: Kendall Hunt, 2006), 73–74.

in the classroom that can be equally beneficial (or harmful) to the learning environment.

Student to Student

Peer pressure is one of the most influential factors in classroom/group activity and performance both positively and negatively. This is true for both adults and children. Some researchers use the term "group climate" to refer to affective student interaction. Although research in this area is limited, some results indicate that positive social and emotional ethos among students leads to better academic outcomes. Aritzeta et al. state that

> students may be especially sensitive to the emotional meanings of their academic experiences, as well as to the experiences of their classmates, who are in such close proximity and are socially relevant. Although research has shown that teachers have the strongest and most direct impact on students' psychological experience in the classroom, peer emotional relationships also have an important effect on [a student's] attitude towards both school and themselves.[27]

They go on to say, "Academic performance would be indirectly affected by a context in which the motivation to engage with the learning process may be increased by the emotional characteristics of the group."[28] From this, we may deduce that a healthy emotional intelligence both individually and among the students will lead to better learning outcomes. This would be an illustration of positive and healthy peer pressure.

What can teachers do to facilitate positive emotional intelligence in student-to-student relationships to benefit the learning process? Le Métais and Jordan give several suggestions:

1. Involve students in setting social as well as [learning] expectations and targets for individual and group activities.

---

27. A. Aritzeta et al., "Classroom Emotional Intelligence and Its Relationship with School Performance," *European Journal of Education and Psychology* 9, no. 1 (2016): 3, accessed August 26, 2023, https://psycnet.apa.org/doi/10.1016/j.ejeps.2015.11.001, 3.
28. Aritzeta et al., "Classroom Emotional Intelligence," 3.

2. Make students aware of how their behavior is perceived by others and how it affects others.
3. Help students develop empathy and negotiating skills in order to resolve conflict and promote their own and others' learning.
4. Monitor each student's behavior towards others and their contribution to achieving collective objectives in the case of group work.[29]

As students learn to interact and work together in a healthy emotional climate, the academic results will improve. And lest we forget, "Two are better than one, because they have a good return for their labor: If either of them falls down, one can help the other up. But pity anyone who falls and has no one to help them up" (Eccl. 4:9–10 NIV), and "Do nothing out of selfish ambition or vain conceit. Rather, in humility value others above yourselves, not looking to your own interests but each of you to the interests of the others" (Phil. 2:3–4 NIV).

Unfortunately, there is a negative side to student-to-student interaction that can impact a student's emotional state and adversely affect learning outcomes. This is particularly evident in youth and children's classes. It is called *bullying*. Bullying occurs in face-to-face interactions but also can exist on social media. The results can lead to avoiding attendance, poor spiritual growth, lack of focus, exclusion from social gatherings, depression, anxiety, and, on rare occasions, suicide. This is all the more reason for a teacher to be aware of students' emotions (skill #3) and seek to provide help through emotional management (skill #4). It is essential for the teacher to have to necessary resources and training.[30]

---

29. Joanna Le Métais and Don Jordan, "Emotional Intelligence and Student Behaviour," *International Electronic Journal for Leadership in Learning* 1 (1997): 4.
30. The following are recommended resources for teachers and parents dealing with bullying. Jonathan McKee, *The Bullying Breakthrough: Real Help for Parents and Teachers of the Bullied, Bystanders, and Bullies* (Uhrichsville, OH: Shiloh Run, 2018); The American Academy of Child and Adolescent Psychiatry, Bullying Resource Center, accessed August 16, 2023, https://www.aacap.org/aacap/families_and_youth/resource_centers/Bullying_Resource_Center/Home.aspx; Teach.com, "Bullying Resources for Educators and Parents," accessed August 18, 2023, https://teach.com/online-ed/counseling-degrees/online-masters-school-counseling/bullying-resources/; NEA.org, "How to Identify Bullying," accessed August 26, 2023, https://www.nea.org/professional-excellence/student-engagement/tools-tips/how-identify-bullying.

CONCLUSION

There are countless stories of students positively impacted and influenced by teachers. Their classrooms were transformed from places of informational lectures into relationally interactive labs enabling life-transforming learning experiences. Were such results from highly motivated students? Possibly. But more likely from a highly motivated, emotionally intelligent teacher. A teacher who can effectively put into practice the four emotional intelligence skills—emotional self-awareness, emotional self-management, awareness of students' emotions (empathy), and managing emotions in students—can create a classroom environment that is conducive to both emotional health and improved learning outcomes. The students' lives will be enriched, and the teacher's life will be impactful.

REFLECTION QUESTIONS

1. Do your emotions impact your ability to teach effectively?
2. Can you accurately perceive the emotions of your students?
3. What are you doing to become a more emotionally intelligent teacher?
4. How well do you listen to your students?
5. How well do you connect relationally with your students?
6. What is your level of spiritual maturity?

RECOMMENDED READING

Brackett, M. A., and N. A. Katulak. "Emotional Intelligence in the Classroom: Skill-Based Training for Teachers and Students." In *Applying Emotional Intelligence: A Practitioner's Guide*, edited by Joseph Ciarrochi and John D. Mayer. New York: Psychology Press, 2007.

Goleman, Daniel. *Emotional Intelligence: Why It Can Matter More Than IQ*. New York: Bantam, 2006.

Malphurs, Aubrey. *Developing Emotionally Mature Leaders: How Emotional Intelligence Can Help Transform Your Ministry*. Grand Rapids: Baker Books, 2018.

Patti, Janet, and James Tobin. *Smart School Leaders: Leading with Emotional Intelligence*, Dubuque, IA: Kendal Hunt, 2006.

Scazzero, Peter. *The Emotionally Healthy Leader: How Transforming Your Inner Life Will Deeply Transform Your Church, Team, and the World*. Grand Rapids: Zondervan, 2015.

CHAPTER 16

TRAINING SKILLED BIBLE TEACHERS

Sue Edwards

You may not consider yourself a teaching "master," but as you hone your craft, God expects you to pass it on to others.

> What you have heard from me, keep as the pattern of sound teaching, with faith and love in Christ Jesus. . . . And the things you have heard me say in the presence of many witnesses entrust to reliable people who will also be qualified to teach others. (2 Tim. 1:13; 2:2 NIV)

It is one thing to teach well; it is an entirely different skill to teach others to teach well. But Paul commands effective teachers to raise up future generations of equally effective teachers.

Remember in the time of the judges, "After that whole generation had been gathered to their ancestors, another generation grew up who knew neither the Lord nor what he had done for Israel" (Judg. 2:10 NIV). Throughout Judges, we observe a cycle of rebellion, retribution, repentance, and finally restoration. Each generation is always in danger of their children no longer loving or knowing God. Without skilled Bible teachers, that falling away is almost assured.

DIFFERENT TEACHING CONTEXTS

The local church, parachurch ministries, and missions agencies need men and women who can teach God's Word in a variety of venues and to different age groups. Regardless of the venue, teachers need training. Kindergartners need Bible lessons based on sound doctrine and Bible accuracy just as much as college students or senior adults. Capturing the attention of junior high school students as well as busy working women requires an understanding of creative methods and how different people learn. The equipping of someone periodically teaching a Bible story to elementary age children will look different from that of someone teaching books of the Bible to adults using in-depth Bible lecture along with interactive discussion. You'll need to adapt the principles set forth in this chapter to your particular context, but in general, most of the ideas and suggestions can help you design and implement helpful teacher training whatever your context.

We will take a three-pronged approach to training teachers. All three elements are needed to ensure quality: (1) screening, (2) cognitive content, and (3) apprenticeship.

SCREENING

All believers need to learn to articulate their beliefs, but not all Christians are called to be Bible teachers, regardless of their desire. Once when I was overseeing a megachurch women's Bible study, a new convert approached me after my message, asking to join the teaching team. Two years prior, a ministry to help sex-trafficked women leave that life had rescued her. She had accepted Christ, was working as a secretary, and was on fire for Jesus. I was thrilled at her Christian growth and loved her dearly.

However, when she asked me if she could train to be a Bible teacher, I knew she was not ready. She may have observed gifted teachers being honored and yearned for those accolades herself. For those who struggle with self-worth, this desire is common and understandable. What she did not know was that although those accolades can enrich one's sense of making a real difference for the Lord, they also come with a downside that requires wisdom and maturity to navigate. And I had not had time to discern whether she possessed the spiritual gift of teaching or if her lifestyle reflected an authentic faith in Christ. She needed time to mature in Christ, and I needed time to observe whether she was cut out for the demanding endeavor of teaching God's Word. Her past life did not disqualify her; it was simply too soon to even consider this possibility.

I was able to guide her into serving in a different capacity and in time we both realized that her gifts, abilities, and passions lay in leading small groups and walking with women one-on-one. I still see her occasionally, more than twenty years later, and she is still in those roles, loved and respected by many women who have grown strong in Christ under her leadership and care. I would have done her a disservice if I had granted her initial wish.

On a different occasion, I had recruited another woman to my lead team, and she was leading that ministry well. Soon, she also requested training as a Bible teacher. Again, I hesitated and prayed fervently for God's direction. You see, although she was now married to a policeman and had a son, she had left a lesbian lifestyle some ten years earlier. I felt it was better to wait a few more years, and I gave her some upfront opportunities so I could observe her further. I'm glad I did, because the next year she left her husband and son and returned to her former lesbian lifestyle. Our ministry would have been severely damaged if she had taken on the label of "Bible teacher."

James counseled us, "Not many of you should become teachers, my fellow believers, because you know that we who teach will be judged more strictly" (James 3:1 NIV). That's a sobering verse! Why did James write these words under the guidance of the Holy Spirit? Because effective teachers will likely acquire an influential platform. If so, they enter a "fishbowl" life that has its hazards. Whether they teach in youth ministry in a tiny church or become a worldwide conference speaker, their students and God's good name are at risk if they fall away. They walk a tightrope of being vulnerable so they can relate to those they teach and walking their talk so that they do not dishonor the Lord. Apostate teachers often take weaker brothers and sisters with them, and they muddy the name of Jesus to the outside world. A teacher's words can be powerful, but they can also be dangerous, so screen those you identify to teach prayerfully and carefully.

The Joy and Privilege

Now that you have been sufficiently warned about the need to screen those you equip, be encouraged. Teaching others to teach is a privilege resulting in extreme personal joy and satisfaction. James was not suggesting that no one should teach the Scriptures. God empowers specific people to do just that, and he expects them to develop and use those spiritual gifts.

> We have different gifts, according to the grace given to each of us. If your gift is . . . teaching, then teach. (Rom. 12:6–7 NIV)

> Christ himself gave the apostles, the prophets, the evangelists, the pastors and teachers, to equip his people for works of service, so that the body of Christ may be built up until we all reach unity in the faith and in the knowledge of the Son of God and become mature, attaining to the whole measure of the fullness of Christ. Then we will no longer be infants, tossed back and forth by the waves, and blown here and there by every wind of teaching and by the cunning and craftiness of people in their deceitful scheming. Instead, speaking the truth in love, we will grow to become in every respect the mature body of him who is the head, that is, Christ. From him the whole body, joined and held together by every supporting ligament, grows and builds itself up in love, as each part does its work. (Eph. 4:11–16 NIV)

Paul writes this to the local bodies of believers in Rome and Ephesus. He instructs every Christian there to discover, develop, and use whatever gift Christ has assigned, and Paul expects that many of these gifts will be used to minister to that local church. Otherwise, these church bodies in Rome and Ephesus will never attain the strength to be the light in their communities that God desires. Nor will yours (Phil. 2:15b-16). Otherwise, the lost will remain lost. Children will not be prepared for the challenges to their faith they will face when they venture out into the world on their own. Believers will remain infants and be vulnerable to charlatans who feed them lies (Col. 2:8).

God's design is clear. In general, real people from within those churches, in contrast to Christians outside, are raised up in individual church bodies to do the work of the ministry. This means that today believers are still responsible to minister to those in their own local communities. Thus, an occasional video series, guest speaker to complement incarnated ministries, or attendance at a national parachurch conference is fine, but it should never replace real people who are part of that local body. People with skin on create authentic communities where regular folks step out in faith to identify, develop, and use their spiritual gifts. This requires that the ministry is not done by "professionals" or by businesses who make a profit selling their goods to churches but by the regular people in that local church. Certainly, it is fine to use curriculum developed by experts, but real, live people capable of connecting in relationships need to teach God's truth to students. This creates a beautiful ethos where believers are active and influential in the lives of other believers, ultimately growing a mature local community of faith that inspires others there to step out and serve in their giftedness too.

Before God called me to academia, I led a ministry to women in a church where women of the church put on a high-quality women's conference each year. The team that created and implemented the conference worked on it all year, using their varied spiritual gifts, forming a united and joyful ministry community. The weekend was jam-packed with workshops, worship teams, and serving ministries led by the women in our church. The goal wasn't to make money, but to cover conference costs; yet each year, as attendance grew, the conference made more and more profit. We rolled that profit into childcare costs for the weekly Bible study that met year-round, benefiting local women who attended. The last year of the conference, profits covered two full years of childcare—a lot of money that churches and families did not have to provide so wives and mothers could attend Bible study without paying childcare workers!

However, as businesses saw the dividends they could earn, they stepped in and offered national conferences, shutting down opportunities for us and other local churches. We grieved not only at the money that no longer went back into ministry but also at the lost opportunities for local women to develop their gifts where they could see God use their efforts to benefit others. I contend that people grow spiritually as much from identifying, developing, and using their spiritual gifts as they do in any other way.

In every local church, some people are endowed with the spiritual gift of teaching. But to put in the hard work to equip for that ministry calling, they need to know they will be given opportunities. Local churches must provide these opportunities instead of relying on businesses to supply professional teachers who are not part of that local body. And to develop and use their spiritual gifts, someone must train these people. That is the responsibility of every seasoned Bible teacher. It takes hard work and time, but it is central if local churches and ministries are to flourish and live up to their potential.

What Do You Look For in Potential Teachers?

> I remind you to fan into flame the gift of God, which is in you… For the Spirit God gave us does not make us timid, but gives us power, love and self-discipline. (2 Tim. 1:6–7 NIV)
>
> There are different kinds of gifts, but the same Spirit distributes them. There are different kinds of service, but the same Lord. There are different kinds of working, but in all of them and in everyone it is the same God at work. Now to each one the manifestation of the Spirit is given for the common good. (1 Cor. 12:4–7 NIV)
>
> Each of you should use whatever gift you have received to serve others, as faithful stewards of God's grace in its various forms. If anyone speaks, they should do so as one who speaks the very words of God. If anyone serves, they should do so with the strength God provides, so that in all things God may be praised through Jesus Christ. To him be the glory and the power for ever and ever. Amen. (1 Pet. 4:10–11 NIV)

Consider these three main qualities to look for in potential teachers.

1. The spiritual gift of teaching:[1] Not everyone who teaches the Bible where armies of volunteers are needed must possess the spiritual gift of teaching, although if they do, they will probably be more effective and love what they do (see chapter 2). However, men and women with that spiritual gift who embark on a lifetime of teaching the Bible in vari-

1. See chapter 2 for additional discussion of the gift of teaching.

ous age-specific ministries, Sunday schools, Bible studies, and more in-depth venues should be given preference.

How will you identify them? Since spiritual gifts are manifested through the Holy Spirit and contain a supernatural element, they are not easily measured. Jesus described the Spirit to Nicodemus in John 3:1–21 by comparing it to the wind. "The wind blows wherever it pleases. You hear its sound, but you cannot tell where it comes from or where it is going" (v. 8 NIV). The same dynamic is true in assessing whether a teacher is spiritually gifted or not. It is powerful, and you know it when you see it. That's not particularly helpful to the novice, but it is reality.

It is helpful to ask others' opinions. Watch the response of particular people, ones who are mature in their faith and look for depth of insight as well as clarity. See if they sit up, immediately attentive, when a potential teacher opens his or her mouth. I have observed this phenomenon in completely inexperienced or nervous people—yet they capture the room with their voice. Something in their spirit connects with the spirit of others and a wonderful transfer of insight and passion occurs. Renowned DTS professor Howard Hendricks wrote:

> Passion is the most important quality a teacher can have. Those hungry to teach will get knowledge and skills one way or another, whatever price they have to pay. And their passion makes their teaching compelling and winsome. The good news is that there are more people in our congregations with the potential for passion about teaching than we realize.[2]

People without the gift of teaching can be trained to teach the Bible and will often do this to respond to a temporary need or as part of their lifelong ministry, generally to complement other spiritual gifts. For example, I have been team teaching with a colleague for two decades. She likes to teach, but it is not her "sweet spot." She does not like to be away from people long enough to invest the time it takes to create excellent content and to be well prepared. She's incredibly gifted working

2. Howard Hendricks, "Training People to Teach," in Roberta Hestenes, Howard Hendricks, and Earl Palmer, *Mastering Teaching* (Portland, OR: Multnomah Press and Christianity Today, 1991), 135.

one-on-one and has come alongside numerous wounded women over the years and nursed them back to health. I, on the other hand, love to teach, and even more, I love to teach others to teach. Teaching has been my primary ministry for almost half a century, and I have taught many people to teach the Bible. I enjoy leading small groups and one-on-one, but I lack my colleague's patience and fortitude for that kind of ministry. I would rather teach.

When our department chair assessed each of our gifts, strengths, and weaknesses twenty-five years ago, he was astute enough to discern where we would each thrive and make the most impact long term for the Lord. Neither of us were particularly ready for the challenges ahead, but he prayerfully and carefully placed each of us according to our gifts and passions. He placed me as full-time, tenure-track faculty and my colleague as administrative faculty focusing on meeting the spiritual and emotional needs of women students. Although some place more value on some ministries over others, God does not see it that way. Our department chair simply placed us according to our giftedness.

As you will see after digesting this chapter, training up teachers is a long-term investment, and you may not have time or resources to do that for everyone. For those embarking on a long-term teaching ministry, ask the Lord to give you his insight and wisdom as you identify people with the spiritual gift of teaching. Then equip them.

2. Budding spiritual maturity: A potential candidate may be spiritually gifted but lack the maturity at present to handle the ups and downs that accompany a teaching ministry. Look for people who have walked with God for a while. Surprisingly though, the choice is not dependent on age, although we would expect that the more years one walks with Jesus the more mature that person ought to be. Sadly, that's not always true.

Look for character qualities evident in the Bible, but remember, as Edith Schaeffer said, "When people insist on perfection or nothing, they get nothing."[3] We are all in process. However, your trainee will need authentic faith, integrity, humility, and a strong work ethic. Also look for someone who can tolerate stress, is not always in crisis, and has a healthy support system and a teachable spirit.

3. Edith Schaeffer, *What Is a Family?* (Grand Rapids: Baker Books, 1997), 41.

3. *Bible knowledge*: Candidates need a working knowledge of the Bible, sound theology, and an ability to use available or provided resources. They must know the basics concerning how to study a text thoroughly (see chapter 3 for guidance). They must take their role seriously. They must be willing to take the time to prepare well and to invest relationally in their students.

For those desiring to teach the Bible over a lifetime, a seminary education is a definite advantage, although many excellent teachers are self-taught. I taught the Bible before I earned seminary degrees, and I found a formal biblical education regularly cut my preparation time in half. Not everyone has that opportunity, but if God provides that advantage, he expects you to share what you learned with others.

Overcoming the Fear Factor

"About 77% of the general population fears public speaking. Public speaking fear is highly prevalent and manifests itself as a significant burden in society through lower educational achievement, occupational impairment, and increased health care utilization."[4]

This means that the majority of people feel nervous or anxious when speaking in public. The underlying fear is that of being judged and rejected by others.[5] Most people would almost literally rather die than teach or make a public presentation. It is scary for most people to stand up in front of others and attempt to say something valuable.

This fear can be overcome with support and practice. Unless the fear comes from deep, unresolved issues requiring therapy, it is often worthwhile to invest in someone who struggles initially with nervousness. Humility is preferable to overconfidence.

When working in church ministry, consider giving volunteers as much time up front as possible. They need to be seen as leaders instead of paid staff. In our morning and evening Bible studies I insisted that the class administrators give the welcome and announcements each week. One year, the morning class administrator almost refused to accept the position if she had to stand up in front of hundreds of women and say

---

4. T. Furmark et al., "Social Phobia in the General Population: Prevalence and Sociodemo graphic Profile," *Social Psychiatry and Psychiatric Epidemiology* 34, no. 8 (1999): 416–24, https://doi.org/10.1007/s001270050163.
5. National Social Anxiety Center, "Public Speaking Anxiety," https://nationalsocialanxiety center.com/social-anxiety/public-speaking-anxiety.

something. I assured her I could help her learn to do this. She trusted me and reluctantly agreed.

The first day she turned splotchy red, and I was concerned that she was going to pass out in front of the microphone. After class, we sat down and wrote out word for word everything she wanted to say the next week. I told her, "Just read the words on the page." The next week she still turned red but no fainting scare. She read her welcome and announcements for several weeks, and then I encouraged her to write out bullet points. She took to this readily. By Christmas she was up there relaxed and natural, telling jokes and ultimately taking more than her allotted time. We both laughed when I explained she needed to rein it in a bit. Most people can overcome this kind of fear through preparation and practice.

A prayerful, careful screening process is wise because as you'll soon see, the next steps are demanding for both trainer and trainee, but they can lead to a lifetime of quality teaching that God uses to transform countless lives, resulting in joy and satisfaction for the teacher as well as abundant glory for God.

COGNITIVE CONTENT

Some local churches desperately recruit volunteer teachers for their children's and youth ministries, Sunday schools, small groups, and Bible studies, only to lose them through experiences like the one below.

> A young woman, an award-winning interior designer, saw that her church needed a Sunday school teacher for one of the children's classes. She volunteered. They put curriculum in her hands and said, "If you can read it, you can teach it." She couldn't. She tried, she read, she stumbled through some classes—and she quit. Though it has been years since, she was traumatized by the experience, and if anyone asks her to teach, she responds with a decisive, "No!"[6]

Retention trumps those heart-wrenching seasonal pleas for volunteers that everyone dreads. How will you retain capable, willing people like the young woman above? For maximum retention, offer

6. Hendricks, "Training People to Teach," 129.

training that involves both cognitive content and apprenticeships. They will need information and a chance to practice with oversight by a more experienced teacher. We'll examine apprenticeships in the next section.

There's no magic formula concerning when and where to offer cognitive teacher training. You will need to discern what will work best in your context for your students. Initial workshops are seldom helpful unless they are followed up by short spurts of additional reminders through the year. Also, finding creative ways to involve your teachers as they learn together is far more effective than just content dumping and expecting them to remember any of it. In addition, helping teachers relate personally to one another provides a supportive team ethos that enhances retention. They need to share their lives, what's working with their students, and prayer, especially as they encounter challenges.

Initially, your teachers need a basic database about the Bible and how to study the Bible for themselves. Even if you give teachers a curriculum as a guide, the best teachers incorporate other elements that personalize and bring their lessons alive. They will also need to know how people learn, creative teaching methods, how to illustrate the principles they want their students to remember, how to tell stories well, and how to organize the material so it is easy to comprehend, hold onto, and live out. Hendricks recommends that we teach our teachers "how to deliver a message in a way that it sizzles. Just as a chef who knows the science of cooking can make the most out of a book recipe, so a skillful Sunday school teacher can optimize the curriculum."[7] Jesus taught that "every teacher . . . who has become a disciple in the kingdom of heaven is like the owner of a house who brings out of his storeroom new treasures as well as old" (Matt. 13:52 NIV).

This book is full of helpful instructions regarding how to help your teachers in training cognitively retain what you teach them about how to teach. But be careful not to overload your teachers with so much information that they feel overwhelmed. Hendricks learned this lesson the hard way:

> How full does the database need to be before you put teachers in a class? When I pastored in Aurora, Illinois, I developed a

7. Hendricks, "Training People to Teach," 133.

> detailed, eight-month teacher training program. Twenty-seven volunteers faithfully attended the whole course. At the end of those eight months, after they had been sufficiently informed of the basics for teaching Sunday school, I asked for volunteers to teach a class. Of all those thoroughly prepared, eminently qualified people, not a single one volunteered. They were paralyzed. I had taught them so many things to avoid, so many principles to follow, so many do's and don'ts, they couldn't imagine themselves succeeding in the classroom. The more I had taught them, the more threatening the classroom had become. Since then I've learned not only to tone down the information I share but intermittently to involve recruits in assisting a mentor before they finish their classroom training.[8]

Effective teaching requires more than information. It is a skill like playing the piano, designing with computer graphics, or baking the perfect pie crust. You may know all the facts, but skills require multiple hands-on opportunities with expert feedback. The best way to enable recruits to become masters is to have them spend time as apprentices.

APPRENTICESHIP

An apprentice, someone who wants to learn a particular skill, partners with an expert who, through real-world experience, helps the apprentice practice and improve through feedback. Some people call this kind of relationship "mentoring" or "coaching," but the word *apprentice* is preferable because teaching really is as much a skill as anything you can learn out of a book, like electrical work or plumbing. When you hear the word *apprentice* you may think of an expert blacksmith taking on a boy to learn the tricks of the trade. Skills training like shipbuilding, carpentry, and welding all have a long history of using apprenticeships to pass on their skills. Jesus learned carpentry from his father Joseph. Throughout time many people learned their life work this way.

This practice is making a comeback today and still works. In 2021, more than 241,000 people nationwide began apprenticeship training, and in that same year 96,000 graduated, having obtained the skills they needed

8. Hendricks, "Training People to Teach," 132.

to build financial security.[9] Today multiple churches and parachurch ministries offer these kinds of hands-on opportunities to give people a chance to get their ministry hands dirty, and most seminaries require that students put their learning into practice through internship programs.

In my experience of training Bible teachers for more than forty years, I have found that the best way to prepare them is a combination of cognitive content and apprenticeships. I adopted apprentices during my years in church ministry, and I have taught seminary courses over twenty years, and still do, to help students learn to teach the Bible using this method.

Ministry Approaches to Apprenticeships

To equip children's ministry or youth ministry teachers, this approach may be as simple as partnering each one with a seasoned teacher in a similar context for a period of time to help newcomers learn how to engage and work with children and youth. You may want to create a formal program or keep this informal, since "new" teachers may have had previous experience, and some may need more time than others working with an experienced teacher.

Men and women who teach adults may need more time as apprentices to ensure that they are astute regarding complex biblical and theological issues, able to communicate effectively to adults, and prepared for challenges that can come when working with adults. Time with a seasoned teacher is an invaluable gift to give a novice and makes his or her long-term success more likely.

Scaffolding

As mentioned in previous chapters, seasoned teachers may want to consider taking their apprentices through a series of opportunities to practice—experts moving their novices toward their own proficiency. This method is known as *scaffolding*. A scaffold is a structure built for workers to stand on when they want to reach high parts of a building. Scaffolds are often built platform upon platform, as craftsmen gradually work their way to the top.

9. FY 2021 Data and Statistics, "Registered Apprenticeship National Results Fiscal Year 2021 US Department of Labor, accessed August 27, 2023, https://www.dol.gov/agencies/eta/apprenticeship/about/statistics/2021.

Imagine a potential Bible teacher standing at the base of a fifteen-story building, looking up. The top of the building symbolizes the expertise they dream of reaching, but right now they feel overwhelmed, wondering how they will ever climb that high. I remember feeling that way when I taught a mini-lecture to a group of Bible study leaders for the first time. But bit by bit, step by step, the teaching leaders of that ministry partnered with me in an apprentice-like relationship until, fifteen years later, I was taking on apprentices myself.

I had been speaking to hundreds of women in Bible studies and conferences when I began learning to teach in a seminary, an entirely different context. The men in our department started me off slowly, simply having me observe them for a semester and occasionally giving me sections to teach. Later I stepped into team-teaching roles before I began teaching solo. I remember thinking—as I watched my colleagues stroll around the classroom in extemporaneous expertise—that I would never be able to teach without notes the way they did. But today, more than twenty years later, I teach that way myself. These seasoned teachers used scaffolding to help me reach what seemed impossible heights. The same principles apply in any ministry setting.

Alber defines educational scaffolding as "support[ing] every student by breaking learning up into chunks and providing a concrete structure for each."[10] Do not think of these learning structures or platforms as necessarily sequential. But these general stages can give you a sense of strategies as you work with apprentices.

Observation: Once you have identified your apprentices, be sure they are exposed to experts in action. Another term for observation might be "modeling." They might sit under your teaching for a time or be asked to watch others who model proficiency. I try to facilitate observation after apprentices have been exposed to some cognitive content so they know what to look for and are able to distinguish good teaching from bad. Some form of follow-up, either on paper or in an informal discussion, ensures the apprentice understands what makes teaching effective.

Tier one: Praxis by mimicking: Praxis is practice distinguished from theory. For apprentices with little or no experience, begin with "first

---

10. Rebecca Alber, *Teaching Strategies*, "6 Scaffolding Strategies to Use with Your Students," January 24, 2014, Edutopia, https://www.edutopia.org/blog/scaffolding-lessons-six-strategies-rebecca-alber.

steps." Assign them a part of your lesson, such as an illustration or story. You may want them to write out what they plan to say so you can evaluate it, or give them a practice run ahead of time. Make sure they time what they plan to say, or you may find them using up your time. And after the actual teaching session, evaluate their part. When working with Bible study or Sunday school teachers, I practically turned joyous cartwheels where they excelled. In areas apprentices need improvement, you can graciously point out an area "where they could strengthen the message" rather than saying something like "you really did poorly in this area."

In addition, prepare them ahead for a healthy perspective on evaluation. If an apprentice is particularly sensitive, buffer your comments on how to improve by reminding them that they are unconditionally loved by God and by you and that their value does not depend on their performance. But don't shy away from being honest about how to help them improve. If you invest well in the relationship, most apprentices are able to take your comments in the way they were meant—to move them up to a higher platform.

In time, everyone develops their own style of teaching, but initially you want your apprentice to master the basics. An artist must learn how lights and shadows affect their paintings. A writer must learn to excise "to be" verbs and replace them with strong action words. And teachers must master certain tried-and-true principles before they are ready to tweak the rules and strike out on their own. It is reasonable to insist that apprentices exhibit a knowledge of the basics as they begin their climb to higher scaffolds.

Here is an approach you can adapt in any ministry setting. In one of my seminary courses, early in the class, I divide the students into pods of four or five that we call "sound bites," led by a professor or seasoned veteran of the course. We limit each participant to a strict three-minute message and spend time afterward encouraging and then pointing out a distraction, like filler words, a lip click, shuffling feet, poor flow, or swaying. We repeat this process three or four times to prepare students for the view as they stand up in front of the class, and also to create a social learning community of future cheerleaders when they give their practice messages to the entire class. By the fourth sound bite, most students have acclimated to the view from the front and are ready to tackle a higher scaffold.

Tier two: Praxis with oversight: As apprentices become more comfortable scaling up the tiers, offer them one or more whole lessons to teach on their own, but assure them that you will continue walking with them, still providing oversight and accountability. Of course, some apprentices need more attention than others; it is a delicate tightrope to provide enough freedom for them to try their wings while still answering to the trainer for theological accuracy and effective communication skills. Adapt these patterns to each individual apprentice and your ministry context.

Consider asking our apprentices to write out word for word what they plan to say so you can evaluate it. Many will not manuscript what they teach later, but it is invaluable in teaching wordsmithing, and it is much more difficult to evaluate the message before they speak if they do not write it out. However, instruct them not to memorize the manuscript but to internalize the message and speak it naturally and with good eye contact. Initial manuscripting raises the level of tight, effective word choice immeasurably. And this process, although time-consuming for both apprentice and trainer, adds a level of confidence that gives the teacher wings when apprentices stand up to minister to their fellow classmates.

Climbing higher but with a safety net: When I trained women speakers and Bible teachers in the church, I only had the time to work with one or two at a time, using the process described above. But as each one progressed, they knew that I was always there if they needed me, and we continued to work together informally and coordinate our messages.

As the minister to women, at first I taught all of the weekly Bible messages. By the time I left to minister in the academy seven years later, I only taught about one-third of the Bible lessons. My four apprentices, now masterful teachers themselves, taught the other two-thirds. I never heard a complaint about the quality of the Bible teaching. We were all different but all astute at our craft. And when I handed over the leadership to others, they grabbed the baton and are still running. Today, they have equipped a new generation of Bible teachers to add to their team.

Each trainer will vary their approaches according to their own teaching styles and availability. But some form of accountability works wonders with unsure novices until they are ready to scale the heights themselves.

CONCLUSION

> I am a teacher at heart, and there are moments in the classroom when I can hardly hold the joy. When my students and I discover uncharted territory to explore, when the pathway out

> of a thicket opens up before us, when our experience is illumined by the lightning-life of the mind—then—teaching is the finest work I know.[11]

Renowned educator Parker Palmer beautifully expresses the delight of guiding students into the magical moments of exploring God's Word together. However, passing the baton to others can be equally and deeply satisfying. How sweet to know that the God you love will be honored by others and your labor of love will continue because of your investment in future teachers! So if God calls you to teach, teach with all your heart, mind, and strength, but don't stop there. Raise up the next generations and feel God's pleasure.

REFLECTION QUESTIONS

1. Why is it important that skilled teachers pass on their craft to others?
2. Name three elements needed to equip effective future teachers, and tell why each is necessary.
3. What qualities should you look for in potential future teachers?
4. Why is simply passing on information about teaching often not adequate to raise up exemplary teachers?
5. What is the role of "scaffolding" in training future teachers?

RECOMMENDED READING

Hestenes, Roberta, Howard Hendricks, and Earl Palmer. *Mastering Teaching*. Portland, OR: Multnomah Press and Christianity Today, Inc., 1991.

Johnson, Keith. *Teacher Training on the Go*. Loveland, CO: Group Publishing, 2003.

O'Carroll Drake, Susan. *Teacher Training with Jesus: Ten Lessons from the Master*. King of Prussia, PA: Judson, 2018.

11. Parker Palmer, *The Courage to Teach: Exploring the Inner Landscape of a Teacher's Life* (San Francisco: Jossey-Bass, 1998), 1.

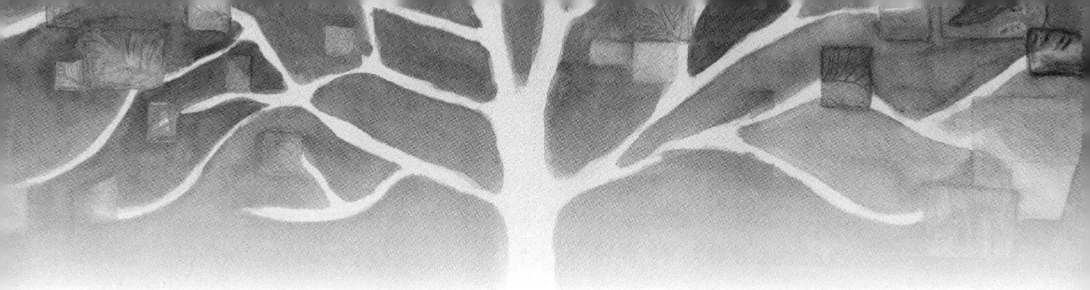

CHAPTER 17

TEACHER-STUDENT RELATIONSHIPS

"Relationships are at the heart of everything Christian."

Michael S. Lawson & Sue Edwards

"Are you kidding me? You're complaining about small classes?" I (Mike) had just arrived at a small Bible school in Athens to teach for a week. As a courtesy, my missionary friend had just apologized for his tiny school and the expected class size of between five and ten, although we actually exceeded his expectations by drawing twelve students. Because I was a visiting professor from a school with about 1,500 students at the time, my friend felt his school was insignificant due to its small size. Really? Is that the way he should feel? Wherever God sends us to teach the Bible, we are called to love our students well, regardless of how many. And sometimes smaller groups facilitate that priority.

How do we know caring relationships are God's priority? The Christian faith belongs to the intrinsically relational triune God, who ooze love for one other. Healthy, loving connections are emphasized in everything Christian because the Trinity exists in an eternal love relationship that God desires to reproduce in us. That includes the student-teacher relationship. Richard of St. Victor (c. 1110–1173) remarked:

> If God were just one person, he could not be intrinsically loving, since for all eternity (before creation) he would have had nobody to love. . . . Being perfectly loving, from all eternity

> the Father and the Son have delighted to share their love and joy with and through the Spirit. It is not, then that God *becomes* sharing, being triune, God *is* a sharing God, a God who loves to include. Indeed, that is why God will go on to create. His love is not for keeping but for spreading.[1]

We often ask students to describe their most influential teacher. Invariably they characterize one who knew their names, believed in them, cared for yet challenged them, and inspired them—someone who loved them well. This relationship often leads to a shared love for the subject matter. The Bible teacher God uses to transform students prioritizes relationships, just like the Trinity and Jesus's teaching ministry on the earth.

Beginning with Jesus's teaching modeled in the Gospels and continuing with his disciples through the epistles, we observe love demonstrated in effective Bible teaching. That love implanted into humans affects every kind of relationship. We expect to find that love benchmarking marital and family relationships. Loving our enemies catches us off guard while repeatedly exposing our deficiencies. How delightful to expect God's love to permeate our ministries and our classrooms.

Unfortunately, student-teacher relationships have a checkered history. Teacher personalities can range from those with a Napoleon complex to those who remain soft and tender no matter how chaotic the classroom becomes. We've seen both in the church and in schools. We have been greatly attracted to teachers with high expectations who also possess a passion that students understand the subject matter. We have been repulsed by very nice teachers who did not care enough about education to maintain some sense of order. Similar dynamics influence a teacher's effectiveness in a Bible study, at a camp, or in a small group.

In this chapter, we emphasize the power of the student-teacher relationship to expand learning beyond sheer information. That relationship lies at the very heart of Christian education as modeled in the New Testament. We recognize that highly motivated students can learn almost any cognitive content on their own. But true Christian

1. Richard of St. Victor, as cited by Michael Reeves, *Delighting in the Trinity, An Introduction to the Christian Faith* (Downers Grove, IL: IVP Academic, 2012), 31. Richard of St. Victor was a young Scot born in 1110 and died in 1173. He entered the Abbey of St. Victor sometime in the 1150s. He was one of the most influential authors of his day.

education combines information with relationships to propel students toward life transformation. Christian education ought to be guiding us through changed character, and with the Holy Spirit's enablement, toward an alignment with Christ's image. If our students don't love Jesus more after our teaching ministry, we've done them a disservice. Writers speak of this process with different labels: spiritual maturity, spiritual formation, discipleship, Christian growth, spiritual life, Christian life, and so on. In the process, students need both information and examples. The most powerful teachers live out the very truth they proclaim.

THE TEACHER AS SERVANT OF ALL

During his disciples' arguments about who was the greatest, Jesus admonished them by describing the current Gentile kings who lorded their power over their subjects. "But you are not to be like that," he insisted. "Instead, the greatest among you should be like the youngest, and the one who rules like the one who serves. . . . I am among you as one who serves" (Luke 22:26–27 NIV). In the Gentile culture, maturity was revered, and children were not considered as valuable as they are today.[2] Thus, to be the "youngest" meant you were at the bottom of the social ladder. Jesus taught an upside-down economy when it comes to greatness. The following example illustrates this principle.

Albania, a totalitarian atheistic country until the 1988 revolution, had just opened up, and one young refugee made his way to Athens. For reasons he could not explain, he began to wonder about God. His curiosity prompted him to ask around for, in his words, a "study for God." No one seemed to know until one friend recalled hearing about a school that at the time was in Kastri, north of Athens.[3] He caught a bus and then asked for help from local residents until he located the small school, housed in an old home. Stopping by the receptionist after entering the front door, he announced, "I want to study for God." She led him to the academic dean's office. After a brief introduction, the dean invited another faculty member to join him. Together they discerned that the young Albanian had no idea what he was talking about except that he "wanted to study for God," a phrase he repeated frequently.

2. Alfred Edersheim, *The Life and Times of Jesus the Messiah* (Grand Rapids: Eerdmans, 1986), 226–28, 252.
3. Since this time the institute has changed its name to Greek Bible College and moved to Pikermi, Attiki (Greece).

Very carefully, the two American missionary teachers explained the gospel until they were convinced that he understood his need to accept Jesus's death as payment for his sin. Preparing for the customary prayer to receive Christ, the two professors left their chairs, got down on their knees, closed their eyes, and began to lead in prayer. The young Albanian, very confused, asked, "What are you doing?" They responded, "We are praying to God." The shock of seeing two "proud" (his word) Americans on their knees overwhelmed him. He concluded there must be a God and if so, then he too wanted to know him.

The notion of teacher as servant contains overwhelming power. Some teachers seek to *rule* over their students, but great teachers understand they *follow* the Master Teacher who expects them to be "servant of all."

CHRISTIAN TEACHERS EXEMPLIFY THEIR MESSAGE

Jesus taught us that "the student is not above the teacher, but everyone who is fully trained will be like their teacher" (Luke 6:40 NIV). That could be taken as a self-evident truth. In other words, of course a student will be like his teacher. After all, the teacher provides both information and models.

Two more stories illustrate this beautiful truth. First, the full impact of Jesus's words never hit me (Mike) until one day in church a young man said, "Pastor, I want to be just like you." What a terrifying thought! Of course, I wanted him to be a student of the Bible and a minister if that was what God wanted. But "just like you" has a dark side, and I knew only too well what that looked like. I am comfortable with asking students to become like Jesus; I am very uncomfortable thinking they will become like me. The teacher-student relationship has powerful overtones with strong undertows as well. If anything ever motivated me to always be checking my behavior and my motives, it was those words that still echo in my mind, "I want to be just like you." That reality should haunt everyone who aspires to teach.

Second, a kind young pastor once wondered if I had time to preach in his church on Sunday. The schedule would be tight as I already had commitments that day, but with a little work, I could squeeze it in. The open-air building suited the Sri Lankan climate perfectly, and the auditorium would seat six hundred comfortably. While preparing in my mind for this last-minute sermon, I managed to get a little backstory.

The young pastor had grown up in Colombo's impoverished district. Sri Lanka is a poor country; but this area is unspeakable, and no school exists for children there. Along with other boys, he managed to get into all kinds of trouble. One day, a kind man gathered a group of boys, including the boy who was now a pastor, and offered to teach them. "Why not?" they thought, since there was nothing else to do. They knew that the ability to read and write would mean better jobs in the future.

What they did not know was this native Sri Lankan evangelist had ulterior motives. Not only did he teach them to read and write, but he also led them to Christ and faithfully discipled them in the Scriptures. He selected certain boys from time to time to include in his church planting ministry. After the church was well established, he would turn it over to one of the young men to pastor, and he would move on to plant another church. Like Melchizedek who moved seamlessly in and out of the biblical record, this man moved around the impoverished district discipling generations of boys and planting numerous churches. No one seemed to know where he came from or what happened to him, but he left behind a living legacy.

That story left me breathless, and I wondered how I would stay focused on preparing my sermon. To gain time to breathe, I commented on the wonderful size and organization of the young pastor's Sunday school. He gave credit to his wife, who obviously had some Christian education training. The adults were seated in groups with open Bibles discussing the text, unlike many American adult classes that imitate the pastor with only lectern and lecture. At that moment, he delivered the punch line I will never forget. "Yes, and if you teach in our church on Sunday, you will teach the same lesson in the poor neighborhood church on Thursday."

The words of Jesus in Luke 6:40 can turn out for good if we carefully provide a wholesome model along with our information. The teacher-student relationship has profound implications not just for our immediate students but also for students in the next generation.

THE DYNAMIC NATURE OF TEACHER-STUDENT RELATIONSHIPS

In the Christian world, the teacher-student relationship is fluid rather than static and moves toward specific goals. Our relationships within the teaching-learning context are dynamic as we help our students first grow as our disciples, then they become our friends, and finally some become family.

First, the Student as the Teacher's Disciple

Matthew ended his gospel with a familiar command that most Christians relate mainly to evangelism. "Therefore go and make disciples of all nations, baptizing them in the name of the Father and of the Son and of the Holy Spirit, and teaching them to obey everything I have commanded you. And surely I am with you always, to the very end of the age" (Matt. 28:19–20 NIV).

Certainly, part of the call is to "go," but the primary command in the Great Commission is to "make disciples." In fact, the only imperative verb in the passage is "make disciples." To do that, Jesus requires that converts be taught, and the curriculum is vast—everything Jesus taught. Whatever part you play in fulfilling the Great Commission—as evangelist, missionary, minister, pastor, preacher, or teacher in a church, parachurch ministry, academy, or school—you are fulfilling the Great Commission. Your students are your disciples. Your role is to move them from cognition to obedience. Thus, we not only pass on critical information, but we must model what an authentic disciple looks like. Students must be close enough to their teacher to observe their relationship with Christ as well as their lifestyle. We are always teaching whether we are instructing or not—we are raising up disciples for Jesus.

The Teacher as Encourager

Burned into my (Sue's) memory are two examples from my early seminary years. As one of the few women on campus, I felt extremely intimidated during the first few years of my seminary training, and I never spoke up during class discussions. However, one day I was late, and the only vacant seat was in the front row. We were studying Romans 7 and 8, and Dr. Bill Lawrence asked us how the two chapters related. Without thinking, I started to raise my hand and then quickly withdrew it, but not fast enough. The professor saw me, called on me, and I had no choice but to blurt out my explanation. His brow furrowed, he sauntered over to me, bent down so we were almost nose to nose, and bellowed, "Mrs. Edwards, don't you ever hesitate to give an excellent answer like that again." Those words vanquished my fear and unleashed my courage. From that time on, I took his advice.

Another time, one of my professor, Dr. Bob Lightner, asked to meet with me. I felt like I was being summoned to the principal's office. As I sat waiting for who-knows-what, he peered at me over his huge desk and handed me an exam I'd taken the week before on Trinitarian theology. He instructed me to turn to page four, but when I did, I noticed the pages had stuck together and page four was blank. I had failed the exam. But then he handed me a pencil and sent me to the next room to finish it. I aced the exam. That kindness yielded a grade point average that played a part in my acceptance to my chosen doctoral program, which led to my ultimate acceptance onto the full-time tenured faculty of the seminary where I trained. Although he is now with the Lord, I will always think of Dr. Lightner as someone who had my best interest at heart and modeled grace when he could just as easily have given me a failing grade. Both these men took a personal interest in my life and illustrated the character of authentic disciples, qualities I've tried to emulate and pass on as a Bible teacher and seminary professor. As Howard Hendricks often said, "You can impress people at a distance but you can only impact them up close."[4]

From Disciple to Friend

On the night before he went to the cross, Jesus comforted his disciples saying, "I no longer call you servants, because a servant does not know his master's business. Instead, I have called you friends, for everything I learned from my Father I have made known to you" (John 15:15 NIV).

Solomon described a friend as someone who "loves at all times" in Proverbs 17:17 (NIV). A teacher has multiple opportunities to exhibit love within the teaching context as well as outside that context. Love means that you have the other person's best interest at heart. You want to see them excel and thrive. You express those sentiments in the way you interact with your students before and after the ministry or the class. Your tone, words, and actions speak volumes as you answer questions, encourage, and take time to explain a difficult concept.

I (Mike) knew he had to be a visitor. No one ever came through the front door of our church. The big guy had his wife and two little girls in tow. I introduced myself and as soon as he introduced himself, I

4. Howard G. Hendricks, "The Teacher as Leader," in *The Christian Educator's Handbook on Teaching*, ed. Kenneth O. Gangel and Howard G. Hendricks (Grand Rapids: Baker Books, 1998), 251.

recognized his name. His neighbor had our church praying for him and his family. After helping his daughters into the appropriate children's class, I led Jerry and Diane to the sanctuary for the service. I offered seating choices of back, middle, or front, and he definitely wanted to sit in front! I accommodated his request by sitting him and Diane not only in the very front row but directly in front of the pulpit. He had never been in a church for any reason, and this Sunday would be his introduction to Jesus Christ.

Jerry's conversion was not only clear and definitive, but he also wanted to grow. We met that week, and I gave him a small book on the spiritual life.[5] He was back in my office the next day saying, "That was nice, what else have you got?" Surprised, I picked a larger and more substantial volume entitled *Grace*.[6] That satisfied him for a few days, but he came back hungry for more. I decided to see if I could slow him down just a little, so, I selected volume 1 of Lewis Sperry Chafer's seven-volume systematic theology.[7] That certainly slowed him down, but only a little. The next time we met he chastised me for holding back "the good stuff."

In addition to his newfound love for theology, we both shared a love for bass fishing. In that arena, he was the teacher, and I was the student. He offered to teach me how to bass fish from a boat if I would continue to teach him theology. We sealed the arrangement. Obviously, the Lord had his hand on Jerry. His love for the Bible drew him to seminary, and his love for the ministry led him to minister in several churches over the years. We now meet virtually on Mondays for prayer and sharing with another mutual friend. What once was a teacher-student relationship has moved into a lifelong friendship.

From Friend to Family

Paul instructed Timothy to treat other Christians as family. "Do not rebuke an older man harshly, but exhort him as if he were your father. Treat younger men as brothers, older women as mothers, and younger women as sisters, with absolute purity" (1 Tim. 5:1–2 NIV). Jesus also used family terms to describe his followers. Consider his response to his mother and biological brothers in Matthew 12:46–50 (NIV):

---

5. Lewis Sperry Chafer, *He That Is Spiritual* (Grand Rapids: Zondervan, 1967).
6. Lewis Sperry Chafer, *Grace* (Grand Rapids: Kregel, 1995).
7. Lewis Sperry Chafer, *Systematic Theology, An Unabridged Original Study of Systematic Theology from a Biblical Viewpoint*, 7 vols. (Dallas: Seminary Press, 1947).

> While Jesus was still talking to the crowd, his mother and brothers stood outside, wanting to speak to him. Someone told him, "Your mother and brothers are standing outside, wanting to speak to you." He replied to him, "Who is my mother, and who are my brothers?" Pointing to his disciples, he said, "Here are my mother and my brothers. For whoever does the will of my Father in heaven is my brother and sister and mother."

Jesus came to create a new kind of family. Not a family related by a common genealogy but a faith family, and what great news for those of us who did not grow up in a healthy family. This kind of familial relationship can blossom between teacher and student, as teachers take particular students under their wing and serve as champions, coaches, or mentors.

I (Sue) experienced this, along with my colleague Joye Baker, after we were students of Mike Lawson (this chapter's coauthor). We affectionately refer to him as "Grandpa Mike." He and his dear wife, Tish, invited students and colleagues into their home for fish fries. He sponsored many of his students as they pursued ministry and teaching careers. He championed us as future professors, paving the way as we progressed from disciple to friend to family. As adjunct professors and before Joye and I had earned our doctoral credentials, Grandpa Mike, amid a busy schedule as department chair, for two years sat in on a course we taught as the resident professor since we were not yet qualified. He coached us like a caring father, calling us out gently where we could improve and encouraging us when we excelled. He insisted that I coauthor this chapter with him. Teachers do not have the time or energy to invest in all their students at this level, but when they can and do, the impact is immeasurable. Taking the teacher-student relationship into the familial realm is one of the greatest joys of teaching. Make it more than a classroom experience whenever and wherever possible. Make your ministry more like a healthy home.

THE EFFECT OF GENDER ON THE TEACHER-STUDENT RELATIONSHIP

Wise teachers acknowledge that gender differences impact learning and they intentionally include both genders as participants in their courses. They take the time to study about learning differences between men and women and base their treatment of both on research rather than stereotypes. Consider the insights below.

Be Aware of Many Women Students' Tendencies to Underestimate Their Abilities and Value

In her book on motivation, Deborah Stipek paints caricatures of some female students as "Hopeless Hannah" or "Safe Sally." Hopeless Hannah exhibits a firm view of herself as incompetent and assumes there is simply no domain where she can excel. Safe Sally makes straight A's, meticulously follows directions, and is well behaved and highly motivated, as long as the learning requires no risk of failure. She systematically plays it safe, resists trying anything new or tapping into her creativity. Learning is something you do in school, brings no joy or excitement, and the desire to become a lifelong learner will be abandoned upon graduation.[8] If Hopeless Hannah or Safe Sally becomes a Christ follower and you become their teacher or minister, you will need to help them overcome obvious hindrances to grow strong in Christ.

Regardless of the reasons, for typical women who easily find fault with themselves and lack confidence, your influence as a teacher/minister—what you say, how you say it, and what you do—carries tremendous weight for good or ill, especially if you are male. Realize that for women without a strong male voice in their lives, you could make a significant difference to many women who yearn for encouragement and to feel valued by a man they respect.

Expunge Harmful, Reductionist Stereotypes

Two grave errors exist as we consider masculinity and femininity. If you want to help women become fully devoted, all-in disciples of Christ, resist both.

The first error exaggerates the differences between men and women. Have you seen the long lists of theoretical masculine and feminine characteristics? Often the list describes qualities like: men are thinkers and women are feelers, men are independent and women are dependent, men are initiators and women are responders. If these lists suggest or imply that God created men and women this way, and they often subtly

8. Deborah J. Stipek, *Motivation to Learn: From Theory to Practice*, 2nd ed. (Boston: Allyn and Bacon, 1993), 2–5.

do, then it sounds like deviation from that norm goes against God's intentional design. The problem is that every man and every woman is a unique creation made in the image of God, and none fits the cookie-cutter lists that make all men very much alike and all women very much alike. These lists cause great inner conflict and guilt to people who don't fit the list, and in one way or another, that is most of us.

Over the last forty years, researchers have produced mountains of literature on women, and some shed light on how women learn, although again we must be aware of the dangers of overgeneralization. For example, a 2002 study by Gabe Keri said that more women than men are collaborative learners (also known as innovative learners), and some are—but certainly not *all* women. [9] How do I know that?

Almost every semester I (Sue) teach an introductory course on educational ministries. One of the sessions exposes students to varied learning styles so they will use creative methods to reach the different people God will entrust to them in their future ministries (see chapter 10). To prepare for our time together, I ask each student to take a learning style assessment to acquaint them with their own predominant learning style. At the conclusion of the session, I divide them up into groups according to their learning styles and ask each group to explain to the other groups what methods are more advantageous to use with their learning styles. I tell them they are representing all the future students those future teachers will teach. The groups create insightful presentations that inform and inspire the other groups, cementing the concepts we've studied in theory, and we have lots of fun.

One of the groups represents innovative learners. These learners are caring, compassionate people who like to discuss what they are learning. Through more than a decade of teaching this course, I've observed the gender breakout, expecting to see the innovative group packed with females, and some end up there. But we usually have an equal number of men in the innovative group. And a fair number of women test out as other types of learners. Some are analytics, more focused on analyzing information. Others are common sense learners, insisting the learning be useful and practical. Still other women are dynamic learners, dreaming of new ways to use what they've learned. Again, we must be

9. Gabe Keri, "Male and Female College Students' Learning Styles Differ: An Opportunity for Instructional Diversification," *College Student Journal* 36, no. 3 (2002): 433–42.

careful not to pigeonhole people. Each person is unique. Nevertheless, some generalizations can be worth considering as we attempt to teach the women within our learning communities.

On the other hand, the second error denies *any* difference between men and women, except for physiology. The truth is that God designed men and women to be different, and it's beautiful. However, we are not nearly as different as we are sometimes portrayed. Gender differences are real, complex, and the result of a variety of factors, including heredity and biology, our family of origin, and the culture and environments where we live. We must be careful not to adopt a reductionist approach to gender. There is as much diversity *within* a group of women or *within* a group of men as there is *between* men and women. In spite of popular nomenclature, he is not from Mars and she is not from Venus.[10] We have much more in common than we have differences. Most importantly, we are human beings, brothers and sisters in the family of God.

Neither do our differences imply inferiority or superiority. However, with the explosion of brain research, we now see that male and female brains are organized differently.[11] Additionally, some physiological differences are undisputed. For example, the male retina is substantially thicker than the female retina, true in every male and every female including animals.[12] But some long-held assertions, such as the familiar notion that all men have superior navigational abilities, turn out to be false. Women typically navigate using landmarks while men often prefer maps: true for me and my husband but false for my friend Kay, the map guru, who drove us around Boston without a hitch. It's complicated. Many of the stereotypes that we held onto were merely a reflection of personal beliefs or political or religious agendas that have been disproven.

> The bottom line is that the brain is just organized differently in females and males. The tired argument about which sex is more intelligent or which sex has the "better" brain is about as meaningful as arguing about which utensil is "better," a knife or

10. John Gray, *Men Are from Mars, Women Are from Venus: The Classic Guide to Understanding the Opposite Sex* (New York: HarperCollins, 1992).
11. Bruce Goldman, "Two Minds: The Cognitive Differences Between Men and Women," *Stanford Medicine Magazine*, Spring 2017, https://stanmed.stanford.edu/how-mens-and-womens-brains-are-different/.
12. Leonard Sax, *Why Gender Matters: What Parents and Teachers Need to Know About the Emerging Science of Sex Differences* (New York: Broadway, 2005), 20–21.

> a spoon? The only correct answer to such a question is: "Better for what?" A knife is better than a spoon if you want to cut through a piece of meat, while a spoon is better if you're facing a bowl of chicken broth. [13]

You are not teaching stereotypes. Approach each student, whether male or female, as first a person made in the image of God and uniquely designed.[14] You will likely observe similarities among many of your women students, but exceptions abound. Our task as ministers or teachers is to see each one as a daughter, sister, or mother in our spiritual family, all placed under our care for a time to love, nurture, and challenge as she takes another step on her journey to becoming an all-in, fully devoted disciple of Jesus Christ.

Watch Words, Jokes, Expressions, and Illustrations

Over the years we've observed some attitudes, actions, and words that devalue women:

- a missions agency that was not interested in the wife's abilities or potential contributions even though she had the same calling and equipping as her husband;
- the female college professor who was included in a conversation about family but excluded when the conversation turned to theology;
- the male leader who introduced his female colleague as "sweetie" and the "prettiest face on the team" while ignoring her academic credentials even though he listed all the men's.

These kinds of words, actions, and attitudes are part of the reasons we are losing more women from our churches than any other demographic. In 2009, 48 percent of women attended church at least once a week, but in less than a decade that dropped to 31 percent. During the same

13. Sax, *Why Gender Matters,* 3
14. Up until about forty years ago, all research on learning was done on men, with women seen as an aberration. Then gradually we began to see studies coming out that helped us understand some of the differences with women's learning. As such, most general learning research studies reflect male learning patterns unless otherwise specified. See Sax, *Why Gender Matters*, and Michael Gurian, *Boys and Girls Learn Differently! A Guide for Teachers and Parents* (San Francisco: Jossey-Bass, 2001).

period of time, the number of men who attended church at least weekly declined 12 percentage points. There is no longer a gender gap in attendance. However, since 2012 attendance has declined significantly for both men and women.[15]

Many Christian women have learned to do the mental gymnastics required to constantly turn male pronouns and stories into applications that work for women. We know men who speak and act this way are usually well intentioned; we love our brothers, and we give them the benefit of the doubt. But women who can do that are usually mature, grace-giving, and confident. Many grew up in healthy Christian families and churches. However, with the breakdown of the nuclear family and the secularization of the culture, more and more women come out of unhealthy homes and skewed environments. Fewer grew up in healthy Christian homes.

Some are disappointed in the men in their families who should have been there to protect and nurture them but instead took advantage of them, marginalized them, neglected them, or even worse, abused them. For many of these women, trust comes slowly, offense quickly. And this is true for some Christian women as well as nonbelievers.

How might we unintentionally offend some women? Consider these examples:

- an off-color or demeaning joke about "dumb blondes" or silly women;
- reading Bible verses that seem to apply only to "brothers";
- off-the-cuff comments like "It will make a man out of you";
- stories that always feature topics of interest to men;
- only talking about male heroes from Scripture; and
- only quoting male authors.

To many women, these words, actions, and attitudes only reinforce what they have been hearing for years: *"Stay away from Christianity—it's a hierarchical male-dominated institution that doesn't care about women."* But Jesus loves these women and wants them to come

15. David McClendon, "Gender Gap in Religious Service Attendance Has Narrowed in U.S.," Pew Research Center, May 13, 2016, https://www.pewresearch.org/short-reads/2016/05/13/gender-gap-in-religious-service-attendance-has-narrowed-in-u-s/.

into an intimate relationship with him. Why would we want to create unnecessary hindrances for these women to come to faith even if it means reevaluating any prejudices and giving up some of our own preferences? Only Jesus can heal their brokenness and calm their anger, but he needs an army of godly Christian men to step into the roles of fathers and brothers. These women need to see different kinds of men, teachers, preachers, and ministers who truly value their sisters, teaching and treating them with the brotherly care they have yearned for. In the Gospels, women flocked to Jesus because he treated them with dignity and respect, and godly men who treat women like sisters in Christ today continue to exert this kind of healing power in their female students' lives.

Expect Many Women, More Than Men, to Desire Affiliation with the Teacher and Peers

I (Sue) have observed that most women seem to view life through a relational lens, thus supporting the broad findings that many women live in a relational web while many men see life from a more individualistic, separate perspective.[16] I'm a good example. I'm an even mix of analytic/dynamic on the learning differences assessment. On leadership inventories, I score off the charts on whatever term they use to describe a strong natural leader. I'm type A, bottom line, goal-oriented, all qualities often on the list of masculine traits, but I'm feminine in my appearance and demeanor. However, when I view my life, I see it through a relational lens, first with my beloved Lord, then with my husband, children, and grandchildren, then with my students and colleagues at work and in my church family.

As a result, I love to learn in community and, during my student days, I valued relational connections with my teachers and professors. Thus, when you teach, you may find that your women students desire an appropriate affiliation with you. If you invest in those personal connections, you will create a culture where they will learn better. You will find that they will stop thinking so much about the impression they are

16. Karen A. Longman et al., "The Secret Sauce: How Developmental Relationships Shape the Leadership Journeys of Women Leaders in Christian Higher Education," *Christian Higher Education* 18 (2019): 54–77; Alice H. Eagly, "Once More: The Rise of Female Leaders," American Psychological Association, September 8, 2020, accessed September 2, 2023, www.apa.org/topics/women-girls/female-leaders.

making on others, relax, and begin taking risks in their thinking. They'll be open to trying out new ideas, delving deep into dynamic discussions, helping others learn, searching for answers together, listening respectfully to opposing viewpoints, and enjoying the process. You'll start to hear comments like "The time in our class just flies by" and "I never knew this could be so interesting." These kinds of cultures are petri dishes for learning that move most female students into becoming all-in, fully devoted disciples of Christ.

If you are male, personal relationships with female students may scare you. Were you taught that they are "taboo temptresses" and you better ignore them and focus on the guys? I understand your concern for your reputation, but notice I said "appropriate" relationships. Navigating that balance is beyond the scope of this book, but resources exist if you need help figuring out what healthy relationships with sisters looks like.[17]

Beware of Her Response to High-Pressure Ethos

Over the years, I (Sue) have observed the differences in what motivates most men and most women in learning environments. Many men are more energized by a confrontational, in-your-face approach and by time-constrained tasks. Fewer women thrive in high-pressure, do-it-in-thirty-seconds-or-you-lose activities. Although some women love competition, many find it stressful and prefer an ethos where everybody works together and everybody wins. Research backs up these observations and may be why men generally score higher than women on time-constrained standardized tests while women often make better grades, engage more quickly in the classroom, and are quicker to ask for a teacher's help. Both are smart; they simply excel in different ways.[18]

When you communicate that God cares for women, values their contributions, and calls them to develop their gifts to serve Christendom in various capacities, God will use you to empower at least half of the body of Christ. From the upper room to the Great Commission, Jesus set the standard for teacher-student relationships. As we read the epistles, we sense that when the disciples taught, they understood and

17. Sue Edwards, Kelley Matthews, and Henry J. Rogers, *Mixed Ministry: Working Together as Brothers and Sisters in an Oversexed Society* (Grand Rapids: Kregel Academic, 2008).
18. Sax, *Why Gender Matters*, 77–92.

tried to love their students well just like their Mentor. They understood that relationships are at the heart of everything Christian. So does the effective Bible teacher today.

THE TEACHER-STUDENT RELATIONSHIP IN THE VIRTUAL ENVIRONMENT

The virtual environment of online teaching easily limits the powerful nature of teacher-student relationships. (See chapter 14 for further discussion.) But Christian education possesses an "X" factor because the Holy Spirit works in both the teacher and the student as well as in their relationship.

Effective Bible teachers and ministers who lead online Bible teaching venues or small groups must equip themselves to teach on the multiple platforms that became necessities during the 2020–22 COVID-19 pandemic. There is no going back. Admittedly, this endeavor is hard work and can require more of a time investment than when a ministry or course meets regularly face-to-face. There, we easily connect for in-person discussions, laugh together, enjoy breaks when natural conversation tends to erupt, and help one another with challenges. These connections naturally occur in the time and space of the shared face-to-face experience, but it is worth the extra effort to facilitate meaningful personal connections in the virtual environment. I (Sue) have found that when we do, students feel heard, respected, and cared for, which promotes better learning and overall satisfaction.

Methods to Promote Online Relationships

Sochacki insists that, "If you would like to create a community of engaged learners within your classroom, it takes more than regurgitating the most compelling content, and it goes beyond collaborative pedagogical practices. The secret to inspiring and transforming students rests in the power of building a community of learners."[19] First, because it is harder to have casual conversations online, teachers and ministers must find creative ways to enhance one-on-one connections. In face-to-face situations we can chat with our students about what is going

19. The Albert Team, "How to Build Relationships Virtually: The Ultimate Guide for Teachers," Albert.io, November 24, 2020, accessed September 1, 2023, www.albert.io/blog/building-relationships-teaching-remotely/.

on in their lives or families, but on the screen students come online together, ruling out private interactions. Everyone can hear everything. Thus, teachers are seldom privy to the kinds of information that can lead to more intimate relationships, creating barriers to the kinds of connections that can move relationships toward becoming friends and family. In addition, students are not as likely to connect with each other since the opportunity for private chats is also limited. A possible solution might be to use breakout rooms or waiting rooms or any platform that has features that give students the opportunity to talk with each other, the teacher, or minister in smaller groups.

Second, we often find that supplementing content with related activities, discussions, games, case studies, or other creative methods helps concepts stick and aids in application, but these methods are often limited when students are confined to squares on screens. Moving, interacting, and exploring together can build rapport, but these methods are difficult to replicate online, and physical touch is impossible. You might try asking students to prerecord videos, and then you can splice them together for a fun activity or create a game that can be played online. Again, you can break up students into smaller groups in chat rooms to discuss case studies and then join back together for continued interaction. Be alert to additional tools that will make these kinds of options doable in the future.

Third, exemplary ministers and teachers achieve a unique ability to be fully present with their students. They can "read" what's going on by observing the body language and facial expressions of their students. They move around the room, using their eyes, face, and voice to secure student's attention, to motivate, and to communicate passion and care for everyone. This presence is easily lost in a virtual environment. Especially when lecturing or sharing their screen, the teacher cannot clearly see everyone on the screen at one time. Students are easily distracted by what's going on wherever they are—dogs bark, children need help, or technology gremlins interrupt. Also, students often differ in their technological skill, making them frustrated and confused when their laptops will not comply or the teacher or minister asks them to perform a task out of their comfort zone. When the student's attention is diminished, community and learning is endangered. Be patient with students who are not as computer-savvy and give clear and slow instructions when moving to other platforms or asking students to perform a task they may not be familiar with. Use something like Microsoft's Gallery view whenever practical so everyone can see everyone else and give clear instructions ahead of time to help students who are not as skilled technologically.

Additional Methods

Dr. Crystal Wong, professor at San Francisco State University where she teaches in the writing program, insists we must offer students both voice and choice in their own learning, and these strategies are particularly needed in online learning.[20]

> This means students can choose topics that are interesting and culturally or professionally relevant to them, can demonstrate their learning in different ways (e.g., a paper, video/visual presentation, or podcast), can choose their readings within a topic or theme, and can give input on the assessment criteria.[21]

In online courses or Bible studies, it is helpful to break students up into smaller groups of four and meet with them periodically in addition to the times for group instruction. This approach makes students feel they are receiving personalized attention as well as individual assessment.

I (Sue) can evaluate if students are struggling and help them catch up. They can interact with classmates. Any format that allows personal interaction tends to create those powerful connections both with me and other students. Even when these groups are optional, I've found attendance fairly consistent, revealing distance students' hunger for personal involvement and relationship.

Wong also encourages teachers to find ways to help the class connect through social interaction.

> We can open our online class with a "question of the day" that asks students to share a piece of themselves each week—their interest, talents, pets, playlist, upbringing, friends, family, social media, identities, future goals—and by the end of the semester,

20. Crystal O. Wong, "Building Relationships: How to Connect from a Distance," October 14, 2020, Faculty Focus www.facultyfocus.com/articles/online-education/online-student-engagement/building-relationships-how-to-connect-from-a-distance/.
21. Wong, "Building Relationships."

> we come to see each other as a whole person. When communicating with students, we could make an effort to write and speak in a friendly tone, address students by name (including emails), check-in with each student at different points of the semester (one-to-one emails), solicit feedback on our teaching, reply promptly to emails, and give individualized feedback.[22]

As we all become more and more skilled at online teaching, remember to include as much interactivity as possible without frustrating your students. Also, attempt to keep up with innovations that promise to make online learning more and more functional for everyone.

CONCLUSION

In building teacher-student relationships, the teacher must initiate the process by creating a safe environment. A personal story or two may connect with those in the class. Sometimes those stories reach back into our childhood to expose our humanity. If the teaching extends over weeks or months, mixing in stories that reflect both our successes and failures help strengthen the growing bond between teacher and student. However, I never tell a "failure" story about my children or wife. Our goal as teachers is to be approachable. If at all possible, our students ought to sense we are all in this Christian struggle together. Then, in the same breath, sense our hope as the wonderful Savior carries us along one step at a time.

REFLECTION QUESTIONS

1. As a student, how have you been shaped or influenced by a teacher-student relationship? Can you recount the story?
2. As a teacher, now or in the future, how will you foster mentoring-discipling relationships with students?
3. The teacher-student relationship is indeed developmental. How would you celebrate the "close" of the teacher-student relationship? What could you do when the student is no longer your student?
4. In an online learning environment, how can you better foster teacher-student relationships? Identify three ways.

22. Wong, "Building Relationships."

RECOMMENDED READING

Barkley, Elizabeth F., K. Patricia Cross, and Claire Howell Major. *Collaborative Learning Techniques: A Handbook for College Faculty*. San Francisco: Jossey-Bass, 2005.

Belenky, Mary Field, Blythe McVicker Clinchy, Nancy Rule Goldberger, and Jill Mattuck Tarule. *Women's Ways of Knowing, The Development of Self, Voice, and Mind.* New York: Basic Books, 1986.

Brookfield, Stephen D., and Stephen Preskill. *Discussion as a Way of Teaching: Tools and Techniques for Democratic Classrooms*. San Francisco: Jossey-Bass, 1999.

Johnson, Donald W., and Frank P. Johnson. *Joining Together: Group Theory and Group Skills*. 10th ed. London, UK: Pearson, 2009.

Scazzero, Peter. *The Emotionally Healthy Leader: How Transforming Your Inner Life Will Deeply Transform Your Church, Team, and the World*. Grand Rapids: Zondervan, 2015.

Smith, Donald K. *Creating Understanding: A Handbook for Christian Communication Across Cultural Landscapes*. Grand Rapids: Zondervan, 1992.

SUBJECT INDEX

F

G

H

I

J

K

L

M

N

P